Gwyn A. Williams

# WHEN WAS WALES?

## A History of the Welsh

Penguin Books

Penguin Books Ltd, Harmondsworth, Middlesex, England
Viking Penguin Inc., 40 West 23rd Street, New York, New York 10010, U.S.A.
Penguin Books Australia Ltd, Ringwood, Victoria, Australia
Penguin Books Canada Ltd, 2801 John Street, Markham, Ontario, Canada L3R 1B4
Penguin Books (N.Z.) Ltd, 182–190 Wairau Road, Auckland 10, New Zealand

First published by Black Raven Press 1985
Published in Penguin Books 1985

Printed and bound in Great Britain by
Cox & Wyman Ltd, Reading
Typeset in Baskerville

PELICAN BOOKS

# WHEN WAS WALES?

Gwyn A. Williams is Professor of History at University College, Cardiff. He has written *Medieval London* (1963), *Rowland Detrosier, a working-class infidel* (1965), *Artisans and Sans-culottes: popular movements in Britain and France during the French Revolution* (1968), *Proletarian Order: Antonio Gramsci, factory councils and the origin of communism in Italy* (1975), *The Merthyr Rising* (1978), *The Search for Beulah Land: the Welsh and the Atlantic Revolution* (1980), *Madoc: the making of a myth* (1980), *The Welsh in their History* (1982) and *Goya and the Impossible Revolution* (Penguin 1984). He also translated and edited Paolo Spriano's *The Occupation of the Factories: Italy 1920* (1975).

Who seeks another kingdom
Beyond the common sky?

Idris Davies, *Gwalia Deserta* (1938)

## Welsh History

We were a people taut for war; the hills
Were no harder, the thin grass
Clothed them more warmly than the coarse
Shirts our small bones.
We fought and were always in retreat,
Like snow thawing upon the slopes
Of Mynydd Mawr; and yet the stranger
Never found our ultimate stand
In the thick woods, declaiming verse
To the sharp prompting of the harp.

Our kings died, or they were slain
By the old treachery at the ford.
Our bards perished, driven from the halls
Of nobles by the thorn and the bramble.

We were a people bred on legends,
Warming our hands at the red past.
The great were ashamed of our loose rags
Clinging stubbornly to the proud tree
Of blood and birth, our lean bellies
And mud houses were a proof
Of our ineptitude for life.

We were a people wasting ourselves
In fruitless battles for our masters,
In lands to which we had no claim,
With men for whom we felt no hatred.

We were a people, and are so yet.
When we have finished quarrelling for crumbs
Under the table, or gnawing the bones
Of a dead culture, we will arise,
Armed, but not in the old way.

R. S. Thomas, *An Acre of Land* (1952)

This fine poem expresses some historical truths. It also sanctifies a monstrous historical lie. The people who inhabit the two western peninsulas of Britain which have lived for a millennium and a half as Wales, and anyone who may be interested in their history, need to take possession of those truths and to identify that lie. I hope this essay helps them.

Gwyn A. Williams

# CONTENTS

## MAPS

## GRAPH

# ACKNOWLEDGEMENTS

Anyone who attempts a book like this becomes painfully aware, as the late David Williams phrased it, that he is putting his sickle into other people's corn. They will be no less painfully aware when I cross their fields. It has been an exhilarating experience, for whatever the twentieth-century Welsh will be remembered for, they will surely be remembered for their historians; it is an honour to be counted one of their company.

None of them, of course, is in any way responsible for the use I make of their work. My debts remain. The oldest and most wide-ranging I owe to my fellow-townsman and the dean of Welsh historians, Glanmor Williams, to my former chiefs now gone, Thomas Jones Pierce and David Williams; to the late A. H. Dodd, Emrys Bowen, R. T. Jenkins and Griffith John Williams; to Brinley Thomas, Thomas Parry, E. D. Jones and Gwyn Williams (Trefenter). My newest are to those heralds of a revolution, Dot Jones, Anne Jones, Deirdre Beddoes, Angela John and Carole Harwood.

My most desperate debts are to Wendy Davies, David Dumville, Glanville Jones, Leslie Alcock, the late John Morris (and Peter Salway had better be promoted to a Welshman for the occasion); to Llinos and Jenkyn Beverly Smith, Rees Davies and Ralph Griffiths; to the late Frances Yates and David Matthews; to J. Gwynn Williams and Geraint Jenkins; to Philip Jenkins and Peter D. G. Thomas; to Ieuan Gwynedd Jones, David Jones, Hywel M. Davies, Brian Davies, Siân Rhiannon Williams and David Howell; to Ken Morgan, Merfyn Jones, David Smith, Hywel Francis, John Davies, Peter Stead, Phil Cooke, Kevin Morgan, Robert Griffiths, Gareth Miles and Dafydd Elis Thomas. My most recent is to D. Hywel Davies, who signs his book from Dowlais. Time may be mending.

Two men were the original begetters of this book; Emyr Humphreys has been an enormously encouraging and challenging Einion Offeiriad or Regulator of the Rule of Taliesin and Richard, lord of Dinefwr, has been a patron as genial and stimulating as The Lord Rhys, lord of the same place.

Finally, I owe debts which are none the less real for being elusive. I would like to pay tribute to the Moving Being Company of Cardiff for their brilliant theatrical presentation of The Four Branches of the Mabinogi, which in my old age, I experienced as a shock of recognition, and to my friends and colleagues Colin Thomas, Peter Thornton, Paul Gaydon, Margaret Griffiths, Medwen Roberts, Anne Jones, Terry Elgar and his crew, to Wynford Vaughan Thomas and to the rest of our HTV team which is trying to translate the history of the Welsh into television, in our version of the craft of the *cyfarwyddion* – a Fifth Branch?

The author and publishers gratefully acknowledge permission to use copyright material in this book:

H. Idris Bell (trans.): Extracts from 'The Woodland Mass', from *Dafydd ap Gwilym: Fifty Poems* (Hon. Society of Cymmrodorion, 1942). Reprinted by permission of Idris Christopher Bell.

Joseph P. Clancy (trans.): Two stanzas of 'Canu Llywarch Hen', from *The Earliest Welsh Poetry* (Macmillan/St Martin's Press, 1970). Reprinted by permission of the translator.

Anthony Conran (trans.): Extracts from 'Trouble at a Tavern' by Dafydd ap Gwilym, from *The Penguin Book of Welsh Verse* (1967), pp.142-4, Copyright © Anthony Conran, 1967. Reprinted by permission of Penguin Books Ltd.

Idris Davies: Extracts from *Gwalia Deserta* (Dent, 1938). Reprinted by permission of Ebenezer Morris.

Rolfe Humphries (trans.): Extracts from 'The Girls of Llanbadarn' from *Nine Thorny Thickets: Selected Poems of Dafydd ap Gwilym* (1969). Reprinted by permission of The Kent State University Press.

R. S. Thomas: 'Welsh History' and 'The Welsh Hill Country', both from *An Acre of Land* (1952). Reprinted by permission of Grenada Publishing Ltd.

W. B. Yeats: 'A Coat', from *The Collected Poems of W. B. Yeats* (Macmillan). Reprinted by permission of Michael Yeats and Macmillan London Ltd.

They also wish to thank Dr Roy Lewis and Mr Michael Jones of the Geography Department of the University College of Wales, Aberystwyth for their assistance in the preparation of the maps and Dr J. H. Williams, Deputy Head, Dynamic Analysis Group, University of Wales Institute of Science and Technology, Cardiff, for compiling the graph.

Land over 600ft (180m)

—·—·— Boundary between
England and Wales

------ County Boundaries before 1974

Amlwch
Holyhead
Llandudno    Rhyl  Prestatyn
Llangefni   Beaumaris    Conway   Colwyn Bay   Rhuddlan   Holywell
Bangor              St. Asaph   Caerwys      Flint
Bethesda              Denbigh            Mold    Chester
Caernarfon                 Llanrwst           Ruthin      Brymbo
Snowdon           Betws-y-coed   Llanarmon-yn-Ial        Wrexham
(Eryri)                   Penmachno              Rhosllanerchrugog
                Blaenau Ffestiniog          Corwen      Ruabon
Criccieth   Penrhyndeudraeth   Rhiwlas        Llangollen
Nefyn  Pwllheli   Porthmadoc                  Bala
Harlech                Llanuwchllyn                Oswestry

Ø Bardsey            Dolgellau
             Barmouth    Cader Idris   Mallwyd        Shrewsbury
                                 Welshpool   Wroxeter
                        Llangadfan      (Trallwng)
                   Tywyn   Llanbrynmair      Montgomery
                   Aberdyfi   Machynlleth
                              Newtown
                        Pumlumon
             Aberystwyth   R Rheidol   Llanidloes
        Llanbadarn Fawr                      Ludlow
                                          Knucklas
                   Mynydd Bach              Brampton
                                            Bryan
        Aberaeron
Newquay         Tregaron        Llandrindod Wells
             Llanddewi Brefi
        Llanwenog  Lampeter       Builth Wells
        Rhydowen                  Llanwrtyd Wells
        Newcastle Emlyn  Llandysul       Hereford
Fishguard                   Llandovery         Trefeca
        Preseli                         Brecon
St. Davids   Carmarthen              Brecknock Beacons
        St. Clears                           Abergavenny
Haverfordwest        Llandeilo   Abercrave         Monmouth
Narberth   Kidwelly  Ammanford  Glyn Neath  Dowlais  Tredegar  Ebbw Vale   Raglan
Milford Haven        Burry Port        Aberdare  Merthyr Tydfil  Abertillery  Usk  Forest
        Pembroke  Tenby   Llanelli  Loughor   Neath  Treorchy  Treharris  Bargoed  Pontypool  of
                    Llanelli         Mardy  Abercynon  Blackwood       Dean
                 Swansea  Maesteg      Pontypridd   Caerphilly  Llanfaches  Chepstow
                 Port Talbot            Llandaff          Newport   Caerwent
                      Bridgend   Cowbridge       Cardiff
                 Porthcawl            Llancarfan  Barry  Penarth
                      Llantwit Major      Barry Island

0        10       20  Miles
0    10   20   30  Km

1.  WALES: TOPOGRAPHY

# 1 · PROLOGUE TO A HISTORY

Somewhere around the middle of the sixth century BC a man made a journey from the Greek colony of Massilia (Marseille) through the Straits of Gibraltar to the trading city of Tartessos, near where Seville stands today. He reported in his *Massiliote Periplus* that the Tartessians traded with the Oestrymnides, the coasts and islands of present-day Brittany, and that these, in turn, trafficked with the inhabitants of two large islands called Ierne and Albion. These are the first recorded names of Ireland and Britain. They are Greek versions of Irish Celtic names, probably derived from an earlier and now lost language.

The adjective 'Celtic' is something of a misnomer. It is used to describe a confederacy of very different peoples, embraced in a Europe-wide Celtic language family, probably originating in small warrior dynasties to the east who boasted an advanced iron culture and made use of the horse. This confederacy became a powerful civilization with a vivid art, whose peoples once challenged Rome, sacked Rome, and finally succumbed to Rome to form the human fabric of the first great European urban polity in the north-west. Clearly, by the middle of the sixth century BC the peoples of these two offshore islands had been absorbed into this European complex and at least one of their official languages was that form of Celtic which produced Irish.

The names Albion and Ierne passed into use among Greek geographers, but in 325-323 BC when one of them, Pytheas of Massilia, made a journey along the western sea-route, he described the islands as Pretanic. This survives in the word *Prydain,* used by the Welsh to describe their own island. It is a genuinely Celtic name and derives from a form of speech which became Brittonic, the language of the island of Britain. The Romans may have mispronounced it; in Latin, they called the island Britannia and its peoples Britanni.

We know of no names for the inhabitants of these two western peninsulas of Prydain/Britannia until the advent of the Romans brings them into history. The invasions of Julius Caesar in 55-54 BC were confined to the south-east of Britain, but he heard tell of the westerners as a wild people, growing no corn, living on milk and flesh, clothing themselves in skins and

1

believing themselves to have grown out of the ground, since they were the oldest people on the island. While this report seems reasonable, it was inaccurate in that those peoples certainly practised an arable agriculture. Where it may strike a chord is in its sense that these were the oldest people. They probably were.

It was after Claudius launched his serious invasion from AD 43 that they come into sight. By the fifties and sixties the legions were fighting them. Five named tribes were to be significant. What had been the heartland of Britain before the rise of a civilization called Belgic in the south-east – the hub of the chalk uplands and the good land ranging out from Salisbury Plain – was settled by a people called the Dobunni. Separated from them to the west by dense forests whose survivor is the Forest of Dean, but closely connected to them and to the lands straddling the Severn estuary and the Bristol Channel, were a fierce tribe, the Silures. Tacitus said they resembled, in their swarthiness and curly hair, the Iberian peoples who were to create Spain. Beyond them, where the better land opened out again from the stranglehold of the mountains, were a people called the Demetae, facing the Irish Sea. North of the Silures and spread out widely across the fertile lands which lay below the mountains were the Cornovii. To the west were a people called the Ordovices. It is not clear where they were actually located; some maps coolly print their name across some of the most inhospitable country known to human beings. If the Ordovices actually lived in what was later known as the Wilderness of Wales, nobody else has managed to do so since. They seem to have been scattered over what is today central and north-east Wales and were probably concentrated to the east. Along the northern coast were a people called the Deceangli. There is something of a void around present-day Ynys Môn (Anglesey) which one would expect to have been quite populous. It is said that the later name for this region, Gwynedd, derives from the Brittonic form of the name of an Irish tribe, the Féni; this, however, was much later and if there was such a migration, it has left little trace.

From these peoples emerged the human matrix of the Welsh people. No such matrix existed in those early times, of course. There was no such place as 'Wales'. How could there be?

## Place

This is the first point to grasp about the history of this people. Wales is impossible. A country called Wales exists only because the Welsh invented it. The Welsh exist only because they invented themselves. They had no choice. A tiny handful of people occupying two western peninsulas of Britain had, in the Bronze Age, lived for perhaps a thousand years (maybe even longer) as an integral element in some kind of human society which made Stonehenge a focus. For perhaps six or seven hundred years they had lived in a fragmented and warlike Celtic-speaking society as four or five tribes within a British complex of tribes. For a further four hundred years they lived under Rome; for half that time, their freemen as Roman citizens of Britannia, in at least three city-state Romano-British commonwealths. With the breaking of Britannia, they emerged in a welter of little British kingdoms, gradually shaking out as four major polities, one of them controlled by immigrants from Ireland, another probably by an intruder dynasty from elsewhere in Britain. By the eighth century they found that Britain had been removed. They were stuck in their peninsulas behind a great dyke and rampart raised by an alien people who called them foreigners – in that alien language *weallas* – Welsh. By that time they themselves were beginning to call what was left of the Britons *Cymry* or fellow-countrymen. Pretty soon there was nobody left to call *Cymry* except themselves. Their stronger kings started to hammer the whole bunch together and to make a country called Cymru: Wales.

And a hard time they had of it. The country which became Wales stands at the heartland of a highland belt of Britain which stretches from the Humber to the Severn. Its core is a central massif rising from 700 to over 3,000 feet, with an annual rainfall of over sixty inches, all rocks and coarse grass. It is beautiful; in our days it is cherished for its beauty. But it cannot support community. Around that core, the land is fragmented into valley settlements, often ribbed apart by hills and mountains. From the Severn valley some fertile cwms thrust into the hills, but only in the south is there a notable extension of the British lowlands. A tongue of good land thrusts from Salisbury Plain and the soft south Severn through Gwent and the lowland of Glamorgan, pinches through the Margam Gap where the hills come down to the sea, lurches and trips on to the Vale of Tywi and then broadens out again in Dyfed in the south-west. A parallel coastal strip in the north is much narrower and the whole north-west is blocked off by three great concentric ring-bastions of mountains which shelter a fertile Anglesey behind. River valleys, a Wye, an Usk, a Teifi, a Tywi, a Conwy, a Clwyd, a Dee, thread some decent living into the hills, though in early times people tended to shun the more dark, forested and haunted depths.

Until people conquered energy in the eighteenth century, this environment imposed its own ineluctable discipline on the men and women who crawled across its bony surface. Firstly there was poverty of people

3

themselves. The land could support only so many, at a given level of technology. Famine would correct any excessive ambition. It is too often forgotten even by their historians that the Welsh were always very thin on the ground. Before the late eighteenth century there were never more than half a million of them. Often there were very many fewer. At times the population of Wales was minimal.

Then there was poverty of resources. Until the land's mineral wealth was expropriated, usually by other, luckier people, and harnessed to human skills, largely native, many of the communities of the Welsh were condemned to the margins and to that piracy which is freedom to hill peoples. The history of Welsh kings, lords and princes is largely the history of men made ruthless in the hunt for resources; usually their best resource was people, and slavery lasted longer in Wales than most places, even when its strutting, braggart freemen, and many of its women, boasted of their liberty.

This has meant dispersal, sometimes amounting to division. The little local homeland, the *bro* ('les clochers de mon pays'), has been and still is, as central to a Welsh man or woman as the *patria chica* is to the Spaniard, that other survivor who has had to live in the interstices of mountain, plateau and moor. The first thing to know about any Welsh person still is where he or she comes from; that alone will tell you a lot. The knowledge needs to be particular. It is necessary to distinguish between Upper Cwm-Twrch and Lower Cwm-Twrch. These days they may even talk a different language.

Any kind of unity that can be called *political* does not come easily and never has. The country has no natural capital. For centuries, its operative centre lay in the borderlands where the roads run easy. Its present capital, Cardiff, is the offspring of artificial insemination, or possibly of a transplant that has difficulty taking. Until recently this used to be considered a major source of weakness among the Welsh. Times change; people read André Gorz and Rudolf Bahro;* maybe it will be less of a hindrance from now on. Up to the present, however, it has meant that any person seeking to unify Wales politically has had to make himself a wizard and a monster (it has always been a 'he').

It has also meant that the sea has been important. For hundreds of years it was much easier to get around by water than by land – and the Welsh

---

*André Gorz, *Farewell to the Working Class*, trans. Michael Sonenscher (Pluto Press, 1982) and Rudolf Bahro, *Socialism and Survival*, trans. David Fernbach (Heretic Books, 1982), two former marxists who have adopted an ecological world-outlook. Their work is central to any effective analysis of Wales and its prospects of survival.

have been a mobile people. It has been along the coasts that most of human life has pulsed. The Irish Sea and the people who sailed on it have imposed a human shape on Wales. The Atlantic and its commerce virtually created early modern Wales. And the shape of the land has helped to shape human minds. For millennia, Gwent-Glamorgan and their lowlands have been a human as well as a physical extension of the Wessex civilizations of Salisbury Plain, always quicker to change, always most prone to adapt Welshness, always most liable to lose it. It is harder in Snowdonia. There is an old saying here that the south innovates and the north preserves.

It is at this point, however, that one rebels. 'A remote corner' the Tudor bishops called St David's, capital cathedral of Wales. Remote from what? Remote from London, certainly, but we have not always been ruled from London. In the sixth century St David's was a veritable Crewe Junction of the sea-routes which laced the Irish Sea and the Western Approaches; that is why it is where it is. Snowdonia may have been remote from Westminster. It was hardly remote from Liverpool when its slates were coming out; it has never been remote from the commercial world of the Atlantic in modern times, nor was it from the pirate Atlantic of the Northmen, a thousand years earlier.

Landscape does not make history; men and women do. Hills may dictate where a road may run but not why a road should be made at all. Forests may mark people off; if they get fed up with that condition, they will remove the forests. As early as the Romans, human beings were shaping the landscape to their needs.

Men and women make their own history. But they do not make it in circumstances chosen by them. It has been the interplay between the often terrifying power of human ingenuity, ambition and desperation and that brute, dumb, starveling and beautiful country which has made history here. And in Wales the people whose land it was had to confront a sight more than mountains. In consequence the Welsh have made themselves. They have made themselves over repeatedly because they have had to make themselves against the odds. There were not enough of them and there were not enough resources around to keep out much more numerous and much more powerful peoples. From birth, they lived with the threat of extinction.

Until our own days, they have survived. They survived by making and re-making themselves and their Wales over and over again. So far, they have survived for over a millennium and a half: one of the minor miracles of history. They are still one of the oldest peoples in this island even if they are now unrecognizable. Their patron saint is St David from that 'remote' south-west. But their patron spirit they captured in their lavish wealth of imaginative stories (the quickest way over the mountains), some of which survive in the *Mabinogion*.* The presiding spirit of Welsh history has been the shape-shifter Gwydion the Magician, who always changed his shape and always stayed the same.

## People

It is at the entry points into these two western peninsulas that we catch our first glimpses of human societies. They were scattered all along the great western sea-route and their culture stretched from Spain and possibly even the Berber lands of North Africa right through the Irish Sea. These were the megalith builders, the builders of the stone tombs, little people, probably dark, who were giants, carrying the rest of human history on their shoulders. They dismissed from that history the Old Stone Age hunters who, before them, had chased arctic animals and collected anything they could eat from caves along what is today the coast, people who had perhaps lived that way for something over 50,000 years in the longest time-span for any human grouping. These vanished as the New Stone Age people established the first rudimentary agriculture and enabled society to begin.

It used to be the practice to explain all these changes in terms of migrations and invasions, but prehistorians have become chary of this. It only takes one person or one family to carry a bright idea and many societies undergo

---

*\*Mabinogion* is the common title for a collection of eleven Welsh stories long recognized as a masterpiece of medieval European literature. The word is modern, employed by Lady Charlotte Guest of Dowlais as the title for her celebrated English translation of 1838-49. It is a misnomer but has passed into common currency. The core consists of four interlocking stories, written down in their present form in the second half of the eleventh century, which described themselves as the Four Branches of the *Mabinogi (Pedair Kainc y Mabinogi)*: Pwyll Prince of Dyfed, Branwen Daughter of Llŷr, Manawydan Son of Llŷr and Math Son of Mathonwy (*mabinogi* derives from *mab* (youth); it seems to have meant, first, a 'tale of youth', finally little more than 'a tale'). These probably represent a survival and an oral reworking of a lost epic about Pryderi, a prince of Dyfed. With these are associated four independent stories: Culhwch and Olwen (one of the earliest Arthurian tales, possibly dating from the tenth century), The Dream of Macsen Wledig, The Dream of Rhonabwy, and Lludd and Llefelys. There is an abundance of echoes from all eight stories in early Welsh verse. There are three other and later Arthurian romances, distinctly French in style: The Lady of the Fountain, Peredur and Gereint Son of Erbin.

Gwydion the Magician, who flickers through the early verse and the Triads, figures largely in the Fourth Branch of the Mabinogi, Math Son of Mathonwy (for a scholarly treatment, see Rachel Bromwich, *Trioedd Ynys Prydein: the Welsh Triads* (University of Wales Press, 1978)).

All the references to Welsh folk-tales in my book are to the classic and superb translation by Gwyn Jones and Thomas Jones, *The Mabinogion* (Everyman, London, 1949; paperback 1972 and successive editions).

parallel evolution. What we can say of the several millennia after the invention of agriculture is that human settlement was most obvious along the coasts from Pembroke to Anglesey and that there was normally a denser cluster on the better lands in Gwent-Glamorgan, usually in close contact with cultures on the chalk focus in Wessex. A Bronze Age Beaker Folk, named after their drinking vessels, who in Europe seem to have been precursors of the civilization called Celtic, do seem to have come in, directly from the Netherlands, to change burial rites and raise standing stones, the *meini hirion*. The fundamental human society in Britain took shape during that Bronze Age. The western peninsulas were then a commercial hub for the trade swirling around the Irish Sea in the gold, tin and copper of Ireland and Cornwall and possibly south-west Wales. The centrality of Stonehenge, which seems to have built up and repeatedly changed its functions over at least 1,500 years, is very striking. Even more striking is the fact that the controllers of Stonehenge should not only have selected a particular kind of bluestone as necessary for their purposes, but should have been able to identify the only source of those stones – the Preseli Mountains in present-day Pembrokeshire in west Wales – and to arrange for their transport and erection; this monumental effort most strongly suggests some kind of very wide unity.

Some time during the first millennium BC that unity seems to have dissolved into warring tribal complexes who shared a fairly common culture but had no political coherence. This change is usually associated with the emergence of the brilliant, warlike, flamboyant Celtic civilization grounded in a superior technology based on iron. Once again the hypothesis which suggests successive waves of invasion has largely been discarded. Some of the features once thought peculiarly Celtic – some round houses, some small, square fields, some hill-forts – are now known to be much older. We know there was an intruder group in what is now Yorkshire, the Parisii who shared a name and some styles with a group in northern Gaul; we know that shortly before the coming of the Romans there appears to have been a cross-Channel migration which created an advanced culture called Belgic in south-eastern Britain, with kings issuing coinage and people living in what amounted to primitive cities. What certainly seems to have happened is that, probably in the first instance through the movements of irresistible adventurer bands of warriors with their chiefs and priests, tribal groups were carved out which were integrated into the sweeping European cultural empire of the Celts. Certainly Britain and Gaul operated as virtually one civilization; Anglesey was a centre of the Druidic religion which seems to have trained acolytes from all over the Celtic world.

In so far as we can tell, the tribes centred on what are called hill-forts. This again is a misnomer: some do not seem to have been forts and some are not on hills. But most were large, fortified enclosures within massive ramparts and ditches, which served as foci for more scattered settlements. Most of them lie between the 200-foot and 1,000-foot contours along valleys, coastal plains and foothills. Their culture in the west was backward compared to similar structures in the lowlands, often still strongly bronze. But there are signs of a more advanced culture in what became south-east Wales and some very rich hoards have been found in lakes. One in particular, Llyn Cerrig Bach in Anglesey, a low-lying and relatively fertile land without forts of note and strategically placed on the critical trade routes to Ireland, was extraordinarily rich in very fine metalwork, harness fittings, slave-gang chain and shield ornaments. They were deposited over an extended period and come from every corner of Britain; they strongly suggest votive offerings at the heartland of Druidism.

Later evidence makes it clear that the hill-forts were generally the core of agricultural estates worked by slaves or serfs. This system was often very old indeed and Celtic-speaking society in Britain seems to have been based on a slave and serf arable and mixed agriculture supporting small classes of cattle-raising freemen-warriors and their chiefs. There is evidence that the standard European ruling family group, the four-generation kin notionally descended from a common great-grandfather within which chieftainship circulated, was normal. Queens, however, were as prominent in their ruling classes as goddesses were in their religion. Boudicca (Boadicea) of the Iceni and Cartimandua of the Brigantes would have been rather difficult to ignore!

We know very little of their culture, apart from its brilliant, fluid, complex and spiralling art forms; most of what we know comes from the Roman and post-Roman period, when it had already been transmuted into something British and distinctive. Their religion, with its fixed calendar of festivals, many of them later Christianized, had hundreds of deities often associated with natural objects, particularly springs, streams, sacred groves, mistletoe. Many of them were as human as the Greeks' but distinctly more grisly. It is notable that the horror with which the Romans confronted the Druids and their human sacrifices, their wild women, all flowing hair and rent robes, whom they called Furies, was the kind of horror particularly reserved for heretics rather than unbelievers. Celtic deities seem to have blended very quickly with the classical and they slipped down into mythological heroes in British-Welsh folklore with equal rapidity. Once again, the female seems to have predominated. We have to work primarily

8

from the example of Ireland, where Celtic life was at its most independent and developed, and from what we know of European example, where again Mediterranean influence was strong.

The great god, who was usually a tribal god, was a horrific character, a grotesque male figure carrying a massive club (in Ireland he often had a little waggon to wheel the club around on), probably represented in the huge and priapic carving of the Cerne Abbas giant. His prime function appears to have been to clobber his people with sundry disasters and challenges, though he could also reward them from his huge cauldron of rebirth. He worked in close union with a goddess who was less tribal and more concerned with the land itself. She displayed both fertility and destructress aspects and seems to have operated in close rhythm with the god and the tribal kings. As the rule of the king waxed and waned so the goddess seems to have turned from a fertile woman into a hag who presided, in the early days at least, at the king's ritual execution. There was an interesting goddess of panic. There were other major gods, such as a universal kind of craftsman god, who was probably Lludd in Brittonic, and the ubiquitous shepherdess and fire goddess who became St Bridget or Braid of Christianity. Shape-shifting was frequent, particularly among the goddesses, who were often also linked with creatures – a raven goddess of battles, a mare goddess of a horse-using people, swiftly assimilated by the Romans, to appear as Rhiannon Great Queen in Welsh legend. The Celtic Triad constantly appears, among both gods and goddesses, but it is notable that the deity of victory, to whom Boudicca sacrificed her prisoners, was a goddess and so, apparently, was the greatest deity of them all, a Mother and Triple Mother. This, the visible role of queens in historic times and the unusual status of women, in Wales and above all in Ireland, sets the brain to race.

They were all appeased by human sacrifice, of the eternal victims, maidens, babies and kings, sometimes of a mind-boggling and shape-shifting complexity, apparently conducted by Druids in sacred groves and enclosures. It is possible that the sacrifices were being commuted to animal sacrifices as the Romans came in, but the latter's shock was real enough. There appear to have been among, or dependent on, the Druids not only magicians dedicated to the customary frenzy, magic and shape-shifting but shadowy orders of heraldic and remembrancer poets, givers and interpreters of the law and soothsayers, astronomers and regulators of the seasonal life rhythms who cultivated medicine and a form of science.

All this, together with the secular traditions of battle, often as much theatre as slaughter, the poem-chanting and mead-drinking around the great fire in hall, the boasting and the word-play, the kindred pride (none of these in themselves particularly Celtic) was certainly transmitted into the Heroic Age culture of the British who became Welsh. Very striking, however, on the larger island, is the speed with which their deities succumbed to the world religions of Rome with their single Gods, like Mithras or Jehovah, and were transmuted into myth-heroes like the god Brân the Blessed, just as their kin feeling was soon charged with the Roman obsession with a precise science of genealogy. The *Mabinogion* stories of the Welsh are as loaded with memories of Romano-Celtic Britain as with those of an older Celtic pantheon. For it was through the fusion of Celtic ways of life with the European civilization which stemmed from the extension of imperial rule that these peoples' personality was shaped.

That imperial rule had not come easy; the western tribes of Britain fought the Romans long and hard. The celebrated Caratacus (Caradoc), son of Cunobelinus (Cynfelin, Cymbeline), fled from the kingdoms of the south-east to lead a resistance in the west before his betrayal by Cartimandua. He became a warrior hero of the Silures and the Ordovices. When a British kingdom emerged from the Romano-British commonwealth of the Silures four hundred years later, its origin-legends named among the early kings of this new Gwent a Caradoc and a Cynfelin. Caradoc could be counted the first historic hero of the later Welsh.

The Silures inflicted so many defeats on the Romans that one general proposed their extermination; they managed to settle their leading people in a little city instead. The Ordovices fought so hard that they nearly were exterminated. But by the mid-seventies it was over. These Celtic-speaking peoples passed into the first urban civilization of the European west. It proved to be a creative experience. Their god Lludd became a myth-hero and for what was he remembered? – the building of one of the greatest cities of the Roman west as the capital of one of its wealthiest and more important provinces. It was Lludd, in British-Welsh tradition, who refurbished Londinium and gave it the name of Caer (*castrum*) Lludd . . . 'and at last Caer Lundein. And it was after the coming of the foreign folk thereto that it was called Lundein or otherwise Lwndrys . . .'

In the Second Branch of the *Mabinogi*, there is a magnificent Welsh story, *Branwen verch Llŷr* (Branwen daughter of Llŷr), one of the most brilliant and poignant folk-tales in any language. It is dominated by the Celtic motherland of Ireland and immersed in the magic other-world of the Celts. But when the survivors of a futile and fratricidal war break their fourscore years of forgetfulness in a Shangri-La in Dyfed by 'opening the door that looks on Cornwall', so that . . . 'they were as conscious of every loss they had ever sustained, and of every kinsman and friend they had missed, and of every ill that had come upon them, as if it were even then it had befallen them . . .', it is to the White Mount in London that they have to carry the head of the great Brân the Blessed so that the Island of the Mighty, the Island of Britain, may be preserved from harm.

Whatever these peoples were, going into Rome, they came out of it Britons.

**military sites**

- ■ legionary
- ▪ auxiliary
- ▪ fortlet
- □ early
- ▽ marching

**civil sites**

- ◉ capital
- ● other
- ▲ villas
- ○ non-imperial
- ——— roads
- ·········· conjectured roads

Caergybi ( Holyhead )
Din Lligwy
Aberffraw
Tre'r Ceiri
Llystyn
Segontium ( Caernarfon )
Kanovium ( Caerhun )
Bryn-y-gefeiliau
Tomen-y-mur
DECEANGLI
Dinorben
(Varis)
Deva ( Chester )
(Leg. XX)
Mediolanum
Rutunium
Caer Gai
ORDOVICES
Pennal
Forden Gaer
Viriconium ( Wroxeter )
Caersws
Buckton
CORNOVII
Bravonium
Trawsgoed
Llanio
Castell Collen
Beulah
Dolaucothi
Llandovery
Magnis
Y Gaer
Cwm-du
Aricon
Moridunum ( Carmarthen )
Coelbren
Gobannium
Blestium
Pen-y-darren
Burrium
DEMETAE
SILURES
Leucarum
Nidum ( Neath )
Gelligaer
Caerphilly
Venta ( Caerwent )
(Bomio)
Isca ( Caerleon )
(Leg. II Aug.)
Cardiff

N

| 0 | | 20 miles |
| 0 | | 40 km |

## 2.  ROMAN WALES

(after fig. 30, from Wendy Davies, *Wales in the Early Middle Ages*, Leicester University Press, 1982).

# 2 · BRITISH WELSH*

Roman power came thrusting into these two western peninsulas of the Britannia it was creating as a military and exploitive force. A manager of mines was clawing at the lead of the north-east even before the Deceangli had been defeated and, as soon as the Silures had been broken, the army with its convict labour moved on the goldmine at Dolaucothi in the south-west. They trenched big reservoirs and scouring channels, washed away hillsides, burned down forests and drenched the district in acid rain. They built a conduit seven miles long, a bath-house for workers and a small fort. They drove the miners deeper into the caverns and worked the site hard well into the second century, to be succeeded by civilian exploiters, as the garrison dwindled to a merely ritual size. In Anglesey they were working copper to the end, outside any original fort system.

It is military occupation which has left the clearest imprint on the land and on the minds of its chroniclers, but the rule of soldiers was short-lived. The base of the Second Legion at Caerleon, rebuilt in stone from the second century, became one of the three major military establishments of Britain, with at least one and probably more large and flourishing civil settlements, whose cosmopolitan population threw up two early Christian martyrs and the only centenarian on record in Roman Britain. The *caer* of the legion was to be duly identified in the legends of British and Welsh as their Camelot, the court of Arthur of Britain.

From Caerleon, roads with their strategically placed forts laced the land of the Silures, running along the coast through Cardiff and Neath (Nidum) and on to the new capital of the commonwealth of the Demetae, the base and civil town of Carmarthen (Moridunum), arcing inland in a network

---

*So scarce is the evidence for this period, so elusive its nature and so fundamental the debate among historians, not least about their very sources, that the proper, professional course for a proper, professional historian would be to say nothing at all about eight hundred of the most critical years in the history of the Welsh. This would be an intolerable dereliction of duty on the part of a historian who is trying to speak to his own people and anyone else who cares to listen about that history. I have therefore tried to read and think as widely and as deeply as I can and to make up my mind. With the qualifications which still seem to me unavoidable, here I tell you what I think happened.

focused on Y Gaer near Brecon. From Chester (Deva), base of the Twentieth Legion, the northern coastal road ran through Caerhun to the other major western centre of Caernarfon (Segontium, the *'caer* in Arfon'), to circle inland through mountain wastes. A road with minor stations snaked down the west coast, while in the east, along the edge of the high country, a major highway linked Chester and Caerleon and ran through Wroxeter (Viriconium), capital of the commonwealth of the Cornovii. Minor roads nosed tentatively into the probably empty central massif.

Those roads put backbone into amorphous societies and were to serve as a skeleton for the societies which succeeded them. It was easier to move around Wales in Roman times than it had been or was to be for centuries; and these western peoples, however poor and primitive some of them were in comparison with the rich Romano-Celtic life of their eastern neighbours, were swiftly integrated into the new British reality. The roads, together with the Britain they knit together, lodged limpet-like in the memory of the Welsh peoples who emerged eight hundred years later. They named them Sarn Helen (Helen's Highway), after an appropriately 'Welsh' wife with whom their mythological history endowed a usurping Roman general Magnus Maximus, appropriately rechristened Macsen Wledig, a British and hence Welsh Emperor of the west.

For the forts the roads served were soon empty of soldiers on permanent station; from the second century, the western garrisons were run down to a merely routine commitment. Apart from its customary and quite significant role in provincial civil life, the army was preoccupied with the permanent threat from the unconquered north beyond Hadrian's Wall and the sporadic menace from eastern and western seas which made Britain something of a frontier province with a strong garrison; above all this big army was enmeshed in the often violent internal politics of the Empire, as Britain's growing wealth and power made it a key factor in the struggle of international factions, a province renowned for its independent temper and the ambition of its generals. These political tensions apart, there was little trouble with the Britons. In the west there was none at all. Settlement and activity in abundance are reported from western promontories well outside any notional military quadrilateral: mineral working and clusters of stone huts serving as the core of land-holdings in Anglesey and comfortable villa estates in the douce land of Dyfed, with a scattering of traders and perhaps settlers from Ireland in both.

Not until the general crises of the fourth century do towns and settlements start to don the medieval livery of fear, as Cardiff, Holyhead, Caernarfon, are refortified to face the sea, old hill-forts are brought back into action and the army returns in some strength to the coasts. The threat they feared then came from outside.

## Britannia Prima

The peoples of western Britain, ultimately embraced in the province of Britannia Prima with its capital in the Dobunni city of Cirencester, were subjected to that remorseless process of assimilation and reorganization which, with all its regional peculiarities, characterized the entire Roman Empire. After AD 212, every free man in that Empire enjoyed the full rights of a Roman citizen. A hundred years later, this old and originally crucial discrimination between citizen and non-citizen had itself yielded to the more realistic legal distinction between upper classes (*honestiores*) and lower (*humiliores*). For while in every province the imperial core was provided by the civil service and an army entrenched in the state industries, the ruling classes of the native peoples, often living by the intense exploitation of slaves and serfs (who at the moment of truth frequently preferred the barbarians) were assimilated into a European class of notables and aristocrats, many of whom owed allegiance to Romanism (*romanitas*) rather than Rome.

Organized at first around the *civitas*, the theoretical city-state form which Rome initially imposed on its peoples, their social power shifted in the late Empire to landed oligarchies within those commonwealths who often came to resent the burden of the Imperial presence. From the early fourth century there was a sustained, if interrupted, effort to impose Christianity as the official religion. Although this met resistance, a powerful, originally urban Catholic hierarchy took shape, ultimately to replace an Imperial with a Christian Rome, an emperor with a pope. This relentlessly advancing religion was soon strong enough to generate its own anti-Catholic heresies which proved politically significant, not least in Britain, one of the richest and most powerful provinces, already notorious for its military adventurers.

The Empire began to crack under its self-imposed burdens, as slaves rebelled and peoples the Romans called barbarian pressed on the frontiers, as the army and the administration were penetrated by Germans, many of whom were settling within the borders as client people or peoples, and its division between Constantinople and Rome bred multiple usurpers and civil wars. Within this late Empire it is already possible to detect the outlines of those Christian warrior-landlord kingdoms which were to be its successors. In what became Wales, for example, every little piratical dynasty of kings which emerged after the wreck of Rome arose from the ranks of the Romano-British notables of the late Empire.

Standard Roman procedure was certainly applied to the Silures, the Demetae and the Cornovii and probably, in the appropriate form, to all the western peoples. The Silures were moved out of their hill-fort capital of Llanmelin and settled in their own Venta Silurum, the town of Caerwent. This was inevitably a small, but a fully operative, Roman town, with the standard equipment of forum, basilica and baths. Its strip-houses with their long plots may at first have been the town houses of rural notables, but from the second century Caerwent became more effectively a town. It was very prosperous and indeed highly fashionable; some of the most sophisticated Mediterranean-style houses of the Empire were to be found among its private residences. It had a guild of merchants and craftsmen, a patron of high rank commemorated in inscriptions; above all, it had the full panoply of civic self-government in its *ordo* of a hundred councillors and its proudly proclaimed status as a *respublica;* it was the capital of the commonwealth of the Silures. It undoubtedly shared in the decline of the towns in later years, but some kind of settlement persisted there for two hundred years after Rome had gone. It had supported religious cults which married the classical god Mars to Celtic deities imported, like many of its consumer goods, from the Rhineland, but it was also an early Christian site. The origin-legend of the British kingdom which succeeded it had the first king handing over what was left of the town to a monastery.

Country estates the commonwealth had in abundance; some of them, like those at Llantwit and Ely, were big; when one of them emerges into history it covered 6,000 acres, while several ranged up to 1,000 acres. The pattern of land-holding was complex: later evidence from Ariconium (Ergyng) in the east to Dinas Powys, near Cardiff, indicates that the economic base of the Silurian notables was a complex and probably old system of multiple estates worked by serfs and slaves on which a small class of free people and their leading families rode in power. It was people like this who were to create the succcessor British kingdom and it seems appropriate that the heartland of that kingdom took its name from Venta, the little Roman town which had spawned it; it called itself Gwent.

The commonwealth of the Demetae in the south-west would no doubt have travelled much the same road, had it not been for an inflow from Ireland in the last years of Rome. Villas and estates there certainly were, and in the fourth century there was heavy residential development in the little town of Carmarthen which seems to have followed a familiar pattern of takeover from outside by powerful individuals and groups within the local Romano-British aristocracy who had dodged the heavy tax burden of orthodox town citizenship. It was a typical late-Imperial landlord commonwealth which was commandeered at the end by Irish incomers bearing some kind of Roman authority. Its notables were to provide the new kingdom with an influential intelligentsia in its powerful Christian Church. No less typically, a monastery was to nest in what was left of the town.

The Ordovices and the Deceangli are much more difficult to detect. The former had been nearly wiped out in the original conquest and human settlement in the area assumed to be theirs did not revive until the third century. The Deceangli seem to survive only in the name of Tegeingl, a district in north-east Wales. The lands associated with the two tribes, however, were embraced in the medieval Welsh kingdom of Powys, which was itself the survivor of a distinguished and long-lasting British polity which stretched from the West Midlands and the Shrewsbury region into what is today Wales. It seems probable that this kingdom emerged from the commonwealth of the Cornovii. One source for the name Powys could well be the Latin *pagenses*, related to the *pagi*, which were rural districts of government. It is possible that the two tribes or their survivors were ruled from the Cornovian capital of Wroxeter (Viriconium) which in the late Empire certainly gives the impression of a town transformed into an administrative village by the power of its local landed notables. Such evidence as we have from the region is familiar. At Dinorben, near Rhyl, an estate with a core worked by slave or serf labour formed around a very ancient hill-fort whose origins can be traced to the tenth or ninth century BC and which assumed its form in the sixth or fifth century BC. Between AD 260 and 360 a large circular house was built within it, probably to serve as the centre of the estate of a Romano-British magnate.

We know nothing about the form of government in the north-west, which was to be the homeland of the strongest dynasty in medieval Wales. In late Roman times the military re-established themselves in some force in Caernarfon, Caerhun and Anglesey to counter pressure from Ireland similar to that in the south-west. The British general Maximus, who briefly made himself the ruler of the Western Empire, took soldiers from Caernarfon with him into Europe. The origin-legends of this region's dynasty assert that, to counter the Irish incursion, the Romano-British authorities transplanted an allied tribal dynasty from the Edinburgh district as federates and that Maximus granted self-government to the leading families of the peoples. Whatever the truth about the form of government in the area, there was certainly a land-owning class ready to exercise power. Estates were fairly thick on the ground. Some sites, such as Tre'r Ceiri in the Llŷn peninsula, a large, fortified, hill village of 150 stone houses, were pre-Roman and still primitive, but in other places there are clusters of stone huts, several hundred of them, solidly built, often with paved floors and drains which, while crude, look very like a 'native' or 'northern' version of the villas of the lowlands. Din Lligwy in Anglesey, Cefn Graeanog on the mainland and several other groups seem to have been centres of estates of mixed farming and cattle raising and there is evidence of communities of slaves or serfs concentrated around some centre of authority like a hill-fort, old or new, and serving as the human base for free families and notables. Most striking of all is Aberffraw in Anglesey, the site of a late Roman fort and naval base directed against the Irish. The fort was refurbished and the settlement of serfs there was to emerge as the very *caput* or royal demesne of the British successor kingdom of Gwynedd.

Outside the south-east and a few other favoured districts, these people were, of course, poverty-stricken and relatively primitive backwoodsmen by comparison with the densely settled peoples of the British lowlands in their striking and distinctive Romano-Celtic culture. The population of Britain, already fairly large in the late Iron Age, may have risen to between 4 and 6½ million; not many of those would have lived in the harder regions of the west. The Brittonic language, present everywhere, would have been stronger and more prestigious, its traditions vividly alive. When Rome lost its grip, these peoples were to slither rapidly into a Heroic Age anarchy of strongly 'Celtic' character. *Romanitas* here was largely a matter of style.

But this is only one side of the picture and perhaps the least important. At a basic, material level, it is becoming clear, as the results of excavation filter through, that we have underestimated the extent of Romanization even in the austere uplands; certainly the international trade and mass-produced commodities of Europe were present, even during the century after the end of formal Roman rule. The Latin language was everywhere and left a notable imprint on Brittonic and its Welsh successor, Cymraeg; it achieved permanence, of course, in the Christian Church, the real inheritor of Rome – and it is beginning to look as though much of the population, no doubt following its social superiors, was already at least nominally Christian by the fifth century. But Latin also dominated the secular world of rulers. For centuries after Rome had gone, memorials to notables and royal monuments all over Wales are in Latin, and often the Latin of scientific genealogy which was one of Rome's most characteristic professions. As late as the sixth century, a man of Penmachno could call himself a *cives*, a 'citizen' of Gwynedd. These are matters of the mind, but in some respects it is the mind which is important here. For what it enshrined was that intense consciousness of Britain, Ynys Prydain, the Island of the

Mighty, which so charged the writings of the Welsh for centuries to come. However steeped it was in older mythologies, their Britain was the Britain which Rome had created. Nowhere was the sense of it stronger than among the men of power and the poets and story-tellers they patronized. It is impossible to say whether these were new people or direct descendants of pre-Roman notables, but what is clear is that by the fourth century and within the structure of imperial government, a class of land-owning magnates had assumed social power throughout the two western peninsulas, to take their humble place in a Romano-British ruling class.

From the late fourth into the fifth century, this class moved through multiple crises to establish its own independent state.

Britannia with its great city of Londinium – Caer Lludd – was at this time a diocese of four or five provinces, incorporated in a prefecture of the Gauls along with Gaul and Hispania, which was run from Trier in the Rhineland and provided an arena for ambitious generals. Unlike the Gallo-Romans, its notables tended to shun the imperial service and many had adhered to the Christian heresy of Pelagius, a British cleric who stressed the idea of grace and whose creed seems to have become the ideology of those discontented with imperial administration. They were living in a time of troubles. From the late third century onwards, as the economy began to shuffle out of an international urbanism, barbarian attacks intensified, Picts from the north coming over the Wall, Scots and others from Ireland hitting the west, German tribes breaking in across the Saxon shore. There were plenty of Germans within the frontier, serving in an army repeatedly engaged in European adventures and possibly as settled federates.

The cycle of terminal crises hit Britain in 367, when an unprecedented conspiracy, taking advantage of imperial difficulties, struck Gaul and Britain simultaneously. Britain was overrun by Picts and Scots, serfs and slaves rebelled, an entire province seceded from the Empire. The general Theodosius had to fight his way across the island to restore order. He undertook a major programme of reconstruction which seems to have opened up a period of unprecedented prosperity for the upper classes. By now the latter were thoroughly disenchanted, however, and they responded when another cycle of troubles precipitated by the Emperor Gratian's Christian onslaught on paganism and the classical cults provoked yet another army coup in Britain. In 383 the army in Britain raised Magnus Maximus, ironically a persecuting Christian himself, and struck for the Empire.

Maximus was a native of Hispania; it is possible he came from Celtic Galicia and spoke a kindred language to the Britons. He had served with

Theodosius, won a victory over Picts and Scots and earned the support of important classes. He took an army over the Channel, won control of the prefecture of the Gauls, assumed imperial power and in 387 marched on Milan to extinguish the rival emperor, only to meet disaster and death in the following year. But such was the support for Maximus in Britain that the imperial regime found it difficult to restore the situation. The British returned to their allegiance only after renewed raids by the Picts.

For the purpose of legend, at least, this man had the makings of a hero of the Britons. He was certainly to be a hero to the Bretons on the continent in later years. What is remarkable is that he was to become absolutely central to the historical traditions of the Welsh after they entered history hundreds of years later. Gildas, a west Briton writing in the sixth century, dated the fall of Roman Britain from the 'withdrawal of the legions' by Maximus. Welsh tradition was to assert that Maximus had done something wonderful for the Welsh people. He certainly took soldiers from Caernarfon with him and he was said to have transferred government to British notables. The origin-legends of the dynasty of Gwynedd in the north-west had Maximus transfer their legendary founder Cunedda from the waist of Scotland to Anglesey and the dynasties of Gwynedd were to be central to the history of the Welsh; the Welsh princes of Wales derived from them. The early poetry and traditions of the Welsh are steeped in the heroic legends of North Britain and suffused with memories of Maximus. In *The Dream of Macsen Wledig* (Macsen the Emperor) he is the pivot of one of the most jewelled stories in the *Mabinogion*. He was supplied with a wife from Caernarfon, Elen or Helen Luyddog, Helen of the Hosts, sometimes conflated with St Helena, the mother of Constantine the Great; they named the Roman roads after her. Nearly every dynasty which was to claw its way to power in Wales took pains to construct genealogies which linked their names with that of Maximus.

In a very real sense, Wales can be said to begin with the British hero Maximus. Wales is born in AD 383 with Macsen Wledig.

However, this is a Wales of the mind, created much later. There was almost certainly a strong oral tradition, but the Macsen of the history of the Welsh was manufactured in the ninth century, by royal genealogists in the service of the second dynasty of Gwynedd which had just come to power. To those ninth-century minds, what had become their country, Wales, began with Macsen the British Roman Emperor. It had taken five hundred years for that Wales to appear on the ground. It emerged then out of the ruins of an independent British state which Romano-Britons created and of whose creation Macsen Wledig had been a herald.

The Welsh, like most of the peoples and nations of Western Europe, struggled painfully to birth as bastard children of the late Roman Empire.

## The Wars of British Independence

In AD 409 Britain broke free from the Roman Empire. For nearly four hundred years it fought for its life. The Welsh come into history as its survivors and inheritors.

In 402 Stilicho the Vandal, who was military commander of the west under the emperor Honorius and who had reorganized Britain's defences in depth, was forced to withdraw troops from the island to cope with Visigoths and other threats at the centre. At much the same time the Imperial court removed to Ravenna and the flow of Roman silver coinage into Britain abruptly ceased. This dislocated the military and civil establishment and their associated industries and pitched the classes dependent on them into the dustbins of history. The landowning magnates continued to enjoy prosperity, but in 405 there was a massive onslaught from Ireland. The disaffected army growled into action again. They raised a soldier in 406, killed him, and replaced him with a British civilian. While they were at this work, on the last day of the year 406, a horde of Christian German tribes burst across the Rhine, swept through Gaul and broke over the Pyrenees into Spain.

The army promptly killed their civilian and again raised a soldier, who was to become Constantine III. Like Maximus before him, he led a force across the Channel and took the prefecture of the Gauls, shifting its capital to Arles. But order in Gaul collapsed in wars between Constantine, Gerontius, his British general in Spain, and Stilicho, each using barbarians against the others. The western Empire began to dissolve into warring polities out of which the embryonic kingdoms of the west were to emerge. More tribes streamed across the Rhine, Burgundians began to settle and in 410 Alaric the Goth sacked Rome itself. Probably as part of this general surge, pagan Saxons descended on Britain in 408. The Britons organized their own defence and beat them off.

They had had enough. The Romano-British notables, led by Pelagian magnates, broke with Rome and took power. They destroyed the imperial civil service in Britain in a bloody purge.

Those who have freely shed the blood of others are now being forced to spill their own . . . Some lie unburied, food for the beasts and birds . . . Others have been individually torn limb from limb . . . Their judgements killed many husbands, widowed many women, orphaned many children . . . Now it is their wives who are widowed, their sons who are orphans, begging their daily bread . . . *

The Greek historian Zosimus, writing a hundred years later, catches the moment . . . 'The Britons took up arms and, fighting for themselves, freed the cities from the barbarian pressure; and all of Armorica and other provinces of Gaul, in imitation of the Britons, freed themselves in the same manner, expelling the Roman officials and setting up their own administrations as well as they could . . .' In Armorica, the western peninsula of Gaul, they did not do so well; they were engulfed in a peasant revolution. Confronted with a vengeful and resurgent imperial power, they turned for mediation to St Germanus of Auxerre. This man had been a barrister and a provincial governor and stood high in the Church; after the military commander Aetius had restored some semblance of Roman power in Gaul, he sent Germanus with the Bishop of Troyes to Britain, to root out the Pelagians and bring the island back to its allegiance. That visit, in 429, gives us the only glimpse we get of Britain after twenty years of independence.

The centralized administration had gone and Britain was ruled by the leaders of its commonwealths. Germanus visited the shrine of St Albans and found Verulamium flourishing under a leader bearing the authority of a Roman military tribune. Power had passed to the landed aristocracy, resplendent in their rich and multicoloured dress, supercilious in their Pelagian arrogance and surrounded by a 'fawning multitude'. Germanus debated with their spokesman, the son of a bishop. To defeat a joint Pict-Saxon raid, he mobilized an army, taught them the Christian warcry 'Alleluia!' and led them to victory. He had to baptize them; they may have been pagan mercenaries in the employ of the magnates, Britons who were pagans or Britons who had to be restored to Catholicism.

Military power was already passing to other hands. Another opponent of Germanus was the man whom sixth-century Gildas called the 'proud tyrant' of these councils. Tyrant was a word then used to describe a person without legal, that is imperial, authority. Saxon sources identify him as Vortigern (Gwrtheyrn), who was to loom large in the demonology of the Welsh. The name may have been a personal one, but it carries overtones

* From *De Vita Christiana*, a Christian tract which came out in Britain in AD 411, only two years after the break with Rome. This text, which itself forces a rethinking of the entire concept of 'the end of Roman Britain', was first brought to our notice by the late Dr John Morris and is discussed in Peter Salway's *Roman Britain, Oxford History of England* vol 1 (1981), p. 441.

of 'overlord' or 'high king'. Gwrtheyrnion near Builth seems to take its name from his; the 'tyrant' figures in the royal genealogy of that kingdom. More significantly, Vortigern was acknowledged as a founder by the dynasty of the important kingdom of Powys. He may have been a strong man of the Cornovii. With imperial authority displaced, power would pass to the organized commonwealths, but it is easy to envisage a situation in which, with order collapsing all around, a local strong-arm would take over, as insecurity drove people to seek what protection they could – from someone who controlled a hill-fort, for example. The Roman styles they used could legitimize such action. In Europe men like this, whether Roman or barbarian, would soon start calling themselves kings. Vortigern's presence in 429 probably heralds their imminent entry into Britain, if they had not appeared already in the west.

The notables contained the threat from Germanus but within fifteen years they were done for. Around the year 452 a chronicler in Gaul identified the year 441/2 as the year in which Britain, long disturbed, 'passed under the dominion of the Saxons'. Taken literally, this is gross exaggeration, but it reflects a reality. Some time in the middle of the fifth century, Britain suffered a disaster which left tracts of the east under Saxon control. Gildas, supplemented by the Saxon origin-legend of Hengist, is the source of the traditional story.

Prosperity in Britain ended in plagues, the renewal of Pictish attacks and, above all, in civil war. Vortigern countered the Picts by hiring Saxon federates and, besotted with Hengist's daughter, gave them Kent as bride-price. The Saxons took advantage of the civil wars among the Britons, rose in revolt, brought in thousands more of their unspeakable kin, betrayed a peace conference in a massacre which was to prove deathless in Welsh annals as the Treason of the Long Knives, ravaged a decapitated Britain from end to end and finished up in command of half of it.

All the greater towns fell to the enemy's battering rams; all their inhabitants, bishops, priests, people, were mown down together . . . Horrible was it to see the foundation stones of towers and high walls thrown down bottom upwards in the squares, mixing with holy altars and fragments of human bodies, as though they were covered with a purple crust of clotted blood, as in some fantastic wine-press . . .

The rhetoric of Gildas finds a chilling echo in a report he cites from the fifth century itself, the appeal of the Britons to Aetius somewhere between 446 and 454 . . . 'the barbarians drive us to the sea and the sea drives us back to the barbarians . . .'

Discounting the hypnosis doubtless exercised by Saxon blondes and certainly exercised by sixth-century rhetoricians, there seems to be some reality underlying this. There is evidence of Germanic settlement in the south-east and it is from the middle of the fifth century that much of a Britain still in important senses Roman ceases to be archaeologically recognizable. There were almost certainly civil wars. Conflict is reported between an associate of Vortigern, Vitalinus of Gloucester, a Dobunni leader, and an Ambrosius (Emrys) who presumably represented the Catholic and Imperial connection which Germanus would have organized. A history of the Britons written by a Welshman in the early ninth century says that Vortigern was threatened by 'the Picts and the Irish, by a Roman invasion and not least by fear of Ambrosius'. * By this time Aetius had built up a confederacy of friendly barbarian powers in Gaul and was threatening Britain with thousands of mercenary Huns. Saxon federates in Kent would have been a defence against him and the Ambrosian party rather than the Picts. In response to the British appeal, Aetius sent Germanus back to the island. He and the Bishop of Trier negotiated with a person who was 'first of his region', presumably another of those 'tyrants' who would be appearing everywhere. Pelagianism had been discredited; an alteration in the dating of Easter, settled by the Catholic Church in 455, was easily accepted in Britain. There was quite intimate contact in terms of trade and Christianity between the continent and at least west-central Britain (and perhaps London). Mediterranean pottery was coming into Wales.

The European dimension is central. Aetius sent Germanus and not an army because he was heavily engaged with the Huns under Attila. Not until the mid-450s did the Hunnish horde break up and by that time Aetius had been murdered by his own Emperor. This moment was probably critical to the Saxon success in Britain. Through the 460s, however, under a new commander, Ricimer, two able men, the Emperor Majorian and Anthemius, a distinguished officer from the eastern Empire, won many victories and re-established a Roman presence in Gaul. And central to the force which Anthemius led against the Visigoths in 467 was a powerful army of Britons under Riothamus, king of the Armoricans.

Large groups of Britons, driven by the plagues, the Saxons and recruitment by the Romans, were crossing into Gaul. They seem to have moved in organized communities; in 461 one of their bishops attended a

---

*The *Historia Brittonum* of 829/830. It is no longer thought that this was composed by the monk Nennius; see David Dumville, ' "Nennius" and the *Hist. Brittonum*', *Studia Celtica*, 10–11 (1975–6).

conference in Tours. It grew into a mass migration which continued over many years, another of those 'migrations of the peoples' which characterized the times. These Britons seem to have swallowed up whatever was left of the Armoricans and they were present in force along the Loire. They played an important role in a confederacy which buttressed a Roman enclave around Soissons. Not until 496 did the new power of Clovis and the Franks extinguish this last survivor of the Empire in the west.

The incomers finally settled in Armorica. By this time its whole population were known as Britons. Their language was Brittonic and in due course produced Breton, close cousin to the Cymraeg of the Welsh. Brittany was central to the history of those Welsh: indeed Riothamus has been put forward as a candidate for the historical Arthur. Churchmen crossed and recrossed endlessly between Brittany, Cornwall and Wales; lives of the Welsh saints were produced in Brittany and the earliest known collection called or calling itself the Canon Laws of the Welsh came out of Brittany. The connection remained intimate for generations. And it was this sequence of temporary Roman success along the Loire which initiated that brief but potent period in the history of the adjacent island which it is difficult to avoid calling the age of Arthur.

The mass migrations following on the Saxon settlement must have ripped the heart out of that Britain which the action of 409 had created. But a Britain remained, focused now on kings who had emerged from the commonwealths; supported by events across the Channel, they fought back. Gildas describes the late fifth century as an epoch of battles, culminating in 'almost the last' battle at Mount Badon, which stopped the Saxon advance for a half-century and opened a time of peace and prosperity, the time in which he was writing.

The person Gildas names is Ambrosius Aurelianus, another Emrys, Emrys Wledig, Emrys the Emperor, member of a family which had 'worn the purple'. It has been suggested that he might even have been related to the family of Ambrose, the powerful bishop of Milan. He came from the same kind of stable as Germanus and the Ambrosius of that earlier time, who may, or more likely may not, have been the same person. In due course he, too, was to lodge in Welsh tradition.

Gildas does not mention Arthur and of all our writers he is the most likely to have known of him, or indeed to have known him, had he existed as a historical person. Apart from some oblique hints, the earliest direct references we have date from the ninth century, where we encounter the catalogue of his celebrated twelve battles, including Mount Badon. From the start he is very much a figure of legend. An extraordinarily rich oral tradition was to grow around him and so mighty, magnificent and attractive is that tradition that most people have been very reluctant to accept his exclusion from real history and have gone to remarkable lengths to find some possible anchorage in reality. The most plausible suggestion, which has early warrant, is that he was not himself a king but fought (presumably with a warband, germ of the later 'knights') for the kings of Britain as a kind of *dux bellorum*, a Roman-style military commander, and in a manner which would have been familiar in the later years of the Empire. It is entirely plausible, in turn, that such a person could have existed at such a time. Both Ambrosius and Riothamus, in some senses, could be interpreted as playing that role. And it is precisely here that Arthur should be located. The legend, which became central to the Welsh assimilation of their own history, expressed precisely that kind of perception of the times which later British-Welsh writers made the very stuff of their own identity. In this sense the legend in its original Welsh form is no lie; on the contrary, it expresses a truth.

At the time Gildas wrote, the Britons were governed by kings. Gildas's work is one long denunciation of them for abandoning Latin, *romanitas* and Christianity and lapsing into what he saw as barbarity. Almost in passing he names a few of them; at least two ruled in what was becoming Wales. There was Vortipor, 'tyrant' of the Demetae in the south-west, who was Gwrthefyr, king of Dyfed, placed precisely in the mid-sixth century on a memorial stone raised in what is today Carmarthenshire and inscribed in both Latin and the ogham script of the Irish. And there was Maelgwn Gwynedd, ruling Gwynedd in lavish, magnificent and Celtic style from a court at Degannwy on the north Wales coast, but who had been trained in the decidedly Romano-British monastery at Llanilltud Fawr (Llantwit Major) in the Vale of Glamorgan in the south-east; according to both Britons and Saxons, he was the most powerful of the kings of the Britons.

After Gildas the curtain comes down. From the late sixth century the mixed peoples of the east, generically labelled Anglo-Saxons and organizing themselves in kingdoms, resumed their advance. It was a long, slow, piecemeal business; some of the advances may not represent straightforward conquests and there is evidence of the transient existence of peoples who were literally mixed. But it was remorseless. The foundation of kingdoms in the north opened an epoch of battles with the North Britons which were to be central to later historical traditions among the Welsh. After a battle near Bath in 577, the kings of Gloucester, Bath and Cirencester were gone and Saxon power reached the Bristol Channel, to press on into the south-west. Almost a century later, in a bewildering maze of triangular struggles between Mercians, Northumbrians and West Britons, the newcomers entrenched themselves on the northern shores of the Irish Sea. It took another century to establish the power of Mercia in the Midlands. Britain, in its shifting form, and uniquely in Europe, fought the barbarians for nearly four hundred years before it was lost. It was late in the eighth century that Offa of Mercia, first of the Saxon kings to adopt imperial styles, drove his Dyke from sea to sea, to shut out the West Britons from their inheritance as 'foreigners' – the Welsh.

East of a line from the Yorkshire wolds to Southampton, there is precious little evidence of British survival, even in river names. West of that line, however, into the upland watershed, there is much evidence. Place-names remain strongly Celtic, though often transmuted; Brittonic, now rapidly changing and splintering into different languages – one of them Cymraeg, or Welsh – survived as a subject tongue. Early laws of the kingdom of Wessex make specific provision for a whole British hierarchy within its society. Further west still beyond this line and up to the rooted Celtic lands of north-west Britain, Wales and Cornwall, British survival under Saxon control seems to have been substantial, perhaps even massive. As English settlement inched up to the Wye and the line of the Southern Dyke, there may have been almost as much fusion as conquest.

It was in these latter regions that the rising kingdoms of Northumbria, Mercia and Wessex took shape between 600 and 800. And it was in those districts that a recognizable Wales was defined.

## West Britons

From the fifth century the western regions of Britain drop out of history; they do not climb back in until the ninth century. Apart from the references in Gildas, we have a few clues from the sixth century at the earliest and a scattering of memorial stones and place-names, difficult archaeological material. Furthermore the written material we have from the ninth century was intended largely to justify the situation which then existed and to provide it with a respectable history. These ages are dark ages because we cannot see anything clearly. All we can do is make intelligent guesses.*

Some things *are* clear. Whatever the reality on the ground, these peoples and their witness-bearers were governed by memories, interpretations and projections, not of Rome, but of that Britain which Rome created. Very

*The essential works here are Wendy Davies, *Wales in the Early Middle Ages* (Leicester University Press, 1982) and David Dumville, 'Sub-Roman Britain: history and legend', *History*, 72 (1977).

visible in the Church, in memorial stones, in the origins, styles and practices of its early kings, this persisted even as these little kingdoms were driven back on themselves. When they emerge in the ninth century and start to write their own history and to explain themselves to themselves, they are totally British in their perception.

Most striking is the marked divergence between the north and the south. Perhaps here lies one explanation for the differing forms of Welsh spoken in the two regions. In the south, despite Irish dominance to the west, the kingdoms which emerge, to crystallize into two of the four 'ancient kingdoms' of Wales, Morgannwg and a Dyfed expanding into a Deheubarth, are recognizable as an evolution out of late Roman Britain. Moreover, the dreaded Saxons do not loom very large; the incomers here are Irish and there is for long an intimate connection with Cornwall (scene of some of Arthur's legendary triumphs) and Brittany. To the north, on the contrary, while the two kingdoms, Gwynedd and Powys, certainly come out of a late Romano-British context, it is more difficult to relate them directly to Romano-British units of government. The Irish are present to the west but not in the dominant force they acquired in the south. Most notable of all is that the Saxon presence is overpowering. North-eastern Powys was enmeshed in complicated dealings, both hostile and friendly, with emergent Saxon powers in the Midlands, while, in a quite startling manner, Gwynedd in north-western Wales seems to be at the very heart of great battles in northern *Britain*. So much so, that when a perspective becomes visible in the ninth century, it seems dominated by North Britain. To employ utterly anachronistic modern terms, it would seem as if the first Welsh poetry to survive, from the sixth century, was written in Scotland about a battle in Yorkshire. This would be a meaningless statement (not least because Wales, Scotland and Yorkshire did not in fact exist) but it does catch something of the travail in which these people (and their historians after them!) slowly turned themselves from West Britons into Welsh.

We know most about the south-east, largely because of the survival of some very old material in the charters preserved by Llandaff, which was to become the episcopal see of the region, and by Llancarfan, an important monastery of ancient foundation.* These charters are themselves significant. They follow a standard late Roman pattern; until the eighth century land was changing hands in the south-east in the terms and the

---

*Wendy Davies, *An Early Welsh Microcosm* (Royal Historical Society, 1978), a superb, scholarly, massive and meticulous study which has transformed our understanding of this, the most difficult of all periods.

vocabulary of Roman Britain. Not until that century do the big estates seem to fragment into smaller units and the terms characteristic of the later Laws of Wales appear. In those charters there are kings, landlords, dependants and slaves; there is no trace of the ordinary freemen who loom so large in the later Laws, nor indeed, of the kindred, the *cenedl*, that structured family and kinship group which was central to later Welsh life and tradition (it does not appear either in the so-called Canon Laws of the Welsh which came out of the Church in Brittany somewhere between the sixth and eighth centuries).

These latter omissions are probably deceptive and accidental, stemming from the specialized nature of the charter material itself. The operation of the kindred can certainly be detected within the families of kings and notables. The influence of the Church was a major factor, and in south-east Wales the Church is very visibly a direct descendant of the Romano-British Church. Clusters of dedications to a particular local saint in Wales tended to form recognizable 'provinces', and in the south-east the saints commemorated are early and strongly Romano-British. Dyfrig (Dubricius) had a cluster concentrated in Ergyng (Archenfield), a British community, called a kingdom, which crystallized out of the district of Roman Ariconium in present-day Herefordshire; tradition associated him with St Germanus. The major figure was Illtud, remembered in the notable monastic foundation of Llanilltud Fawr (Llantwit Major), one of the mother churches of Wales. Illtud was said to have been born of a noble family in, characteristically, Brittany and is presented as a blend of late Roman gentleman and Christian monk. So is Cadoc, associated with the house of Llancarfan, not far away, a man of similar temper, a Romano-British aristocrat versed in Latin culture. Their foundations, particularly Llanilltud, became renowned for learning; Maelgwn Gwynedd himself, when that devil a monk would be, is said to have put in a stint there. Later ages could see such places as 'universities'. And the dedications of these saints quite clearly form a province which is identical with the kingdom of Morgannwg.

That Morgannwg in turn stretched from Ergyng through Gwent and Glamorgan to Gower and was probably bounded to the north by the Brecknock Beacons. This is the land of the commonwealth of the Silures and it persisted until the Normans.

Kingship in early Wales, however, resembles that Welsh magician who constantly changed his form while remaining always the same – and was a good teller of tales with it. Origin-legends certainly have a king emerging from Caerwent and creating the kingdom of Gwent and we may suspect that after 409, while official authority may have passed to the acknowledged councillors of the commonwealth, real power passed to the men who could grab it. In a time of sharply declining population there was no land shortage; labour was a different matter. The Romano-British notables on their big estates with their slaves and serfs would have commandeered whatever labour they could. Slavery persisted long in Wales and actually strengthened in the ninth and tenth centuries; the earliest forms of serf labour known to later Welsh law are severe. Slaves and serfs, who must have formed a substantial proportion if not a majority of the people of Wales, simply disappear from Welsh history and tradition. The estates, we know, clustered on the good lands along the coast. We catch a brief glimpse at Dinas Powys near Cardiff (*din* or *dinas*, an old name for stronghold, features strongly in settlements all over Wales at this time) of a small but effective cluster in an old hill-fort, eating well – pork, beef, poultry, shellfish, salmon, sea trout, puréed vegetables – working their own iron smithy, stocking up with Mediterranean imported pottery in the fifth century. In the sixth century the Llandaff charters refer to a minor king ruling a small enclave in the vicinity of Cardiff.

Those same charters in the same period locate kings in Ergyng and in Gower to the west; and kings of this kind constantly reappear, sometimes operating in an area of little more than fifteen miles' radius. Highly significant here is the fact that what became the standard legal term for high status, for an 'aristocrat', *breyr*, derived from an older form, *brogorix*, which meant king of the *bro* – the little local homeland. Kings of the *bro* appeared all over Wales. The larger units they created hardened into intense local loyalties and it was out of such shifting material that the major kingdoms were built.

The first visible kings to appear in the record do so in Gwent, the old heartland which probably commanded loyalties. Gwent figures as a recognized realm quite early in the literature and an Iddon, king of Gwent, appears in the Llandaff charters in the sixth century. Whether his Gwent corresponded to the Gwent of the Silures, however, is not clear; the charters locate him in a particular area of northern Gwent and cite these other very localized kings at much the same time. From the early seventh century a new dynasty makes an appearance, that of Meurig ap Tewdrig, which begins in the rich coastlands around the mouth of the Wye. The growth in the power and influence of this family can be traced through the charters until it extends throughout the whole south-east, the kingship held by one person or shared by several, brothers and cousins. The consolidation of kingship and territory reached its peak when Ithel ap Morgan of this family ruled as sole king of the whole kingdom from 715 to 745. By this time the realm was known as Glywysing, after an alleged founding father, and the name persisted. After Ithel, minor kings reappear until another branch of the family starts its own climb, to climax in the tenth century, when Morgan ab Owain, Morgan Hen (Morgan the Old) established his own sole power and the kingdom assumed its familiar name of Morgannwg, Morgan's land (Glamorgan). By that time Gwent had become the name of a region, though it resurfaced as a kingdom in a final fragmentation on the eve of the Norman conquest.

Moreover the status of these kings seems as restricted as their actual ambitions were boundless. In the early charters, their authorization is necessary for the transmission of land; this is a very Roman concept and makes them little emperors, *gwledig*. But they had no specific political nor legislative powers. Assemblies of local notables are often associated with them and, indeed, in the borderland of Ergyng such groups of notables were the voice of the Welsh in their dealings with the English. Many of these nobles were as powerful as the kings. They, too, seem to have operated that four-generation family group within which kingship circulated and they were as obsessed with family descent, blood and honour as the kings and, indeed, as the shadowy freemen were to prove. It is possible to detect here traces of an old Celtic style which had been transmuted under the governance of the genealogy-obsessed Romans.

For, in reality, these kings originating from among their peers of the Romano-British notables, living the same culture and in effect constricted by that culture, were driven into an arbitrariness, violence and irresponsibility which proved permanent. They built themselves up any way they knew, laying hands on land, men and women, rights. They surrounded themselves with warbands of young men who would shift after the latest hero. They would hire their court poets to sing songs around the fire and the mead, the lavish hospitality of their hall; they would build up a loyalty around Heroic Age virtues. The people subjected to them had a different view. The ordinary, living as slaves and serfs, had no voice. The loyalty of free commoners tended to be to the realm these kings created. The Church, which viewed the great hero Arthur himself with a somewhat jaundiced eye, often regarded them as little more than a bunch of pretentious thugs. And their power rested on a very fragile base; they had constantly to strike a balance within their own kin and between them and the notables who were as ferociously obsessed with kin and descent and the status they brought as they were themselves. All kingships in Wales lived in this permanent tension, with greater kingdoms building themselves up on lesser ones and then, by some accident of inheritance or usurpation, shivering back into their fragments again. Out of this process, what emerged as the unchanging bedrock was the later administrative unit of the *cwmwd*, the commote, the permanent pawn of Welsh politics, the rooted sphere of the *bro*; beyond it there were small kingdoms living a fluctuating political existence but commanding an enduring loyalty. Out of these were built the four 'traditional' kingdoms, persisting but changing their form as often as Gwydion himself.

In the south-east, the ghost of the old Silurian commonwealth repeatedly reappears as Glywysing-Morgannwg; this was the arena for all its kings. It seems singularly obsessed with itself. There is report of battles against the Saxons, but in fact the frontier seems to have settled fairly easily along the Wye. Along that river there was for a time in the Dunsaete a people who actually seem to have been a mixed people, with elaborate laws about passing from Welsh to English territory, from the west Saxons to the 'Wentsaete'.* The old connection with the lowlands seems to have been resumed. Saxon influence, particularly after the formation of Wessex, seems to have been present, but Saxon pressure does not seem to have been severe. Glywysing-Morgannwg may well have been wealthy enough in Welsh terms to sustain this introspection; it is a stranger to Welsh politics until the tenth century. Only then is it drawn fully into the life of medieval Wales, as it becomes a target for kings to the north and itself provides a base for one of its own kings to try for command over the whole of the south. But it is in that period too that the process of dissociation inherent in its kingship lurches into another cycle of fragmentation, so that when the Norman bandits come over the border, its kings go down like ninepins and their Morgannwg is wiped off the Welsh map.

Nowhere else in Wales is there this relative wealth of detailed, if oblique, evidence and nowhere, of course, this degree of 'Roman' presence. But the tendencies which can be documented in Gwent and Glamorgan were present everywhere: the late Romano-British origins, the emergence of kings from shaped communities of notables, the building of minor kingdoms, the crystallization of traditional kingdoms with traditional capitals, existing in permanent inner tension, and, most notably, the lapse from the Roman peace into endless war, great and small. Central to the Laws of Wales as they emerge was the king's right to a third of the booty

---

*Glanville R. J. Jones, 'Early historic settlement in border territory. A case-study of Archenfield and its environs in Herefordshire', *Recherches de Géographie Rurale: hommage au Professeur Frans Dussart*, tome 1 (Université de Liège, 1979).

of a raid; in some texts some kind of war appears to be an annual event.

In the south-west the Romano-British commonwealth of the Demetae gave its name to the kingdom of Dyfed and its patron saint to Wales, but here it is the Irish presence which is overpowering. There is a dense cluster of Irish place-names throughout south-west Wales, particularly intense in what are today Cardiganshire and north Pembrokeshire, extending east deep into Carmarthenshire. The memorial stones raised in honour of local notables carry inscriptions in the ogham script of Ireland as well as in the customary Latin; some are bilingual. Gildas names Gwrthefyr (Vortipor) as king of Dyfed, a memorial stone calls him Protector and the genealogies give him ancestors with Irish names, some of them carrying Roman titles as names. Independent Irish genealogies agree. There is an Irish tradition of a tribe called the Deísi who seem to have been expelled or to have quit Ireland in these times and the evidence suggests that migrations, growing out of slave raids, occurred shortly after 400, when Britain was still nominally subject to Rome. They came into a commonwealth which would have been accustomed to an Irish presence and their early kings exercised an authority which was in some sense 'Roman'. They may even have been planted as federates or colonists at the time that the origin-legends of Gwynedd have Cunedda coming down from North Britain to expel or subdue Irish immigrants there.

In Dyfed there was evidently fusion with the natives. The Church provides the best evidence. St Samson, an ascetic who ultimately established himself in Brittany and achieved a European reputation, came from a Romano-British family of magnates and royal officials in Dyfed; so did St Teilo, commemorated in Llandeilo, and above all Dewi himself, St David, who established what was to become the centre of the Welsh Church at 'remote' Tyddewi. In the sixth century, of course, St David's was in no sense remote; on the contrary, it was a hub of those western sea-routes along which the monkish missionaries moved in that seaborne enterprise of which the great Irish Church was the exemplar. Certainly Dewi (who evokes memories of Patrick) moved in a very Irish climate; at one stage he confronted an Irish magician king-in-a-castle Boia, whose slave girls stripped and pranced lasciviously about David's monks in an attempt to suborn them (they failed, naturally). Samson, Dewi and Teilo were very much in that puritan, semi-hermit style which was displacing the older and more comfortable style of Cadoc and Illtud but which stemmed no less from the late Roman Church, which found its model in St Martin of Tours and informed the breathtaking Irish missions. These religious and secular phenomena in Dyfed are the most striking symptoms of that reincorporation of Wales into the world of the Irish Sea which was henceforth to be central to it.

The core of the kingdom which emerged, Dyfed, was the area between the Tywi, the Teifi and the sea but it extended well to the east along the Tywi. Furthermore, the memorial stones in ogham march along the Roman roads to cluster again in the area around modern Breconshire. A kingdom emerged in this area, Brycheiniog (Brecon), which claimed one Brychan as founder and was also Irish in style, the entire royal family being anointed Christianizers in the Dewi manner. Ceredigion (Cardigan) to the north, whose dynasty claimed (or was forced to claim) descent from the Cunedda clan of Gwynedd, lived bursts of independent existence and was remorselessly drawn into the orbit of Dyfed. For an historically brief period a kingdom called Seisyllwg, named after a putative founder, may have embraced Ceredigion and Ystrad Tywi, a region on that river. What seems clear is that there was a tendency to cohere around Dyfed. The cult of Dewi grew relatively early into something of an all-Wales cult, the monastic centres of St David's and Llanbadarn in Ceredigion became important foci of early scholarship and letters and it is possible to trace the Dewi – Teilo cult marching inland right across south Wales to invade the south-eastern region of Cadoc and Illtud. Ultimately Llandaff itself was to be dedicated to St Teilo. No doubt the power of Dewi and his church was a major reason for the fairly rapid disappearance of Irish Celtic (though not its legends) and the full assimilation of Dyfed into the British life of Wales. The oscillating pattern of relationships between major and minor kings can be traced, though not within Dyfed itself; rather within that vast if somewhat ramshackle realm which emerged later as another ancient kingdom, the slightly artificially named Deheubarth (the Southern Part) with its capital at Dinefwr (Dynevor). Dyfed-Deheubarth shared with Morgannwg an apparent distance from any Saxon threat.

The central power in early Wales, and its central mystery, was in the north-west, the traditional kingdom of Gwynedd. When Maelgwn Gwynedd appears in the dyspeptic pages of Gildas, he is already something of a giant, educated at Llanilltud but living a wilful life of power, holding court in the sea fortress of Degannwy, surrounded by his 'bawling bards' and the warriors drawn by his fame. He was known among Britons and Saxons in the North, his court was a focus for a northern Celtic world and there were contacts with Europe. This 'island dragon', as Gildas called him, 'first in evil, mightier than many both in power and malice, more profuse in giving, more extravagant in sin . . .' ruled from Degannwy, though the centre of the dynasty's power was in Anglesey; Degannwy itself was later (and perhaps earlier) the stronghold of a different branch of this dynasty, whose sub-kingdom of Rhos lived a fitful independence. Later still it was associated with the distinct kingdom of Powys and in the early ninth century could be called the *arx* or citadel of that realm. Moreover, the power of Maelgwn stretched deep into the south. Ceredigion's rulers claimed descent (or were forcibly associated with) the same legendary dynasty of Cunedda, and the presence of the king of Gwynedd may even have been temporarily established on the south coast. One has the distinct impression of an unusual power sprawling across what came to be traditional frontiers and occupying a distinctive place in the confederacy of British kingdoms which ran through the north-west into what is today Scotland.

For some generations this condition persisted. An early seventh-century memorial at Llangadwaladr, near the *caput* at Aberffraw in Anglesey, records the king Cadfan in appropriate Latin: *Catamanus rex sapientisimus opinatisimus omnium regum* (Cadfan, most wise and most renowned of all kings); his son Cadwallon, 'king of the Britons', appears as a savage tyrant in Bede and fought all over the north; *his* son Cadwaladr was in turn to figure in legend as the last British king. It is only after the decisive victories of the Saxons in what is today north-western England, and the dislocation of the northern and western chain of British kingdoms, that Gwynedd shrinks back to recognizable Welsh proportions and, in what was becoming a traditional Welsh manner, shudders apart into its component kingdoms.

It is difficult to trace both the polity out of which this dynasty grew (and it is becoming increasingly clear that we need to make some distinction between kingdoms and the dynasties who ruled them, sometimes in a parasitic manner) and the sources of its power. The north-west showed all the familiar characteristics: small, episodically independent minor kingdoms splutter repeatedly into life in Rhos, Rhufoniog, Dunoding; Meirionydd (Merioneth) in its mountain fastnesses often lived separate under its own kings. Within the heartland of the dynasty itself there was frequent conflict, with Anglesey-based kings combating others on the mainland and often resorting to what was becoming a Welsh royal tradition, the strangling of a cousin or brother in the interests of good government. The saints' dedications in the north lack the strong regional concentrations visible in the south. There were a myriad strictly local saints. Only Beuno begins to build up into a real cult; very much in the Dewi style, he was said to have been trained in Tyddewi, to have started in the north-east but to have ended up closely associated with Clynnog in Gwynedd. In the north, as in some regions in the south, it is the dynasties themselves who are dubbed Christianizers; Cunedda's multitudinous brood were saints to the last man and woman.

Nor is it possible to trace any local base from which the dynasty could have started; we know of nothing in late Romano-British north-west Wales to correspond with the Silures, the Demetae, the Cornovii and Ordovices of other regions. And while Anglesey was certainly prosperous – in later years it was called Môn Mam Cymru, Anglesey Mother of Wales – and the Snowdonia ranges were an incomparable defence buttress, there is nothing to suggest that it was in any meaningful way richer or more powerful by nature than any other region. The 'energy' which is sometimes attributed to this dynasty is meaningless; such energy as this was the occupational disease of any kingship. It could be translated into effect only by command of slaves and serfs, of land, and, perhaps critically, the warband of loyal followers who needed keeping. 'Fair Cei,' says the Arthur of the folktale *Culhwch and Olwen,* surrounded by that incredible band drawn from the four corners with which Welsh writers and story-tellers equipped him in significant style, 'We are noble men so long as we are resorted to. The greater the bounty we show, all the greater will be our nobility and our fame and our glory . . .' Where had Maelgwn's warband and bounty come from as he hammered an intensely fissured and particularist region into a kingdom? It is difficult to avoid the impression that the dynasty itself virtually invented Gwynedd and with resources wider than the local.

It was precisely in order to explain the northern connection and the distinctive power that the genealogists and remembrancers of Maelgwn's dynasty invented the story of Cunedda and his sons. They asserted that the royal house took its rise from Cunedda Wledig, Cunedda the Emperor, a leading man among the Votadini who inhabited Manaw Gododdin, north of Hadrian's Wall in the vicinity of the Firth of Forth. This tribe lived in a fluctuating relationship with Roman authority; genealogists gave Cunedda's immediate ancestors the Roman names of Eternus, Paternus and Tacitus while three of his alleged sons bore Brittonic versions of Romanus, Donatus and Eternus. In the last years of Roman Britain, to counter an inflow of Irish into north Wales, Cunedda was transplanted to Anglesey; he and his warband expelled or subdued the Irish, commandeered the whole tract of western Britain between the Dee and the Teifi and established a dominant dynasty. The names of many of the small sub-kingdoms of northern and western Wales were explained by reference to Cunedda's alleged eight sons.

This story, which bears all the familiar stigmata of an explanatory origin-legend, was constructed by men who were competent craftsmen and who used the correct Latin terms with precision. They had to work with mythological material and to produce propaganda but it was not their fault if their historical horizon could not extend back beyond the sixth century. In the first version of the story, which crystallizes in the ninth century, the genuinely historical figure of Maelgwn Gwynedd is made the great-great-great-grandson of Cunedda; the span of time between his reign and the migration from the north is precise – 146 years. This places the transplantation nicely in the year 388 – when Maximus was in power! In the tenth century, however, there is a change. Remembrancers in the service of the second dynasty of Gwynedd and, in particular, of one of its members Owain of Deheubarth who actually ruled in south Wales, decided (no doubt after much poring over Gildas, Bede and the *History of the Britons*) that it would be more effective to locate the migration in the early fifth century. So they juggled the genealogies to have Vortigern, not Macsen Wledig, effect the transfer!

It is necessary to repeat, however, that there *was* something to be explained: the northern connection (which in diluted form, reappears in the second dynasty). These early texts are full of northern material, including a collection of northern annals (also used by the Irish) at St David's. Most notable are the early poets, Aneirin and Taliesin, who have inevitably moved into tradition as the first Welsh poets. So difficult is the dating of these texts, so insoluble the problems involved in the shifts from Late British into Old Welsh and their orthography, that historians now refuse to use this poetry *at all* as evidence on the dark ages. Its message, however, is unmistakable. *Hwn yw y Gododdin. Aneirin ae cant.* (This is the Gododdin. Aneirin sang it.) That is the title appended to a poem in typical Heroic Age style which describes a late sixth-century sortie of noble warriors, drawn like Arthur's from the four corners of the British kingdoms, including a man 'from the south', from the land of the Gododdin against Catterick (which had been a Roman fort) and which ended in one of those noble disasters which punctuate the history of the Welsh. The twelve poems generally ascribed to Taliesin, a master poet associated with both Powys and North Britain and made into an ideal figure, come out of the same northern world. These are full of the significant lists of heroes we find in the stories of the Mabinogi and Arthur, the same virtues and vices, the gold-givers, the sword-wielders, sons of noble fathers, 'boundary-extending, conquest-seeking'; the ravens feasting on corpses, with their sometimes timelessly memorable images – 'His sword rang in the heads of mothers. . .'And after all, Maelgwn Gwynedd and his immediate descendants had in fact been enmeshed in the battles against the Anglo-Saxons of the north. However legendary the explanations, the connection existed; it was intimate and perhaps organic.

We know that north-west Wales was refortified and remilitarized against the Irish in the fourth century. We know that Maximus pulled the soldiers out. We know that, in north Wales, Irish settlement (presumably the Féni) is most visible in Anglesey and we know that, stemming from a Romano-British root, Anglesey was the base of the new dynasty. We know that the story of Cunedda was a legend but we know that this dynasty was in truth involved in northern struggles. We know also that organized migrations of kings and peoples, however unlikely they may seem in the context of north Wales and the waist of Scotland, were common in the Europe of the late Empire and the sub-Roman period (Britons were moving *en masse* into the Loire valley). It is difficult to avoid the suspicion that something unusual probably did happen in north-west Wales in the days of Macsen Wledig. What is certain is that the dynasty which created Gwynedd emerged as the southernmost member of the confederacy of British kingdoms in north-western Britain and that it was after the disruption of these kingdoms that Gwynedd, in Welsh style, fell apart, to await the next hammer-fisted unifier who, in turn, could draw upon an established tradition of power and supremacy.

In the north-east the emergence of the traditional kingdom of Powys is beset with the same problems of locating dynasties, but these seem to stem from the actual processes of history-making among the literate Welsh of the early ninth century. The first notice we have of kings associated with Powys comes from some Welsh annals in Latin whose contemporary entries date from the eighth century. They pinpoint three Powys kings at the battle of Chester around 616, a grandfather (who also appears in Bede), son and grandson. The middle member, Cynan, is credited with power in a ninth-century praise poem *Canu Taliesin*, staging raids from the north-east all over Wales. The main source of information is a corpus of poetry from the ninth century, dramatic and haunting, with a very memorable elegy, the *Canu Heledd*, itself part of a wider collection attributed to Llywarch Hen, who was counted a major poet and associated with Powys. The central verse laments the fall of a great kingdom of Powys in the seventh century. The speaker, a princess, mourns the deaths of her brothers, with Cynddylan the most prominent. The poem is quite unusually precise in its topography. The loved lands, now empty, were by the river Tern in modern Shropshire; the lost town Pengwern was identified (not least by Gerald the Welshman, Giraldus Cambrensis, in the twelfth century) as Shrewsbury, though it looks more like timbered Wroxeter (Viriconium) to me; places within the power of Cynddylan include the Severn, the Wrekin, Ercall, Baschurch deep in what is today England and, equally deep in Wales, Manafon and Newtown. An earlier poem made Cynddylan a ruler in Dogfeiling, a strip in north-east Wales running from Deeside to the north coast, and had him and his brother fighting at Lichfield from beyond the Tern. A poem from the same collection makes Cynddylan into an ally of Penda, the pagan king of Saxon Mercia, in a battle near Oswestry – and the west Britons did indeed get enmeshed as allies of Penda in triangular struggles between themselves, Mercia and Northumbria at this time and in this region.

None of these people, however, find a very secure anchorage in any of the later genealogies. Early in the ninth century Cyngen, king of Powys, raised a striking twelve-foot memorial, the Pillar of Elise, recounting old victories against the Saxons, which is now near Llangollen. On it he blazoned his pedigree in correct Latin terms. The founder of the dynasty is given as Gwrtheyrn; so he is in some of the genealogies, so he is for the kingdom of Builth to the south, which became a sub-kingdom of Powys. Gwrtheyrn is Vortigern. There could have been a man of that name who had no connection with the person who fought against Germanus and Ambrosius. But within these kingdoms Vortigern would figure as the Betrayer of the Island of Britain.

In the *History of the Britons* composed around 829/30, however, a different origin is provided for the kings of Powys. It is now becoming clear that this was the product of a clerical imaginative exercise common in the Middle Ages. The local saint of one core of Powys was Garmon (Germanus), with a mother-church in Llanarmon-yn-Iâl (Yale). Cyngen, the king who raised his Pillar of Elise, was the son of a Cadell, and a story came out, probably from Garmon's church, that the founder of the dynasty had been a Romano-British slave or serf Cadell, who had been raised to the kingship by St Garmon. A Latin 'Life of St Germanus' was circulating among the literate Welsh and it was fatally easy and fatally attractive to assimilate the local preacher Garmon to the illustrious St Germanus of Auxerre himself. It was one way, after all, of getting around a by-now highly embarrassing Vortigern! The story grew to epic status; in legends Germanus and his agents go pursuing Vortigern all over the Island of Britain and the story left a deep impression on genealogies and poetry. One of the poems in the Taliesin group hails the three kings at the battle of Chester as descendants of Cadell – the Cadelling – and the Cadell attribution figures in the genealogies. On the Pillar of Elise Germanus is used to bless Vortigern's patriotic son, and for good measure, Vortigern himself is made the son-in-law of Macsen Wledig!

In fact, if the intrusive early Cadell installed by the local Garmon is eliminated, the picture which results is internally consistent and quite plausible. The core of the original Powys was the Commonwealth of the Cornovii (and a Vortigern connection there would not be at all implausible); the lands in north-east Wales, perhaps stretching as far west as Degannwy, were lands associated with the Deceangli; those in mid-Wales have been attributed to the Ordovices or whatever was left of them. The story seems to resemble that in Glywysing-Morgannwg in the south-east. There may well have been local kingships of fluctuating fortunes, but Powys emerged out of those Romano-British polities. It became embroiled with the advancing Saxons, was enmeshed in the complex struggles in the north-west, and finally went down before the rise of Mercia, leaving the Powys of Wales to struggle desperately for survival.

And it is from the fall of that great house that there come what are for me, the most memorable words to come out of these darkest of ages, the poems which put words in the mouth of Heledd who had been a princess in Powys – 'Heledd the hawk I am called'. Now, in a thin cloak and goatskins, she leads one cow into the hills and remembers her dead brothers, in their golden plumes, who defended the White Town:

> White town between Tren and Trafal,
> More common was blood on the field's face
> Than ploughing of fallow.

> The hall of Cynddylan, dark is the roof,
> Since the Saxon cut down
> Powys's Cynddylan.*

The hall she remembers above all, focus of so much warmth and song and enjoyment in everything written in this Wales, not least about Arthur.

> Stafell Gynddylan ys tywyll heno
> Heb dân, heb wely,
> Wylaf wers, tawaf wedi.

> Cynddylan's Hall is dark tonight
> No fire, no bed
> I'll weep awhile and then be silent.

*Original Welsh in Ifor Williams (ed.) *Canu Llywarch Hen* (University of Wales Press, 1935); translated J. Clancy, *The Earliest Welsh Poetry* (Macmillan, 1970). There is another English translation in Anthony Conran (trans. and ed.) *The Penguin Book of Welsh Verse* (1967).

*Wylaf wers, tawaf wedi.* There is a lot of Welsh history in those four words.

## Aliens in their own Land

As these bickering kingdoms climbed out of the wreck of the province of Britannia Prima and ran into a Mercian wall which shut them out from the land of which they had been a province, they found some tentative unity in their distinctive Christianity.

In the multitudinous saints' lives, several early and several from Brittany, most of them late and written in the rat-race of the Norman imposition of the Roman Church several centuries later, the sixth century emerges as an age of saints, of ascetics ceaselessly traversing the western sea-routes. Monasticism was certainly known in Britain as soon as it appeared in western Europe, and while the churches in the south-east were recognizably Romano-British in style, the British Church itself was influential on the Irish, which became celebrated for its wide-ranging monkish missionaries. In Welsh records, unlike the Irish, there is no mention of an actual conversion of the population. They may already have been nominally Christian. But one recollects the use which Germanus made of the people against the Pelagians, and it was clearly this monastic mission impulse which was decisive.

St Samson in the sixth century certainly followed a classic pattern. Born into a family of Dyfed notables, he embraced the dedicated life of an ascetic. He tried the famous monastery at Llanilltud, found it too comfortable by half and moved to a harsher one on Caldy Island near Tenby. Still discontented, he moved to a cave on the Severn (where his iron rations were brought by servants). Then he was off, on the seas, founding houses, to enter posterity as the saint of Dol in Brittany. There were a sufficient number of such people travelling, seeking out islands or lonely valleys like Llanthony's, leaving small groups of disciples behind. Some could range far. One Briton became a bishop of Celtic Galicia in Spain; a Welsh tradition has curraghs peopling the western sea, carrying the saints to Bardsey Island (Ynys Enlli) for burial. The very pre-eminence of St David's itself, a sea-girt communication hub, testifies to the reality.

This mission wave, however, spent itself in the sixth century. What was left were houses, mostly small but some substantial, which built up a federation of daughter churches as members of a saint-cult together with individual churches dependent on that centre – the familiar *clas*-church, the *classis* corporation, monastic in title and style, with its daughters, possessed or supervised. From the first, however, this Church of monasteries was controlled by bishops.

Partly because the Normans tried deliberately to wipe it out of the world, it has left very little physical trace. We are certain of only thirty-six Celtic church sites in Wales, with perhaps a dozen more possible. There were certainly more than this. From the Llandaff charters, it is possible to detect thirty-six monasteries in the south-east alone, with thirty-eight others described by the ambiguous *ecclesiae* (churches). The great majority were in the Wye Valley, only eleven were in Glamorgan, which would more closely resemble the rest of Wales. Many of these were clearly tiny, with numbers ranging from a handful to a dozen, but there were big houses, such as Llanilltud and Bangor-on-Dee, which must have had the air of a small town. For they were the core of settlements and the *llan* place-name, so common in Wales, could indicate both a church and an enclosure belonging to a church elsewhere. The houses operated according to rules which varied but followed a common European pattern of austerity. Their records soon began to list the customary officers of the monastery and the list grew longer – scribes, teachers, reeves, smiths, craftsmen. The houses themselves must have acted as foci of settlement. Those we know of are located exclusively on good lands, around the sea coasts, along the valleys, near usable roads. Very few can be found, like Llangurig, in the high uplands. Though the picture may be distorted by later obliteration, there is little sense here of the 'little white churches' scattered out among a population in hamlets and isolated homesteads (which may, indeed, be itself the consequence of later population shift). The Laws of Wales as they developed, however, automatically assumed the presence of a *llan,* a church, in every commote.

While disciplinary rules, canons of penance and the whole lifestyle of the monastic life were operative, the distinction between monasteries and other churches was rapidly blurred. A memorial stone at Llantrisant in Anglesey commemorates a 'most holy woman' who was the wife of a bishop. While the familiar horror at sexuality, particularly its female variant, was widely and loudly voiced – Samson was reluctant to enter the house of his sick father because he himself had been 'carnally born' there – the monasteries in fact teemed with women and children; women found a niche, there was talk of mixed monasteries and clerical marriage was ubiquitous. The houses were small *clas* corporations, owning property. A hereditary interest developed; abbots succeeded their fathers. In time, a distinction was made between the nominally monastic church settlements served by priests and people described as celibates. For this Church, with *clas* churches like Llandeilo and Llandaff building up their federations of daughter houses, was enmeshed in the world of the aristocratic kindreds and their kings.

Bishops had appeared early and exercised the usual duties, supervising the clergy and making visitations to monasteries. What the Church lacked and what made it seem strange and aberrant to St Augustine, newly arrived from the Roman heartland, was a strict and defined territorial structure. There was, however, a definite structure of authority. There had been a bishop's establishment at Mynyw (St David's) before the monastery was established, and Gerald the Welshman in the twelfth century could present a list of forty-four bishops of St David's before the Normans. The Church acquired land, rights, the recognition of the inviolable protection and sanctuary it offered, central to the preoccupations of the time. Its leaders were men of political substance; its literate clerks kept the records; in substantial centres like St David's and Llanbadarn in Ceredigion, they were creating the history of the peoples. Major churches called bishoprics quickly emerged, the earliest on the Wye, soon displaced by Llandaff, ecclesiastical capital of Glywysing-Morgannwg. Llandeilo was a bishopric, so was Bangor. While there was a church at Llanelwy (St Asaph) and a big monastery at Bangor-on-Dee (where monks were massacred by the Saxons), there is no trace of an incipient see for Powys, but this may simply be an accident in the survival of documents.

Pre-eminent from an early date was St David's. Dewi, a *dyfrwr* (a man who drank only water), puritan in Irish style and reputedly a great traveller, outshone all others. A famous story had him addressing a synod at Llanddewi Brefi, to find the ground rising beneath him so that he towered over all. His cult marched across Wales. The centre at St David's, notable for piety, learning and, increasingly, wealth, had seven bishop-houses in dependence; Llanbadarn and Llandeilo subsided into its discipline. Dewi was already a force throughout Wales by the eighth century. Asser, the cleric from St David's who spent half his time at the court of King Alfred of Wessex and wrote his life, could call his kinsman back home an archbishop.

This Church could hardly be called isolated; the historians at their writing tables could employ material from much of the western world. Yet by the eighth century, in the disruption of that world, it had evolved differently from the continental church which was passing under the dominion of Rome, and it passionately cherished that difference. When St Augustine reached England in 597 on his mission to convert the Saxons, there was conflict. Bede reports that two conferences between Augustine and the

Welsh bishops over 602/3, at the mouth of the Severn and near Bangor-on-Dee, broke down in mutual intransigence and alienation.

There was a range of differences over such matters as the tonsure of monks and the practice of baptism and a complete closure of minds over a married clergy. Augustine pronounced himself ready to tolerate what he regarded as the peculiarities of the Celtic Church, providing it accepted the Roman calculation of the Easter cycles and co-operated in the conversion of the Saxons. The Welsh and Irish had remained faithful to the calendar and the practices established in the early fifth century. In the meantime, however, the Church which was passing under the control of the Bishop of Rome had adjusted its practices to that control and had changed the dating of Easter, a critical moment to the whole Christian year, adapting the movable feast of the Jewish Passover to the Christian Sunday. By 600, the Celtic Easter could anticipate the Roman by a week or fall as much as four weeks later; in the island of Britain, one set of Christians could be celebrating the Resurrection while another remained sunk in Lenten austerity. The rhythms of the Christian life could be dislocated, even rendered absurd.

The Celtic Church as a whole resisted Roman pressure. Nowhere was this resistance more sustained than in these two peninsulas which were becoming Wales. The Welsh bishops totally rejected the Roman Easter, refused to accept the primacy of Augustine and scorned his mission to their enemies. At the Synod of Whitby in 664, the newly converted Northumbrians went over to the Roman rites; most other Celtic churches submitted to Rome in the course of the seventh century. Not until 768 did a Bishop of Bangor secure the agreement of the Welsh Church to the Roman Easter and most of its distinctive practices it retained to the death, until the Normans came to blot it out and expel it from human memory.

No less significant in that report from the Severn was the total refusal of the Welsh (unlike the Irish) to have anything to do with any conversion of the Saxons. Those no doubt somewhat rough-hewn Christian gentlemen, their churches the very fabric of their kingdoms, could not bring themselves to secure an entry into heaven for those landless Saxon pirates who, through their Treason of the Long Knives, had robbed them of their Britain.

In their monasteries their scholars were elaborating a history for their kingdoms. They were joined by the poets and the story-tellers who erected a hypnotic and fabulous structure of memory, legend, myth and history into a perception which was Welsh and was expressed in a language which was moving out of Late Brittonic to become unmistakably Welsh. This was the world which was offered to any man and woman of the kingdoms who could raise their eyes above the *bro* – or indeed listen to a story over a fire. And it was a world which carried them straight back into the other world of Macsen Wledig and Vortigern and Germanus and Ambrosius, a world dominated more and more by the giant figure of Arthur. This few and fragile people took the whole inheritance of Britain on their shoulders. And late in the eighth century they were confronted with an imperial Offa, king of the Mercians, who had the effrontery to score his Dyke across their land and shut them out as foreigners.

In a valley right under Snowdon, near Beddgelert, a dramatic, rocky outcrop dominates all passage through. Here, in these dark ages, rose a typical hilltop fort-settlement, the nucleus of some little king of the *bro*. It had its imported Mediterranean pottery, it smelted its own iron, it made its own jewels, working gold, glass and enamel. It called itself Dinas Emrys (the fortress of Emrys). To later generations, what Emrys could this be but that other Emrys, Emrys Wledig, Emrys the Emperor, Ambrosius Aurelianus? Here it had been, then, that magic lake in which the Red Dragon of the Britons and the White Dragon of the Saxons had fought for dominion over the Island of Britain.

The Welsh, as a people, were born disinherited.

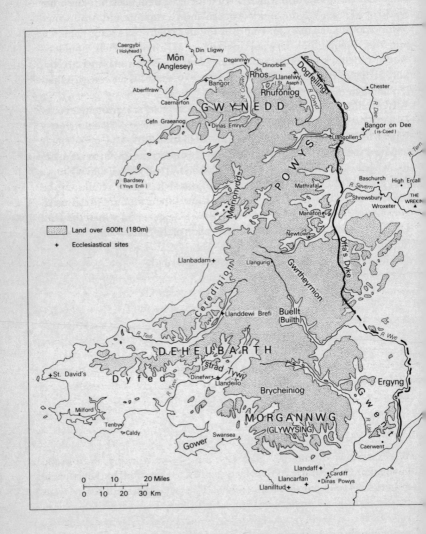

Caergybi
(Holyhead)
Môn
(Anglesey)
Din Lligwy
Degannwy
Dinorben
Aberffraw
Bangor
Rhos
Llanelwy
(St. Asaph)
Caernarfon
GWYNEDD
Rhufoniog
Cefn Graeanog
Dinas Emrys
Dogfeiling
R. Clwyd
Chester
R. Dee
Bangor on Dee
(Is-Coed)
Llangollen
R. Tern
Bardsey
(Ynys Enlli)
POWYS
Baschurch
High Ercall
Mathrafal
R. Severn
Shrewsbury
Wroxeter
THE WREKIN
Manafon
Land over 600ft (180m)
Newtown
Ecclesiastical sites
Llanbadarn
Llangurig
Gwrtheyrnion
Offa's Dyke
Ceredigion
Llanddewi Brefi
Buellt
(Builth)
R. Teifi
DEHEUBARTH
R. Wye
St. David's
Dyfed
Strad Tywi
Dinefwr
Llandeilo
R. Tywi
Brycheiniog
Ergyng
Milford
Gwent
Tenby
Caldy
Swansea
MORGANNWG
(GLYWYSING)
Gower
Caerwent
0        10        20 Miles
0    10    20    30 Km
Llandaff
Llancarfan
Llanilltud
Cardiff
Dinas Powys

3.   EARLY MEDIEVAL WALES

# 3 · THE FIRST CRISIS OF IDENTITY

In the ninth century the political order which had emerged among the peoples west of Offa's Dyke broke down. The ruling dynasty of Dyfed-Deheubarth ran out in 814, that of Gwynedd in 825, and of Powys in 855.

Into the vacuum stepped a new breed, the High Kings of all Wales. The first of them took over all Wales outside Glywysing by 878; he fought Vikings and English and though he was cut down in battle, he set a precedent and created a dynasty, grounded in Gwynedd, which took all Wales as its patrimony. He was Rhodri Mawr, the only king in Welsh history called Great. The second set up the dynasty in Dyfed-Deheubarth and by 950 ruled all Wales outside Morgannwg. He presided over a great codification of the laws of Wales, which henceforth bore his name. One Wales was to have one law. He was Hywel Dda, the only king in Welsh history called Good.

At much the same time a written literature emerges, in charters, annals, scholarly works, histories, poetry and prose, in Latin and in a language which was now unmistakably Welsh. These people were giving themselves an identity.

They were creating a *Wales*. But their Wales was born under a dark star. A hundred years after Hywel, the Welsh people were fighting for their survival.

## A People and its Kings

We can see what kind of Wales these kings were working on from the lawbooks. The actual texts date from a much later period, but the archaic material in them, particularly in the south, where the Law of Hywel went into suspension under the Normans, refers to these times when the arbitrary rule of self-made kings was being drilled into a system. Early and later kings were literally peripatetic; king, household, retinue of hungry young men would eat out one estate and move on to the next. At their approach, people were known to take to the woods; the Church called them a plague of locusts. The lawyers (always a multitudinous brood in Wales) took this reality and out of it invented units of government, of taxation, of social control.

Wales was a land of commotes.* In the laws, these basic human communities were averaged out. A commote (*cwmwd*) was deemed to hold fifty *trefi*, small townships or vills. Two commotes made a *cantref*, literally a hundred *trefi*, probably copied from the Saxons and often corresponding to a small sub-kingdom. Within every commote, certain lands were reserved for the king. The king's lands were organized around a multiple estate called a *maenor* in the south and a *maenol* in the north. He had one *maenor* of seven unfree *trefi* in the lowland and another in the upland. In the commote were three other *maenors*, held by free notables. Each of these had twelve *trefi* spread over lowland and upland, plus one *tref* which the lord held free from royal demands.

The reality underlying this was that form of agrarian exploitation which had taken shape in late Roman times. The land was exploited in large tracts covering twelve miles and more; the people settled in the *trefi*, where they lived and from which food rent and serf labour were delivered to their masters. Large blocs like this could integrate upland and lowland, fit arable, meadow and woodland together with summer and winter pasture in a more or less self-sufficient economy of mixed farming and cattle raising. Of course, no particular community would correspond precisely to the legal model. Already in the south-east, the big estates were breaking up; there were groups of townships with no visible bond between them apart from taxation. There was to be a major growth in royal land and its serfs and also in settlements by freemen and notables which dispersed people over hamlets and homesteads. But some such pattern as this governed both agrarian life and primitive royal organization in the early kingdoms.

This society was built on the bent backs of the unfree. They worked at the king's *tir bwrdd* (literally the land which supplied his table). They managed his upland waste and looked after his cattle. They paid a *dawnbwyd* (food render) twice a year. They built the halls, made the camps for his soldiers, supplied those soldiers with pack-horses and axe-men. They also maintained his queen, officers, falconers, huntsmen, young men on military training and any one else he fancied, for the notables had their bond people, too. Headquarters was the chief bond *tref* near the *llys* (court) and the *llan*, the twin powers of King and Church; run by a *maer* (reeve) it was called the *maerdref*.

There were slaves and it looks as though there were plenty of them. They hardly figure in the record; they were taken for granted. Slavery remained

*Essential here is the work of Glanville R. J. Jones, particularly 'Ancient British settlements in their organizational settings', *Paysages Ruraux Européens: travaux de la conférence Européenne permanente pour l'étude du paysage rural* (Université de Rennes, 1979).

common in Wales long after it had withered in the rest of Europe. There are few reports of any of them being set free. Slave raiding was a common motive for war and got worse during the Viking attacks. The most dismal spectacle in dismal late tenth-century Wales were the gangs of men and women being shunted all over Wales by the Northmen and avariciously desperate Welsh kings. They were sold off, exchanged in human commodity markets with other hard-pressed and hard-nosed kings, all hungry for the raw human material with which to win power, glory and a propagandist poet. Welsh law records little labour service beyond humping stuff from one place to another. There was no need to.

More visible and much more numerous in later years were the serfs. They were men without pedigree, without descent and therefore outside the real community (the women are invisible). They were bound to the soil and held land in primitive community. It was shared out equally between all adult males except the youngest in each household. This was called *tir cyfrif* (reckoned land) and the reckoning was done by the reeve. These people cultivated the commonalty of the oppressed. There were also unfree people of higher status. They occupied what was called *tir gwelyog*. This reflected the freemen's notion of the *gwely* (in modern Welsh, a bed) and its *gwelygordd*, a kindred group which held, or at least presided over, the use of land. The unfree people on this land, land 'like a *gwely*', hereditary land, had a legal kin and some sense of personal property. People on the reckoned land had to pay a fixed render and, in legal theory at least, they had to pay the same amount even if their community had dwindled to one man. On hereditary land the kindred offered some protection, and in later years, serfs on reckoned land made pathetic attempts to claim, usually vainly, that their holdings were 'of the nature of hereditary land'. Serfs or the half-free on hereditary land tended to increase in number, since it was they who generally worked the land handed out to the Church and the notables.

The only people recognized by the lawbooks as truly Welsh were freemen of status. 'Every Welshman born to Welsh parents *(Kymro vamtat)*' declares the texts, 'will be a gentleman innate *(bonheddig cynhwynawl)* without taint of servility.' What this overpoweringly male and aristocratic concept of full existence fixed as the defining notion of a Welsh man was his *braint,* (status), decided in turn by his 'blood', his free descent. Freemen were aristocrats and, in early days, were probably a minority among the Welsh.

These people owed dues to their kings and lords, a *gwestfa* (food rent), some services linked to the *cylch* (the circuit of the royal court), occasional demands like a *commorth* (aid) or a *treth* (tax). These were not assessed on their land but on their persons and were basically communal; it was the community of freemen who paid. The freeman's status, which defined his whole life, his *braint,* was therefore critical. It was assessed in terms of currency (usually cattle) and it was fixed, not originally by wealth or achievement (though clearly these, and particularly the former, helped) but by birth. Every man and woman, therefore, had his or her price and central to its maintenance was the notion of *sarhad* (insult, trespass, loss of face). Such an offence had to be compensated. It was this, rather than any concept of 'crime', which originally governed the maintenance of law. And here the status-conferring kin of the person was central. Offences were compensated by a payment in kind made by the family of the offender to the family of the offended. This could be extended into every field, even to a person's tools and clothes. It was extended in particular to homicide, where it was used to prevent long-lasting blood-feuds (a central feature of life, or rather death, of most communities in Europe). To pay a person's *galanas* or blood-price, the family of the killer out to the fifth cousin was responsible to the family, similarly computed, of the victim.

So the central institution was the *cenedl,* a structured, measurable kindred group. It was decided by male descent. A woman had her own kin, which she did not lose on marriage, and there were complex regulations relating to a mother's kin. But a woman existed in the *braint* of her husband. The law invented a kindred focused on the individual which moved outwards in concentric circles from that individual. At first sight, it would seem to require a nation of mathematicians to work it. In practice, the key group was the standard four-generation kin, notionally descended from a common great-grandfather and extending to second cousins. This was certainly the kin most involved in land transactions. For the freeman was also a *priodor,* an owner of land. His ownership of that land, however, was conditional on his membership of a family group and became firm only in the fourth generation of occupancy. On the death of such a *priodor* his land was divided between his sons *(cyfran);* if the sons failed, it went to first and then second cousins within the four-generation group. Originally, it seems then in the event of failure of male cousins, to have passed to daughters, but quite early, with the advance of lordship and of an anti-female Christianity, it instead escheated to a lord who had levied an *ebediw* (a death-duty), at the moment of succession.

The obvious threat of the fragmentation of holdings was checked in early days by its operation within these large multiple estates; lands would not have been subdivided into units smaller than the constituent townships. In later years, however, as population and political pressures built up, this practice of subdivision called *cyfran* was without doubt a factor in the growth of that scattered settlement in hamlets and homesteads considered typical of Wales. While nuclear families seem to have formed the essential human core, the role of the *cenedl* was therefore critical; it had to strike the balance between its members and to make sure that land remained within the kin. It tended to cultivate an attitude which made land into a kind of revocable trust. An escape from rigidity was provided by the practice called *prid*, which was not common in early days but became central later. A *priodor* could grant his land to another for payment for a fixed period, usually four years, and the grant was renewable. A form of mortgage, this could in fact conceal outright alienation clean out of the clan, which was legally unthinkable. At first a marginal practice, probably to handle emergencies, it was to become all-important.

The *cenedl* or kindred was, then, ubiquitous, and it was also central to civil actions and the laws of the person. The notion of *sarhad* could be extended to every form of trespass, and the notion of kindred, in different computations, was applied to an increasingly complex set of actions. In effect, it tended to evolve into a practice of deciding guilt by compurgation, sets of oathtakers in support of the credibility of a person, carefully computed from kindreds, who had to follow very strict procedures, since any slip would be taken as an unmasking of the will of God intervening in human justice. In this area, in fact, Welsh practice was not very different from that of the Saxons and most other peoples and it evolved increasingly differentiated, complicated, indeed sophisticated forms of legal action. It was the land law of the kin which was peculiarly Welsh. The law, in effect, was a community law, enforced through kindreds, a 'people's law', subject to that people's kings and, increasingly, its lords.

This kind of society, fanatical from necessity in its obsession with blood and descent (which ultimately threatened to turn the Welsh into a nation of genealogists) bred an anarchic kindred liberty and independence among the free and a cockiness in the face of superior persons, which later Welsh writers were to eulogize as the very essence of the freedom-loving Welsh. It was libertarian in style, if not always in content.

This was a verdict in which its women would without doubt concur, because the role of women in this society was highly ambiguous. As usual, they were considered weak and inferior, in need of a protector. They did not wage war, the central prerogative of the free (and even the half-free), they carried the babies and looked after the children; they managed the house, did most of the sordid work and if they were good, kept quiet. When the celebrated writer Rhigyfarch made an analogy with the hive, he replaced the queen-bee with a king! This was effrontery even from a Christian Church whose Fathers sometimes talked as if God had created woman out of sheer spite. Their status was symbolized in *amobr,* a fine which women paid to their protector for the loss of their virginity. This extraordinarily curious but universal attitude (at least in Europe), enormously reinforced by a misogynist Christianity, would seem at first sight to indicate an unnatural yearning for species suicide; it in fact made female virginity or 'purity' a male property. The fine of *amobr* became a badge of female degradation which, under colonial rule later, was the most telling symptom of an alien-imposed Welsh racial inferiority.

Yet Welsh women came to be identified as the gift-givers and while they were not apparently as free as their Irish cousins, they seem to have been more free and independent than many ordinary women of the Europe of the time. Marriage, while arranged as was universally customary, seems to have been a reciprocal business. The husband paid his wife's *amobr* to whoever was her protector and the bride brought gifts from her kin. The husband gave her a *cowyll,* a morning gift in recognition of her gift of herself, which remained her own property. If the couple separated before seven years, the wife got her *agweddi,* a kind of dower, and after seven years she was entitled to half her husband's property (a right which English and later Welsh women do not seem to have acquired until very recent times!) There were the most elaborate rules on separation (which provoked much vulgar not to say strictly petty-bourgeois mirth in Marx and Engels much later) and there was no real concept of 'bastardy' or a birth which was 'illegitimate'. The obsessive preoccupation with legitimate descent seems to have been interpreted in strictly biological terms. This civilized and human acceptance of 'children of the brake and brush' as they were called, was one of the 'abominations' cited by the thirteenth-century English to justify their extirpation of Welsh law. Women had land at their disposal and widows were much respected. They even appear occasionally at official *cyfran* share-outs of land and as official witnesses. And while they generally had no official place in public life, they seem in practice to have acted as the remembrancers to this community which so badly needed a collective memory. 'My memory is a surer safeguard than thine,' says Blodeuedd the woman made of flowers to her husband in the story of *Math vab Mathonwy,* and the *achau* (the family trees) were securely filed away in the heads of Welsh women right down to very recent times. The central figure in the kindred of the Welsh was its head, the *pencenedl* with his special status as an 'elder'; his wife would have been a far more important person than one might guess from the laws.

Most free and most anarchic were the men at the top, later called *uchelwyr* (higher men). They riveted lordship on the kindreds. They took their cut of all fines from death-duties to virginity fines and demanded their voice in kindred transactions. They could get or be awarded land, serfs, powers at will. 'Could I have a share of those little fellows?' cries a horseman to Iddawg the Embroiler of Britain as he trails his bunch of followers in *The Dream of Rhonabwy*. The bigger fellows were the real power in the communities. They were enmeshed in their own aristocratic kindreds and cultivated an intense class-consciousness. They practised fosterage, the putting out of sons to be reared in other aristocratic families, with a semi-professional class of wet-nurses to assist. Kings went looking for 'a woman with breasts'. This knit an upper class together – foster-brothers figure constantly in the tales and poems – and provided a mechanism for the initiation of useful newcomers. Gerald the Welshman (the celebrated Giraldus Cambrensis) in the twelfth century could explain the weaknesses of south Wales's kings by the bald statement that their great men were ungovernable. Indeed, such people may well have created these kings in the first place. There is a suggestion in Gildas that the first kings after British independence were chosen, elected by their peers and anointed by priests, an echo of both Celtic chieftains and Roman 'dictators'. For what were these kings but a bunch of aristocratic kindreds themselves?

## Kings and King-makers

From the beginning, kings in Wales trod the familiar road of kingdom-builders all over Europe. They tried to get their hands on as much land, as many serfs, as many powers as possible. They tried to root that power by passing it on to a chosen heir. They tried to thrust their officers into a community law enforced by kindreds. They tried to build a bureaucracy supported by specific revenues out of their literate men, their clergy, their retinue and warband, whom they called their *teulu* (family). They paid their genealogists and historians to give them a respectable past and their poets to legitimize and honour their present and their future. When they found no legal word in Welsh law to signify a recognized heir, they took one from the Saxons and called him an atheling, an *edling*.

For succession was the critical point. These kings had emerged from the kindreds and were constrained by their practice. The oscillation of kingship between sons and cousins, the perpetual division of both royal land and royal sovereignty, indicate that the four-generation *cenedl* and the practice of *cyfran* imprisoned kings no less than commoners. The very culture they lived by enforced that imprisonment. What were its virtues? Those of the Heroic Age: intense pride in descent and royal blood – shared of course by their kin out to their second cousins; valour in battle, generosity towards followers, foster-brothers and of course the poets who lived by it – shared by everyone with power over the 'little fellows'; chivalry towards women, honourable enemies and the weak – the commonplaces of poets and preachers. Justice was praised, but in peculiarly individual terms; it is the churchmen and later chroniclers who talk of peace and good government and only one king in Welsh history is called good.

To become real kings, these kindreds who had seized command had to break out. One instrument was the king's control over 'aliens' – outsiders – who were many in a mountain country with a footloose population of young men – and his *teulu*, which success could make a focus of attraction and which could in turn give the king the support he needed to shape the aristocratic kindreds who strutted as cocks of his own commotes. The *teulu* was a heartland of royal power, endlessly celebrated by the poets and tale-tellers and enshrined in ideal form in Arthur's brilliant band . . .

'My trusty gentles and my warband and my foster-brothers,' cries Gronw Bebyr, a king confronted by a death-challenge in *Math vab Mathonwy*, 'is there one of you will take the blow in my stead?' 'Faith, there is none,' said they. And because they refused to stand taking one blow for their lord, they are called, from that day to this, one of the Three Disloyal Warbands . . .

Disloyal warbands abounded, for the establishment of a kingship required constant struggle against or accommodation with brothers, cousins, local kings, *uchelwyr* (higher men), the Church and outside powers like the Vikings and the English. This system, if it can be called that, offered some opportunities to a strong or clever man; it offered more to the adventurer. It looks less a system than a set of systematized instincts enshrined in a culture which was all-embracing, attractive and difficult to convert into institutions. There is a characteristic passage in *The Dream of Rhonabwy* –

Madawg son of Maredudd held Powys from end to end . . . And at that time he had a brother. He was not a man of equal rank with himself; he was Iorwerth son of Maredudd. And he felt great heaviness and sorrow at seeing the honour and power that were his brother's whereas he had naught. And he sought out his comrades and his foster-brothers and took counsel of them what he should do about it. They decided by their counsel to send some from amongst them to demand provision for him. The offer Madawg made him was the captaincy of his warband and equal standing with himself, and steeds and arms and honour. And Iorwerth rejected that and went harrying into Lloegyr (England) . . .

It was the excluded and resentful brother of the king who became the standard Iago figure of the Welsh political drama, always open to the whispered promptings of that king's enemies, even if – or perhaps above all if – that enemy were the King of England, whose tall shadow fell across every royal household in Wales.

And it was precisely in that shadow that the High Kings of Wales emerged.

## High Kings and Hard Facts

In north and west Wales the growth of the landed power of the Church and the notables which undercut kingship in Glywysing was probably at work, but it was the failure of male heirs which opened a route for intruders. Gwriad, an unknown who claimed descent from Powys notables and a useful distant origin in north Britain, edged his way into the Gwynedd dynasty by marrying one of its daughters. When the male line gave out in Gwynedd, his son Merfyn Frych took over the kingdom. Powys was now crumbling; the English had swarmed over much of the north-east and destroyed Degannwy. Merfyn took the chance and married its princess Nest. And when the male line gave out there, Merfyn's son Rhodri, who had inherited Gwynedd, assumed control of Powys as well; it was not to resurface until the late eleventh century. Down in Dyfed-Deheubarth, where the male line had given out in 814, intruders had married in. So did Rhodri, taking Angharad of Ceredigion as wife. With all north Wales at his command, he earned his spurs by defeating Gorm, king of those new intruders the Danes, and took over the southern kingdom.

By the time of his death all Wales outside the south-east was at his command. Like everyone else, he was desperately hard-pressed by the new Viking threat – at one stage he had to flee to Ireland – and by the rising power of the English, who in the end killed him. But it was the dynasty of Rhodri which was now the major force in Wales.

His sons followed up by driving into the south, sending its kings scuttling for shelter to the court of Wessex, but, riven by the usual inner conflict, they were themselves driven to that same shelter to buttress their power. The centre of gravity of the dynasty shifted to Dyfed-Deheubarth. Hywel, a grandson of Rhodri, had married Elen of the Dyfed line. In the early years of the tenth century he extended his power over Deheubarth. He made alliance with Wessex the lynchpin of his policy. He won a respite from the Vikings with this support and in 942, when the succession ended in Gwynedd, he beat down resistance and took over the north as well. He was going to make Rhodri's one Wales a reality. He was the first Welsh king to strike coins bearing a *Hywel Rex* (though he had to have them struck in Chester) and he gave this united kingdom its unified law. The traditional story has him summoning six men from every *cantref* to a parliament at Whitland, consulting the best lawyers, making a pilgrimage to Rome. This is fanciful fabrication, but there is little reason to doubt that a codification occurred under his supervision. This was the essential step, common to Europe, in the transformation of a monarchy into a nation.

A nation was in fact beginning to emerge in the written literature of this people, which dates from the ninth century. In their monasteries they were annotating Boethius's *Consolation of Philosophy* and Ovid's *Ars Amatoria,* the fourth-century Gospel poem of Juvencus and the fifth-century treatise on education by Martianus Capella; St David's produced its *Annals,* the historians their propaganda genealogies. An unknown historian, in his *Historia Brittonum,* wrestled with Isidore of Seville, Prosper and Victorinus of Aquitaine and a clutch of Welsh, English and other sources to create a disjointed history of the Britons. The history with which he equipped the Welsh was the history of Maximus, Vortigern, Germanus and Ambrosius, and, above all, of Arthur of Britain.

So did their poets, so, more than anybody, did their story-tellers, the *cyfarwyddion*, lower in status than the poets but far wider in their reach. They tapped a vast wealth of oral resources through their Triads, a grouping of material in threes to serve as an index or device to jog the memory. The universe they unlocked, written down in final form in the eleventh century, was a brilliant and breath-taking world of myth, legend, half-history, folk-tale, and sheer, marvellous invention, circling around a lost saga of Pryderi of Dyfed which broke up and re-formed as the *Four Branches of the Mabinogi* (Pedair Kainc) and four accompanying stories which are steeped in Arthur and his Britain. Two are devoted to Macsen Wledig, the British emperor, and to Lludd, Celtic god transformed into a Welsh mythical hero. He it was who rebuilt London as Caer Lludd (still obscurely remembered in Ludgate and its King Lud pub).

In the days of Hywel Dda, this tradition became politically operative and got a bite to it. Myrddin – Merlin, poet and guru to Arthur – had prophesied the Return of the Hero; one day a British king would sit in London again. And around 930 this challenge was thrown into the arena and at Hywel Dda himself. Out of south Wales came a dramatic and vivid poem, *Armes Prydein,* parading St David as a national patron and calling on the Welsh to ally with the dread Danes, the Scots and anybody else who would join, to expel the Saxon pirates from the Island of Britain. Just such a confederacy took shape in 937, when kings of the Scots and the Strathclyde Britons joined the Danes of Dublin, only to be smashed by Athelstan at the battle of Brunanburh.

And it was precisely Athelstan who had provoked *Armes Prydein*. One of those Wessex kings who were making an equally novel England, he had hammered Cornwall, summoned the Welsh kings to the Wye, fixed the frontier there, exacted tribute from them and settled disputes among them as if he were Macsen or Arthur himself. His writers were calling him a *basileus*, an emperor of Britain. It was this which summoned up atavistic spirits from the historical imagination of the Welsh. In so doing, it precipitated a head-on, if only half-conscious, conflict of traditions among them. Because in 930, *Armes Prydein* was dissident propaganda from an angry cleric. Even as he wrote, his own High King Hywel was at Athelstan's court attesting his charters.

He had been driven there, like so many others, by 'The Fury of the Northmen'. Over two centuries the impact of Danes and Norwegians, first in their devastating raids, then in their settlement and commerce, unhinged the British Isles. In England, settled in strength in the Danelaw, they propelled the country into a Scandinavian orbit even as they conjured up the new and English power of Wessex. On the western seas, they turned Iceland with its admixture of Celts into a centre of exploration which reached out to Greenland, Labrador and Newfoundland. They dominated the Irish Sea, planted colonies in Ireland and the Isle of Man. They surged repeatedly into Wales and drew its people into the Celtic-Scandinavian world of the west.

They left a permanent imprint. Swansea and Anglesey are Scandinavian names and there is a scattering of such all around the coasts. There may have been small settlements on the commercial routes at Milford Haven and Swansea. By the twelfth century, Cardiff men with Norse names were citizens of Dublin. It was the Irish connection which proved crucial. From the tenth century, mercenary bands of Northmen from Irish bases were central to the wars of Wales; one helped drive out Normans from the north. Irish and Viking enclaves offered refuge to Welsh kings on the run. A stint among Irish and Northmen became part of the normal political education of a Welsh princeling. In the end, there were Welsh Vikings; Gruffydd ap Cynan himself, of the old Gwynedd dynasty, was one such. The celebrated later legend of Madoc, a Welsh prince said to have discovered America in the twelfth century, has its origins here; he was made Gruffydd's grandson.

The initial impact, however, was destructive and unhingeing. Wave after wave of raids hit Wales, especially the peninsulas of north-west and south-west. In 878 a host wintered in Dyfed; in 896 another moved from England virtually to occupy the south-east. The Norsemen in Chester were a permanent threat. In 914 a Viking raid went deep up the Severn, ravaged the south and kidnapped the bishop of Ergyng.

It was in response to this threat that Wessex had climbed over the other kingdoms to establish its hold on England. It was this which now drove the Welsh to that same centre of power. Mercian raids had been thrusting deeply into Wales, but under Alfred of Wessex there was a significant shift. Asser of St David's, one of the leading academics of his day, was invited to Alfred's court from a monastery which had been pounded without mercy by the Northmen; he wrote a life of the great king. Hywel Dda was to be no less an admirer. The southern kings had fled to Alfred from Rhodri's sons in Gwynedd; the latter soon trod the same path themselves. At Buttington in 893 and elsewhere, Welsh and English had to fight side by side against a common enemy. It was an English king who ransomed the Bishop of Ergyng. There were cultural exchanges, gestures of reconciliation. Welsh kings made formal submission to the king of England. At that ceremony on the Wye in 927, Athelstan was an over-king; the Welsh kings were *sub-reguli*, sub-kings. Their leader was Hywel Dda, High King of Wales.

In the long perspectives of the history of the Welsh, this is a significant moment. The codification of their laws, the first advance towards the creation of a Welsh nation and the submission of the High King of Wales to the King of England, were one and the same process. In objective terms, it represents the abandonment of the kind of vision expressed in *Armes Prydein*. *Britain* continues to govern the imagination of the Welsh but it is banished from their reality. The realities of fewness and fragility have their own logic. *Wales,* as a political entity, comes into existence as a junior partner in a *Britain* run by England.

## A Crisis of Survival

The political life of this new Welsh nation, even in the ambiguous form it assumed at birth, was brief. The century after Hywel was sheer, and horrible, anti-climax. The kingdoms of Wales become cockpits in which fratricidal brothers, usurpers, Welsh, English, Danes, Irish fight over the bodies of Welsh people like blind rats in a cage. This, at the moment when the new England was entering its tenth-century renaissance.

Under the year 1043, a Welsh chronicle records that a king of Glamorgan had died in his old age; it was a rarity worthy of note. Between 949 and 1066 at least thirty-five Welsh rulers died by violence, generally at the hands of their own countrymen. There was a yearning for an end to all this. Time after time, chroniclers run to some strong-arm who emerges from the ruck to hail him as the new Rhodri: Maredudd, a grandson of Hywel who took Gwynedd from the south, bought off the Northmen and imposed a thirteen-year peace, new men like that Gruffydd who took south Wales from a base in Gwent, an Aeddan who reduced Gwynedd to order, only to be killed by another intruder. They are hailed in traditional terms: 'In his time, there was no desert place in hill or plain and but three townships left solitary in the whole of Wales...' a chilling glimpse of the reality of famine, slavery and political breakdown which was their kingship's final legacy to the Welsh.

Beneath the political instability, with the recurrent incursions of the Northmen now part of the texture of Welsh politics, some underlying trends may be detected. The south-east is at last drawn fully into Wales, as its resources become the target of kings to north and west and themselves support adventurers who kidnap Dyfed and briefly rule all the south. The south-west flexes its muscles as Anglesey passes under the Northmen and Gwynedd is eclipsed. The cult of Dewi becomes the Welsh national cult of St David, the stories of the *Mabinogion* are written into literature in Dyfed, and Deheubarth grows into the strongest power in Wales. The dynasty of Rhodri remains central. Based essentially now in the south, with ambitious men marrying into it, Deheubarth provides the springboard for its leaders to launch themselves at Gwynedd, their ancestral base, in an attempt to restore the old hegemony.

It was from this region and in this manner that the last High King appeared. Gruffydd ap Llywelyn, offspring of a strategic marriage into the southern branch of the Rhodri dynasty, used Northmen as ruthlessly as anybody else, killed the king of Gwynedd in 1039 and took his kingdom. He ruled Wales for twenty-five years and throughout those years, in the words of the chronicler, 'he hounded the Pagans and the Saxons in many battles and he prevailed against them and ravaged them.' He did indeed. He hounded the Welsh no less. He hammered the Welsh into a kind of unity. For the first time, the power of a High King stretched into every corner of Wales. He launched great raids into western England. He at least ensured that an old Wales ended with a bang. Yet his reign seems nothing but one endless battle, against English earls, Danish freebooters and Welsh kings. Shield and Defender of the Welsh, as they called him, he ended as he had begun. Earl Harold, his own eye on the English crown, drove a big army into Wales. In what was becoming another Welsh royal tradition,

Gruffydd was finally killed by his own men. More ominously, Harold would permit his half-brothers to inherit only after they had sworn allegiance to Edward the Confessor.

> We were a people taut for war; the hills
> Were no harder, the thin grass
> Clothed them more warmly than the coarse
> Shirts our small bones...
>
> Our kings died, or they were slain
> By the old treachery at the ford...

A modern Welsh poet, 'remembering', laments. Some Welsh nationalists claim to detect among the Welsh a specific type of inferiority complex, a self-questioning suspicion that the Welsh people, as opposed to individuals among them, inherently lack political capacity. If such a feeling exists, its roots presumably lie here, in some alleged failure of the Welsh to find an independent political form for their distinctive ways of living.

Presumably such people are more concerned with quality than mere quantity. In historic truth, any people of that small number which the Welsh were, in that predicament, would have found it impossible to achieve a genuine political independence, had they been endowed with the political wisdom of a millennium's sages. The inherent weaknesses of Welsh kingship are obvious, but there is no reason why, in reasonable detachment, one Welsh kingdom should not have absorbed the rest in the manner of the English and so many other peoples. There is nothing very mysterious about it. The decisive factor was the sheer numerical weight, wealth, power and presence of England among a people few in number and in a political situation made unstable by the intrusive ubiquity of Danes and other marauders. In such a situation, all the disruptive tendencies inherent in Welsh kingship, including the very culture by which it lived, were given free play.

At the time of Hywel the question really at issue was whether the Welsh could find a viable political form for their highly individual polity within a 'Britain' dominated by England. A hundred years later, that was no longer the issue. The question was whether a distinctive Welsh people was going to survive at all.

A mere three years after the Shield and Defender of the Welsh went down before the English, the English kingdom itself went down before William the Bastard, Duke of Normandy, and his army of iron-fisted and greedy adventurers. A year after Hastings, William fitz Osbern was Earl of Hereford; three years later Roger of Montgomery was Earl of Shrewsbury and Hugh of Avranches Earl of Chester. A few years after that, Caerleon, the *caer* of the legion, Arthur's court, was a Norman castle; there was another at Caernarfon, the *caer* in Arfon, court of Helen wife to Macsen Wledig; kings had run away to Ireland . . . 'Our limbs are cut off . . . chains are loaded on our arms . . . liberty and self-will perish . . .' And in 1093, Rhys ap Tewdwr, legitimate king of Deheubarth, was killed by Normans outside their new castle at Brecon.

'From that day kings ceased to bear rule in Wales . . .' proclaimed an Anglo-Norman chronicle. The Welsh Chronicle of the Princes agreed . . . with Rhys, 'the kingdom of Wales was overthrown.' Neither was in any meaningful sense accurate. What they indicate is that, in both Welsh and Norman eyes, a whole epoch had come to an end. In that, they were correct.

# 4 · EUROPEAN WELSH

The Normans made the Welsh a European people. They prised Wales out of the Celtic-Scandinavian world of the Irish Sea and incorporated it into Latin Europe. They brought feudalism, the baron and his knights, castles and manors; they brought the first truly large-scale farming, towns, trade and a money economy; they brought the European Church, European monasteries, Canterbury and the Pope; they brought chivalry and the literature of Europe.

In response, the Welsh exploded into self-expression and self-assertion. Adopting the methods of the intruder and adapting their own, they carved out a distinctive polity, entered European politics and at one historical moment were set fair to create their own feudal state around Gwynedd. They turned their oral culture into a scintillating literature, retaining its Celtic core but glossing and enriching it from the new world which had, perforce, been opened to them. Furthermore, through the Norman March or Borderland, they gave Europe itself the initial form of what became one of its more brilliant and abundant literary-historical traditions.

It was through a March that they transmitted it, that potent society whose analogue can be seen in border zones elsewhere in Europe, for the Normans also drew a frontier across the bony face of Wales. That frontier, in different form and circumstance, has appeared and reappeared as a shadow line across its human landscape. It exists today, more visible than ever.

In one sense, it has been a frontier beween two different human communities, as one people, split by a political demarcation line, developed into two divergent societies operating to different historical chronologies, with different laws and different loyalties, threatening sometimes to become two embryonic 'nations'. Human beings, wrenched apart into divergent historical experiences, interiorized those experiences and those divergences as custom, memory and tradition. Consider the Serbs and Croats, close kin, indeed ethnically one, who under the radically different disciplines of Habsburgs and Turks, evolved into two distinct and mutually hostile 'nations'. The dividing line in Wales was nothing like as hard and impenetrable as this, but even as a political frontier, it lasted for nearly five hundred years. Nations have been born, lived a span and died in less time. Over centuries, the process of differentiation was to be reinforced by successive waves of innovation, agrarian modernization and merchant capitalism, the infiltration of English Puritanism, the massive implantation of industrial capitalism, the English language, all rooting themselves in the easier, more open lands of what had been Marcher Wales. In our own day that shadow line, once again looming ominously out of the past across the languages we speak, has sometimes seemed a Berlin Wall between two civilizations.

In other equally vital areas of human experience, however, the frontier has been as substantial as gossamer. From the beginning, brides as well as raiders crossed the border, the Church of the European papacy strode over it; from the beginning, practices and styles flowed both ways over the border in mutual interaction. New species of human beings emerged, as much Welsh as Norman; families on both sides were inextricably intermeshed; the French language inserted itself between Welsh and Latin to make important sectors of society trilingual. Above all, periodic surges of feeling and action, pulsing up from the Welsh people themselves, no matter what rulers they were subjected to, have swept away the line in repeated reassertion of an irreducibly Welsh identity which has survived the buffetings of a millennium and a half, in one of the minor miracles of history.

In 1163, during a big military expedition into south Wales, Henry II, ruler of the European empire of the Angevins and king of the English, asked an old Welshman of Pencader, who had joined his army against his own people, 'because of their evil way of life', what chances there were of victory. The old man replied,

My Lord King, this nation may now be harassed, weakened and decimated by your soldiery, as it has so often been by others in former times, but it will never be destroyed by the wrath of man . . . Whatever else may come to pass, I do not think that on the Day of Direst Judgement any race other than the Welsh, or any other language, will give answer to the Supreme Judge of all for this small corner of the earth.

Gerald the Welshman, a distinguished member of the new establishment, descended from Norman lords and a Welsh princess, using very different language in very different style in his great struggle for the independence of the Church of St David, said much the same thing. More significantly, it was Gerald himself who reported the old man; it was his speech he chose as the climax with which to conclude his equally celebrated *Description of Wales (Descriptio Kambriae)*.

Nevertheless, anyone who looks objectively at the history of this precarious people cannot fail to observe the repeated re-emergence of a shadow line which was first drawn as a border in the eleventh century. In recent times it has been visible in matters great and small, as the line between a Wales which innovates and a Wales which persists, between a Wales which officially refused alcohol on a Sunday and a Wales which did not; in our own day it is the essential border between two languages. When Welsh people made desperate today propose a last-ditch stand in a *bro* or heartland which they intend to preserve Welsh-speaking and immaculate, it is in old Pura Wallia, 'Welsh Wales', as opposed to the March, that they root themselves.

The persistence of this frontier through all the changes of eight centuries testifies to the force of the European impact and to its historical congruity.

## The Frontier

It was established by brute force and colonial cunning. The Norman conquest of England was a joint-stock enterprise by a syndicate out for loot, power, glory and the favour of Heaven, for the Normans also came to redeem an English Church considered heretical. Appalling Christians but very good churchmen, they found the Celtic Church incomprehensible and abolished it.

Wales was attacked by an independent provincial family of the parent mafia. An adventurer, under licence, cut through the forests with his mailed knights and men-at-arms, beating off clouds of Welsh guerillas, to throw up a quick motte-and-bailey castle. The target was the local king of the *bro* and the aim was to take over a profitable enterprise in decent working condition. The advance was commote by commote, often supplemented by strategic marriage into some local Welsh dynasty. The forts were in time replaced by square towers and later by those massive and extensive fortresses which are still so visible and which they had to maintain for three hundred years. In time, they were ubiquitous, almost as numerous as that other Welsh architectural phenomenon, the chapel. No corner of Wales would be complete without one, ruins become picturesque, in whose brutal functionalism one can still sense the grim terrorism which raised them.

Once established, these well-born bandits introduced all the paraphernalia of the world familiar to them: the manor with its great open fields, its lord's demesne and its serf-tenant strips where possible, the nearest approximation when it was not. They imported citizens for their little towns with their money and market economy. They brought in Black Monks for their Benedictine monasteries, in more genial counterpoint to the castles but with no less colonial a purpose. They obliterated the Welsh Church, banished its saints, tried to turn its *clas*-churches and their daughters into European canons and Roman parishes, to impose the familiar European hierarchy and to subject the whole apparatus to Canterbury. They generally held on to the unfree Welsh people in the lowlands and along the coasts, shipping in anyone they could get hold of to form a polyglot population (which, in fact, was not particularly English). Some of the more affluent Welsh were turned out at swordpoint, others negotiated with. The Welsh in the uplands with their Law of Hywel they generally left alone, provided they kept their proper stations and paid tribute.

From this crude beginning, the Norman lordships of the March grew into a complex and multiracial society and a power in their own right. The lords succeeded Welsh kings and owed little beyond allegiance to the English Crown; they were often decisive in the politics of England and Western Europe. Very rapidly they became hopelessly enmeshed with the Welsh in marriage, lifestyle, temporary alliance. A new and hybrid culture grew up in the March with quite astonishing speed. Plenty of Marchers over time were cymricized; as in Ireland, several became more Welsh than the Welsh. Numbers of their descendants were to turn out three hundred years later alongside Owain Glyn Dŵr in the last Welsh war of independence.

The formation of so peculiar and potent (and long-lasting) a society was the direct result of Welsh survival and recovery. At first, nothing could stop the Normans. Two legitimate kings, Gruffydd ap Cynan in Gwynedd and Rhys ap Tewdwr in Deheubarth, and their sons after them, lived lives out of some implausible Hollywood epic. Now in jail, now restored to the favour of a king of England worried by overmighty Norman subjects, now in victorious revolt, now on the run, they found Ireland a refuge. Several – Gruffydd ap Cynan in particular – became almost as much Irish leaders as Welsh and half-Viking with it. But in the end it was the restoration of their realms in Wales which drew them back – and into a feudal world.

The first smash-and-grab thrusts from Chester, Shrewsbury and Hereford overran the north and penetrated deeply into the south-west. William the Conqueror came down to St David's, to pay his respects and to assert control, but after his death and the killing of Rhys ap Tewdwr, the robber barons swarmed all over Wales. The shattered dynasties of Wales, with their backs to an Irish wall, using their own weapons and stealing the Normans', fought back. They beat the bandits out of the west, only to bring the power of the English king down on their heads. Henry I rolled his power into Wales over Welsh kings and Norman lords alike.

He confiscated Shrewsbury and took the Montgomery booty in the south-west, making Carmarthen the first royal lordship in Wales. He imported Flemings and planted them in southern Dyfed. They transformed its agrarian economy and launched the Little-England-Beyond-Wales, behind the landsker line which shut the Welsh off in their upland north. But on Henry's death England lurched into civil war and the Welsh seized their chance.

Owain Gwynedd, son to Gruffydd ap Cynan, ruthlessly eliminating all rivals, Norman and Welsh (for the traditional fratricidal strife among the Welsh continued unabated, indeed, intensified), rebuilt Gwynedd into a power and drove it across north Wales. He thrust south into Ceredigion. Powys, in full revival and trying to re-create its old kingdom out of its ruins, was confronted with a new and permanent menace. In the rubble of Deheubarth in the south, the king's sons fought Normans and each other to win personal control over as much as they could reconstitute, and the legitimate Rhys ap Gruffydd began to make headway.

In 1154 the English civil war ended with the accession of Henry II as commander of a great European power-complex, the Angevin Empire. In two big land-sea campaigns he brought the resurgent Welsh to a halt. Owain in the north dropped the title 'king' and pulled back west of the Conwy, while in the south a hemmed-in Rhys made sortie after sortie from his traditional base in Dinefwr (Dynevor). In the 1160s, with Henry immersed in the Becket struggle and troubles in Europe, Rhys's raids grew into a war and Gwynedd joined in. Owain moved to the head of what was virtually a national coalition. Henry in response mobilized a massive expedition in 1165 'to destroy all Welshmen'. It collapsed in the Berwyn mountains in bad weather, guerilla resistance and logistical breakdown.

Owain Gwynedd cut loose to the Dee while Rhys in the south took Ceredigion, Ystrad Tywi and much of Dyfed. Powys, threatened with renewed extinction, rallied to the English crown. But by 1170 Owain was dead and his sons slithered into the traditional civil war. Henry, sensing the moment, went for settlement. Rhys was formally confirmed in his possessions and, entering a peculiarly personal relationship with the king, was made a Justiciar of South Wales. The first recorded gathering which looks like an eisteddfod, embracing north and south, was held under his auspices. All Welsh rulers took the oaths of fealty and homage to the king even as a bunch of Marchers were diverted into a strong-arm invasion of Ireland. By the end of the twelfth century, the frontier which had emerged over two generations had settled.

The old kingdom of Morgannwg-Gwent had vanished, to be replaced by Monmouth and Glamorgan, two of the strongest bastions of Norman power in Wales. The diminished lordship of Powys faced a struggle to survive, torn three ways between Gwynedd, the English Crown and nostalgia for its own past greatness. It proved remarkably tenacious. In the end, Powys split in two, the southern Powys Wenwynwyn rallying normally to Westminster, the northern Powys Fadog (which was ultimately to produce the last Welsh prince) to Aberffraw. A core of the old Deheubarth had been re-established, but it was ringed by Norman lordships with a strong base in Pembroke and a royal presence in the region. Much of the south and east and their resources had passed into permanent alien control. Only Gwynedd had ultimately emerged relatively unscathed. Under Owain and some of his successors it grew into a major force, the strongest power in Welsh Wales and, in time, a contender for power in Wales itself. Under the spur of necessity, its ruling house of Aberffraw exploited to the limit its natural mountain barrier and its Anglesey granary and applied the newly learned modes of feudal warfare. Its pre-eminence began to register not only in the texts of the Laws of Hywel which its lawyers were continuously modifying, but in the political terminology of the land. Everywhere in Wales kings had disappeared; all that were left were lords owing allegiance and fealty and doing the critical homage to the king of England. There was a temporary Welsh overlord in The Lord Rhys, Yr Arglwydd Rhys, of Dinefwr. In Gwynedd, however, there was a 'prince', an imprecise term which could be charged with a constitutional significance.

And to the east and south, embracing much of the best land and expropriating much of the potential for growth, marched the Marcher Lordships in a great arc. From the pivot of Chester, they stamped their imprint from north to south, a seed-bed of the powerful families, Montgomerys, Mortimers, Bohuns, Clares. They stretched deep into mid-Wales, where their Brecon was entrenched. Glamorgan was immensely powerful, later the fief of the Clares. They ran west along a rich and open coast, planting towns, peopling the plains with an unfree and sometimes alien population, to cluster in force in the fist of Pembroke and southern Dyfed with its revolutionized economy.

There was a permanently disputed shadow zone and endless border raiding but there was also a fine mesh of intermarriage and fluctuating tactical alliances. The beautiful princess Nest of Deheubarth could play the role of a Helen of Troy, precipitating wars over her person.

And in this tension there was some equilibrium, a certain nervous stability. In 1188 Archbishop Baldwin could preach the Crusade and impose his will on the new cathedral churches on his grand tour through both the

March and Pura Wallia, the tour made immortal by its chronicler, Gerald the Welshman. Gerald was one of the new breed, grandson of Nest and her Norman husband Gerald of Windsor, son of Nest's daughter Angharad and her husband the Norman knight William de Barri. Norman by male descent, then, Gerald was also the great-grandson of Rhys ap Tewdwr, the last legitimate king of Deheubarth. He was a man who could impartially advise each people on how to defeat the other (almost impartially, at least, there is no Norman equivalent to his old man of Pencader!) Scholar, administrator, author and something of a scientist, known in Rome and of European stature, he has left some of the most vivid testimony ever written on a medieval people. It was this Norman-Welsh mandarin who was to fight a great, losing battle for an independent Welsh Church with its own archbishop in St David's – himself, naturally.

For the most startling and perhaps unexpected consequence of this confrontation was the entry into history of a brilliant new literary culture, simultaneously Welsh and European and itself without doubt the product of a new civilization in Wales.

## A New Civilization

Once again, the Welsh had to define themselves in response to a challenge from outside. The consequence was a literary renaissance in several languages; many of the Welsh classics date from this confrontation. There was a veritable explosion of the immensely popular *Lives of the Saints* as Welsh churchmen fought for their cherished houses in the total reorganization forced by the Normans. The old Celtic *clas*-clans went out in some glory, in the learned families of Bishop Sulien along the St David's–Llanbadarn axis and of Llancarfan in Glamorgan; Rhigyfarch, author of *David's Life*, with his brother Ieuan, were supported by scribes from Llangranog in Ceredigion to Llangybi in Gwent. The new Latin monasteries, particularly among the intensely Welsh Cistercians and Augustinians, despite their alien origin, came to marry the traditions of European cloister and the old Welsh *clas*; the largest single body of medieval Welsh ecclesiastical manuscripts comes from the Austin canons of Llanthony, down near old Ergyng (Archenfield), now lost in Herefordshire (an area which was to remain Welsh-speaking into the nineteenth century and to produce so many Welsh notables that it begins to look like some lowland Snowdonia with a West Country accent!) The chronicle of the kings, which had started at St David's, moved to Llanbadarn and then shifted to the Cistercian house of Strata Florida, whose *scriptorium* came to be served by every one of its sister houses from Caerleon in the south to Conway in the north, to produce a magnificent collection of literary and historical material, culminating in the great *Brut y Tywysogion,* the masterful *Chronicle of the Princes.*

Even more active were the equally popular friars, with their close connections with the universities. It was along the communication networks of the friars that Welshmen were filtered into the Europe of the scholars; along the same route, the ideas of Europe were filtered back into Wales. Adam of Wales and Philip Wallensis, who found their way to the University of Paris in the twelfth century, initiated a tradition. Young Welshmen made their way there and, in greater numbers, to its offshoot in Oxford, where they established a permanent and highly visible presence. Thomas Wallensis and John Wallensis in the thirteenth century served as regent-masters to the friars in Paris and Oxford and the former was ranked with the great Grosseteste himself by Roger Bacon. Some found their way even into the closely controlled episcopate, where Cambro-Normans like Gerald found a niche; no fewer than three bishops were descendants of the evidently potent Nest of Deheubarth, the 'Helen of Wales'. Under such people as Adam of St Asaph, a friend of Peter Lombard in Paris, men of Welsh sympathy within even this Church poured out a mass of manuals and sermon collections in Latin for the priests and of devotional, evangelical, and miracle literature in Welsh, including translations of the Paternoster and the Creed. The native Welsh, to a quite striking degree, were admitted to much of the now rapidly developing learning of Europe; there were Welsh works on that old Celtic preoccupation, medicine; there was a beginning in science.

More particularist in its Welshness was the secular work of the poets. In a revival directly arising out of the struggle, the bardic order seems to have been reorganized. Bardic schools were arduous and apprenticeships in the strict metres long. Gruffydd ap Cynan was credited with the initial impetus, possibly systematized in eisteddfods under that Maiestawd Dehau, Majesty of the South as he was called, The Lord Rhys, Justiciar of the King, who exercised some shadowy, theoretical authority over every lord in Wales, whether Welsh or Norman, and whose eminence endowed the Welsh language and its poetry with prestige. This was the age of the *gogynfeirdd*, the court poets. Every court and many a sub-court had its official *pencerdd*, the master-poet who sat next to the prince's heir in hall, and its *bardd teulu*, the household poet (who was a bit simpler, for the benefit of 'little fellows' and women!) For the poets had official functions, they were the remembrancers to a dynasty and its people. They evolved a complex, difficult and powerful tradition which was, like the cathedrals, architectural in structure, leaving as little room for individuality as the latter. A renaissance tone enters; princes like Owain Cyfeiliog and Hywel the son of Owain Gwynedd were themselves poets and they permitted themselves some occasional licence, the latter, for example, cherishing wild mountains and the sea, which was unusual. But most, like the great Cynddelw in the twelfth century, bent their talents to the service of a mission. We get an odd glimpse of a more plebeian world, a sword of three meltings, those glass windows through which the girls used to peep at Cynddelw himself, splendid figure that he was (to quote) or of Einion, fed to the teeth, 'weary am I of the service of princes. . blessed are they, monks in churches'. But mostly it is a poetry of praise, morality, exhortation and legitimation addressed to a strictly traditional concept of the prince and lord, which was not much liked by the Church. The most vivid touches reflect raids and skirmishes; Owain the prince-poet sheathes his sword and counts his stolen cattle and day breaks – 'Lo! the long hillside and the valley were full of sun!'. . .in Mathrafal the sods are trampled under the feet of proud horses, and after a night raid on the Severn border, with the 'tall, powerful eagle on the Long Hill' (Long Mynd) and the delightful smile of men on the Severn, 'we are welcomed with drink under stars and moon by a generous bloodstained warrior . . .' This clearly derived from the Heroic traditions of the Welsh and the British and their kings, adjusted to a world of lords and princes. What we hear is what they themselves called The Old Song of Taliesin. It is a mutation of that British Arthurian tradition which is the longest tradition in the writing of the Welsh.

It was even stronger among the lower-caste *cyfarwyddion*, the story-tellers. An Irish *ollamh* had to know no fewer than 350 stories, orally transmitted. His Welsh colleague with his Triads would have been no less well equipped. It is as the Normans ride in that some unknown genius finally writes down his version of those *Four Branches of the Mabinogi*; the others follow – and they follow directly into Europe via the remembrancers and translators of south Wales, Bretons, Normans, Flemings, English, Welsh. What a superb collection this is! Four branches of a complex tree of legend and narrative, four independent tales and three romances rather French in style. This is essentially a Welsh Land of Xanadu; there are Irish elements in many stories and a French mode copied from the continental transmission of the Arthur cycle, but the whole is unmistakably Welsh in provenance. The rough, tough Arthur of the British moves in and out of the world of Celtic mythology to ride side by side with the Arthur of Camelot and his Round Table Knights with their French accents.

For this renaissance stopped at no frontier. Norman lords soon succumbed to the charms of court poets, harpists and singers. Gerald made a special note of the part-singing characteristic of the Welsh: 'when a choir gathers to sing, which happens often in this country, you will hear as many different parts and voices as there are performers, all joining together in the end to produce a single organic harmony and melody in the soft sweetness of B-flat . . .'

A motley lot themselves, with Bretons strongly represented, the lords created whole schools of translators, particularly in Glamorgan and Monmouth. Flemings were some of the earliest to transmit stories of Arthur and Merlin into Europe along the clerical network. Peter Vostaert produced a Dutch version of the story of Gawain; clerics made many Latin versions which Dutch-Flemish patrons in the Low Countries had rendered into Dutch, with their Celtic origins acknowledged. Willem of Ghent, a troubadour who produced the Dutch version of *Reynard the Fox,* the most successful in the Germanic lands, spent some time in Britain and Wales and was a friend of Walter Map, himself a racy jongleur, one of whose Arthurian romances was translated by a Brabantine in the employ of the major Dutch patron. In the late twelfth century Willem wrote a romance, *Madoc*, which went down well in Champagne and Poitou and seems to have been derived from Welsh stories of a Welsh seafarer, perhaps someone like that Freeman of Wales who raided their settlements so effectively from Lundy Island that he lodged in the *Orkneyinga Saga* of the Icelanders themselves in the days of Owain Gwynedd. Walter Map himself, a Herefordshire man and a friend of Gerald of Wales, could speak of 'my compatriots the Welsh' and share their culture.

Out of this world came the astounding *History of the Kings of Britain* written by Geoffrey of Monmouth in the early twelfth century. A Breton based in Gwent, it was Geoffrey who created the classical form of what passed down centuries as the British History, rooting the Britons in a history started by Brutus the Trojan, already outlined in the ninth century, giving them their great hero Arthur, who now bestrides Europe and the northern seas of the Northmen, broadcasting a wealth of rich, largely mythical but compulsive history and a prophecy of redemption when an Arthur would once again sit on the throne of Britain. The Matter of Britain swept the French-language universe and a continent. It became a European best-seller, even as other versions of the Arthurian traditions entered the discourse of Christendom to be transmuted at the hands of such as Chrétien de Troyes and others into something rich and very different. This became one of the most potent story-cycles we have known. By 1180 Arthur was a hero in the Crusader states of Antioch and Palestine – 'The Eastern peoples speak of him as do the Western, though separated by the breadth

of the whole earth. Egypt speaks of him, nor is the Bosphorus silent . . .'
The Welsh were assiduous in translating this World Hero back into the
language he had started in! Even as 'history', and in spite of all the spirits
who cried in pain out of their commonsense rationality, Geoffrey's Arthur
lived long. Under the Tudors, he was to power a new and highly effective
British national mythology. He has come to life again in the film studios.

This dramatic creation of a Welsh-European culture mirrored the growth
of a hybrid society in the March. For a long time the Norman hold over
the upland Welshries was merely military and often precarious. In 1158,
according to one story, one of the minor lords of upland Glamorgan, Ifor
Bach – so called because he was short – threatened by the Earl of
Gloucester with the loss of his 'strip of mountain and forestland', scaled
the walls of Cardiff Castle in the teeth of 120 guardians and carried off the
Earl, his wife and son, to hold them in the woods until they let him and
his lordship be. This story may also reflect the fact that, with so much of
the good land and its serf population in the Englishries, native society,
penned up into the hill country, was becoming more markedly a society
of freemen; a process which was also happening in Welsh Wales, running
counter to a growing concentration of princely power based on bond people.

The originally sharp distinction between Englishry and Welshry, though
maintained in legal practice, began to blur, however, particularly in the
south, as a money economy and a small but lively urban and mercantile
community, increasingly tuned to cities like Bristol, began slowly to
transform the old economy, itself undergoing modernization in forest
clearance and new settlement. Over generations, Welshmen became
citizens and merchants and knights, even as local lords found a place in
castle society. Henry le Waleys from Chepstow could serve as a royal mayor
of London and Bordeaux; Welsh merchants nosed into the Gironde as did
Welsh students into Oxford. As even the Welshries of the March grew feudal
in style and the people were acclimatized, loyalties as powerful as those
once directed to old kings could be offered, under compulsion, to Clares
and voluntarily to the more genial Bohuns and Mortimers.

Less direct but no less powerful was the process of interaction across the
shadow line. The abrupt emergence of the Welsh into a European historical
visibility – it is no exaggeration to call it an explosion – sprang from their
need to get to grips with both Norman power and European culture, to
survive them and integrate them into their own self-expression. This is
no less true of saints' lives, chronicles and vernacular religious texts. It
is true above all of that other monument to the creativity of the medieval
Welsh, the multiplying and increasingly complex texts of the Laws of Hywel

Dda. It was from the twelfth century that lawyers, no less than poets and chroniclers, settled to the job of defining their own society and justifying it to themselves and the world. In consequence, from about 1200 or so, this tiny people the Welsh produced a corpus of medieval law, which was, relative to the disparity in population, at least as bulky in volume as that produced by the contemporary English.

They produced it because they had to. The law of the Laws is the law of a society undergoing continuous and radical change.

## Welsh Wales

In 1280 Edward I established a commission to examine Welsh law, in order to justify his obliteration of Gwynedd. Several Welsh witnesses before that commission asserted that the princes of Gwynedd in the thirteenth century who dominated Welsh Wales or Pura Wallia had abolished *galanas*, the blood-price fine for homicide, and indeed had forbidden the practice of the Law of Hywel. The reality, reflected in the editing of the lawbooks of Gwynedd, was a radical transformation in Welsh law during the thirteenth century: the motor forces were the growth of human settlement and land exploitation in Wales, the challenge posed by the revolutionary change in contemporary English law and, above all, the attempt by the princes of Gwynedd to construct a Welsh feudal state.

The most striking feature of the lawbooks of thirteenth-century Gwynedd is a sharp increase in the power of the ruler in the ideal or model commote of fifty townships. The multiple estate, the *maenol*, is now smaller, holding four instead of seven *trefi* or townships; the king's table land itself looms less large, but it is still yoked to an estate of townships in the upland (usually bond settlements around the summer pastures). There are now four other multiple estates linked to the central bond township, the *maerdref*, and two others attached to the prince's local officers, the reeve and an officer called a chancellor (*canghellor*). The overall effect was to increase the share of royal land worked by the most subject serfs, those on reckoned land (*tir cyfrif*) to nearly *double* what it had been in the model commote of earlier texts.

In contrast to this tendency towards the concentration of an unfree population, this model commote now allowed for six multiple estates, attached to free notables, in which freemen seem to have predominated and in which the unfree were the half-free on hereditary land (*tir gwelyog*). This reflects what we know from other sources. The rise in population during the twelfth and thirteenth centuries, the advance in settlement, the loss of so much good arable land to the Normans, drove the princes of Gwynedd on the one hand to exploit their resources of limited arable and serfs to the limit, while on the other free kindreds moved out within and from already complex estates to open up new land in largely pastoral districts; and lordship, developed in a semi-feudal manner by the princes, spread over all. This seems to have reduced the proportion of the unfree to the population as a whole to a maximum of about 30 per cent. While this strengthened the free character of Welsh society, it probably severely handicapped the princes and drove them into expansion and a ruthless manhandling of Welsh traditions.

This process subjected a 'people's law' to intense pressure. The expansion of settlement and extension of cultivation created shifting patterns of ownership, lordship and subtenancy within a highly complex mosaic of tenures. Individuals and families claimed overlapping rights to occupancy, to the commons, to co-sharing; all rights were anchored in the kindred, the *cenedl*, as well as to the *priodor*, the individual holder. In expansion, operating under the law of *cyfran*, division of land on a father's death, and the practice of transhumance, with cattle moving seasonally between the old township (*hendref*) and the summer station (*hafod*), the kindred had to strike a very careful balance between shares in new and old homesteads, clearings from the waste, claims to pasture, gleaning, meadow and other assets. The use of *prid*, the renewable four-year mortgage which could become a concealed sale, spread among a population evidently developing a stronger sense of personal proprietorship, within a country which was still poor and characterized by cattle raising, raids and rustling.

As a result, the Law of Hywel, in its civil law and in personal actions (for *prid* was capable of wide extension) quickly developed a high degree of diversity and sophistication, with the practice of oath-taking by kindred computation budding off all sorts of technical devices. It developed, in truth, in a style similar to that emerging in the revolutionary changes in English law. Most of the new civil and personal actions in English law found their rough parallel in the Law of Hywel. But, while *prid* could produce a land-law in Wales not dissimilar to that of some English procedures, the basic kindred structure of land-holding with its *cyfran* found the primogeniture (inheritance by an eldest son), the entail and the rigidity over 'legitimacy' of English law alien, and during the thirteenth century apparently had little use for them.

It was very different in criminal law. The most revolutionary change in English law during the late twelfth and early thirteenth centuries was the development of the petty jury and its extension from land and civil to criminal actions. This proved immensely popular among an English population which in its folk practices had not really been all that remote from the Welsh, and the attraction of the 'law of twelve' stopped at no border. Welsh in the March were petitioning for it by the end of the thirteenth century. In Welsh Wales the lawbooks themselves reflect a dissatisfaction with traditional practice and a demand for individual responsibility and probably for the jury. By mid-century under David, the first Gwynedd ruler to call himself a Prince of Wales, the original *galanas* blood-price system for homicide had gone, to be replaced by individual guilt; verdict by jury was being resorted to within the kindred pattern.

These processes bred a particular mentality among the Welsh, some aspects of which were to prove permanent. Much of the hard work in townships in which property and other rights were intermingled was done in common. People got together to plough, to raise new buildings, to launch a newly married couple. From this sense of commonalty sprang customs which persisted over centuries as popular tradition: *cymorthau* (mutual aids not unlike the American barn-raising), and bid-ales, later called *cwrw bach* (literally 'little beer'), mutual community loans wreathed in fellowship and liquor, not unlike the American 'shower'. Practices under this name were early systematized into a kind of tax in both Welsh Wales and the March, but the popular realities underlying them outlived the taxes. This co-existed with an intense awareness of individual rights; those rights, the claims of the kindred and of women, were rigorously protected by the law which developed into a sophisticated instrument serviced by a corpus of lawbooks.

In consequence, there was an intense public life in the commotes where the 'good men', the *gwyrda*, and 'wise women' preserved the records of the community in their heads and staffed the embryonic jury, while the head of the kindred, the *pencenedl*, was a key figure with specific duties, notably admission to the kindred, specific perquisites and a higher personal value, for the principle expressed in the *galanas* was still widely operative. These people were intensely litigious, with a genealogical cast of mind. This generated a collective mentality which simultaneously cultivated on the one hand a strong sense of commonalty, and on the other an individualism worthy of a Castilian hidalgo; an intense pride in pedigree which became well-nigh universal, and an alert but narrow sense of the past, a tunnel vision. In varying forms these seem to have become permanent legacies.

Most striking in the lands controlled by Gwynedd, however, is the appearance within this 'people's law' of professional lawyers and of a professional judge, the *ynad*, who is no longer merely an arbitrator but actively intervenes to make the *llys*, the local royal court, a focus of initiative. Princely power had uprooted the old procedure in homicide; it intervenes in all *galanas* action, to take its share of any fine, imposing the idea of 'crime' against a community embodied in its prince. The whole multitude of offences compensated by the kindred swiftly changes its character and becomes a common law under princely administration. New officers appear, a *rhaglaw* and a *rhingyll* (bailiff and sheriff to the English), a rudimentary police force.

The princes start to concentrate their serf townships, to amalgamate estates and lordships. They exploit *prid* to break up kindred holdings where necessary. They use their control over *alltudion* or 'aliens', a class which could be large in Wales, with its fosterage, the taking of hostages in peace treaties, the internal migration of a mountain country in which population pressure and concealed unemployment were building up. The princes planted out favoured men and endowed them, enforced lordship upon the kindreds and charged it with a semi-feudal character. By the end of the thirteenth century, at least in the core districts of Gwynedd, serf vills were growing into the beginnings of miniature 'towns'; and with the increasing use of money, and that ultimate modernization, the commutation of dues into money payments, a market economy had begun to appear. Over this society in the throes of painful and often coercive change, appear a higher class who are recognizably quasi-feudal lords in kindred trappings, complete with coats of arms and all the mumbo-jumbo of chivalry, typified in its 'royal tribes'.

In final symmetry, the princely household began to follow the practice of all such households everywhere, to differentiate its functions and to elaborate a bureaucracy. A chancery appeared early to conduct an active foreign policy focusing on Westminster, Paris and the Rome of the papacy, but which could range from Ireland to Norway and the Holy Land. An exchequer took shape as revenues were organized; stewards, marshals, a seneschal in charge of military mobilization, driven to unheard-of lengths in embattled Gwynedd. The seneschal of Llywelyn ab Iorwerth (the Great), Ednyfed Fychan, created an official dynasty which acquired estates in England and which was ultimately to place one of its members on the throne of England itself. Summons went out regularly to the great men of the localities to join this official class in its deliberations: the germ of a parliament.

It was precisely here that the princes encountered their major difficulty, the Church. The Church, with its literate servitors and its command of the universal language of Latin, was the seed-bed of every bureaucracy, but the Welsh Church was under the thumb of Canterbury. The sheer autonomous power and limitless ambition of the reformed Church of the

Gregorian papacy drove across every Welsh frontier, with its appeal to the deepest instincts of men and women and its attraction to minds ill at ease with the essentially rude culture of princes and lords. The new bishops dismantled the Welsh *clas*, dismissed its saints, carved archdeaconries, rural deaneries and parishes out of its fluid organization; they imposed tithes. It was a slow process, not completed in some parts until the fourteenth century. But everywhere those bishops in the end took the oath to Canterbury. It was relatively easy in Glamorgan's Llandaff, in the arm-pit of Cardiff Castle; for decades it proved impossible in Gwynedd's Bangor; the first Norman bishop was chased out by his flock and Owain Gwynedd resisted to the end, sending his bishop to Ireland to be consecrated. It was finally achieved even there. St Asaph, in a frontier zone of Powys, was not erected until 1143 but served its turn. A Norman was installed in St David's, but disconcertingly took up the native cause of independence for the see, to the no small consternation of the Church's controllers. Welshmen and more often Cambro-Normans did get to sees and there was a powerful undercurrent of Welsh feeling among the lesser clergy. The overpowering sentiment, however, was the crusade for clerical independence from lay power which set Empire and Papacy at each other's throats. Anian, Bishop of St Asaph, defended his church against all comers including his kinsmen who were princes of Gwynedd; though Welsh in sympathy, he proved to be one of the worst opponents those princes had to face. As for the episcopate of Bangor, in the heart of Gwynedd itself, it must have seemed to the princes a veritable fifth column in their own capital. The Bishop of Bangor was most often to be found in the ranks of enemy armies.

. The long struggle of Gerald the Welshman at the turn of the century for an independent metropolitan Archbishop of Wales at St David's offered the last chance to escape from this trap. It was a great fight, an endless wrestle with Canterbury, involving repeated pilgrimages to Rome, a sustained exercise of his skills often against Welsh disunity, particularism and resistance from what had become a conservative clergy within his own see. The lay rulers of Wales were slow to perceive the significance of the fight; only his local princes supported him at first. It was in the final struggle that Gwynedd and other Welsh laymen took a hand, too late; it was the usual story – the Welsh were too few to carry any clout in Rome. Rome remained in some ways their hope; the practice of papal provision to clerical office, advancing in the teeth of royal resistance, could be and was used to place useful men in useful positions. But by and large the secular church, which was the standard recruiting field for ambitious kings, was in large part denied to the princes of Gwynedd.

It is this which, in part, accounts for the sensational rise of the Cistercian Order of White Monks in Wales. They were a papal order, free from the control of Canterbury. They were sheep-raisers, who could fit themselves into the economy of Welsh Wales and stimulate it. From the start, in their penetration of west Wales, beginning at Whitland in 1151 and spreading north and east through Strata Florida, Strata Marcella, Cwm Hir, Valle Crucis, Conway, the monastic houses moved in a thoroughly Welsh environment. Their earlier foundations to the east, Margam, Neath, Basingwerk, at first located in a Norman ambience, felt the pull, too, though episodically; Tintern never did. The Order was cherished by all Welsh princes, endowed and favoured by them. It was these men, followed by the friars, who peopled the prince's councils and his diplomatic missions.

By the late thirteenth century, what amounted to local states had emerged in Wales. At the opposite pole to Gwynedd, the Glamorgan of the Clare dynasty was building itself into a kingdom within a kingdom, with a power which could challenge that in the north-west. The overlords of Glamorgan had exercised precise control only over the vicinity of Cardiff; even in the Vale of Glamorgan, the mesne lords enjoyed much independence. Overlordship in the hill fiefs of the Welsh was largely tribute. Under Earl Richard and Earl Gilbert between 1240 and 1267, the lords of Glamorgan totally subjected the mesne lords in the Vale, dispossessed two Welsh rulers and jailed another. They riveted control on the hill-country and built their new castles at Llantrisant on the edge of the Vale and Morlais in the heart of the hills. Finally in 1267, the year that a prince of Gwynedd got himself recognized as a Prince of Wales by the King of England and some of the hill people in Glamorgan showed signs of a Welsh restlessness, Gilbert built a giant and highly advanced castle at Caerphilly. His lordship had driven into every corner; its income quadrupled and the structure of its government became semi-royal.

In Welsh Wales it was Gwynedd which towered over all, with its feudal insignia, its quasi-feudal lords, its tiny half-towns and little shipping fleets, its first market economy. The kindred was still dominant, but the princes, backed by a growing structure of officialdom, were making great inroads upon it. At the level of sovereignty, they laid brutal, indeed desperate, hands on what had become hallowed traditions. They did not shrink from using feudal primogeniture, full inheritance by an eldest or chosen son. Other Welsh lords had tried this, within the traditional four-generation pattern, but none had ever gone so far as to make a Welsh *edling* into a feudal dauphin and to root his power in the most potent feudal sources of warranty, an English king and a Roman pope. The princes were, in effect, conjuring a feudal order out of the kindreds and trying to transform the *de facto* control they were establishing over Welsh Wales into a state.

The drive was without doubt instinctual; while there is in the last Llywelyn a powerful sense of a 'Wales' (essentially only Welsh Wales) that his strength and craft had created, there is not a trace of any wider or more imaginative loyalty to anything other than his Gwynedd, which was creating that 'Wales' by conquering it. The court poets of Gwynedd, while devoted to the standard and unstinted praise of patrons, were to some extent trapped within their own culture, which had scruples over *trais* (oppression) and *traha* (over-reaching): 'all over-reaching is a pulling down . . .' When Owain Gwynedd moved into Powys on the death of its Madog ap Maredudd, its poet Cynddelw had expressed opposition: 'one should not hold anything in this world that does not come from God . . .' This tone of voice was soon lost in the intoxication which accompanied the rise of Gwynedd above the crippled survivors of the other Welsh kingdoms. Llywarch Prydydd y Moch revels in the ruthlessness of Llywelyn ab Iorwerth: *Ac ar bob terfyn – torri!* (On every frontier, break!) It was those who withstood the boundless claims of his prince who were over-reaching. And as for the permanent resistance of Powys, 'Let the Powys people realize who he is – the king of a strong people. Is it better to have a Frenchman than a generous Welshman? . . .' Moreover, his power was the 'uncovering' (*dadanhudd*, a legal term akin to *mort dancestor*, an action to secure lawful inheritance) of the right order of things foretold by Merlin. The response from Powys may be imagined! Here is the authentic and timeless voice of imperialism, albeit in a miniature Welsh arena. Such propaganda from the poets of Gwynedd evoked not a single echo elsewhere. Indeed, in the last days, a majority of the Welsh nobility rallied against it and Welshmen comprised a majority of the soldiers who fought against it.

In those same years, some lawyers around the court of Aberffraw were inserting into their texts the assertion that the other rulers of Wales had owed tribute to their house since time immemorial, or at least the time of Maelgwn Gwynedd, an exercise in the manufacture of a history. The past was being made usable, for what was emerging from Gwynedd's mobilization against the English Crown was a feudal Principality of Wales to be erected upon the subjection of all other Welsh rulers.

## Principality

The achievement of such a Principality was a political and military exercise. By the thirteenth century there were four centres of power in Wales: Welsh lords, Marcher lords, the prince of Gwynedd and the king of England. The purpose of Welsh and Marcher lords alike was simple: it was to survive, which meant maintaining feudal order and the principle of aristocracy. The purpose of the kings of England was to reduce every power in Wales to the status of a mere lordship, to push royal justice into the lordships and integrate them into their realm. All the rulers of Wales owed the king fealty and the more significant homage, which carried with it claims on land and the profitable exercise of justice ('Justice is big money' ran the proverb). All the major powers in Wales, except Gwynedd, ranked as tenants-in-chief of the king; this gave the crown useful leverage, including that of escheat, the reversion of a lordship to the Crown in the event of a failure of heirs, unsuccessful treason or some other disaster; it might be able to extract homage from sub-tenants. Marcher and Welsh lords resisted this process as best they could. The position of Gwynedd was ambiguous. While many Welsh lords sported the title 'prince', the ruler of Gwynedd charged it with fuller meaning: he refused to accept tenant-in-chief status, he drew comparisons with the king of Scotland, he offered shelter to the king of England's enemies, a royal prerogative. At the same time, he did homage to the king for Gwynedd, of necessity.

The prince of Gwynedd's purpose was to win permanent recognition of special status within the homage pattern of the Crown, to extend his physical power over Welsh Wales and, if he could, over the Welshries of the March; above all, to divert the homages of all Welsh lords to himself; the prince would then do homage alone to the king for his Wales. In practice this would have meant a degree of independence which no king of England could stomach.

The struggle was determined by hard political realities. Around 1200, with an absentee Richard and a John locked in civil war, Llywelyn ab Iorwerth was able to take over most of Welsh Wales and to make inroads into the March. He trafficked with the baronial opposition in England, with France and with Rome. He took as wife John's 'bastard' daughter and married one of his own daughters to a Mortimer (ultimately to provide one of the Welsh strains in the present royal house). He achieved a stunning success. By the time of Magna Carta, he towered over Welsh Wales. The English chancery accorded him special status; Welsh chronicles not given to constitutional niceties called him 'Prince of Wales'. He became Llywelyn Fawr, Llywelyn the Great.

He himself was far more cautious. He literally moved heaven and earth, king and pope, to secure the undisputed succession of his chosen son David, son to an English mother who was a king's daughter. This ran counter to

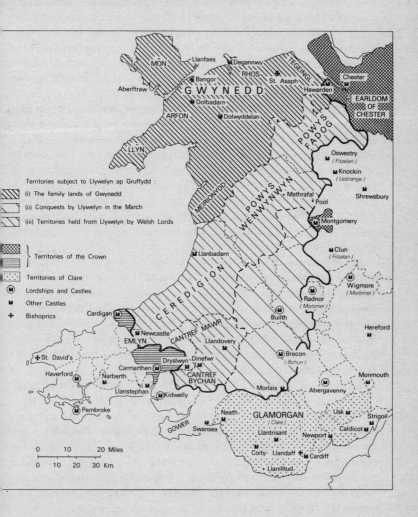

4. THE PRINCIPALITY OF WALES, 1267
(after William Rees).

much cherished Welsh practice; many Welsh lords within Gwynedd favoured David's half-brother Gruffydd, *mab y Gymraes* (son of a Welsh woman), illegitimate in English eyes, but not in Welsh. During a truce which lasted a generation, Llywelyn won the king's recognition of David in 1220, the pope's confirmation of his disinheritance of Gruffydd in 1222; in 1226 the magnates of Welsh Wales recognized David, who did homage to Henry III in 1229 and married a Marcher heiress.

By this time, however, Gruffydd, something of a hero to old-fashioned warband and foster-brother Welsh, was running amok in traditional style; in 1228 his father jailed him for six years. By 1238 Llywelyn's health was failing and he entered into negotiations to transform the truce into a peace. A great assembly of all the lords of Welsh Wales was summoned to the favoured Cistercian house of Strata Florida, to do homage to David. At once the royal chancery sprang into action and strictly forbade any Welsh lord to transfer his homage. Llywelyn had to make do with oaths of fealty and his last days saw the formation of a pro-Gruffydd party among Welsh notables.

In 1240 the essential precariousness of the imposing structure Llywelyn the Great had built was exposed. As soon as Llywelyn died, David and Gruffydd went to war. The former, in a conspiracy which exploited the Bishop of Bangor, captured Gruffydd and jailed him. The Bishop, enraged, laid Gwynedd under the terrible interdict and fled to Henry III. Henry took up Gruffydd's cause and parading as a defender of good order, including Welsh tradition, whipped up so much Welsh support that David's power collapsed overnight.

The total, almost bloodless success of Henry, achieved essentially with Welsh armies, is a vivid microcosm which illumines the realities of power in Wales. Among David's enemies were not only traditional opponents like the lord of southern Powys but the rival lord of northern Powys and others noted for their collaboration with Llywelyn the Great. They represented a Welsh tradition much older than any newfangled Principality and they were prepared to fight for it. It is a striking demonstration of the resistance which traditional Welsh aristocracy both outside and within the core of Gwynedd itself could offer to new concepts of feudal authority. In the event, those people were soon taught the new realities of power in Wales. The Crown imposed the principle of escheat on Gwynedd, began to demand military service from David and to refuse him any special status. Exploiting the process of arbitration set in train by the peace, Henry's men raised castles and enforced royal control; royal justice penetrated Welsh and Marcher lordships alike. Within months Welsh lords were shouting about tyranny. Once the countervailing power of Gwynedd had been diminished, there was little to stop the Crown.

In a convulsive shudder, many of the Welsh lords rallied to David. The death of Gruffydd, liberated from a Welsh jail only to be installed in the Tower — 'we have all been too oppressive for a long while,' said the poet Dafydd Benfras – released inhibitions. In a long, hard war over two winters in the 1240s, the worst Welsh war yet, David became the first Welsh ruler formally to proclaim himself Prince of Wales. He could not hold. Winter, sustained blockade, the customary defections, finished him. When he died, the entire realm of Gwynedd in theory escheated to the Crown of England. Henry was too careful to go that far, but he divided Gwynedd between brothers in good Welsh tradition and reduced both to the status of a lordship.

In a matter of years, the pendulum swung hard the other way. England, having lost Normandy and turned in on itself, began to grow English, even though its ruling class still spoke French and the city of London excluded the English language as vulgar. The kingdom broke into passionate conflict over the meaning of the 'community of the realm', to precipitate the first civil war with a serious political content. Its rebels emerged briefly under Simon de Montfort — 'St Simon', a stepfather of the English Parliament – as an ally of Gwynedd against the king. In Gwynedd, Gruffydd's son Llywelyn had driven to power in the customary ruthless, strictly traditional manner. In all other respects he was far from traditional. He used the old skills, joining with the rebels in England, helping to form a European coalition against Henry and his hard-nosed son Edward, marrying the daughter of Simon de Montfort. He developed new skills, ruthlessly exploiting Gwynedd, screwing down hard on the people under his own control, dispensing a strictly provisional largesse to those who were not, employing an abrupt terrorism where necessary. With a modernized army and his own increasingly charismatic appeal, he swept the west and broke into the March. When he reached the Brecknock Beacons, some of the hill lordships in Glamorgan tried to break away from the Clares. Behind him he mobilized Gwynedd and strained its developed but limited resources to the edge. Finally, in alliance with a Montfort trailing his captive king, he forced the helpless Henry to recognize his formal title. Even after the death of Montfort and the restoration of Henry III, this could not be reversed, with the struggle still raging in England against the rebel Disinherited and the international Montfort clan. By the Treaty of Montgomery of 1267, the king of England formally recognized Llywelyn ap Gruffydd as the first Welsh Prince of Wales to be 'legal' in English eyes.

The Principality lasted for ten years; the real reasons for its fall are still unclear. Edward I, now in power, was certainly committed to a new and far more thoroughgoing imperialism than any predecessor, directed first at Gascony and Ireland, now at the Welsh and the Scots. It was also novel in its selfconsciously English expression. But there is no sign, in the 1270s, that any total expropriation of Gwynedd was planned. The early intransigence came from Llywelyn. He totally refused to compromise on any of the disputed articles of the peace treaty; he repeatedly refused to do homage in person. He may have been involved in the actions against Edward undertaken by the Montfort clan from France to the Crusader states in Palestine. Certainly Edward kidnapped his chosen bride Eleanor de Montfort as a blackmail weapon. The breaking point, however, was a crisis in Wales. During those ten years a poet like Llygad Gŵr could hail Llywelyn as a king of the Welsh whose quarrel was with an alien nation of foreign speech and talk of a Cymru Fawr (Greater Wales); some of the lesser lords in the south may well have welcomed an overlord who was Welsh. But many were sullen in their subjection. Dafydd, Llywelyn's brother, in his oscillations, was almost a caricature of the Disinherited and Dissident Brother of Welsh tradition. He joined with the long-hostile lord of southern Powys in a plot against his brother's life and when it failed, fled to England, where Edward gave him asylum. Llywelyn responded in kind, and war, unexpected on the English side, broke out.

That war passed into the military textbooks, with Edward's seaborne assault on Anglesey synchronized with attacks on the mountain front, supported by Welsh auxiliaries and a massive programme of forest clearance and fort-building – one of the first major 'counter-insurgency' actions we know. The war of 1276-7 was bitter and prolonged. But it exposed some serious weaknesses in the Principality. Numbers of Welsh lords rallied to Llywelyn, but others had been made aliens in their own land; what they considered tradition had been breached repeatedly. The prince of Gwynedd enrolled twelve-year-old boys in his armies, screwed every ounce out of his subjects, built castles on their backs. The resources of his Principality, unaided, could not sustain his ambition. Even so, Edward had to mortgage the crown to Italian bankers, to mobilize the merchants and to start the revolutionary change in English military society towards a contractual 'bastard feudalism'. In a long, amphibious campaign without precedent, he finally broke the prince.

This was the end of the Principality but not yet of Llywelyn. Gwynedd was stripped of power over Wales, divided savagely, and severely diminished in status. Edward, however, did not deprive the prince of all precedence and it does not seem as if anything total were contemplated at that stage. By this time, however, what amounts to a school of colonialist thought had built up in England around Archbishop Pecham. This conducted a major campaign, partly through Edward's commission of 1280, against Welsh law as barbaric and blasphemous, teeming with abominations. It preached the elimination of the independence of the Welsh and their incorporation into the 'civilized' orbit of English law.

What brought law to the forefront were the disputes arising out of the peace. Were they to be settled by Marcher or Welsh law? To the end, Llywelyn stood intransigent for the right of the Welsh to have their own law, and for his realm to enjoy the same privileges as Scotland and other free peoples. Even at seven hundred years' distance, some of his letters make very moving reading. In these years he lent a Welsh dignity to his Principality which had not often been visible earlier. Edward even tried to buy him out of his country with an estate in England. In the end, his hand was forced by his brother Dafydd who rebelled against the new royal oppression which characteristically plagued the conquered lands, including those he had been allotted.

Llywelyn faced an impossible choice; he was called on to crush the rebellion. Instead, he joined it. The final days are very obscure. It is possible that the Pecham campaign, developed through the Church, secured some support. English law was much more favourable to personal accumulation. There is vague talk of a 'treason in the belfry of Bangor'. In any case, the writing must have been on the wall. The war of 1282 was at first as hard as that of 1276-7, but there were soon defections. Much of the official aristocracy of Gwynedd, led by the family of Ednyfed Fychan, seneschal to Llywelyn the Great, ultimately went over to Edward. In 1283 Llywelyn was killed after a battle in south Wales; his head duly adorned the Tower. Dafydd took up the leadership but was hideously executed at Shrewsbury. Independent Gwynedd was obliterated and Edward took pains to secure all insignia and any other symbols which might service a revival, to take action against the poets and to wipe out whatever trace of a Welsh state remained.

With the fall of Llywelyn ap Gruffydd an epoch ended, the Wales of the Princes. The Welsh passed under the nakedly colonial rule of an even more arrogant, and selfconsciously alien, imperialism. Many historians, aware that the feudal principalities of princes have elsewhere made nations, have largely accepted the verdict of nineteenth-century Welsh nationalism and identified the house of Aberffraw as the lost and legitimate dynasty of Wales. Llywelyn ap Gruffydd has become Llywelyn the Last. In fact, Wales of the Princes had to die before a Welsh nation could be born. That Welsh nation made itself out of the very tissue of contradictions which was the colonialism which choked it. And it chose its own prince.

# 5 · THE LAST PRINCE

At the Council of Constance in 1415, in the midst of the upheaval in the Universal Church which had ranged the Pope at Rome against the Pope at Avignon, the English delegation proposed that voting should not be by dioceses or provinces but by *nationes* (nations). A French delegate thereupon objected to the inclusion of the Welsh within this English nation. The Welsh, he said, were not part of that nation, they were themselves one of the *nationes particulares;* the Welsh were a *nation.*

At that Frenchman's elbow stood a remarkable Welshman, Dr Gruffudd Young. He was an exceptionally able and talented cleric who was crippled in English eyes by his 'illegitimate' birth. He had tried to make his way within the Church, offering his loyalty in turn to both Richard II and his murderer Henry IV; at every stage he was blocked. By 1404, with many other Welsh churchmen, he had rallied to Owain Glyn Dŵr (Owen Glendower), who had broken into revolt in 1400 and was by then the leader of a national rebellion. In Glyn Dŵr's service, he helped to shape a sophisticated administrative and diplomatic team; he led the mission which secured an alliance with France and the Avignon papacy; he was made Bishop of Bangor by Benedict XIII and would have headed the independent Welsh Church at St David's; he was the prime mover behind a celebrated project, the Pennal policy, which was breathtaking in its sweep and has caught the imagination of posterity. By 1410, after ten of the most destructive years of war since the tenth century, the revolt had collapsed and Glyn Dŵr had disappeared. Gruffudd Young was still active in his cause in France in 1415 and staged the last stand at Constance. Ultimately, he had to give up and make his repentant way to Rome, where the Pope provided him with a bishopric.

At much the same time back home, the government published an Act in 1413, which had to be repeated in 1429, directed at an obnoxious practice by which Welshmen were exploiting the use of Welsh law in the courts of Wales to hound those many Welsh people who had fought against Glyn Dŵr; they were forcing them to prove their innocence by one of the harshest proofs known to the Law of Hywel, the oaths of no fewer than 300 witnesses. One of the men so pursued was Llywelyn ap Hywel of Brecon. His family had once been princely in the Welsh kingdom of Brycheiniog but had found a niche in the Marcher lordship which displaced it. Einion ap Rhys (called Sais, the Englishman) stood by the Bohuns and resisted the transfer of his allegiance to Llywelyn ap Gruffydd, Prince of Wales. His descendants were no less loyal to the Bohuns and the House of Lancaster of Henry Bolingbroke after them. Llywelyn ap Hywel resisted Glyn Dŵr; he was harassed, the houses of his sons were burnt. One of those sons, the celebrated Dafydd Gam, fought the rebels, was captured and ransomed by them. When Henry V went forth to Normandy, Dafydd Gam went with him, with three men-at-arms, in one of those French campaigns from which the leek is said to have emerged as a Welsh national emblem, derived from the taste of hungry Fluellens. Dafydd Gam died heroically at Agincourt, having been knighted on the field by Henry. Back home, his compatriots, who had been governed by his family for generations, were hounding his father from pillar to post, in revenge for their lost leader.

Owain Glyn Dŵr was the first, indeed the *only,* Welsh prince to command wide popular and spontaneous support from every corner of Wales. The revolt was many things. It was a quarrel in the March which ignited a race war; it was a civil war; it was an explosion of anger and hatred from the unfree and oppressed; it was a peasant *jacquerie;* it was a rebellion by rising squireens against the restrictions of an archaic regime; it was a revolt of frustrated intellectuals within the Church; it was a feudal war to create some kind of Burgundy within Britain. These all fused, like so many rebellions we have seen since, into a war of national liberation against a colonial regime riddled with contradiction.

What it was *not* was an attempt to 'restore' an old Wales gone beyond recall. Over a generation before the revolt, Welsh society had abandoned the Law of Hywel in a wholesale transfer to English law; every Welsh class above the unfree was split down the middle by the Rebellion. It was wreathed in the mythical history and redemptive prophecy of the Welsh; no one was more versed in it than Glyn Dŵr himself. He was a man who wrote Merlin's prophecies into his diplomatic correspondence and his peace treaties. But this ancient British-Welsh tradition - *brut* as the Welsh called it - was to provide a recognizable identity to something novel; the Welsh were to become one of the *nationes.*

The Rebellion of Owain Glyn Dŵr was not the last stand of an old Wales, but the explosive entry into history of a new one.

## The Contradictions of Colonialism

In the fortress of Rhuddlan in 1284, Edward I, contemplating a Gwynedd whose dynasty had been destroyed and every symbol of its governance eradicated, whose countryside was dominated by fourteen monstrous castles rising to spread-eagle a people on its back and to shelter little *bastide* towns peopled by an organized transplantation of English endowed with a sense of racial superiority, issued that Statute which an English historian has justly called the first colonial constitution.

'The land of Wales' had been 'annexed and united . . . unto our crown of the aforesaid realm as a member of the same body . . . ' 'We have caused to be rehearsed before us', thundered the English Justinian, 'the laws and customs of those parts . . . which being diligently heard and fully understood [Welsh historians envy him his mastery!] . . . we have abolished certain of them, some thereof we have allowed, and some we have corrected . . .'

Thousands of Welsh people could be pardoned for not appreciating this indulgence; in the sharp legal discrimination which immediately came into operation throughout Wales, they were classed as *meri Wallici* (mere Welshmen); across the apartheid line were the *Anglici,* who were privileged, who were not to be condemned in law by the oaths of Welshmen alone, who were to be tried only by English law and never in the Welsh language, who were authorized to exclude every Welsh person from their towns as *forinseci* (foreigners).

To build the new boroughs in Gwynedd, 5,000 acres of the best agricultural lands were confiscated and their numerous inhabitants, mostly serfs, turfed out. The people of Llanfaes, one of the miniature new 'towns' being created by the princes of Gwynedd, were ordered out to worse land twelve miles away. They staged a sit-in led by a local doctor, Master Anian. They were driven out. Even in their new place, Rhosfair, they had no peace; it was renamed Newborough. At Dryslwyn in the Tywi valley in the south, the new town was formed by expropriating the demesne land of the former court, the *llys,* and the homesteads of freemen. It was the same in the new lordships of the March. Welsh free tenants were thrown out to make the borough of Holt. There was massive transfer within the lordship of Denbigh, with whole districts being turned into English preserves. The law of escheat was ruthlessly exploited; people working 600 good acres in Ystrad were evicted to make a park. Sometimes this was at sword-point; more often in the March, it was done with a mathematical equity of South African precision; in exact acreage compensation, the Welsh were removed from the fertile vale of Clwyd to the rain-drenched lands of the Hiraethog mountains, 1,500 feet above sea level. The memories of these evictions rooted themselves in folklore, as they had done earlier in the south. Rhys ap Gruffudd of Afan in Glamorgan could remember in 1365 how his people had been evicted 250 years earlier; in north-east Wales, the Greys were still hated men in 1379 for what they had done after 1284.

This is an Irish situation. One of the sharpest distinctions between the Irish people and the Welsh in their experience of English rule has been that the latter before the coming of industrial capitalism were not dispossessed *en masse* like their cousins. For a generation and more after 1284, it looked as though they were going to anticipate the fate of the Irish. What stopped it in the end was not only native resilience and ingenuity or the slow process of assimilation which had already softened the southern March, but those devastating crises of population and economy in the mid-fourteenth century which unhinged this whole system. The Black Death killed many Welsh people but it seems to have prevented their progressive disinheritance.

The settlers were a mixed bunch. Many were soldiers, craftsmen who had built the castles, clerks to the garrisons, members of royal and noble retinues; two cooks of the Earl of Lincoln got handsome estates in the Clwyd valley. Many were adventurers, some of whom carved new land out of the waste and, like the Flemings and others planted much earlier in the south, were much more alive to the commercial possibilities of Wales than the natives. Some struck roots; some went native. Names which were to figure years later among Welsh gentry and, indeed, Welsh patriots, figure in the incursion: Salisburys and Thelwalls, Hanmers who ultimately gave Owain Glyn Dŵr a wife, Pulestons who had provided Simon de Montfort with a loyal supporter and were to do the same for Glyn Dŵr. But most held themselves aloof across the shadow line and cultivated their connection in England. This was particularly true of the towns which repeatedly reasserted their alien and anti-Welsh character through to the union between Wales and England and even beyond. Although social realities could not be resisted and Welsh people eventually found their way within the walls, they were liable at any moment to be confronted, as were forty-three established residents of Ruthin in 1364, with the challenge to explain by what right they, as 'mere Welshmen' presumed to trade in the town. The Englishness of the boroughs was a bedrock; the burgesses of Aberafan in Glamorgan, who were hopelessly Welsh, existed legally as the 'lord's Englishmen', and towns above all were the targets for Owain Glyn Dŵr's 'barefoot scrubs'. The experience helped to make the Welsh a peculiarly non-urban people and bred an attitude among them which was to prove disabling.

And after their land went their law. It was widely believed that Edward had abolished Welsh law; Welsh criminal law was certainly dismissed as an abomination but the whole range of English civil and personal law, fully described in the Statute of Rhuddlan, was offered for voluntary choice. The change in criminal law, while total, was not, however, dramatic. Individual responsibility for killing had long been established as had the jury in such cases. A certain nostalgia for the Law of Hywel survived among a people who, like so many others, seem to have found judicial execution worse than murder itself. Two centuries later, the poet Dafydd ab Edmwnd, after seeing a public hanging, compared the harsh 'law of London' with the gentler law of Hywel, and cases over *galanas* occur in the March as late as 1468. It is possible that a number of cases involving homicide were settled out of court according to the old principles. In one pleasing poem, 'Ymgêl, wen, o'm galanas', a poet dying of unrequited love charges his cruel lady with his imminent *galanas!*

But by and large *galanas* faded, as did a host of other offences which were felonies under English law. Nine-tenths of the cases in fourteenth-century courts were settled by jury. In civil cases, in any event, Welsh law had achieved enough sophistication to make the two codes very similar; *mort dancestor* and *novel disseisin* (an action against unlawful dispossession) had close parallels in what had been a rapidly evolving Welsh law. Edward II specifically granted rights to Welsh law and, in fact, a quarter of the working textbooks of Welsh law which survive date from the fourteenth and fifteenth centuries; it remained alive for over a century.

What it had become was the law of an inferior breed and it bore that stigma. Both royal and Marcher justice found it profitable to keep some aspects of Welsh law alive even when the Welsh themselves petitioned for their removal; inferior status for subjects meant more money for their rulers. *Amobr,* the fine paid by a woman for a sexual offence, was peculiarly degrading and it was rigorously enforced in its old Welsh form; judges solemnly ordered unfortunate women to strip off the top item of their dress as a fine; fathers disowned daughters and brothers sisters; women made implausible claims to be English or the daughters of Englishmen in order to cross the apartheid barrier which would have shielded them from the ancient ridicule punishment still embedded in the Law of Hywel.

The authorities similarly maintained the communal basis of much Welsh land law, its old fines and procedures, for financial reasons. Land law, of course, was the crux. English practice was more efficient, clear, swift and convenient. This is generally counted a superiority. It would not necessarily seem so, to defendants at least! One reason for the tenacious hold Welsh law retained was the endless opportunity for delay it offered. Where English law helped, in its succession by an eldest son and its practice of entail, was in the personal acquisition of a private estate, free of the trammels of kindred.

The effects here are not clear-cut. Throughout the fourteenth century there was increasing pressure from people trying to break out of inferior status. The family which became the gentry dynasty of Clenennau built up its estate from bits and pieces of kindred land by using the flexible Welsh practice of *prid,* the renewable mortgage, and then anchored it by switching to English entail and inheritance law. The beginnings of a squirearchy can certainly be detected, but by and large, before the social crisis of the late fourteenth century, such resort to English law, allied with and often blurred by *prid,* was a fringe activity among a peasant population usually making family arrangements.

What managed to survive was the Welsh attitude towards the children 'of brake and brush', whom English law ferociously excluded as 'illegitimate'. People bought the right to *cynnwys* – the extension of succession rights to such 'illegitimates' – and proved remarkably ingenious at using this, and even *amobr*, to establish family interests across the legal line, basing themselves in Welsh and raiding English law as it suited them. It all cost money and authority found it profitable.

The impact of crises and social disruption in the late fourteenth and early fifteenth centuries, however, radically altered the scene. The ultimate caricature of colonialism in Wales is the spectacle of a colonial people clamouring for the law of the colonists in the face of resistance from colonial authorities stubbornly maintaining native custom to stop themselves going bankrupt! The Law of Hywel lasted longest in the March and south Wales where it had remained very much a community, a 'people's law', free from the professional judges and lawyers of the lands ruled by the princes of Gwynedd. An amateur people's law lasted as long as people wanted it; by the early fifteenth century it had largely gone. Some echoes lived in a folk memory. In the early nineteenth century, in both industrial south-east and rural south-west Wales, squatters used to try to build a house and get a roof on within twenty-four hours in the belief that this conferred freehold. Challenged in court by irate landowners, they cited the Law of Hywel Dda. And, of course, the obsession with kin, indeed the extra-legal practice of a form of *cyfran* – equal inheritance – did not die.

Dispossession and disinheritance, both resisted, modified and even exploited by a subject people, operated within the full administrative structure of the kind of colonial regime Edward had already practised in Gascony. Edward shaped the newly conquered lands into what was in effect one huge lordship which was royal and, from 1301, vested in the king's eldest son as Prince of Wales; this was the Principality, essentially embracing Pura Wallia. The English county system, already operative in royal lordships in the south and even in Pembroke and Glamorgan, was riveted on western Wales. Snowdonia was carved into three shires, Anglesey, Caernarfon and Merioneth, under a Justice at Caernarfon, to run parallel with a Justice at Carmarthen managing Carmarthen and Cardigan. A county was created in Flint under the Justice of Chester. English rule was pinioned by the great castles at Caernarfon, Conway, Harlech and the rest; English society was afforded an entry through the new monopolistic boroughs with an English population and markets which were to give effect to the commutation of all old dues into money payments.

The March not only survived as a separate entity, it was extended. North-east Wales was handed over as a reward and Lacys, Greys and Warennes took their place among the older families. Welsh families who had taken the winning side during the war found a subordinate but secure position. Edward, however, had to take action against the Clare empire in Glamorgan, which was getting out of hand. Not only was Earl Gilbert, from his new castle at Morlais, waging private war on the Bohuns of Brecon, he was trying to commandeer the bishopric of Llandaff, through his brother, Bogo, a chancellor of the diocese celebrated for having once forced an official of the Archbishop of Canterbury to eat his own summons. Edward came down like thunder. He defeated the Clares in Llandaff and at a parliament held in Abergavenny, stopped the private war in Brecon. He followed up by defending the Cistercians at Strata Florida against the Mortimers. He was to clinch his ascendancy over the Marchers during the Welsh revolt of 1294-5. In Glamorgan this took the form of a revolt of the upland Welsh against the encroachments of Earl Gilbert, led by the son of one of the dispossessed, which asserted its continuing loyalty to the king. Edward marched in, received the rebels into his homage, showered pardons and put the lordship under a royal officer for a while. The March was to enjoy its proper immunities under the new dispensation but no more. Its persistence, however, gave a boost to that principle of aristocracy in Wales, which had served the English king so well in Pura Wallia, and deepened its shaping influence on Welsh society.

In this subjected land, Edward had shown some favour to the Church, and with anything remotely resembling a state gone, that Church, ambiguous as it was in a Welsh context, remained the only refuge, particularly for the literate and talented among the Welsh. Edward and the Archbishop staged their triumphal progressions through Wales and firmly established their control over it. More than ever before, that Church was exposed to royal taxation and royal appointment to its offices, countered by the growing power of the papacy which made its own provisions to such bishoprics, canonries and prebends. In time, papal provision was to become embroiled in all sorts of local struggles and, indeed, in the struggle between a people and its overlords. It was from the reign of Edward III, however, that such matters became serious. During the first fifty years of the Conquest, while the high ranges of the Church remained largely closed to Welshmen, men of lesser status, in co-operation with an increasing number of literate and cultivated laymen, produced a body of writing in Latin and, more particularly, Welsh, which, though neglected today, can stand comparison with the prose romances and the secular verse.

Two of the most comprehensive collections of religious, philosophical and even lay romantic writings, the *White Book of Rhydderch* and the *Book of the Anchorite of Llanddewi-Brefi*, come out of this Church in the first half-century of colonialism. So do a host of manuals, prayers and hymns, among the latter the celebrated 'Emyn Curig Ferthyr', a hymn to Curig the Martyr which invoked the Trinity as protection against peril and disaster. The poet Iolo Goch assured his patron John Trefor, Bishop of St Asaph, that he would sing it before the latter went off on a Scottish campaign. The Bishop was to need Curig nearer home; he joined the Glyn Dŵr rebellion after the rebels had burned down both his cathedral and his palace. There were many works of piety, notably *Y Gysegrlan Fuchedd (The Way of Holiness)*, a compilation from French sources and the vehicle of a Catholic mysticism of intensely erotic character, and many dialogues for the laity, like the *Elucidarium*. There was a multiplicity of Visions of Heaven and Hell, Lives of the Saints and a corpus of productions to serve the growing cult of the Virgin Mary. Most striking of all were Welsh translations of biblical texts, the most famous being *Y Bibyl Ynghymraec* (The Bible in Welsh), actually a Welsh version of a synopsis of the historical books of the Bible, whose existence and popularity were to provide an ideological base for embattled Welsh Protestantism many years later.

These mostly anonymous works were produced by clerics, among whom the friars bulked large, even as notable Welshmen or men from Wales made names for themselves in the theological and philosophical battles in Oxford and Paris. They seem to have tapped the services of numbers of laymen and here they ran into the problem of the Welsh romances, the laws and even the poetry, much of which, of course, was alien to the Church and even to Christianity. A striking feature of the fourteenth century is the way these trends were, more or less, harmonized. Prominent among the lay co-operators with the clerics, for example, was Hopcyn ap Tomos of Ynystawe in the Swansea area, an outstanding patron of men of letters; it was probably his brother who persuaded a Glamorgan priest to translate a celebrated Latin *Way of Brother Odrig*. From similar circles, particularly in that south which saw so many of its men march off to the French wars, came the translations of the cycles of Charlemagne and the Holy Grail. Hopcyn ap Tomos, however, was also a 'master of *brut*' and, as such, was to be formally consulted by Owain Glyn Dŵr, no mean practitioner himself of this kind of 'history'.

More striking still, the Church tended to take over the guild of poets, the very heartland of the Old Song of Taliesin and the central formative force in Welsh imaginative life. That guild had been unhinged by the removal of its princely patrons; it was hounded by English officers as a rabble of vagabonds. It dispersed, ultimately to scatter in circuit around the homes of the *uchelwyr*, the greater men, survivors of the princely dynasties and new men shaping into a gentry. Critical at this point was the appearance of a poetic grammar, that of Einion Offeiriad (Einion the Priest), written between 1322 and 1327. This established the canons of Welsh poetry. Praise remained the core, carefully defined in a hierarchy of values from God to maidens. It was this which gave a frame of reference to a renewed outburst of verse which can sometimes look like a compensation for political loss. Religious sentiment now charged traditional verse, both the extremely difficult forms of the master poets and the more accessible couplet *cywyddau* (odes which were still highly complex in their internal rhymes, alliteration and assonance). In contrast and probably in reaction, novel and altogether freer forms of poetry emerged in mid-century, to inhabit a world totally different from anything yet seen in Wales.

The point about this poetry is that it came to focus on the latest substitute for the hall, the *plas*, the seat of a gentleman. Critical to the survival of the Welsh as a people was this class of gentry, often an official if subordinate class within the colonial regime. Dafydd ap Gwilym, the greatest of the new poets, himself came from such an official family and, during years of growing social crisis in Wales, wrote a poetry – and a light-hearted poetry – of summer gardens and even more summery girls.

The first and the most common reaction to this colonial regime was what it was to be throughout history – a massive acceptance of and accommodation to it. Typical of many was that Welsh gentleman who changed his coat of arms at the Conquest from three bloody Saxons' heads to the more tactful three closed helmets. Welsh families suddenly sprouted names like De La Pole and De Avene: keeping up with the Joneses would be an inappropriate but apt comment! In the last days of Llywelyn, there seems to have been a stampede of the established to the winning side. Ten Welshmen of the true blood, including Llywelyn's secretary, presented

Edward I in July 1283 with the richly mounted piece of the True Cross which had been the prince's cherished relic. Dafydd Fychan was given Emlyn in the south-west because he had captured the prince's brother. Foremost in the changeover were the multiple families descending from Ednyfed Fychan, the powerful seneschal of Llywelyn the Great. These had become interlocking clans with estates scattered across Wales and England; they had a lot to lose. Not one of them suffered any loss whatever at the Conquest and they soon turn up as vital agents of the new regime. Among them was one family, itself multiple, which it would be convenient to call by the English-style surname they later adopted, the Tudors.

Such men were essential. It was swiftly recognized that while the upper reaches of the administration had to be kept English, at the face-to-face level Welsh people could be governed only by Welshmen. The Welsh were soon ubiquitous at that level. But the relationship was fragile, tense and precarious. It is in the fluctuations in response of this Welsh subordinate official class that one can most clearly see the increasingly violent oscillations between loyalty and disaffection which ultimately exploded in the Glyn Dŵr rising.

The first years of colonialism were harsh and brutal. The new money economy was enforced before a slowly changing kindred society could adapt to it. There was wholesale default and escheat. The burgesses of the towns exploited their privileges without mercy; they and the alien courts were hated. The unfree were driven desperate. In the upheavals, the serfs on reckoned land had dwindled to a tenth of the population and they paid two-thirds of the Principality's revenues. There were outbreaks of rebellion, one by Rhys ap Maredudd in 1287 and another by Madog ap Llywelyn in 1294. These were old-fashioned Welsh nobles who had actually resisted Llywelyn himself, though they claimed royal descent and sided with Edward. Equally characteristically, the Ynyr Fychan who captured Madog (whose revolt had sparked off a number all over Wales, posing a serious problem to a military depleted by campaigns elsewhere) was rewarded with the commote of Talybont in Merioneth. From him stemmed the potent gentry dynasty of Nannau.

Ynyr belonged to a group around Sir Gruffydd Llwyd in north Wales who owed everything to Edward II. It is a curious but well attested fact that the only two kings who achieved a personal popularity among the Welsh, Edward II and Richard II, were both deposed and murdered by the English baronage. It was probably the crises of the 1290s that had induced Edward I to ease up and stage his propaganda coup of proclaiming his baby son Prince of Wales in 1301. To judge by the claims made later by north Wales gentry, it must have been the most overcrowded delivery room in history, with a multiplicity of nurses and midwives from the best Welsh families. Edward II relied heavily on his Welsh official class, with Sir Gruffydd Llwyd the leader in the north and Sir Rhys ap Gruffydd in the south (both of them descendants of Ednyfed Fychan). They repaid him with total loyalty during his struggle with the baronage; so did the northern bishops. In the southern March, matters were more complex, since it was an arena for the multiple struggles between Edward II, the baronial factions, Mortimer and the Despensers. One product of the prolonged crisis was a Welsh revolt which, though strictly localized, was quite ferocious.

Llywelyn Bren was the son of the last lord of Senghenydd (Ifor Bach's lordship) who had been dispossessed in 1266. He had become, nevertheless, one of the Welsh official class in Glamorgan; there were books of Welsh law and French romances in his house. The extinction of the Clare lordship at Bannockburn put Glamorgan in the hands of royal managers. In the general crisis of revenues and food shortages of those years, the first European herald of an epoch of depression, authority's exactions became intolerable, while the leading Welshmen, defending their communities, were treated like dogs. Llywelyn, like many Welshmen of his kind, became an outsider in his own country and would not tolerate it. He broke into revolt. The result was an abrupt popular rebellion in which, according to local tradition, his wife Lleucu played a leading part. That rebellion became a kind of *jacquerie*, with the hated towns and the lord's mills a major target. When the revolt was crushed, Llywelyn no less typically fled to surrender into the neighbouring lordship of Brecon, where Humphrey Bohun took pains to cultivate good relations with his Welsh. Both he and the two Mortimers wrote to the king, begging mercy for Llywelyn and going surety for him. Instead, he fell into the hands of the younger Despenser who promptly executed him at Cardiff in 1316. Payn de Turberville, the lord of Coety, was ordered to ship all Welsh people in the plains back into the hills, while in Brecon Bohun gave the widow Lleucu a pension; her seven sons were to fight loyally for him. In many respects this highly localized conflict in Glamorgan in 1316 anticipates the conflagration which was to engulf all Wales eighty years later.

It was with the fall and murder of Edward II that the brief summertime of the Welsh official class came to an end. The rule of Edward III and his son the Black Prince subjected Wales to an exploitation which was often brutally insensitive and reintroduced a crisis atmosphere. It was in 1335 that there occurred the first of those recurrent panics which seized authority at reports that the Welsh were about to rise under a Messiah or upon the landing of one of the exiles who had gone abroad to serve France. It was at times like these that the citizens of the fortress town of Aberystwyth dared not go to church in Llanbadarn, all of two miles away, for fear of the Welsh in between.

An explosion did not in fact occur until 1345 but it was then almost painfully symptomatic. After ten years of heavy war taxation and contemptuous treatment of native Welsh gentry by the Black Prince and his Council, north Wales was restless. There was conflict over appointment to the see of St Asaph. The local canons, pointing to the roughness of the land and its inhabitants, begged the Pope to provide a bishop who could speak Welsh. The Pope responded favourably and told them to elect a bishop of their own nation. The Prince was pushing an Englishman. In the middle of the early stages of this struggle, in 1344, the Welsh at St Asaph fair suddenly attacked the English burgesses of Rhuddlan and drove them back to their own gates. Attacks on towns took place all over Wales and in February 1345 the Prince's own deputy Henry Shaldeford was murdered by Tudor ap Gronw and his cleric brother Hywel, Tudors of the Anglesey clan of officials. Allied to them were the Dean of St Asaph and the Abbot of Conway and other clerics prominent in Bangor and Llŷn. The whole town population of north Wales panicked and demanded protection, talking of a general rebellion and invasion from abroad. The usual security clampdown followed, in the middle of which the canons of St Asaph, with papal support, defeated the Prince and installed a Welshman, John Trefor. The Pope intervened frequently in these years and knowledge of Welsh was sometimes a factor in his choice. In 1370 the Pope made his second provision of a bishop to Bangor, each in the teeth of opposition from the Prince; this was of a Welshman Hywel ap Gronw, who may well have been the very same Tudor who had murdered Shaldeford!

The entry of Edward III and his son on the scene opened an epoch of crises for this colonial society, which was to end in a wholesale withdrawal of allegiance.

## A Crisis of Society

The Black Death struck in 1348-50 and the first impact was devastating. Hill and moorland country suffered less than the riversides and the lowlands, but casualties of up to 40 per cent are reported; one distraught chronicler thought half the population of Wales had gone. The plagues returned repeatedly to climax in another bad outbreak in the 1360s. In the Vale of Clwyd, the average mortality rate which had stood at twelve per 1,000 over

1340-48 rocketed to 173 in 1349, fell to thirty-four in 1350 and rose again to sixty-two in 1362. A prolonged economic depression, punctuated by brief bursts of prosperity, ran into the 1370s. In the last quarter of the century there was an upsurge, probably accompanied by a compensatory population explosion, which seems to have shifted the balance significantly in favour of the Welsh, and which turned the 1390s into a decade of economic buoyancy through social and political crises.

Between 1350 and 1450 society and landscape were transformed. There was a major shift in landed wealth, the emergence of a yeomanry, a squirearchy and a mobile labour force; there was a withdrawal from open fields, strips, the scattered settlements of the kindred, a widespread consolidation of estates, great and small, the enclosure of arable land, a major shift into pasture and the growth of a cattle and cloth trade with England. Traditional serfdom and the traditional kindred broke down and there was a striking increase in social and physical mobility, partly funnelled off into the armies of the French and Scottish wars. Between 1350 and 1420 the old legal kindred and its practices virtually disappeared among the Welsh, and a wholesale shift into English law accompanied a major recolonization of areas long lost and a penetration into the towns of Wales and the border counties, and indeed Bristol and London. The Principality and the March both went into a crisis of lordship; both survived and in the March in the 1390s, profits were probably at a peak. It was their control over the profits of justice and taxation which gave them power; their exercise of this power in the teeth of social upheaval proved peculiarly explosive.

The sudden throwing open of a land-market opened the way to the emergent yeomanry and squirearchy. In the west, families both old and new began to piece together estates from the kindred, exploiting *prid* and resorting to English law, while others fell behind in the race. The pressure on the small bond population intensified even as new opportunities opened up. There was wholesale flight countered by severe repression. In the March serfs bargained for their freedom with hard-pressed lords; in Gwent the manor and its serfs virtually disappeared; elsewhere the result depended on the outcome of local struggle and accommodation. But essentially, with infinite local variation all over Wales, the line between Principality and March was eliminated in a profound and sustained class struggle, with fiscal and judicial power being used to keep authority's heads above water. Everywhere the unfree population fell sharply and, in many places, the distinction between free and unfree lost all meaning; those unfree who remained trapped were subjected to repression and exploitation. Among the abruptly more mobile classes a squirearchy emerged, with clerics turned land speculators and money-lenders as prominent as old *uchelwyr,* and new men on the make. Beneath them a yeomanry was forming as richer and more skilful peasants clawed their way up, and thousands of lesser people were pitched into dependence and frustration. Through the middle and third quarter of the century, change was measured and piecemeal; in the last years, it accelerated to achieve one of the most momentous transformations in the history of the Welsh, with profoundly contradictory social effects. Every rising class and group was split wide open by the Rebellion of Glyn Dŵr, but the anger of the unfree and of those who were driven to the wall was its permanent theme. In 1401 the serfs of Abergavenny killed their lord, and the appearance of one of Glyn Dŵr's bands, or even the rumour of their coming, was enough to set off a destructive explosion.

Through the years from the 1340s into the 1370s, which we can now identify as the lurching, shifting, groaning years of basic change preparatory to the breakthrough of the last years of the century, there was what amounted to a significant withdrawal of the Welsh official class from public life within Wales. After Edward II the country became something of a political desert for such people, with some individual exceptions. Many found compensation in foreign wars. Service in the armies of England as in other Celtic lands became a pledge of loyalty and a means of advancement for people denied fulfilment in their own country. From the reign of Edward I began that tradition which was to install Welsh aristocratic and gentry families in the officers' messes, and a legion of Fluellens in the sergeants' and other-ranks canteens. The bowmen of south Wales were to be as celebrated in English writing as the myriad budding Dafydd ap Gwilyms in Oxford. In the March this intensified a loyalty to one's lord which became a political force. Thousands of Welshmen in their proud livery – like Mortimer's men 'all clothed in green with their arms yellow' – were a force to reckon with in the politics of England itself, whenever the Marchers were heavily involved, as they increasingly were.

In that other outlet for service and advancement, the picture was more dismal. From the 1340s the Church in Wales, poor though its dioceses were, with St David's alone offering some reward, became increasingly the preserve of royal patronage offered to dependable servants. The papal provisions which to some extent countered this process, turned the Welsh dioceses into arenas of dispute between congeries of divergent interests. It is notable that the major waves of papal provision in Wales tended to coincide with moments of crisis and outbursts of anti-English feeling:

1316-20 during the social crisis and Llywelyn Bren revolt; 1327-30 in the restlessness after the overthrow of Edward II; the early 1340s during the Shaldeford crisis. From time to time, then, papal provision had in effect served the interests of the Welsh against the Black Prince. But from the 1350s there is little evidence of any such effect and from the 1370s onwards the Welsh Church in its official aspect lost any specifically Welsh character. Hundreds of dedicated Welsh clerics remained, of course, but they found their way to preferment increasingly arduous. The endless struggle between England and France which got enmeshed in the Schism between Rome and Avignon, propelled the English king towards Rome and was to create further trouble within Wales. The Cistercians tended to lapse into a narrow provincialism and there was a rapid decline in the quality of scholarship and cultural service to the Welsh in a Church which had been noted for both. In Church as in State, able Welshmen found themselves barred from advance, second-class citizens, 'mere Welshmen'.

A more congenial expression of this distancing from power was the unprecedented efflorescence of lyrical, naturalist and love poetry in the middle years of the century, in which you would not know there was a crisis on. These are the years of Dafydd ap Gwilym, probably the finest early poet in Welsh and certainly the most accessible and human, not least at divine service in the garrison church of Llanbadarn:

> I am one of passion's asses,
> Plague on all these parish lasses!
> Though I long for them like mad,
> Not one female have I had . . .
> So I fall in love, I do,
> Every day, with one or two,
> Get no closer, any day,
> Than an arrow's length away.
> Every single Sunday, I,
> Llanbadarn can testify,
> Go to church and take my stand
> With my plumed hat in my hand,
> Make my reverence to the altar,
> Find the right page in my psalter,
> Turn my back at Holy God,
> Face the girls, and wink and nod . . .

With little luck, needless to say:

> See that simple fellow there,
> Pale and with his sister's hair,
> Giving me those leering looks,
> Wickeder than any crook's? . . .
> All I'll give him is *Get out!*
> Let the Devil take the lout!*

Dafydd, who proposed to seduce the nuns of Llanllugan, their abbess at their head, and who insinuated that the Pope himself had a way with the women, used to compare his maidens to the Virgin and beg the latter's aid in his proposed correction of this error!

His brilliant lyrical invention was sometimes near blasphemy and there is a powerful naturalism in him, most memorably expressed in his celebrated 'Offeren y Llwyn', 'The Woodland Mass', where he heard the thrush-cock

> With lucid and unfaltering tongue
> Intone the gospel to the throng

and 'for a wafer lift a leaf on high', where

> the slim, bright, eloquent nightingale
> Chantry priest of the listening vale . . .
> Sounded clear the sacring bell . . .

Some of the less personal realities of his Wales occasionally intrude, as in 'Trouble at a Tavern', where his futile pursuit of one of the girls sends him crashing head-first on a table of pitchers while dogs bark to wake the devil:

> In a foul bed, at the wall
> Bothered for their packs and fearful,

*The scholarly edition of Dafydd ap Gwilym's poems is by Rachel Bromwich (Gomer Press, 1982) which has English paraphrases in heightened prose. This translation of 'The Girls of Llanbadarn' is by Rolfe Humphries, *Nine Thorny Thickets: Selected Poems of Dafydd ap Gwilym* (Kent State University Press, 1969); reprinted in Gwyn Jones (ed.) *The Oxford Book of Welsh Verse in English* (Oxford University Press, 1977). It is very free: the first four lines here are a free but fair version of the first four lines of the original; the next four are an even freer but still fair version of lines 13-18 in the original; the following eight lines are a development of lines 19-22 of the original; the remainder is, once more, a very free but fair version of lines 27-34 of the original. Scholars frown on this translation but I think it wholly in keeping with the spirit of the original. There is a more respectable translation in Anthony Conran (trans. and ed.) *The Penguin Book of Welsh Verse* (1967).

Three English lay in a panic  –
Hickin and Jenkin and Jack.
The young one spluttered a curse
And hissed forth to the others:
'There's a Welshman on the prowl!'
 – O hot ferment of betrayal  –
'He'll rob us, if we let him!' . . .*

In him, however, and in a whole school of poets (we are now realizing) who tried to write like him, about the only contact with political affairs we observe is a running undercurrent of anti-clericalism, which gets nasty about friars. There were other anti-clericals among the poets, all hostile to the friars and the hypocrisy of churchmen. Iolo Goch, a more traditional poet, was one of them and even more striking in him was verse unique in this whole canon in that it is an 'Ode to the Labourer' ('Cywydd y Llafurwr'), in which the honest husbandman, so skilful at the plough, is contrasted with the idle rich; in the sanctity accorded to productive labour, Iolo sounds like Piers Plowman.

There was, however, another kind of verse altogether, the mystery and prophetic poetry of the *brut*, which was an underground verse, anti-English, drawing on the vast store of the British Arthurian tradition and the prophecies of Merlin, expressly political and couched in the terms of redemption by a political saviour. It is impenetrable because it is written in a lost code. People have tended to discount it as an obscure grumble, but in fact verse like this was purposely employed in 1485 to create a fifth column at the service of Henry Tudor, and a striking feature of these years is the recurrent security panics which gripped the English administration.

One major source of alarm was those Welshmen abroad who, like the Wild Geese of the Irish, took service with enemies of the king. Outstanding among these was Owain ap Thomas ap Rhodri, a descendant of the dynasty of Gwynedd, who from 1369 led a Welsh free company in the service of France. Owain Lawgoch (Owain of the Bloody Hand, Yvain de Galles), in his proclamations, based his claim on the direct dynastic inheritance of the Llywelyns and announced the imminence of his arrival with a French fleet. Twice he actually sailed from Harfleur, and throughout the 1370s there were ripples of disaffection in his name through north Wales. The

*Translation of 'The Woodland Mass' in H. Idris Bell, *Dafydd ap Gwilym: 50 Poems* (Hon. Society of Cymmrodorion, 1942); translation of 'Trouble at a Tavern' in Anthony Conran (trans. and ed.) *The Penguin Book of Welsh Verse* (1967).

authorities took this threat and others like it in deadly earnest. They sent John Lambe to murder Owain in Mortagne-sur-Mer in 1378 and paid him £20 for the job. Nothing gives a better sense of the permanent insecurity underlying the apparent outward calm in Wales in these years than the repeated security clampdowns, with a coastal watch, the manning of walls, the renewed exclusion of all Welshmen from any office of significance: they happened in 1335, 1337, 1345, 1369–70, 1376–7 and 1385–6.

Little of the poetry, however, has any trace of nostalgia for the Llywelyns; most is directed, in the traditional praise mode, to the gentry, their affluent households, their noble blood and their generosity. One note of discord does come through – a profound dissatisfaction at the treatment of such Welsh leaders in their own country; it cultivates that sense of frustration and unfair denial which had characterized the rebellion of Llywelyn Bren. Gruffydd Llwyd, for example, in one poem which cites history in the terms of Geoffrey of Monmouth, bemoans the lack of honour accorded to Welshmen of merit of the old tradition; only two Welshmen had been knighted that year. Even his own patron, so visibly worthy of such reward, had been slighted. His patron was Owain Glyn Dŵr.

Where the Return of Arthur could find an anchorage in current political reality was the March, among that baronage which so often had Welsh connections of long duration. Outstanding here was the family of Mortimer. A Mortimer had married Gwladus, daughter to Llywelyn ab Iorwerth, in the previous century, and in the last half of the fourteenth century Roger Mortimer, fourth Earl of March, had probably as good a dynastic claim as any to the inheritance of Gwynedd. He became the focus of extravagant hopes among the Welsh gentry. The poet Iolo Goch, who was one of his tenants, wrote a fulsome ode of loyalty, and the battery of the Arthurian *brut* was brought to bear on him. Here was the Hero Returned who would rescue the Welsh from degradation. What made this all the more poignant was that Mortimer had a good claim to the inheritance of Richard II.

For with the coming of Richard in 1377, some of the Welsh official class, at least in north Wales, returned to favour. Prominent among his supporters were the five sons of Tudur ap Gronw who, from their base in Anglesey, through kinsfolk and connections, commanded an influential bloc in north Wales. Gwilym and Rhys Tudor in particular seem to have been personally close to Richard II, who was as popular in north Wales as in Cheshire. This shift came at a critical moment, because it was precisely at this time that the social changes in Wales were beginning to provoke political response. The surge of the renaissant Welsh was meeting judicial resistance.

The Welsh language had started to reconquer the Vale of Glamorgan; Welshmen began to appear in the towns, Oswestry, Brecon, Monmouth; the Welsh were harassing English merchants in the March. A chorus of complaint against them burst from towns not only in Wales but in the English border counties. Nearly every Parliament which sat between 1378 and 1400 demanded stern action against these impertinent scrubs. In 1395 there was an ugly anti-Welsh riot in the University of Oxford − 'Kill, kill the Welsh dogs!' And even as the gentry turned towards Richard II, the upper ranges of the administration in Wales slammed its English doors hard. Between 1372 and 1400, of sixteen bishops appointed in Wales, only one was a Welshman. This reassertion of colonialism in a regime which was breaking down under its own contradictions, thrust to the fore that English-Welsh tension which could provide a scapegoat for so many of the discontented now clutching at the coat-tails of Richard II and the Mortimers.

The shocks of the last years of the century were all the more unhingeing. In 1398 Roger Mortimer died and in 1399 Richard was deposed and murdered by Henry of Lancaster. The usurpation by Henry IV opened an era of instability in the succession in England, interwoven with the repeatedly renewed French wars, which thrust real power into the hands of the baronage, not least those of the March, and was ultimately to break into the Wars of the Roses. The immediate impact of Henry's seizure of power was dislocating. The new king met resistance from important groups among the barons; the affronted Franciscans spread disaffection. In the March there was disturbance as factions moved against each other. When Henry IV made his son Prince of Wales, a French knight commented, 'But I think he must conquer Wales if he will have it . . .' As heavy communal levies were imposed, Lord Grey of Ruthin reported serious 'misgovernance and riot' beginning in the north-eastern March, and demanded action throughout Wales, particularly against Welsh officials who were kinsmen of the troublemakers. By the spring and summer of 1400, the administration at Caernarfon was nervous. It spoke of letters passing between the Welsh and the Scots which talked of a rebellion; men in Merioneth were stealing arms and horses; 'reckless men' of many areas were meeting to plot sedition.

They were certainly doing so in Anglesey. The Tudors, so affronted by the abrupt change in their political fortunes, were planning a protest in their island to tap the widespread dismay. They could call on a small universe of cousins. One of them was a man moving towards revolt in the March, Owain Glyn Dŵr. Joan of Arc, we know, heard angel voices from Heaven. Owain Glyn Dŵr may have heard Tudor voices from Anglesey.

## The Deliverer

Owain Glyn Dŵr was a member of the dynasty of northern Powys and, on his mother's side, descended from that of Deheubarth in the south. The family had fought for Llywelyn ap Gruffydd in the last war and regained their lands in north-east Wales only through a calculated association with the powerful Marcher lords of Chirk, Bromfield and Yale and the lesser family of Lestrange. In 1328 the family abandoned Welsh law and secured its estate through English entail. They thus rooted themselves in the Welsh official class in the March – Glyn Dŵr's grandmother was a Lestrange – and figured among its lesser aristocracy.

The man himself was comfortably placed. He held the lordships of Glyn Dyfrdwy (Glendowerdy) and Cynllaith Owain near the Dee directly of the king by Welsh barony. He had an income of some £200 a year and a fine, moated mansion at Sycharth with tiled and chimneyed roofs, a deerpark, heronry, fishpond and mill. He was a complete Marcher gentleman and had put in his term (possibly seven years) at the Inns of Court. He must have been knowledgeable in law; he married the daughter of Sir David Hanmer of the cymricized Flintshire family, a distinguished lawyer who had served under Edward III and Richard II. He moved freely in such circles and married one of his own daughters into the Scudamores of Herefordshire. In 1386 he appeared at a celebrated court of chivalry in the same company as the poet Geoffrey Chaucer, indistinguishable from the throng of gilded baronial youth. He had served in the wars, in the retinues of Henry of Lancaster and the Earl of Arundel. In the Scottish campaign of 1385, according to the poet, he had worn his scarlet flamingo feather and driven the enemy before him like goats, with a broken lance.

In the troubles of 1399-1400, however, Glyn Dŵr ran up against his powerful neighbour, Reginald de Grey, lord of Ruthin, an intimate of the new king, Henry IV. The quarrel was over common land which de Grey had stolen. Glyn Dŵr could get no justice from king or parliament; Welshmen, as supporters of Richard II, were suspect – 'What care we for those barefoot rascals?' This proud man, over forty and grey-haired in service, was visited with insult and malice. God knows what sort of conspiracies were brewing in the March at the time, but in one sense Glyn Dŵr's response was traditional; like any Marcher, he would avenge his honour with his sword.

But he was more than a Marcher. He was one of the living representatives of the old royal houses of Wales, an heir to Cadwaladr the Blessed, in a Wales strewn with the rubble of such dynasties. The poets and the masters of *brut* would have, indeed already had, reminded him of the fact. Not that he needed them, he was himself steeped in the history. His correspondence suggests that an effort was made to contact the disaffected elsewhere, and when he raised his standard outside Ruthin on 16 September 1400, his followers from the very beginning proclaimed him Prince of Wales; one of them was a poet whom the English called a prophet and a wizard.

The response was startling and may have startled Glyn Dŵr himself. Supported by the Hanmers, other Norman-Welsh Marchers and the dean of St Asaph, he attacked Ruthin with several hundred men and went on to savage every town in north-east Wales: Denbigh, Rhuddlan, Flint, Hawarden, Holt, Oswestry and Welshpool. Rhys and Gwilym Tudor raised a rebellion in Anglesey. Hundreds of people rushed to join, churches followed towns into flame. The lesser clergy in north Wales joined promptly. The Cistercians throughout Wales, in Conway, Strata Florida, Whitland, Llantarnam were to rally. The Abbot of Llantarnam in Gwent, John ap Hywel, joined Glyn Dŵr's army as a Welsh Savonarola and was to fall in battle. The Franciscans, and not only in Wales, embraced his cause; the friars at Llanfaes were ejected by Henry's punitive force and their house ravaged. There was an immediate response from Oxford, where Welsh scholars at once dropped their books and flocked home. Graduates of standing like Hywel Cyffin and John Lloyd were accused of treasonable correspondence. Scholars from 'the merest boys of Wales' to senior figures like David Speckled Eyes (Dafydd Llygaid Brith) were said to have met at Alice Walsh's house to plot 'the destruction of the kingdom and the English language'. Even Adam of Usk, a distinguished scholar and chronicler and a man who was to oscillate in his loyalty over the next few years, was suspected of stealing a horse and taking off. Even more dramatic was the news that Welsh labourers in England were downing tools and making for home. That English Parliament which was so savage against heretics and alien merchants at once rushed ferociously anti-Welsh legislation on to the books. They singled out the poets of the Welsh in particular.

Henry IV marched a big army in a great arc right across north Wales, burning and looting without mercy. He left the pacification to Henry Hotspur who offered general pardons, except to the ringleaders, to soften the heavy community fines. Whole populations scrambled to make their peace. Over the winter Glyn Dŵr, with only seven men, took to the hills.

But in the spring of 1401 as the Tudors snatched Conway Castle by a trick, Owain's little band moved into the centre and the south. Once more, popular insurrection broke around them, hundreds ran to join the rebel army and at Mynydd Hyddgen in the Pumlumon range they won a decisive victory. Carmarthenshire erupted into revolt and so many rushed to arms that the government panicked over an invasion of England. Another royal army trudged in futility through south Wales, guerillas melting before it, to close in again on its baggage trains in the retreat. A powerful onslaught on Caernarfon at the other end of Wales drove the King's Council to consider peace terms.

For the key men were coming over too, the gentry, generally those outside the charmed circle of the official class. There seems to have been a network of supporters even in towns. Glyn Dŵr's letters went to such men as Henry Don or Dwnn of Kidwelly (of whom the poet John Donne was to be a remote descendant). This was a domineering local bully boy of a squireen, who had served John of Gaunt in France in 1371-2 and Richard II in Ireland in 1393-4. He straddled his community and had already had his estates confiscated once, in 1389. He and his retinue of 200 men were said to terrorize the district. He went over to Glyn Dŵr and there were more like him.

It was during 1401 that Glyn Dŵr became aware of this growing power, mushrooming out of any acre his men trod. He addressed naive but powerful letters to the Irish (in Latin) and to the Scots (in French); he reminded them of the prophecy that Wales would not be freed without their assistance and, like the author of another *Armes Prydein,* called upon them to join. In his letters to south Wales he declared himself the liberator appointed by God to deliver the Welsh race from their oppressors.

The twelve-year war which ensued was, for the English, largely a matter of relieving their isolated castles. Expedition after expedition was beaten bootless back. Henry IV, beset by Welsh, Scots, French and rebellious barons, sent in army after army, some of them huge, all of them futile; he never really got to grips with it and the revolt largely wore itself out, in a small country blasted, burned and exhausted beyond the limit of endurance. For the Welsh, it was a Marcher rebellion and a peasants' revolt which grew into a national guerrilla war, its leader apparently flitting so swiftly and mysteriously from one storm-centre to the next that in English eyes he grew to be an ogre credited with occult powers, a name to frighten children with. This probably reflects the operation of widely scattered guerrilla bands operating in his name.

The sheer tenacity of the rebellion is startling. Few revolts in contemporary Europe lasted more than some months; no previous Welsh war had lasted much longer. This one raged in undiminished fury for ten years and did not really end for fifteen. While the guerrilla bands lurked and fought everywhere, Owain could put armies of 10,000 into the field; at one time Adam of Usk credited him with a force of 30,000. The rebels maintained themselves partly by sheer pillage; Owain, 'a second Assyrian' came down with fire, sword and blackmail; whole districts as well as rich men were held to ransom. The royal armies exacted a terrible vengeance in wholesale arson, looting and confiscations, even as retreating rebels scorched their own earth. Many a community was trapped in the grim and, to us, all-too-familiar vice grip of terror and counter-terror. In February 1404 the people of the hill country of Brecon agreed to submit to the king, but only if he could defeat the rebels in their area; if not, they would remain faithful to Owain. It was a civil war. Most of the English in Wales and nearly all the townsmen were implacable enemies; Thomas Dyer of Carmarthen lost £1,000 in the rebellion. Welsh families were split. Robert, Abbot of Bardsey, was a Glyn Dŵr man; his brother Evan was killed defending Caernarfon Castle. Owain's own cousin Hywel tried to murder him.

What is more remarkable than the civil war the revolt inevitably became, is the passion, loyalty and vision which came to sustain it. Glyn Dŵr's men put an end to payments to the lords and the crown; they could raise enough money to carry on from the parliaments they called, attended by delegates from all over Wales – the first and last Welsh parliaments in Welsh history. From the gentry came Owain's best leaders like Rhys Gethin and the Tudor brothers, from the clergy came intellectuals who charged his pirate principality with principle. From ordinary people by the thousand came a loyalty through times often unspeakably harsh which enabled this old man to lead a divided people one-twelfth the size of the English against two kings and a dozen armies. Owain Glyn Dŵr was one Welsh prince who was never betrayed by his own people, not even in the darkest days when many of them could have saved their skins by doing so. There is no parallel in the history of the Welsh.

Within two years of the outbreak it was on the English border that battles were being fought; outside the beleaguered castles Wales had been swept clear. During 1402-3 the revolt was enmeshed in baronial conspiracies in England which were to rally the powerful northern Percys against Henry and to cost Archbishop Scrope of York his life. In 1402, as Gwent and Glamorgan were liberated and three massive royal armies collapsed in the chaos of retreat, Glyn Dŵr captured Lord Grey and Edmund Mortimer. Parliament hurled yet more savage laws against the Welsh on to the statute book and yoked Englishmen who married Welsh women to the scrubs. They agreed to ransom Grey. But Mortimer, through his nephews, had a better claim to the throne than Henry himself, who proved reluctant to redeem him. Glyn Dŵr seized his chance. Mortimer married the Welshman's daughter Catherine and ordered his people to rally.

The years which follow are full of panicky rumours in England of disaffection in the western counties, which were repeatedly accused, and with some justice, of coming to a separate peace with Glyn Dŵr. Shropshire certainly made a peace with 'the land of Wales'; people in Herefordshire and Gloucestershire took supplies to the Welsh when they penetrated western England. The Franciscans were suspected of being Glyn Dŵr's English fifth column; Englishmen were haled into the courts and accused of sending him money. At one wild moment fifty-seven English abbots, priors and other dignitaries were named as his agents!

Something odd was certainly going on in the west. The Herefordshire border and its March had been much disturbed by Lollards and one of their most powerful figures, the Welshman Walter Brut, actually joined Glyn Dŵr. Mortimer's rally to the prince brought over his brother-in-law Henry Hotspur even as the future Henry V put Owain's beautiful house at Sycharth to the torch. Certainly it was only Henry IV's speed against the clumsy co-ordination of the Welsh and their northern allies which led to the defeat and death of Hotspur at Shrewsbury in 1403.

By this time the castles in Wales were beginning to fall; Cardiff itself went. Only those which could be supplied by sea were holding out. And now the ubiquitous English squadrons were being challenged by Henry Dwnn of Kidwelly and David Perrot of Tenby who joined Breton pirates to harass Bristol, while Jean d'Espagne and a French fleet ranged the north Wales coast in support of the Welsh. By this time, too, people in established positions were rallying. Lewis Byford, the candidate provided by the Pope to the see of Bangor, had, like his predecessor, been checked by the king; with Glyn Dŵr's support he was now installed. John Trefor, the Bishop of St Asaph who had hesitated even as rebels burned his church and palace and who had acted as an agent for Henry as late as 1403, had joined Glyn Dŵr by 1404 as had the highly influential Dr Gruffudd Young. It is perhaps not surprising that Owain saw fit at this time to consult Hopcyn ap Tomos, the master of *brut*!

The year of 1404 saw decisive victory; the great castles at Aberystwyth and Harlech fell. Glyn Dŵr now had a base and a staff of civil servants and diplomats, with contacts in Rome, Avignon, Burgos and Paris. There was a takeover by professionals and his correspondence becomes weighty and official. He summoned his first parliament to Machynlleth, in the heart of liberated territory, four men from every commote of Wales, summoned to raise money, ratify an alliance with France – the key to survival – and, in all probability, to witness his formal coronation in the presence of envoys from France, Scotland and Castile. He is now Owain by the grace of God Prince of Wales, with a great seal and a privy seal, showing a figure with a slightly forked beard, seated crowned with orb and sceptre. His envoys to France were Gruffudd Young and John Hanmer. There, disputes over policy proved a disappointment, but aid was promised. A French fleet of sixty ships sailed, but dispersed their efforts along the southern coasts of England.

In 1405, however, as the Countess of Gloucester tried to smuggle Mortimer's nephews into Glamorgan, Owain and his allies drew up the astounding Tripartite Indenture, signed in the house of David Daron, Archdeacon of Bangor. This proposed to divide the realm, with Mortimer taking the crown and the south, Percy the north and Glyn Dŵr a Wales which was to run from Mersey to Severn, embracing great tracts of western England, with a frontier deliberately drawn to include the Six Ashes on the Bridgenorth road where Merlin had prophesied the Great Eagle would rally his Welsh warriors for the day of deliverance. A second parliament was summoned, this time to Harlech, which funded an army of 10,000 men to support an ill-starred rising in the north of England and a small French army of something over 2,000 men which landed at Milford Haven, forced the men of south Pembrokeshire to buy their peace and marched with the Welsh in a triumphal progress across south Wales and deep into England, to halt near Worcester.

This was probably the last chance of enduring success; the tide was beginning to run against Henry's enemies in both Scotland and France. The allies could get no further; they withdrew and many of the French went home, though some stayed, on land and sea, to the end. In 1406, however, came a glittering climax for this new Welsh nation and its prince. In return for their support, the French had required the Welsh to transfer their allegiance to the Pope at Avignon. In response, the Welsh required Avignon to sanction the creation of an independent Welsh Church. At a great synod at Pennal near Machynlleth that Church adopted a sweeping policy designed to equip this new Wales, whose prince had coolly stolen the coat of arms of Gwynedd, probably in a futile attempt to win 'legitimacy' in the eyes of the incorrigibly established, with its own Church, its own literate classes and its own bureaucracy. The Welsh Church was to be free of Canterbury, with its own metropolitan at St David's exercising control over the western English dioceses of the Tripartite Indenture as well. Welsh clerics were to speak the language of their people, Welsh Church revenues were to be devoted to Welsh needs and finally, in a clause which captured the imagination of later generations, two universities were to be created, one in the north and another in the south, to train Welshmen in the service of the new Wales. There was some trouble as the result of the transfer of allegiance from Rome to Avignon: Lewis Byford was a Roman and was replaced temporarily by Gruffudd Young who was, without doubt, the metropolitan designate.

This was illusion; the ground had already begun to give way. During 1406 Gower, parts of the Tywi valley and Ceredigion crumbled, while the island of Anglesey made its peace with the king. During 1407 the Welsh maintained their position but were now fighting against the odds as resistance in Scotland slackened and France slithered into internal conflict. The royal armies carted great guns from Yorkshire through Bristol to batter them, though Aberystwyth under Rhys the Black beat off a fierce attack. Henry, now strongly Roman and seeking European help against the Welsh, was able to expel John Trefor from St Asaph and to push Henry Chichele into St David's in the teeth of resistance from Gruffudd Young.

Disaster struck in 1408 when the castles at Aberystwyth and Harlech fell, Mortimer died and many of Glyn Dŵr's own family were taken prisoner. The last of his northern allies had already been cut down. The Welsh nation which had existed for four years took once more to the woods, with its prince once more an outlaw. Owain, with his son Maredudd and a handful of his best captains, together with some Scots and Frenchmen, was at large throughout 1409, devastating wherever he went; at the end of the year the officers of the north-eastern March were ordered to stop making truces with him. The last big raid came in 1410, when they swooped in Shropshire. They were beaten; Rhys the Black, Philip Scudamore and Rhys Tudor were executed. After that, says a chronicler, Glyn Dŵr made no great attack. The last direct reference comes in 1412 when he or his men kidnapped Davey Gam. Gruffudd Young carried on the fight a little longer in France and at Constance, but by 1410 the longest, fiercest, most popular and the last Welsh war of independence was over.

No one knows what happened to Glyn Dŵr. He simply vanished. One happy guess is that he spent his last days at the secluded manor of Monnington Straddel in the Golden Valley of Herefordshire, sheltered by his son-in-law John Scudamore. Henry V, the new king, who had taken Owain's remaining son into his own service, twice offered the rebel leader a pardon but the old man was apparently too proud to accept. Maybe Henry let him be; he was not born in Monmouth for nothing and there is good men born there, as we all know. No poet sang Owain's *marwnad*, his elegy. He could not die. Like Arthur, he would come again.

In this traumatic experience, which was swiftly expunged from public memory by the successful Welsh who found their redemption in a different Arthur, a people in travail had generated a nation and, in effect, chosen a suitable rebel as their prince. In the process they propelled Wales not only into a war of national liberation but into a civil war. That whole complex of contradictory and often unpleasant attitudes which had characterized Welsh political life since the tenth century assumed permanent and painful form in the minds of most Welsh people. Half-suppressed, for in modern Wales and particularly among people of substance Owain is still something of an outlaw prince, it has helped to make the Welsh the peculiarly schizophrenic people we are.

Since 1410 most Welsh people most of the time have abandoned any idea of independence as unthinkable. But since 1410 most Welsh people, at some time or other, if only in some secret corner of the mind, have been 'out with Owain and his barefoot scrubs'. For the Welsh mind is still haunted by its lightning-flash vision of a people that was free.

# 6 · WELSH BRITISH

The poet Skelton once told a story which was popular at the court of the Tudors. St Peter and the better class of people in Heaven were suddenly overwhelmed by an abrupt influx of the Welsh, driving everyone crazy with their incessant talk. So the Keeper of the Keys arranged for an angel to stand outside the gates and to shout in a loud voice 'Caws Pobi' (toasted cheese, evidently the original Welsh rarebit). The Welsh promptly thundered out in a stampede after their national delicacy and the gates were slammed shut behind them, to everybody's intense relief.

This story would seem to offer a reasonably succinct, if somewhat partial, summary of the history of the Welsh during the fifteenth, sixteenth and seventeenth centuries.

## *The Return of Arthur*

The ferociously racist penal legislation passed at the height of the Glyn Dŵr rebellion turned the Welsh into unpersons without civic rights; Englishmen who married Welsh women followed them into the pit. Even as these laws went into effect, Henry V went into Normandy and many of his captains and his infantry were Welsh. From this period dates Shakespeare's sympathetic image of the Welshman – garrulous, comic, but brave, honourable and congenial; Pistol, after all, eats the leek. The leek itself dates from the French wars, where Welsh bowmen did so well and Davey Gam died. What sort of colonial subhumans would these be? Fluellen's father had probably at one time or other been out with Owain. Successful Welshmen escaped the penal laws by buying letters of denizenship which declared them to be English ('Money is very Catholic; it makes you white', ran a Spanish-American colonial proverb). They earned the contempt of the poets and before long they had little need of such letters. From the middle of the fifteenth century nothing could stop the Welsh, particularly those who had taken the winning side during the Rebellion.

While the revolt had been very destructive and inflicted terrible blows at the structure of both March and Principality, which slithered towards bankruptcy, the Church recovered fairly rapidly in material terms and all the social forces at work earlier accelerated. Wales of the squires rapidly took shape in north and south while the landscape assumed a modern form. Towns, manors, professions lost their English monopoly. The Welsh language surged forward in the Vale of Glamorgan and into long-lost districts. The ports of the south, followed by those of the north, flourished; the cattle, cloth and butter trade with England grew into major export enterprises. The familiar network of families which was to govern Wales for three centuries emerges in the Salisburys, Bulkeleys, Vaughans, Gruffydds and the rest, with the great houses of Dynevor and Herbert rising newly minted from their ranks. The merchant class of Bristol was heavily colonized, Goughs, Lloyds, Howells and those apMeurig-apMeryk-Ameriks who may even have given their name to America. By the end of the century the bureaucracy of colonialism had been taken over by the colonized.

It was to such men that the poets addressed their renewed homage. For while the spiritual life and the culture of the Church shrivelled up into that indifference and inertia which were to make it such a pushover for the Reformation, the late fifteenth century saw the eisteddfod reorganizing the poets' guild under Dafydd ab Edmwnd and no fewer than thirteen major poets in a very striking cultural renaissance. While free forms of verse appeared and horizons widened (in contrast to a dull and lifeless prose), it was the old themes which Guto'r Glyn, Gutun Owain and the rest preached and with sharper emphasis. For while Glyn Dŵr had gone, he himself was not a stranger to the poems, the affectionate *hen* (old) was attached to his name, and the national consciousness he had embodied, with its strong overtones of the old *brut*, was transferred *en bloc* to those patrons who had so often been the victorious families in the civil war. When Harlech fell to William Herbert, the first Welsh-speaking earl, during the Wars of the Roses, Guto'r Glyn had no hesitation in calling upon him to unite Glamorgan and Gwynedd, pardon not a single burgess, and expel all Englishmen from office in Wales. The lives of Welsh Lancastrians he should spare but no children of Rowena were to remain in Gwynedd nor the children of Horsa in Flint.

It was the Wars of the Roses which gave this old Arthurian yearning unbridled rein. With the end of the French wars the baronage of England were unloosed in a self-destructive sequence of conflicts. York controlled the March and Lancaster the Principality and practically every family of substance in Wales was drawn in. At the battle of Banbury in 1469 the flowers of a Welsh forest were cut down and the Marcher lords dismissed themselves into historical limbo. Out of the ruck emerged the new men:

in the south-east, William Herbert built himself up from a 'mere chapman' to become Earl of Pembroke, the ruler of south Wales and father-in-law to the queen's sister. On the side of the Red Rose, Griffith ap Nicolas rose from humble origins to make himself and his family after him 'kings of south-west Wales' and to establish the house of Dynevor (Dinefwr). Gwilym ap Gruffydd saw his Tudor kinsfolk go down with Glyn Dŵr, collared their lands and built the nucleus of the great estate at Penrhyn in the north which managed, with some ease, to survive Henry IV, Henry V, Henry VI, Edward IV, Richard III and Henry VII.

It was the latter, Henry Tudor, who finally brought the cycle to a close and his descendants who saw it safely into the archives of Shakespearean drama; and it was he who was the residuary legatee of the old tradition. The Tudors of Anglesey, in their half-hearted apology for a gentry mansion at Penmynydd, were descendants of those legendary survivors, the kindred of Ednyfed Fychan, Seneschals to the princes of Gwynedd. They were no mean survivors themselves, in which they faithfully represented the bulk of their countrymen. The family's fortunes had been established by Tudur ap Gronw, great-great-grandson to Ednyfed Fychan and it was his sons who fought alongside Owain Glyn Dŵr as his cousins. Rhys was executed in 1412 and the family lost Penmynydd for a while. A brother, Maredudd, who had been steward to the Bishop of Bangor, had to go into exile, but his son Owain (named after his rebel prince of a kinsman) was taken on board as a pageboy by Henry V. Owain ap Maredudd ap Tudur was something of an innovator; he adopted an English-style surname and called himself, after his grandfather, Owen Tudor (had he chosen his father, as most did, Queen Elizabeth I would have been a Meredith). Innovation did not stop there. While bathing naked he caught the eye of his master's young widow, Catherine de Valois. More boldly still, he married or at least moved in with her; when her monoglot Welsh in-laws turned up, she found them 'the goodliest dumb creatures that she ever saw'! Owen's new stepson Henry VI, who seems to have been as generous in spirit as his father, accepted his Tudor half-brothers and made them earls of Richmond and Pembroke.*

The former, Edmund, married Margaret Beaufort, the remarkable woman who founded St John's College, Cambridge and built the 'Stanley churches' in north-east Wales. It was she who brought a claim to the English

---

*This genial tale of upward social mobility, alas, had an unhappy ending. Owen supported his stepson in the Wars of the Roses and was executed at Hereford, remarking as he laid his head on the block that it had been 'wont to lie in queen Catherine's lap'.

throne. Edmund died and was buried in Carmarthen; his son, Henry, was born posthumously to a fourteen-year-old mother and taken over by his uncle Jasper at the great castle of Pembroke, where he lived for fourteen years and, according to report, learned some Welsh and spoke English with a Welsh accent.

The Lancastrian disaster in 1471 sent Jasper abroad with the boy, and the Herberts having been cut down earlier, the poets of the Welsh swung behind Henry Tudor. Led by a celebrated versifier and master of *brut*, Dafydd Llwyd of Machynlleth, the whole underground network moved into action; into the occult verse come the secret signals, the Bald Bull, the White Boar, the Lily for Margaret, the Seagull for Henry Tudor himself. And when Henry and his small army sailed from France on his highly risky venture in August 1485, he depended utterly on a Welsh rally to carry him through to his supporters in England.

He landed from France at Milford Haven, where the French had landed to help Glyn Dŵr; the great magnate Sir Rhys ap Thomas of Dynevor came over. Henry moved north and went out of his way to consult Dafydd Llwyd, as Glyn Dŵr had Hopcyn ap Tomos. His propaganda drenched Wales, the old British tradition in its most modern persona. In mid-Wales the leaders of north Wales came down, bringing huge herds of cattle as in the old days. 'A worthy sight it was to see', says the *Ballad of the Rose of England*, 'how the Welshmen rose wholly with him and shogged them to Shrewsbury.' At the decisive battle of Bosworth Henry unfurled the Red Dragon of Cadwaladr. And to his victory *Te Deum* in London the Welsh came shogging in herds, for Merlin's prophecy had at last come true. Henry VII made sure it would; he called his eldest son Arthur... 'The Welsh', reported the ambassador of Venice, 'may now be said to have recovered their independence, for the most wise and fortunate Henry VII is a Welshman...'

This was play-acting, but it worked. England opened up like the rose it now bore as its badge, and the Welsh poured in. The old order hung on back home in Wales and, in the boroughs, made a last stand against the incoming tide. But by the end of the reign of Henry VII, who kept St David's Day and packed his court's minor offices with Welshmen, nearly every Marcher lordship was in royal hands, overmighty subjects had been cut down and charters of emancipation issued to north Wales. There was nothing Welsh about his successor Henry VIII (except, conceivably, a taste for light verse and theology in between wives), but Wales thrust itself on the attention of the king who was trying to create a Renaissance nation-state with the powerful aid of his minister Thomas Cromwell. From 1529 that state went into action against the papacy. All the clergy in Wales save two took the oath under the Act of Supremacy but as the commissioners moved on the monasteries and their property, with Welsh gentry eagerly joining in, there was cause for alarm. Just across the water was restive Ireland, and Wales itself, as its Marcher lordships collapsed into gangster fiefs, had become a by-word for disorder. Thomas Cromwell, who was closely informed on Wales (and who had as brother-in-law a Williams from Glamorgan who had set up as a brewer in Putney) decided to send in a strong-arm man as President of the Council in the Marches of Wales, an instrument which Henry VII had prudently retained from his Yorkist opponent's initiative.

Bishop Rowland Lee, with no great love for the Welsh, moved into the middle March as a hanging judge, cluttering the landscape with gallows and his reports with a jovially racist contempt. In the process he started to give the Welsh surnames. He wearied of the long strings of *ap* (son of) in the legal presentments of their kindred-trained memory and ordered their deletion. It is from this time that surnames spread from the border region to reach western Wales by the eighteenth century. In the process many of the Welsh got surnames much as Jews got theirs at Ellis Island.

They were saddled with incomprehensible English distortions of Welsh names, nicknames, insults. When they took over the process themselves, most adopted their father's Christian name, but the *ap* was sometimes embedded in it in English, so that, say, Enoch ap Hywel would become Enoch Powell. Since the process was late in Wales, English Christian names ended up as Welsh surnames – Davies, Thomas, Williams, Hughes – as did Flemish pet-names like Watkin and Hopkin. Some surnames were Welsh descriptive terms distorted in English transcription, such as Coch (red) which spawned Gooch, Gouge, Gough, etc., or Llwyd (grey) which could end up as Flood as well as Lloyd, or the infinite variations of Vaughan which stemmed from Fychan (short). Meredith is a visible descendant of Maredudd, but Beddoes stems from its colloquial form Bedo. In western Wales the kindred made a stand as people included their mother's name as well, suitably hyphenated in later times when social inflation had set in, to populate the district with Parry-Joneses and Pritchard-Lloyds. The whole process was enlivened by the Welsh passion for nicknames, but the latter became a necessity when eight out of ten were saddled with a handful of English or anglicized Christian names as surnames. There are fifty-four Joneses in the *Dictionary of Welsh Biography*, but this is a five-finger exercise for anyone who has to locate a Jones in an average Welsh telephone directory (hence the familiar Jones the Fish, Jones the Bread and, in recent times,

Jones the Spy). The recent rise of Welsh nationalism has led some people to reverse the process; even the *ap* is returning. But the most engaging last stand was made in the eighteenth century by a genial bankrupt who signed himself 'Sion ap William ap Sion ap William ap Sion ap Dafydd ap Ithel Fychan ap Cynrig ap Robert ap Iorwerth ap Rhyrid ap Iorwerth ap Madoc ap Ednawain Bendew, called after the English fashion John Jones.'

The Welsh surname has certainly added to the gaiety of nations, not least the Welsh, but its advance from the early sixteenth century was a symptom of incorporation. More was to come. By 1536 Thomas Cromwell realized that a hamfisted coercion would not suffice; as Lee would have put it, to restore order, thieves would have to catch thieves. More prosaically, the law and order of England would have to embrace Wales with the aid of Justices of the Peace drawn from its gentry. A nation-state in formation was faced with the little local difficulty that there were actually two nations in it. One would have to be made invisible. So between 1536 and 1543, the English crown put through a series of measures which have gone down in Welsh history as the Act of Union.

A very old song came to its end. Both March and Principality were wiped off the map and Wales became thirteen counties; the key office of the Justice of the Peace passed to the gentry as kings of the *bro*. Parliamentary representation followed. Since Wales was poor, the burden was reduced to one MP a county, and the boroughs of each of these were grouped into a unique system to supply another. Merioneth was excused borough representation and Haverfordwest, for no very obvious reason except the local rumour that its leading gentleman was Henry VIII's 'bastard', was given its own. Contrary to the original intention, Wales was provided with a distinct system of higher administration and justice, in that twelve of its counties were grouped into four circuits of three for a Welsh Great Sessions, while a Council of Wales survived and was strengthened; it became a species of capital, meeting for convenience in the borderlands, with Ludlow for long the centre.

Wales acquired its historic frontier in the estate boundaries of an oligarchy of its exploiters. Ethnic minorities were left on both sides of the line. Old Ergyng (Archenfield) disappeared definitively into Herefordshire but remained Welsh-speaking for three hundred years and, indeed, supplied a quite disproportionate number of Welsh notables, not least under Elizabeth I. Monmouth became an anomaly. Nearer to London and relatively wealthy, it was saddled with the full parliamentary quota and subjected to the courts of the capital. Always reckoned a part of the Welsh Church, its exclusion from the Great Sessions and the Welsh parliamentary

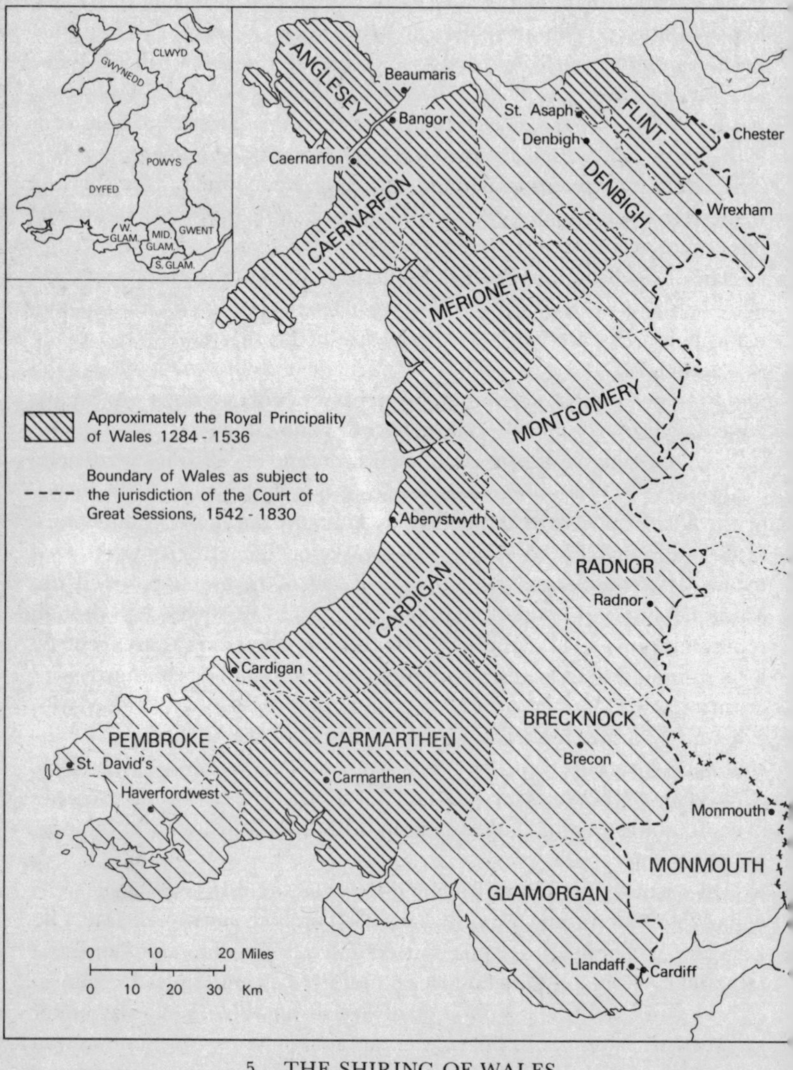
CLWYD
GWYNEDD
POWYS
DYFED
W. GLAM.
MID. GLAM.
GWENT
S. GLAM.
ANGLESEY
Beaumaris
Bangor
Caernarfon
CAERNARFON
St. Asaph
Denbigh
FLINT
Chester
DENBIGH
Wrexham
MERIONETH
MONTGOMERY
Approximately the Royal Principality of Wales 1284 - 1536
Boundary of Wales as subject to the jurisdiction of the Court of Great Sessions, 1542 - 1830
Aberystwyth
RADNOR
Radnor
CARDIGAN
Cardigan
PEMBROKE
St. David's
Haverfordwest
CARMARTHEN
Carmarthen
BRECKNOCK
Brecon
Monmouth
MONMOUTH
GLAMORGAN
Llandaff
Cardiff
0 10 20 Miles
0 10 20 30 Km

5. THE SHIRING OF WALES

*The boundaries of the shires created by the legislation of 1536 – 1543 remained essentially unchanged until 1974, when they were replaced by the new counties (see inset).*

system bred that curious lawyers' hybrid 'Wales and Monmouthshire' as a standard secular description, which English settlement in the eastern lowlands reinforced.

More than Gwent was affected. In this nation-state, English was to be the only official language. The descendant of Arthur proclaimed the necessity to extirpate 'all and singular the sinister usages and customs' of Wales. No person or persons 'that use the Welsh speech shall have or enjoy any manner of office or fees within this realm'. The threat of cultural genocide was not in fact fulfilled; indeed, since if the Welsh could not be made invisible they at least had to be made Protestant, the Crown was forced to accede to pressure and authorize Welsh translations of the Bible, whose 1588 version was to prove the sheet-anchor of a threatened language. The use of interpreters softened the worst impact of this cruel imbecility in the courts, but in effect, a largely monoglot people were made aliens in their own lawcourts and cultivated a corresponding alienation. Welsh ceased to be an official language and had to retreat into the kitchen. Since this happened at a critical moment in the inner history of the culture, its long-term effects were to be very serious.

No such fears beset the victorious leaders of the now self-confident Welsh of the time. The union went through in jubilation and many a sour-faced burgess found himself cheerfully thumped about the head to the cry that Welshmen were now as free as Englishmen. Arthur had returned, perhaps a little earlier than expected, and was reinventing his *cantref* of Britain with a squirearchy for his warband.

## The Invention of Britain

An integrated Britain becomes visible first in a major migration of the Welsh to the centre of power. Dafydd Seisyllt from the Welsh-speaking Ergyng of Herefordshire went up to London as a sergeant of Henry VII's guard. He bought land and installed his son as court page. His grandson was William Cecil, Elizabeth's potent statesman. The Seisyllts, in a transfiguration which was to become commonplace, gave birth to the Cecils, an indestructible dynasty all too much with us still, late and soon. The family of Morgan Williams the brewer who had married a sister of Thomas Cromwell changed its name and its base and, after the customary mutations, produced Oliver three generations later. Spotting these distinctly diluted 'Welshmen' among the elite became as much a national pastime among later stay-at-homes as it was among those British Jews whom in some respects they resembled.

There was a horde of lesser imitators in the first of those recurrent explosions of the Welsh into English society which have characterized modern British history; that Welsh colonization of some English professions, the armed forces and some branches of commerce which in a few sectors became historically significant. The law and education are major examples, drapery and the London milk and hotel trades minor; a disappearance of Welsh teachers would precipitate crises in several English cities today.

In Wales itself there was the first serious exploitation of its minerals since the Romans: brass and copper found their British centre around Neath and Swansea, early tin-plating in Monmouthshire. The Irish Road opened the north to the winds of change. There was a surge of enterprise into many branches of commerce and almost every sector of the Welsh economy found an outlet in a new and much larger market, itself spreading out across the Irish Sea and into the European and Atlantic trade routes. The massive cattle trade with its great drove-herds slogging through England to Smithfield, the cloths moving to Shrewsbury and Blackwell Hall in London, the butter and other pastoral commodities following the same routes, the great gangs of migrant labourers and adventurers, all the exports human and material of the novel merchant capitalism, brought more permanent settlers in their train. It is from this point that the London-Welsh begin to emerge as a distinctive community with a critical economic and cultural role, a surrogate capital for their invertebrate homeland.

Anything from a third to a half of the Welsh people lived on or below the poverty line and much of upland Wales earned its English reputation as a provincial backwater. But among the landowners clustering thick in commercial Glamorgan and Monmouth in the south and along the critical Irish Road in the north were some of the richest squires in contemporary Europe. Like the Wynns in the north-east and the Owens in Pembrokeshire, busily retracing and where necessary inventing their family and regional histories in the fashionable antiquarian-political styles of the day, and carrying many of the multitudinous lesser gentry with them, such people swarmed into the greatest upheaval in the land market Britain had yet seen, as over generations, feudal, Church and Crown possessions passed under the hammer. During what one breeched and booted English historian in the tradition of William Cobbett has nicknamed the Age of Plunder,* the newly minted and semi-capitalist gentlemen of Wales moved resolutely into every conceivable avenue of advancement, from the Court, the Great

*W. G. Hoskins, *The Age of Plunder: The England of Henry VIII, 1500-1547* (Longman, 1976)

Sessions, the Council of Wales, JP patronage and the academy, through minerals, estate industrialization, the merchant marine and its commerce, strategic marriage and tactical politics, to smuggling, piracy, the labyrinths of sweet Old Corruption and their sister profession the law.

The process reached its climax in the reign of Elizabeth I, that 'red-headed Welsh harridan' as A. L. Rowse once called her, when Blanche Parry from Welsh Herefordshire was a key figure in the Queen's household and served as contact for whole coteries of compatriots in legal, naval, academic and professional circles; when Elizabeth's immediate entourage was so heavily Welsh in composition and Welsh intellectuals concentrated in such force behind the first thrust for naval growth, American colonization and empire. Under Elizabeth, for the first time in centuries, the Welsh Church ceased to serve as outdoor relief for deserving hacks; thirteen of the sixteen bishops appointed to Wales were crusading Protestant Welshmen. In 1571 Jesus College, Oxford was created specifically as a Welsh college, an apt symbol of the whole movement.

For if the Welsh were admitted as junior partners to the new state, with its market economy and its merchant capitalism, it was as senior partners that they helped create that new and imperial *British* identity by which the state lived. This new Protestant Britain had to fight for its life and its place in the sun against the Counter-Reformation and its powerful agency, Habsburg Spain, and its monopoly of the New World. Intellectually and emotionally central to the enterprise was the assertion of an aboriginally independent and imperial British identity, whose sources had to be sought in those remote ages when Albion was an empire and its Christianity free from Rome. Here, Welsh traditions were inescapable. The Tudors spent much necessary time hunting out their legitimizing genealogies; Henry VII started it and it took their servants back into the Britain of the Welsh, with its ancient warrant. Geoffrey of Monmouth's *British History* became semi-official doctrine. When it came under attack from the new scientific history at the hands of Polydore Vergil and others of the Italian school, most Tudor Renaissance humanists rallied passionately to its defence. Cogent new scholars from Wales were to the fore, Sir John Price of Brecon and Humphrey Llwyd of Denbigh, himself a brilliant geographer and a protégé of the seminal school of savants in the Netherlands. So did the pillars of the new history based on antiquarian survey, men like John Leland and John Bale, scholars steeped in a British antiquity whose work was to climax in William Camden's magnificent *Britannia*.

The British-Arthurian cycle reached its climax, in learning, poetry, public ritual and propaganda, in Philip Sidney's vision of a Renaissance-

Protestant chivalry in the service of British empire, in the 1580s, the years of Spenser's *Faerie Queene*, when relations between Britain and Spain degenerated into open war, when the enterprise of Drake, Gilbert and Raleigh precipitated the crisis of the Spanish Armada. The Welsh were the most direct inheritors of this British tradition, which had so informed their own identity. At the moment Henry Tudor had marched out of Wales, Malory had printed his *Morte D'Arthur*.

Central to this burst of British imperial energy was that seminal figure of the European Renaissance, the London-Welshman of Radnorshire roots, Dr John Dee, who is credited with the coinage of the very term 'British Empire'. A brilliant mathematician like Robert Recorde of Pembrokeshire before him, foundation fellow of Trinity College, Cambridge, unforgettable lecturer at Louvain and Paris, Dee was a key thinker in the Hermetic tradition and a scholar of major European reputation; in the 1580s, from bases in Bohemia and the German Palatinate, he was to launch a semi-scientific, semi-mystical reform movement of anti-Jesuit character, focused on Elizabeth and the Palatinate, which was cultivating a novel world view. Snuffed out in Europe by the Counter-Reformation and the hideous religious wars, it went underground to live a shadowy and increasingly occult life for centuries, before resurfacing in novel and eccentric form in the eighteenth century Enlightenment. Earlier Dee had been at the very heart of Elizabethan maritime enterprise, corresponding with Mercator and Ortelius in the Low Countries, putting his superb Mortlake library at the service of Frobisher and Gilbert, pouring out maps and treatises, and working with the *'mechanicians'* in the service of the first British effort to break out into the New World.

Dee's new Britain was Welsh Britain transfigured. He traced his genealogy back to Rhodri Mawr, claimed kinship with the Tudors, immersed himself in the traditions of the Welsh, to produce his many tomes grouped under the *Perfecte Arte of Navigation*. When he went, as 'hyr Brytish philosopher', to present Elizabeth with her Title Royal to empire over the North Atlantic and Atlantis (as Dee called America) it was rooted in the old mythical conquests of Arthur glossed with the new geography. More, in Humphrey Llwyd's history of the Welsh (published by David Powel in 1584 as the first history of Wales to appear in print) he came across the old Madoc stories; endowed with a moral character – an old people finding a new start in a new world – after the Glyn Dŵr rebellion, these had been transformed in folklore into a Welsh discovery and colonization of America three hundred years before Columbus. It was Dee who thrust Madoc to the forefront and built a whole Arthurian and scholarly edifice around him.

A whole generation seized avidly on Madoc as a weapon against Spain. His first English advocate, Sir George Peckham, used him in 1583 to justify a scheme to solve the problem of England's Catholics by 'evacuating' them across the Atlantic. Above all, he lodged securely and in the very first pre-eminence in that book which was the voice of the new British ambition, Richard Hakluyt's celebrated *Principal Navigations, Voyages, Traffiques and Discoveries of the English Nation*.

No Englishman, but no Welshman either, saw any paradox in the inclusion of Madoc, alongside Helen wife of Macsen Wledig, Constantine, the heroes of Welsh story-tellers and Arthur (for they are all there, surging up out of the British prehistory of the Welsh) in a celebration of 'English' discovery, just as neither saw any paradox in the demotion of King Edgar as a 'mere Saxon' in favour of the truly British Arthur. In this new Britain and its British Empire, the Welsh could recover a respectable and central identity, the English devise a new and useful one, under those Tudors who *were* the Return of Arthur. To that new Britain, the *Worthiness of Wales*, to quote Thomas Chirchyard, one of its English celebrants in verse, whose sentiments were echoed by Shakespeare, was crucial.

The *brut* was no less crucial to the Tudor Protestant humanists battling at home. At first Protestantism was alien, *ffydd y Saeson*, the English religion. The closure of the monasteries enriched the gentry but was mourned by the poor, the vagrant and the poets. The violent oscillations under Edward VI and Mary produced a handful of martyrs, Catholic, usually well-born, and Protestant, usually humble. Catholicism remained strong in south-east Wales, on the Monmouth border and in the north-east around Denbigh and Flint, largely gentlemanly in character. Its practices, origin forgotten, lived on as irreligious folklore. The first stirrings of a native Calvinism also produced a martyr in John Penry, a Brecon man, who argued for a preaching ministry in Welsh; and perhaps in tiny communities of nascent separatists in what had been the borderland of the southern March, the old Lollard stronghold. On the whole, however, the changes encountered the same indifference which the old religion had suffered from for generations.

It was under Elizabeth that the battle for hearts and minds was fought and won; Welsh bishops appeared in Welsh dioceses for the first time in a hundred years and waged spiritual war against an equally potent and equally humanist generation of Welsh Catholic intellectuals. The tragic saga of the Catholic exiles began, with Welsh clerics basing themselves in seminaries in Rome, Milan, Douai and Valladolid, smuggling men out for training, sending them back into Wales, running a printing press in a north Wales cave, above all producing a whole corpus of devotional literature in Welsh. For many Welsh Catholics the language itself, now under attack at home, became a sanctified vehicle of the faith. Gruffydd Robert was personal confessor to Carlo Borromeo himself and published a celebrated Welsh grammar in Milan on St David's Day in 1567; Morris Clynnog brought out a Christian Doctrine in Welsh in Rome in 1568. In curious contrast to what was then happening at home, the Welsh exiles lost their struggle for special treatment. Outnumbered by English exiles who had the ear of Rome, they clashed with Jesuits whose style seemed to them almost as alien as Protestantism. As usual, the Welsh were too few. Back home the new Jesuits proved too foreign. Gentry houses sheltered the faith but reeled from the execution of their sons caught in futile conspiracies. Strong pockets of Catholics remained along the border, buttressed by a handful of magnate families, and in the early seventeenth century there seems to have been a popular revival in south-east and perhaps north-east Wales. A majority of the Welsh, however, slipped out of Catholicism, even if the anchorage in Anglicanism of many ordinary people, particularly in the uplands, was still insecure. This was a decisive breach between Welsh and Irish, who had in early years shared so similar a history. The pathological hatred of Catholicism, both in itself and in the tyranny it was taken to embody, rooted itself in Welsh Anglicanism and in the Dissent which later displaced it. The Irish, perceived as a quasi-permanent threat from Counter-Reformation Europe, were a human vehicle for this menace. Two Celtic peoples, with very different experiences of self-development under English control, ended as mutually hostile nations, confronting each other across every conceivable divide.

Under the last years of the Tudor dynasty and the first of the Stuart, Protestantism finally began to burn itself into the Welsh mind and spirit. Protestants were in action early. John ap Rhys, of an old Breconshire family and a protégé of the Herberts, established himself at court and became a front-runner in the new generation of Renaissance scholars, producing Latin texts on Welsh antiquities. Laying hands on Brecon Priory and launching its grammar school, he became Sir John Price of Brecon. Over 1546-7, he published the first book in Welsh to be printed, *Yn y Lhyvyr hwnn* ('In this book' – it carries no title), a collection of basic religious texts. William Salesbury, an Oxford lawyer, followed up with more and a call to the Welsh to petition for their own Bible.

It was once more under Elizabeth that the intellectual struggle was joined in earnest. Led by a brilliant scholar, Richard Davies, Bishop of St David's, a cluster of humanists won a stunning propaganda victory. To counter the charge that Protestantism was an alien import, Davies, in parallel to the thinkers in the secular arts, reached back into history and uncovered the quarrel of the Celtic Church with Augustine. 'The Pope came late into Wales and that by the sword of the king of England . . .' This characteristic manufacture of a usable past was to colour Protestant thinking for generations. They followed up with a campaign for a Welsh Bible and secured an Act in 1563, designed also to enable the Welsh to learn English more quickly and shed yet another of their 'abominations'! The first translations were clumsily academic, but a stream of enterprises finally reached a climax in the beautiful Welsh Bible of 1588, produced by William Morgan and a handful of north Wales scholars. An even more striking revision appeared in 1620, the work of Richard Parry and Dr John Davies of Mallwyd, the leading Welsh scholar of his day. Ten years later came the epoch-making *Beibl Bach*, the 'little Bible' at five shillings, destined for that respectable hearth and home which Protestantism had made the focus of religious training. It was accompanied by a tide of popular publications, the most celebrated being *Canwyll y Cymry* (The Welshman's Candle) by the Old Vicar, Rhys Prichard, from Llandovery, an enormously popular collection of carols and verse.

The time of the early Stuarts, in fact, was a kind of golden age for a Wales of the squires in which Anglicanism and royalism were being rooted in the very soil. The coming of the Stuarts tended to displace the Welsh from Paradise, but James I and VI was favourably disposed and loyalties were easily transferred. 'I rejoice that the memorial of Offa's Ditch is estinguished,' cried William Vaughan of Cardiganshire as he poured out learned treatises on hygiene, theology and politics and tried to launch a Welsh colony, Cambriol, in Newfoundland. Sir William Maurice, MP for Caernarfonshire, pressed the Welsh to adopt as their own the king of *Great Britain,* as the realm was now technically called. The useful term Briton was certainly popular, the more nice-minded adopting a Cambro-Briton.

Central to this polity was the presence in power not merely of great landlords under their magnates but the active participation of many of the lesser gentry, multitudinous in Wales in consequence of the kindred. They peopled the Inns of Court and colonized the law. The Council of Wales at Ludlow, later at the households of its Presidents like the Earls of Carbery sprung from the Vaughans of the south-west, or the Marquis of Worcester on the southern border, was a focus for gentry and lawyers and Welsh MPs, those from rich counties like Glamorgan and Monmouth often serving constituencies far beyond Wales. In Parliament such MPs tended to act as a bloc in defence of Welsh interests. These were at base now few, all summed up by the slogan 'religion, liberty, property', essentially a defence of that Tudor settlement which had given them power. For through much of the seventeenth century that power remained under threat. In Glamorgan, for example, the wealthy gentlemen of the Vale could be threatened by lesser men from the west and the uplands as well as by sea-borne enemies, if government should take a wrong turning, and every county had its own pattern of menaces, since gentry rule was in fact contentious and riven by feuds, enmeshed in magnate rivalries at the centre. The focus of all fear was Catholicism and Ireland and the threat from Spain and papist Europe, made all the more real by the Catholic presence under magnate protection on the borders. Less immediate, but growing, was a threat from below posed by radical Protestantism and the dissenting and often levelling creeds it spawned. Above all, then, government had to be held to the safe centre of Elizabethan Anglicanism, which the great Herbert house of Pembroke and its myriad Welsh clients exemplified. The coasts had to be guarded, the Irish Sea cleared of pirates, Ireland itself planted with good Protestants. Those districts in the vanguard of the new economy like Glamorgan, Monmouth, Denbigh, Flint and the beneficiaries of the Irish Road, were committed to the central issues of war and trade; all were solid in the defence of a country which elsewhere was poor and currency-starved. (Archbishop John Williams from Conway, one of the wealthiest and most influential of Stuart Welshmen, called the drove-herds of cattle Wales's Spanish silver fleet bringing back the currency on which much of the western economy depended.)

At home, at least outside the foci of the new commerce, life tended to pulse rather slowly around the gentry households, which carefully taught their sons English but generally made those sons' English wives learn Welsh. They often still patronized the local Welsh poet and Welsh letters generally. But while some of the gentry, like the Glynnes of Glynllifon, tried their hands at verse themselves, others, particularly in that south which was more exposed to the new commerce, now needed a Welsh grammar to talk with their community, and while the Welsh language began to carry the Bible and its controversies into the popular heart of Wales, the more Cambrian among its Cambro-Britons were raising a lament which was to echo for centuries; the quality of the Welsh language was in decline, half its products were translations, Welsh poetry had 'gone all English' and the poets were dead . . .

Between 1580 and 1587, the very years of climax for John Dee's imperial Welsh Britain, when a wholly new tradition of Welsh writing in English was launched, a fierce controversy raged in *cywyddau*, poems in the strict metres, between William Cynwal, master of the poets' guild and a Catholic, and Edmwnd Prys, Archdeacon of Merioneth and a spokesman for the New Learning. The latter called on the former and his friends to abandon a bankrupt tradition and open up Welsh to the Renaissance world; the former found Prys no poet at all. The guild faced a crisis: the new grammar schools within Wales and, more often at Shrewsbury and Westminster; the Inns of Court, the universities, the London season, the exclusion of Welsh from official business, threatened to withdraw the traditional patronage of the gentry. The invention of printing had destroyed the secrecy and exclusiveness by which the poets' guild lived. The advance of merchant and agrarian capitalism and the laws against vagrancy undercut the mode of production which had sustained them. Fraught eisteddfods were held, under royal licence, at Caerwys in 1528 and 1567 to reorganize the guild. They failed. The Old Song of Taliesin threw up few stars after the great days of Guto'r Glyn and Tudur Aled. When Gryffydd Phylip of Ardudwy died in 1666 he was counted by himself and everybody else 'the last of the old poets'. A poetic culture which had been buoyant and innovatory as late as Henry VII, stammered and disintegrated and retreated into folklore.

More significantly, little of creative substance in Welsh replaced it, except characteristically in scholarship and antiquarianism. The new generation of Welsh Tudor humanists came in with a sense of mission. They were deeply endowed, above all, with a *European* rather than strictly English feeling for the classical revival of the new learning; they shared none of the contempt for the vernacular which was common. On the contrary the British tradition and the Old Song of Taliesin seemed to them wholly admirable; they simply had to be modernized. Sion Dafydd Rhys, for example, born in Anglesey and educated at Christ Church, Oxford, spent many years in Italy and travelled to Venice, Crete and Cyprus. He took a doctorate in Siena, taught at Padua, published a book on the pronunciation of Italian at the latter place and a very popular Italian grammar at Venice. Back in Wales by 1580, he practised as a physician in Cardiff, settled in Breconshire, married a Herefordshire heiress, worked closely with Dr John Dee and brought out a Welsh grammar which tried to impose Latin rules on a Celtic tongue.

These humanists had not only learned their Geoffrey of Monmouth, but had absorbed the popular European work attributed to an alleged Chaldean historian Berosus which claimed, among other things, that the inhabitants of Britain before the Trojans were descended from Samothes, grandson of Noah; they had founded orders of Druides, Bardi and Vates from whom the guild of poets of what was thus one of the most ancient languages in the world had descended. This ran into confluence with the work of Dr John Dee (in common with the new scientists in Europe) on the Jewish Cabala, the secret language God gave to Moses, which could unearth a world which predated Christianity and Judaism and in which the ancestors of the Welsh in their vast Celtic realms appeared to have been prominent. Equipped with this kind of vision of a remote and distinguished past (which was to be strongly revived in the late eighteenth century) the humanists moved in on Welsh culture and its Song of Taliesin.

They demanded that it recover its dignity and inherit the new world. It had to shed its guild exclusiveness, abandon its silly pedigrees and its petty praise; the poets should learn European rhetoric and take on board all the new sciences, medicine, history, the art of war; they must become what they were ceasing to be, the remembrancers and educators of a modern people, like those remote Bardi of old. The humanists failed totally. The professionals rejected them and went bumbling on into their graves.

The humanists needed a new kind of patron, a capitalist patron, the amateur and up-to-date gentleman or merchant. There was a beginning in such as Captain William Midleton and the ebullient Captain Thomas Prys of Plas Iolyn (who peppered his work with the salty expertise of the seadogs!); the greatest was Edmwnd Prys himself. In poetry their impulse soon died, but in prose, which had remained alert in Glamorgan, they scored some success, mostly in the field of rhetoric, grammar and dictionary work. Much of their energy, however, was diverted into the great campaign for biblical translation. Their planned Renaissance library of modern and major works in all fields in Welsh never materialized. Where their drive struck root was in the archivization of the Welsh past. John Jones of Flintshire, a genial lawyer who spent much of his life in prison for debt, produced more than a hundred volumes of invaluable transcripts in his own hand, while Robert Vaughan of Hengwrt in Merioneth made a superb collection of early manuscripts. Many a gentleman indulged similar tastes. Not much of it came into print. Welsh culture was retreating into the museums.

The critical factor without doubt was a failure in patronage. The new economy and the new state directed the key men into English. It was not at all that they abandoned the Welsh language in a blind and greedy anglicization (as used to be declared). On the contrary, the old patronage continued, but in an antechamber style. In the last resort what decided their attitude was their changed perception of the very role and function of the Welsh language in Welsh life. They did not seem to want challenge from it, they wanted comfort and familiarity and reassurance. To me, the fate of Welsh in these years resembles that of the Dutch tradition of realist portraiture in painting after its great days of bourgeois self-assertion. The new, capitalist squirearchy faced challenge enough in English and Latin; from Welsh they did not want a challenge, they wanted a mirror, preferably tinted. Since the *British History* was crumbling under the attack of scientific history at much the same time, the Welsh language and its culture quite quickly lost contact with the modern world and shrank back into an amateur world of idle chat in a parlour or argument in a pub eisteddfod. It was the ordinary people who cherished, as central to the whole of life, a language which became increasingly oral, increasingly fragmented into local *patois*, and whose poets' guild dissolved into local *beirdd cefn gwlad* (country poets cultivating the old skills) and a world of almanacs and popular chapbooks, carol collections, interlude popular drama. In that world of the popular language, it was in an intensely religious, devotional and, increasingly, a doctrinal and disputive, culture, that a sophisticated and high-quality Welsh registered. Welsh became peculiarly a sacral language with less and less secular purchase of intellectual substance. In the end, as that people and its religion took over the cultural identity of Wales, they emerged as a People of the Book – and of a Book which was Holy. It stamped an identity on those people which proved tenacious.

It was, then, as a people which had indeed entered into its physical inheritance with the Return of Arthur, but as a people whose sense of identity had become subaltern and subject in the new Britain, that the Welsh faced the challenge of the epoch heralded by the Civil War which cut their Britain off from its Europe and launched it on a highly distinctive career. They faced that challenge, according to the London Puritans, as 'Poor Taffy, up to her knees in blood', led by their gentry in dutiful service to their indifferent king.

## Poor Taffy

In the Civil War, Poor Taffy was certainly Charles the Martyr's most loyal unknown soldier. The fighting in Wales was around its only two parliamentary strongholds, the merchant community in south Pembrokeshire where the Earl of Essex was influential, and Wrexham in the north-east, affected by Cheshire Puritanism and under the influence of the parliamentary Middletons of Chirk who made a fortune in London commerce. Sir Thomas Middleton, who was MP for Denbighshire, was the son of a Lord Mayor of London who had helped finance the Welsh Bible of 1630. Wales as a whole was a bastion of royalism and an apparently bottomless reservoir of men and money. Of the hundreds of pamphlets poured out, not one preached Parliament's cause in Welsh. The fall of Raglan to Parliament signalled the end, and Harlech was the last royalist fortress to yield. Most of the Welsh lived through the Commonwealth as an enemy occupation.

In reality, however, the royalist coalition in Wales was tenuous. Through Charles I's personal rule, county after county in Wales had defaulted on ship-money and while most Welsh MPs in the Long Parliament were royalists, the majority were also moderates. Their mind was probably best expressed by men like John Williams of Conway who was pursued with extraordinary vindictiveness by Archbishop Laud, snatched from prison by the Long Parliament and made Archbishop of York by Charles in his extremity. For what Laudian rigour exposed was a fear of its apparent Romanizing tendency by no means restricted to intransigent Puritans. Coupled with fear of the Irish, which Charles's policy did nothing to assuage, this threw many Welsh loyalists into the 'moderation' represented by the Earl of Pembroke.

They had some cause to fear, since there were Catholic strongholds on their doorsteps. Dominating the horizon was the Catholic Marquis of Worcester in his massive stronghold at Raglan Castle. Worcester had sponsored a Jesuit 'college' at Cwm in Welsh Herefordshire from 1622 and in the uplands of the south-east, notably in Monmouthshire, still hardly touched by Protestant teaching in any depth, something of a Catholic popular movement developed. Worcester was naturally a royalist fanatic – he was said to have lost £900,000 in the king's service – and the image of Wales as similarly fanatical in its royalism in fact derives from a handful of Welshmen in Worcester's entourage, notably the hero Judge David Jenkins and a cluster of related Glamorgan families, both Catholic and Protestant – Kemeys, Stradlings, Bassetts and Turbervilles.

In truth, there was a middle party of very considerable strength, for the south-east, like Denbighshire and the middle border country, also had its 'Puritan squires'. The best way to ward off the Catholic threat, to their minds, was to carry the Word to a still unregenerate people. Rhys Prichard, the Old Vicar whose carols were immensely popular, was a Pembroke protégé and was supported by the powerful family of Mansels of Margam. Together with the Morgans of Ruperra, the Prices of Briton Ferry and many others, they formed a strong Pembroke bloc, some of whose wealthiest members supported radical preachers.

For the first stronghold of Puritanism in Wales was in the south-east. Baptists appeared in the Olchon Valley of Welsh Herefordshire in the 1630s, while the congregation at Llanfaches near Chepstow got into trouble with Laud. Its vicar was William Wroth, a contemporary of Mansels and Lewises from Glamorgan at Jesus College, Oxford. Wroth was an immensely influential figure in early Dissent, not least in the Puritan city of Bristol. He was reinforced above all from Cardiff, which had produced a Protestant martyr in the sixteenth century and whose parish of Roath had become a radical hotbed. The Lewises of the Van, perhaps the wealthiest non-aristocratic family in Wales, sponsored two men at St Mary's in Cardiff whose congregation proved a seedbed of Puritans: William Erbery, who became a friend of Oliver Cromwell, and his curate, Walter Cradock from Usk. The Laudian Church took action against both. Cradock, 'a bold ignorant young fellow' according to his enemies, was deprived of his licence and set out on a career which was to make him a titanic Recruiter; his very name passed into Welsh as a synonym for Roundhead and he is still remembered in a Cardiff pub sign. He moved to Wrexham and converted the schoolboy Morgan Llwyd from Merioneth who was to become another titan, not least in the literature of the Welsh. Chased out, Cradock moved to the Puritan sanctuary of Brampton Bryan, protected by the Harleys, where he converted Vavasor Powell, a youth from Knucklas in Radnorshire. Powell was to become the greatest titan of them all. It was these men, together with some others, who launched the first 'gathered church' of Independents at Llanfaches in 1639. By that time Puritanism had struck roots not only along the border but among lesser gentry around Swansea and Llangyfelach, and was sending its first missionaries into the hill country.

At every stage such men had been supported by ardent Protestants among the Welsh gentry who naturally gravitated into that 'Pembroke party' which, like the ultras around Worcester, long outlived the nobles who were their foci. When the crisis broke in 1642, all rallied around Charles, and the Saints were blown away to Bristol and London. By 1645, however, the royalist coalition in Wales, bludgeoned by repeated levies of men and money, murky deals with the Irish and an inflow of royalist refugees, began to break up. In Glamorgan 'peaceable armies' demonstrated for compromise and throughout Wales there was wholesale defection. By 1646 the 'Pembroke party' was reappearing and working for a compromise peace with the Presbyterians in the face of a radical army. But with that army and its heterodox preachers came Powell, Llwyd and Cradock and the Committee of Plundered Ministers, to eject clergymen from their parishes and launch itinerant preachers at the Welsh. The threat to the Church now came from the Puritans, and moderate royalists, Presbyterians and disgruntled parliamentarians shuffled into an alliance in support of the imprisoned king. Manipulated by the ultras, this led to the rising of 1648 focused on the south Pembroke of the former Roundheads John Poyer and Rowland Laugharne, which spread to north Wales. In a second civil war, it brought down the New Model Army to its victory at St Fagans near Cardiff and the final reduction of Pembroke by Cromwell himself. Early in 1649 Charles was executed and Wales was exposed to the full force of the Republic, which in such a country was a revolution.

For four years the gentry lived through their 'Dark Times'. The country was run by a military puritan clique determined to transform society as radically as their allies were doing in their 'New England' across the Atlantic. Their agency was the county committee: some of the traditional gentry served and lesser branches of major families supplied recruits, but in most counties power passed to a small, often interrelated group, sometimes drawn from lesser gentry. Their regime was one of sustained proscription, confiscation and military dictatorship often scored by corruption. The Earl of Carbery's agents entrenched themselves in many counties, while in south Wales Colonel Philip Jones of Llangyfelach, a distinguished soldier, built himself into a kind of viceroy. A Buckinghamshire linen-draper, Colonel John Carter, got himself 'the best piece of Holland in the country' – Elizabeth Holland, heiress of Kinmel. Conquered Ireland offered further scope for enterprise; Henry Bowen and William Cadogan of Glamorgan carved out estates there – and the Cadogans would be earls in the next century.

But it was by no means simply an orgy of expulsions and confiscations. Many of these men were crusaders. John Jones, a freeholder of Maes-y-Garnedd in Merioneth and a Morgan Llwyd convert, married Cromwell's sister, served the Protector loyally in Ireland and was to die heroically on the scaffold as an unrepentant regicide. Colonel Philip Jones was close to the visionary Hugh Peter and it was this circle who evolved the notion of organizing Wales around a commission to propagate the Gospel. Wales was to them a dark corner and an admirable site for a radical experiment in godly government.

Ironically, therefore, it was this abused regime with its army men and preaching cobblers, drenched in the snobbish Tory spittle of the poets' spite, which proved to be the only English administration to date to treat Wales as a separate nation. The Act for the Better Propagation of the Gospel in Wales of 1650 gave the country a peculiar form of autonomy under Colonel Thomas Harrison and seventy commissioners. There were a few of the established gentry of evangelical temper like Sir Erasmus Philipps of Picton in Pembrokeshire, though most, of necessity, were English military missionaries. Philip Jones and John Jones were prominent, but the core around Harrison were men like Powell, Cradock, Llwyd, John Miles who had created the first Calvinistic Baptist church in Gower, men whom later generations would see as founding fathers of modern Wales.

They threw out nearly 300 clergymen. Their Approvers, dominated by republican intransigents, created the first state schools, fifty-nine of them, open to both sexes and offering Latin and Greek, but trying to preach regeneration to the Welsh in English. They had even more trouble finding replacements for the ministers. In came the itinerants and in came men from the hitherto invisible classes, to battle forward, often in the face of gales of hostility.

The greatest was Vavasor Powell, travelling 100 miles in a week, preaching in two or three places a day. Associated with Fifth Monarchy men who believed in the imminent Rule of the Saints and wanted all laws condensed into a pocket handbook, Powell was probably the outstanding Welshman of his time, a brilliant and fearless man not afraid to address *A Word for God...against Wickedness in High Places* to Cromwell himself. Converts sprouted wherever he spoke. A particular conquest was the uplands of the south and the border. In Merthyr Tydfil, a commercial village in upland Glamorgan, people turned on their curate and gave him a dreadful time; they crowded his church to abuse him, hoisted blacksmiths and God knows who else into trees to challenge him; they stopped his tithes. How gladly would he have rung the bells for Charles II had not his parishioners melted them down! At the height of the persecutions of the Restoration, hundreds from all over the south-east gathered there again to listen to Vavasor, briefly released from jail, before coming to blows again over total immersion in baptism.

In the north there was Morgan Llwyd, a writer of powerful Welsh and author of what became the Welsh classic *Llyfr y Tri Aderyn (Book of the Three Birds,* 1653), a man of mystical temper, a reader of Jacob Boehme, who sent John ap John of Ruabon to contact George Fox and to start the remarkable and often anarchic movement of Welsh Quakers. George Fox, on his own mission, found God raising up a people around Cader Idris in 1657. Cromwell himself thought 'God had kindled a seed' in Wales. As Presbyterians penetrated Flintshire, Baptists, Independents, Quakers multiplied along the eastern border and began to plant in the west.

By the time the Act lapsed in 1653 and the successor Triers were settling out contagious individuals like Stephen Hughes in Mydrim and Samuel Jones in Llangynwyd, such ministers were themselves being denounced as traitors to the rule of the saints. For the enterprise spilled over to produce a myriad sects and creeds, many like the Ranters or Anabaptists, often called 'Quakers', some crossing the line into a freethought, a deism, even an atheism which could draw on old and deep popular traditions of heterodox thinking. Such men, rivalling even the most radical Baptists, offered a serious threat to tithes and all established order. They were appearing in many places, from Dolgellau to the Vale of Glamorgan itself.

It was in a shudder of alarm, therefore, that many of the displaced gentry, clobbered by fines and challenged by new men in a country which seemed full of shouting, began to inch back into the county committees and to try to restore old moderate alliances, as Cromwell made himself Lord Protector and Major-General Berry, former clerk to a Shropshire ironworks, became an efficient and attractive controller in Wales. The Welsh republicans, who had been strong in Barebone's Parliament, moved into opposition. Vavasor Powell, calling Cromwell a perjured villain, tried to organize insurrection in Wales and Ireland, while Walter Cradock rallied to the regime. As the system started to come apart, there was a revival of the old alliance of royalist moderates and ultras who, to forestall the radicals, combined with Presbyterians to engineer the restoration of Charles II, with wine flowing in the conduits of Carmarthen town.

Independents and Baptists, far more numerous in Wales than the Presbyterians, caught the first full blast of repression. Nearly 120 ministers were thrown out of their livings and subjected to harsh controls. The Quakers were pursued like mad dogs. Vavasor Powell died in the jail from which he had published his *Bird in a Cage, Chirping*. Whole communities braved the horrible Atlantic crossings to create their pioneer settlements in a new world. The Quakers, now strong in Montgomeryshire and Merioneth, with their martyrs like Richard Davies of Cloddau Cochion, were to be central to the formation of Pennsylvania. The Lloyd family of Dolobran, gentry converts, supplied William Penn with his deputy. The sects continued to grow even during the repression. The Baptist mother chapel of Rhydwilym in the south-west was formed in 1668. In an arc of southern upland stretching from the Swansea area into Monmouthshire, Dissent rooted itself and began to develop remarkably radical tendencies in Arminianism, Arianism, unitarianism and even freethought. Through the sporadic indulgences offered by Charles II and James II, they persisted until at the Glorious Revolution of 1688, they won a limited but essential measure of toleration (still denied to Catholics and unitarians).

This small minority of second-class citizens, Dissenters who rejected the State Church, numbered perhaps 5 per cent of a population of around 350,000. Independents and Baptists mostly, half of them were in the south-east, in Monmouth, Glamorgan and Brecon. But they also had considerable strength in Wrexham, Flint and the north-east and had planted themselves in some force in the south-west, in Carmarthenshire, parts of Pembrokeshire and the valley of the Teifi. There was a potent bunch in mid-Wales, around Llanbrynmair and Dolgellau. Commissioners in 1684 could find only three Dissenters in Anglesey and north and west were generally a sea of conservative Anglicans, but there was a tough-minded pocket in the Llŷn peninsula and some notable, if isolated, communities elsewhere. They were 'little fellows' for the most part, men almost invisible to history like that Rhys ap Rhydderch of Llanwenog in Cardiganshire who had fought as an officer in Cromwell's army and who at the age of eighty-one led his Baptist people over to the Delaware to create an American dynasty. But they were hardly ever the poor: tradesmen, craftsmen, small farmers; lesser gentry had appeared in their ranks and would multiply, so would men from the professional classes and, in south-east and north-east, industrial artisans.

And after the great storms had passed, there they were in the land of Poor Taffy and his squires, a clutch of chapels, schools, slowly growing communities, with a memory of a time which broke kings, of their state schools, and of that Welsh national college which the Triers had proposed. Into the service of the Word, indeed, many of them moved, into academies and the printing press, to create in themselves and in the communities they were shaping in the American colonies, an alternative society with an Atlantic dimension.

Above them, the gentry returned at the Restoration, its power undiminished and its Toryism undimmed. Beneath the apparent uniformity in the onslaught on Dissent, however, the old pattern of shifts between moderates and ultras can soon be detected, around the Earl of Carbery in west Wales, Lord Herbert of Cherbury in mid-Wales, the Booths in Cheshire, above all in the developing south-east. Philip Jones survived to establish a new county family in Glamorgan and around the Mansels the old 'Pembrokian' grouping re-formed, cool towards the persecution of Nonconformists when all danger seemed to have been removed by 1666, alarmed above all by the growing power of the Somerset family, the Marquises of Worcester, transformed into Dukes of Beaufort, and buttressed by kinsfolk whom James II made Marquises of Powis in the centre and north. The fact that the heir to Worcester's power was now nominally a Protestant made the menace of covert Catholicism seem all the more real, particularly in view of the continued activism of Catholic missionaries in the south-east. The secret Catholicism of Charles II and the open Romanism of James II were difficult to cope with.

In the 1670s as Charles flirted with Dissent to secure toleration for Catholics, moderates in Wales tended to drift back towards old parliamentarians against the ultras. The Welsh Trust, an educational enterprise of Puritan temper which allied moderate Dissenters and Anglicans in 1672 when Charles issued his Indulgence, came to serve as something of a focus for opposition to Worcester and the court. When indulgence ended within a year, to be replaced by the Test Act excluding non-Anglicans from office, Catholics were the target, as the Whigs tried to whip up a campaign to exclude James from the succession. Conflict reached a climax in the hideous outbreak of witch-hunting over the Popish Plot of 1678 and 1679. In a violent action in southern Wales, the Catholic seminary in Cwm was raided and sacked, priests were thrown into jail and there was heavy confiscation. Four Welsh priests, two of them Jesuits, were hanged in a savage persecution. In 1679, eleven of twenty-seven Welsh MPs voted for the Exclusion of James. In these circumstances, many of the old Roundheads came bubbling back to the surface and there were rumours about a return of the Quakers and Vavasor Powell's people. In consequence there was a sharp reaction in the 1680s, a massive renewal of persecution of Dissenters, major emigrations to America and Holland. Not until 1685 was some calm restored to Welsh politics in an uncomfortable reunification of Tory moderates and ultras. No sooner was this achieved than they had to confront a headstrong James II.

By this time it had become clear that Welsh political life, apparently unaltered even in its repeatedly renewed gentry feuds, had in fact experienced a subtle but decisive shift.

In the late seventeenth century, the land market which had been fluid for so long closed up. There was pressure on rents, a reduction in the number of estates, an increasing concentration of landed power and wealth. Wholly new patterns of trade were opening up as new rivalries with the French and the Dutch displaced the old. In the already developing regions such as Denbigh and Glamorgan, this induced shifts of interest and power between greater and lesser gentry and newer professional classes, but over much of Wales something seemed to go wrong: the smaller squire was staggering in the saddle. Hard hit under the Commonwealth and with their mortgages piling up, they found the world closing in. It was the bigger men now, who made the running. Bulkeleys, Vaughans, Middletons, Mostyns and the rest began to monopolize parliamentary representation and the universities. The lesser gentry began to drop out of even the traditional Inns of Court and shrank back to a merely local prestige.

This was a Wales passing into the hands of its greater men, themselves often changing abruptly through accidents in inheritance, a Wales which was finding less and less room for what had been the peculiarly Welsh classes and seemed to be losing an easily identifiable personality. It still sent its top men into positions of power – a Lord Chancellor, two Secretaries of State, two Speakers, a Chief Justice for Charles and nearly all his principal law officers for James. Most of them came now, however, not from Welsh county society or its parliamentary families but from the English law courts and the royal court itself. Some were men of distinction: Sir John Vaughan of Cardiganshire established the right of juries to judge by their conscience; Sir John Trevor was that rare bird, an incorruptible Secretary of State, and so was a successor from humbler origins, who endowed a good school at Cowbridge, Sir Leoline Jenkins. Most, however, were standard Restoration politicians and the best-known Welsh recruit to the world of the late Stuarts (unless Nell Gwynn's surname is significant) was Judge Jeffreys, an unmitigated and murderous careerist, but one who was loyal to the death (preferably somebody else's).

It was a somewhat disoriented Tory squirearchy which had to confront James II who, completely misreading their loyalism, launched his truly revolutionary attacks on every aspect of the Anglican establishment – Church, army, universities, finally the JP lists. To cap it all, in Wales he proposed to make the Catholic Marquis of Powis President of the Council, and unable to find many Catholics for the Bench, permitted the emergence of JPs who were not only Dissenters but survivors of some of the more radical sects of the Commonwealth. There was a mushroom growth of Whiggism and a wholesale if reluctant transfer of Tories to William of Orange. It was this distinctly unhappy political class which had to support the Glorious Revolution of 1688 and to live through the granting of toleration to Cradocks and Roundheads, the creation of the Bank of England, a war against their own James which created what became the Royal Welch Fusiliers and all the sickening lurches between William III, Anne and the Hanoverians.

As they slumped sourly into their Jacobite drinking clubs, they faced a more subtle and long-term challenge. In 1707 by the Union of Scotland and England, a union of crowns became a union of peoples, a significant punctuation point in that process which was to turn two off-shore and out-of-step islands of Europe into the centre of the most advanced capitalist agriculture in that Europe, to create an unheard-of and monstrous capital city in London and to make the new and far more real *Great Britain* into the greatest merchant empire in the world. Wales of the squires found itself a sector of the Atlantic economy and Atlantic empire of an unprecedented Great Britain which was creating a *British nation.*

# 7 · WELSH IN A GREAT BRITAIN

'I am giving you the Patriarchal religion and theology, the Divine Revelation given to Mankind and these have been retained in Wales until our own day.' It was Iolo Morganwg speaking in 1792, a stonemason Bard of Liberty from the Vale of Glamorgan and a leading figure, along with vivacious London-Welsh societies, in a Welsh literary-historical revival. He was announcing to the Welsh the rediscovery of their ancient Druidic tradition; he was giving them, for the first time in two centuries, a coherent vision of their own past, to inform and direct the re-creation of their nation. He was offering them, in his newly minted *gorsedd,* or Order of Bards of the Island of Britain, a democratic organization of their intelligentsia, a cadre of people's remembrancers, as its instrument.

A few months earlier, at one of the eisteddfods which the London-Welsh had revived in order to re-engage an interrupted tradition, in Llanrwst, a market centre of the Atlantic stocking trade of an intensely poor and intensely Welsh mountain people, William Jones, a follower of Voltaire who lived in the village of Llangadfan and worked as a teacher and country healer among the Welsh and Congregationalist weavers of Montgomeryshire, with their overseas markets, circulated a dramatic Address. It announced that the Lost Brothers, the Welsh Indians descended from that brave and peace-loving prince Madoc who had discovered America three hundred years before Columbus, had been found on the far Missouri . . . 'a free and distinct people . . . who . . . have preserved their liberty, language and some trace of their religion to this very day . . .' William Jones read the whole history of the Welsh as one long struggle against English oppression. He was composing a Welsh national anthem 'Toriad y Dydd, (Daybreak), as a counter to *The Roast Beef of Old England,* and he called on the Welsh to quit their Egyptian slavemasters and join their Lost Brothers to re-create Wales in the new Land of Liberty.

A few months later, in 1793, Morgan John Rhys, a Baptist minister of Pontypool in the industrializing south, who published the French freethinker Volney in Welsh translation and would have published Voltaire had not his printer taken fright, brought out the first number of a magazine, *Y Cylchgrawn Cymraeg* (The Welsh Journal), which became the first political periodical in the Welsh language. Morgan John had launched a crusade for Protestant liberty in the revolutionary France of 1792. As the self-appointed Moses of the Welsh nation, he was to ride the length of the new American Republic in 1794–5, to fight for a black church in Savannah, Georgia and for Indian identity at the peace talks at Greenville, Ohio which expelled the Iroquois from history. In 1795 he was to stand on 'the unbroken grass' west of that Ohio and on Bastille Day claim the American frontier as a national home for the Welsh people, a *gwladfa*. In his *Journal* he printed an exhortation from a resurrected and Jacobin Madoc to the renaissant Welsh: *Dyma ni yn awr ar daith ein gobaith* (Here we are now on the journey of our hope).

In the 1790s a handful of intellectuals in Wales, in common with men like them from other 'non-historic' peoples in Europe, those antiquarians, historians, poets, of the Czechs, the Catalans, Serbs and Croats, who were stamping nations out of the ground and weaving new tricolours out of old legends, summoned the Welsh to re-create the nation they had rediscovered. When they encountered indifference, hostility and repression in the Great Britain of the age of the Atlantic revolution, they tried to transport that Welsh nation across the Atlantic.

This nation of the intellectuals was born of an alternative society which had been slowly forming in Wales under the carapace of the gentry–parson squirearchy and which, no less than that *ancien régime,* was a product of the new Great Britain with its Atlantic dimension.


## Great Britain and its Atlantic Province

Great Britain, as a human reality rather than a ritual title, took shape around the union of England and Scotland in 1707 and was built on merchant capitalism, imperialism, naval power, a modernized agriculture and liberal oligarchy. In its sweep to maritime supremacy, its hegemony over the Atlantic trade and its slave economies, the unparalleled productivity of its agrarian society and the unprecedented exploitation of its subject Irish granary, in its uniquely dominant capital of London sucking in talent from the four corners, it evolved a highly unusual structure in which what was in fact a multinational state (with the so-called Celtic Fringe providing 46 per cent of its population) achieved a British uniformity. More, it progressively created a *British* nation, which became a living reality in Scotland and Wales and even in sectors of Ireland, nowhere more visibly than in the land of the original Britons, where its 'Rule Britannia' and its

'Britons, strike home!' struck an old chord. This nation achieved its deep penetration among ordinary people during the traumatic experience of the generation-long war against Revolutionary and Napoleonic France at a peak of its first surge into industrial power, when Wellington and Nelson were erected into *British* heroes and 'God Save Great George our King' (and confound their knavish and Jacobin tricks) into a *British* national anthem. When Lord Nelson and Lady Hamilton reached the Cyfarthfa ironworks at Merthyr Tydfil in Glamorgan to see the men who were making his ships' cannon, Richard Crawshay, a shirt-sleeves-to-the-peerage entrepreneur if there ever was one, took the hero's arm and shouted, 'Here's Nelson, boys! Cheer, you buggers!' Cheer they certainly did and the buggers have gone on cheering ever since.

The battles of the seventeenth century had destroyed absolutism and demystified monarchy, had established a Bank of England, religious toleration, a governing aristocracy which directed the state to mercantile objectives; they had created a powerful civil society and an oligarchical Parliament which could hire kings from the Dutch and the Germans. After the partisan conflicts of the later Stuarts were over, this polity, after disarming the provinces, putting through a prudent restriction of the franchise and taking the heat and the principle out of politics, was able to ride commercial and agrarian growth into an extraordinarily relaxed and informal system of government. It had to tolerate a licensed area of popular anarchy in times of shortage. It erected a law in defence of property and oligarchy which was terrifying in its severity but, except at moments of crisis, tolerant in its application. It won a moment of consent which lasted a century and which acquired popular depth and resonance, particularly during the French wars. The government of this Great Britain reduced politics to the play of predatory faction around a Whig core under a broad, flexible, semi-capitalist, innovatory and episodically ruthless oligarchy which, in its hustings, its licensed mobs, its flexible web of libertarian traditions and its Freeborn Englishman mentality, permitted the commons a voice. Not until the twin challenge of the American and French Revolutions did it have to systematize this peculiar English liberty (duly extended to Britons) into an ideology.

Within this state and its developing nation, the Welsh, like the Slovaks in Austria-Hungary, had disappeared into the dominant partner. Their pattern of response, in resistance and assimilation, was not un-Slovak either, though the organic intelligentsia which the growth of Great Britain created in its Welsh province at the end of the eighteenth century behaved more like Czechs.* For the backward land of Poor Taffy was allotted what was to become its modern role: to serve as the export base of an imperial British economy.

Copper, tinplate and their related industries had been planted in Swansea-Neath and Pontypool since Tudor times. During the eighteenth century 90 per cent of British production was concentrated there and yoked to the mines of northern Anglesey, where Thomas Williams could carve out virtually a world monopoly. This was directed almost wholly to Atlantic export, particularly the West Indies and the world which the slave empire fed and sustained. By 1720 the scattered charcoal furnaces of south Wales were producing a sixth of British pig-iron. The Shropshire iron industry, going over to coal, pulled well ahead and by 1788 was producing twice as much. By that year, however, south Wales had seen the first giant and integrated plants raised on its hill-country coalfield by London, Bristol and local capital derived from the Atlantic slave trade and the Indian empire, and serviced by Midlands technology. It was beginning to use coal, and in the puddling process, 'the Welsh method' had just acquired the key to its meteoric expansion in the 1790s when it established a 40 per cent grip on the pig-iron production of Britain. ** Shropshire, whose technicians were revolutionizing iron production in Monmouth and Glamorgan, was performing the same service for Denbighshire and Flintshire, whose industrial growth at this time was of a southern intensity. There were the beginnings of another centre of monopoly of British production in the slate districts of the north-west and a steady development in the lead of the western coasts and in every exploitable mineral. The ultimate destination of iron and other products is less visible, with Ireland looming large as an early customer, but the great bulk went either into export or into British trades which serviced export or into the service of such trades. This whole sector of the economy, drawing more and more people and indirectly affecting more and more districts, was essentially mercantile-imperial in character.

*Slovaks were much slower to disengage themselves from Magyars than Czechs were from Germans. Czech intellectuals started to define themselves as a Czech nation in the age of the French Revolution; it was these Czech intellectuals who were to initiate the process among the Slovaks themselves. Summary account in A.J.P. Taylor, *The Habsburg Monarchy* (Hamish Hamilton, 1948).

**Puddling, invented simultaneously in Hampshire and Cyfarthfa works, enabled coal to be used to make malleable iron. It was embraced so swiftly and totally in south Wales, that it came to be called 'the Welsh method' and immediately boosted productivity, which was maintained despite the bottlenecks in supply which ensued. A skilled, organized and powerful group of workers emerged around the process; they were for a generation the vanguard of popular action in south Wales.

This was no less true of more traditional, less heavily capitalized trades, which were turning whole tracts of rural Wales into networks of factory parishes. The cloth trade had migrated to mid and north Wales since Tudor times and was subjected to the Drapers' Company of Shrewsbury. Its farm-based production was transforming the country people of a great tranche of Wales, running from Machynlleth on the west coast in a broad arc through Merioneth and Montgomeryshire to Denbigh and the borderlands, into a population of farmer-weavers, rural workers in industry, whose demographic and life-chance rhythms were radically different from those of traditional 'peasants' (one cause of the population explosion in Wales, which was a rural phenomenon). The flannels of Montgomeryshire went out through Blackwell Hall to Europe and the Americas, and even the poorer quality webs of Merioneth and its intense stocking trade which could produce sales of £18,000 in local markets at Bala and Llanrwst, were shipped out through the busy little port of Barmouth to Charleston and the Gulf of Mexico, to serve British soldiers, poor whites and American slaves.

The upland farming of Wales, which had embraced many of its people, was geared to a massive outside market and had developed a major drovers' trade in store cattle which sent great herds seasonally into England, to bring back currency, breed banks and a bunch of sometimes maverick intellectuals who were to prove of some cultural importance. This lively, if porous, merchant capitalism was steadily transforming much of rural Wales, creating pockets of modernization and reservoirs of technical skills, and turning the economy of a country measuring scarcely 200 miles from end to end into a plurality of modes of production. Certainly, if there *were* any 'peasants' in Wales in 1700, there were not many left by 1800. What replaced them was the working population of an export economy to which its working women were central. Women formed the heart and core of a nascent 'working class' dispersed through this economy. Other younger, single women staffed that army of domestic servants who were by far the largest single occupational group.

Characteristically, the largest concentration of people in Wales was around its biggest fair in Wrexham, with 8,000 people in its parishes. Swansea, with some 6,000, had developed into a fully articulated, if miniature, mercantile, social and intellectual capital. The whole of the south and Denbighshire in the north had a scattering of industry and improving landlords; the Vale of Glamorgan and south Pembrokeshire were the nearest approach to the champion farming of the English south. Even the uplands of the south were caught up; Merthyr Tydfil, long before iron had struck root there to take it to 8,000 people in 1801, had an artisan and commercial population on its ninety-three farms, with markets serving a very wide area; it was as celebrated for its auctioneers as for its clock-makers. There was a cluster of little but lively towns, oversupplied with artisan crafts, professional men and printers, such as Carmarthen, Brecon, Haverfordwest, Neath, Denbigh and Caernarfon. There was a numerous and brisk fraternity of seamen and shipmasters along the western coasts facing Ireland and the Atlantic.

This measured but remorseless penetration of merchant capitalism had not yet effected any profound structural change in society or social perception. Ranges of people still worked on traditional small farms and most people were still poor. The Welsh population of about half a million was still pinned to the mountain core of Wales's hollow heart. The stockings which went out to the Gulf of Mexico from Merioneth were knitted by a poverty-stricken people who used to gather over the winter at chosen farmhouses to save candles. Entertained by harpists and singers, they turned the area into a legendary stronghold of Welsh culture as it was later to be of Dissenter ministers and craggy polemicists arguing over biblical texts in the Sunday schools. There was a very similar stocking-trade concentration in the south-west around Tregaron and Llandovery in a land no less legendary in the history and mythology of Welsh-language popular culture and Dissent. This area in the south-west, particularly Cardiganshire, upland Carmarthenshire and north Pembrokeshire, was where a traditional farming persisted longest and traditional farmers with it. But it was also the Galicia or the Ireland of Wales, a land which lived by the seasonal migration of its working people to the lowlands and England; it was to become the human matrix of the industrial society to the east and it was the region of Wales in most direct human contact with the America of the Nonconformists.

Generally, this core of the British imperial economy was itself colonial. North Wales was passing from the control of Shrewsbury into that of Liverpool; Bristol enmeshed the south. The London-Welsh were still the main source of native funds and enterprise to a people of small commodity producers. Many of the Welsh, on their upland farms and at their treadmill of loom and spinning wheel and domestic drudgery, were trapped in a back-breaking poverty and an unremitting colonial dependence which sent great droves of skinny cattle and skinny people seasonally tramping into England to be fattened.

Nevertheless there was a panic over American Independence in Dolgellau in 1775 and it was when Barmouth was closed during the Revolutionary wars that Merioneth, like Denbighshire and Montgomeryshire, lurched into its *Jacobin* crises of proletarianization, pauperization, radicalization and millenarian emigration. Merchant capitalism, with its multiplying array of rural workers, its small concentrations of urban industry, its little colonies of skilled workers, its shipping fleets, its merchants, salesmen and hucksters, its drovers; above all, perhaps, in the crafts and professions it called into existence or nurtured to service it, was sending ripples of insistent change through slow-moving parishes. Throughout the century there is a shuffling but increasingly visible rise in the numbers of artisans, craftsmen, professional agents of the service trades, many of them 'on tramp', and a notable increase in the strength of the professions – lawyers, teachers, doctors, a surprising number of whom were of relatively humble origin; shopkeepers were colonizing whole reaches of society.

This steady rise of what later generations would call a lower-middle and artisan class was accompanied in many parts of Wales by a steady fall in the political status of the numerically strong lesser gentry. The squires had emerged from their fifteenth-century adolescence to enter into their inheritance under the Tudors and early Stuarts, efficiently building up their estates, moving into government jobs, monopolizing JP lists with their parsons, putting their money into trade, giving Wales its most celebrated modern dynasties – Wynns, Perrots, Phillipses, Mansels, Stradlings, Matthews. But from the late seventeenth century, serious landholding became once more an aristocratic business and a thrusting one, requiring expertise, managers, capital. The great estate made all the running. In many parts of Wales the lesser gentry could not stand the pace. They lost their traditional anchorage in the Inns of Court and the universities, in politics and Parliament. They lost their toehold in the dominant culture and shrank back into a merely local prestige. Even there, they were increasingly challenged in their cultural leadership by the multiplying middle orders. In other parts of Wales there was less a drop-out from conventional politics than a shift into newer forms of economy and political action. But everywhere the consequences were serious for Wales's political structure and its sense of identity.

It is possible to present a summary description of Welsh political structure during the prosperity of the mid-eighteenth century. Broadly speaking, some thirty to forty parliamentary families worth perhaps £3,000 to £5,000 a year monopolized Commons seats and the patronage which went with them. Beneath them, the local gentry, the £500-a-year men, perhaps twenty-five to fifty families a county, served as JPs and, with their parsons, ran the place through their country club of a Quarter Sessions. In some affluent shires like Glamorgan and Denbigh, as many as 1,500 men could vote and the forty-shilling freeholder was a force. The tiny boroughs, forty villages in the squires' pockets, were well under control. Voters could be created virtually at will to ward off local malcontents or some new rich 'nabob' horning in. Before the constitutional crises of the late eighteenth century, genuinely political issues were largely absent and rarely disturbed the even tenor of traditional practice among the 20,000 or 25,000 Welshmen who possessed the franchise, though a challenge could turn elections into Eatanswill orgies and precipitate bankruptcies. In a country markedly poorer than England, whose gentry were a joke in the capital, this system, lubricated by Church-and-King ideologies which could find room for Welsh sentiment, if suitably antiquarian or anodyne, worked well enough for its purposes and was to prove durable.

In general terms, such a description is broadly accurate, but it masks highly important divergences in space and time. These have been spotlit in a startling manner by a recent, and revolutionary, in-depth study of the county of Glamorgan and its gentry.* Glamorgan bore not the slightest resemblance to the Welsh gentry of metropolitan mythology. In the first place it was genuinely a gentry society; by 1700 the dominance of magnate families had faded. The most gentrified counties in England were Surrey and Hertfordshire, with a great house every 5,000 and 7,000 acres respectively. Most Welsh counties came nowhere near this: Carmarthen boasted a great house every 294,000 acres; Pembrokeshire, every 393,000 – Glamorgan, with a house every 65,000 acres, stood with the western English counties. In fact, all its great houses were concentrated exclusively in its Vale, which was as gentrified as the English Home Counties.

Moreover, these families were very wealthy. As early as 1700, a dozen men had an income of over £2,000 a year and eighteen over £1,000. A great house like the Morgans of Tredegar in Monmouthshire or the Mostyns in Flint could chalk up £3–4,000 in that period but men with over £1,000 were very rare. The dominant house of the Vaughans in Cardiganshire lived on £1,500; there were ten houses in Glamorgan at that level. During the eighteenth century the wealth of the Glamorgan gentry increased massively. What was counted a large estate in the region of Paris was held by many a yeoman in the Vale of Glamorgan; fifty Glamorgan men held the equivalent of the 'great estate' of the wealthy Republic of Venice. The commercial French nobles of the Toulouse district (an area comparable in size to Glamorgan), 226 of them, held 44 per cent of its land; in Glamorgan

*Philip Jenkins, *The making of a ruling class: the Glamorgan gentry 1640–1790* (Cambridge University Press, 1983).

forty-seven men owned 80 per cent of its territory. There were nineteen men in Glamorgan who owned more land than the seven richest nobles of Toulouse, some of them four, six, nine times as much. The richest marquis in Toulouse owned the same amount of land as the Reverend John Carne of Nash.

In Glamorgan, while there was certainly a concentration of landed power during the century, the lesser gentry did not so much 'drop out' as switch their enterprise (and often their politics) into fields which brought them into contact with burgeoning groups among the 'middle orders'. For the gentry community was totally dedicated to modernization; it developed as many industries as it could – copper, coal, iron, textiles – and located itself squarely in the mainstream of British imperial growth; by the early eighteenth century its interests lay in the 'blue-water' strategy of British commercial imperialism. It was precisely around this commitment that its community achieved a comfortable political consensus from mid-century onwards.

Earlier the feuds of Stuart times had continued, with the mushroom rise and fall of politically favoured families. By the 1720s, while Whigs had appeared, Tories in Glamorgan had organized a fine political network, developed through Freemasonry, and carried considerable clout in both opposition and government circles in London. There was a commitment to Jacobitism which was serious during the crises at the Hanoverian succession. By the Rising of 1745, however, Jacobitism was of little practical account and from mid-century both the Tories and the Whigs built up largely by government support had settled into the familiar pattern of eighteenth-century patronage politics. The fear of Dissent had largely disappeared (they were more alarmed by Methodists who seemed a throw-back to the seventeenth century), indifference and deism were widespread and there was a total commitment to the values of the new imperial and commercial Britain.

By that time, in little more than a generation, the gentry class had been transformed. In 1700 most of the great families had been established for at least two generations and several for three centuries. The Mansels, Herberts, Carnes, Matthews, Bassetts and the rest were the product of steady organic growth. During the early eighteenth century this community dissolved as male lines gave out and heiresses were married off, and there was a remarkable turnover in families. Of thirty-one great estates in 1750, only ten were occupied by males of the original line; only four great houses were occupied by the same families in 1770 as in 1650. The county's ruling elite became much more English. Of the twenty-five greatest gentlemen in the 1760s, twelve came from families with no recent Welsh connections. The Welsh families tended to come from what had been minor stocks and many of those were non-resident. Moreover there was a major return of the aristocracy. A group of very rich peers moved in, Talbots, Plymouths, Butes, Vernons, later still Dynevors and Dunravens.

The ideology of the class was transformed. A great wave of rebuilding from the 1760s testified to the reconstruction of county society. The new men introduced new concepts of property, law and order, to be countered by new forms of popular protest, in riot, sabotage, resistance to the militia and wrecking. The gentry were devising a new-model prison even as they rapidly equipped the county for its industrial take-off. They were, in short, members of a British ruling class, grounded in landed oligarchy, which was adopting the values of industrial capitalism.

And while patronage tended to continue in an older style, it was now that the barrier of language between governors and governed became acute in Glamorgan; they were accused of abandoning the historical and antiquarian concern with identity which had characterized the older elite. Such concerns, indeed, tended to become a hallmark of a new opposition which was no less 'modern'. Stemming from the old 'country' oppositionism of Tories and interpenetrating in Freemasonry, it shifted towards the older and newer middle groups. By the time of the Wilkes troubles and the American War, Glamorgan had generated a Patriot movement very similar to those contemporary Patriot movements in America, Ireland, Holland and England itself. This embraced a wide range of classes and was to fall apart only in the black reaction precipitated by the French Revolution.

No other Welsh county, of course, would reproduce this striking configuration, but many of the forces at work in Glamorgan can certainly be detected in Denbighshire and Flintshire in the north-east which, in some senses, played the role of a Glamorgan in that region. There was certainly a massive magnate presence in the Watkin Williams Wynns of Wynnstay, the 'kings of the north', but there was also early industrialization, absorption in a British mainstream, an increasingly complex society and, in the late eighteenth century, the emergence of a Patriot movement. In Monmouthshire, too, under the shadow of the Beauforts and the Morgans of Tredegar, and later in the century in Anglesey, strong modernizing tendencies can be detected.

It is when you cross the central massif into the west that matters seem to become simpler and more classical; it was here that reaction to the new Methodism and a resurgent Dissent was to be so harsh. Certainly in Caernarfon and Merioneth, the growing concentration of landlordism, the political eclipse of a lesser gentry (some of whom found an outlet in Methodism), the slow rise of the newer middling orders are visible. The same forces were at work in the south-west, but this had its own complexities. Great families could dominate Carmarthenshire, Cardiganshire and Pembrokeshire, but there was much rivalry, which enmeshed lesser gentry and made Carmarthen a by-word for ferocity in faction. The population pressure, heavier here than anywhere in Wales, and that seasonal migration which was a way of life for many of the inhabitants, were differentiating factors.

Throughout Wales, however, though the chronology of change may differ, the same determining forces were at work. There is the heavy commitment to the opposition around 1714, with Jacobitism a major power, its strong societies, the Cycle of the White Rose in the north-east and of the Sea Serjeants in the south-west enrolling many leading figures; there is the build-up of Whigs on government patronage and the great shift from mid-century when Jacobitism, despite the involvement of Sir Watkin Williams Wynn in the Rising of 1745 and the execution of David Morgan of Merthyr after it, goes into eclipse. The demographic crisis of the nobility and gentry was far less serious than in Glamorgan, but a profusion of Welsh heiresses, traditionally marketed during the Bath season, led to the intrusion of English and Anglo-Scottish houses, who together with the greater Welsh clans, Vaughans and Pryses in mid-Wales, Middletons in the north-east, Wynns and Bulkeleys throughout the north, established a political dominance or even monopoly which lasted nearly two hundred years. There are the same shifts and changes among lesser gentry and middling orders, and towards the end of the century, when the west in particular was disrupted by the impact of industrial capitalism and war, the emergence of a new opposition.

Everywhere the process tended to open up cleavages between classes and languages and to empty Welsh political life of any recognizably Welsh content. By 1830 Wales's own judicial system, the Great Sessions, could be abolished with hardly an eyebrow raised. Within the Church, the situation from this point of view was probably worse. That Church has been grotesquely slandered by an inflated Nonconformist mythology from the nineteenth century. There were plenty of dedicated clergymen, dedicated in particular to popular religious instruction, which gave the Welsh press a significant boost and was perhaps the major contribution to Welsh-language literature. But the dioceses were poor, history had shuffled off much of their patronage into lay control which was increasingly indifferent. The episcopate was virtually as blank towards the Welsh as it had been in the fifteenth century and proved to be peculiarly obstructive towards the intensely Welsh Methodist movement stirring within it. Absenteeism and pluralism were spectacular even for this century and the Church as a whole was a broad-bottomed and Whig corporation. One of its bishops was accused of atheism by his own clergy and several others in fact may have been non-Christian. Clergy in the middling and lower ranges and committed laymen, in their evangelicalism, came to feel more and more distanced and alienated. When the challenge became serious from the 1780s, the Church offered no powerful alternative to the multiplying Dissenter and Methodist competitors. Lesser clergy were following lesser gentry into a kind of limbo within their own country. In different regions and often for different reasons and in different ways, men of short purse (whether they were shortening or lengthening), long pedigree (or none), diminished (or potential) prestige, tended to cultivate an alternative system of values.

But an alternative system of values, ideologies, leadership, an alternative society in embryo, already existed in the literally transatlantic world of Dissent and its fellow-travellers, in the strengthening communities of artisans, craftsmen, local professional groups and commercialized farming families with cultural aspirations. The peculiar development of Great Britain in this, one of its marginal yet mercantile provinces, was slowly but remorselessly prising its society apart, opening a gulf between classes and languages, depersonalizing it and creating intellectual and moral space for alternatives.

In the late eighteenth century this Great Britain, with the loss of its American colonies, suffered its first post-colonial crisis which was also in some respects a British civil war of the mind, at the very moment when economic growth accelerated, industrial capitalism massively penetrated Wales and quantitative growth became qualitative. At that moment a freemasonry of organic intellectuals from the excluded classes equally abruptly proclaimed the rebirth of a Welsh nation. They were unconscious heralds of a generation of explosive change which actually created one.

## An Alternative Society

One major source of an alternative society lay in the scattered groups of chapels, societies and schools of Dissent, inheritors of the Puritan Revolution who rejected the State Church, now grouped into three major denominations, the Independents (Congregationalists) Baptists and Presbyterians. Granted a limited toleration, they were still denied full citizenship and at the national level had formed an effective pressure group with a London committee of the Three Denominations directed at the Whigs and Parliament. In Wales they were a small minority but an influential one, rooted in people of some substance and independence in direct contact with humbler classes.

Those 'common people' of Wales, the *gwerin* (folk) as they were later to be called in idealistic salute after their conversion to Nonconformity, were largely monoglot Welsh, though an instrumental knowledge of English was spreading from the borders and market towns. They lived a Welshness in which the old language, excluded from official life, was essentially oral and becoming undisciplined, strongly scored by regional diversity, but in which survivors of the old poets' guild continued to exist as country poets and local patrons and in which popular traditions were shaping into a 'way of life' strongly folkloric in character: muscular games and sports, ballads, story-tellings, wordplay, distinctive communal and marriage customs of informal vigour, popular and generally picaresque festivals erratically punctuated by beery and incoherent 'eisteddfods' and penetrating a printed literature marginal to polite discourse through ephemeral ballad collections and the ever-popular almanacs. Out of this world was growing, under careful tutelage, the complex contrapuntal harp-song called *penillion* (which in the end became as demanding as the *cante jondo* of the Andalusians) and, in more sprawling fashion, a popular drama, beginning as a plebeian kind of *commedia dell'arte*, the *anterliwt* (interlude).

If Dissent were to grow, it needed to penetrate and ultimately capture these people, but it was conscious of what it considered superior intellect, strengthened as it absorbed eighteenth-century science, and to a lesser extent, of its character as a Calvinist Elect. To join Dissent was to distance oneself. During the relative prosperity of the mid-century among farmers and the middle orders of the service trades, from which Dissent drew much of its support, it tended to become absorbed in its own intense intellectual life. This led on to an immersion in the eighteenth-century Enlightenment which was to produce startling results when its evangelicalism was renewed in the challenges of the last years of the century, which made the 1790s an intellectual cauldron of competing ideologies in Wales.

Its intellectual absorption in the early years coincided with a remarkable burst of publishing in Wales in that same service of the Word which had characterized the Commonwealth. From the date of the first printed book in Welsh in 1546 to 1660, 108 Welsh books are known to have been printed. From 1660 to 1730 the output more than quintupled to 545, building up from ten to 180 a decade. Patronage of Welsh letters was clearly withering, particularly in the eastern and southern counties and among the London-

Welsh, where in 1718 Moses Williams appealed in vain to its smugly prosperous Society of Ancient Britons, a Hanoverian loyalist society which sponsored charity schools. While there were houses like the Williamses of Aberpergwm who sponsored work on Wales in both languages, the major antiquarian collections tended to drift from the south into the north-east, to generate much scholarly activity there. The foci of support were in the west and the north.

Out of this marginal world, hardly visible to majority society, came some of the major Welsh classics; Charles Edwards's *Hanes y Ffydd Ddi-Ffuant* (A History of the Faith), with dazzling images, in 1677; Ellis Wynne's *Gweledigaethau'r Bardd Cwsc* (Visions of the Sleeping Poet) in 1703, one of the most brilliant satires in Welsh, based on the Spaniard Quevedo and the Cockney School in England. Theophilus Evans, a mid-Wales vicar, produced the first version of his *Drych y Prif Oesoedd* (Mirror of the Early Ages) in 1716, which faithfully reproduced the mirages of the old *brut*. For as Geoffrey of Monmouth was driven out of respectable life, he found his last defenders here. Patriotism was a prime motive for trying to publish anything at all in a singularly unprofitable language like Welsh. Another was shame at the state of the language and fear for its future . . . was our 'lingua . . . to be English'd out of Wales as Latin was barbarously Goth'd out of Italy'? Overriding all else was the feeling inherited, even by more liberally inclined Anglicans, from the Interregnum, that the Welsh were a dark people to be illumined. Not even some of the most cherished Welsh classics were to be reprinted by these people . . . 'babes must be fed with milk' and with books directed at the family hearth.*

Of the 545 books printed between 1660 and 1730, 205 were devotional and didactic works and 117 were religious verse. Only the eighty-one everlasting almanacs came anywhere near them in number. Before 1695 most of them had to be printed in London, but the relaxation of the licensing laws then allowed Thomas Jones, the son of a Corwen tailor, to open up the first Welsh printing shop in Shrewsbury, to be challenged almost at once by John Jones of Wrexham, an almanac-monger. A ferocious war of the words was transcended by the appearance of the first print-shop in Wales itself in 1718, in the village of Trefhedyn near Newcastle Emlyn in south Cardiganshire. This launched the Welsh printing profession on its amazing career from one of its more amazing centres. Printers seem

*Sentiments widely voiced at the time and quoted from such diverse sources as Colonel John Jones addressing Morgan Llwyd, Jeremy Owen in his *The Goodness and Severity of God* (1717) and William Richards's *Wallography* (1682) in a seminal study by Geraint H. Jenkins, *Literature, Religion and Society in Wales 1660 – 1730* (University of Wales Press, 1978).

to have bubbled in the area; even Lewis Morris who was a north Wales chauvinist had to give up Anglesey in the end and go for what became the first major publishing centre in the busy little town of Carmarthen. The 140 Welsh authors we know of from this period covered an equally wide social range, over seventy from the north and fifty from the south, though an east–west split would probably be more accurate; nominal Anglicans outnumbered Dissenters by four to one, but alongside the forty clergymen authors there were twenty-two Dissenting ministers. This heavy overrepresentation of Dissent stems from the crusading passion generated by such people as Stephen Hughes of Swansea, an ejected minister as many were; a man of total dedication and captivating charm, he more than anyone secured the co-operation of Anglicans in those major drives against illiteracy which characterize the period.

As soon as the first persecution had lifted in 1672, Thomas Gouge, with the help of Stephen Hughes and some Anglicans, launched the Welsh Trust as a charity, and for a short period up to 2,000 Welsh children a year were taught in its schools. The medium it used was English, though it distributed Welsh books and in 1678 sponsored a new Welsh Bible and distributed 1,000 copies to the poor. More serious was the enterprise of the Society for the Promotion of Christian Knowledge which together with the Society for the Propagation of the Gospel and societies for the improvement of manners, embraced Wales within their missionary and Atlantic compass. They achieved considerable success, with the support of patrons like the gentry family of Philipps of Picton Castle and the merchant–industrialist Sir Humphrey Mackworth. Between 1700 and 1740 some ninety-six schools were set up, with a broad and successful curriculum. They started to founder after the 1720s as Jacobitism split the gentry and charges of Methodism were flung around. Although Welsh books were distributed these, too, operated in English; Welsh was regarded as at best a nuisance, at worst a barbaric survival.

Out of this movement, however, Griffith Jones, an Anglican clergyman from Llanddowror who had been one of its schoolmasters, invented a distinctive system of itinerant teachers. With a minimum curriculum of biblical reading and the use of mobile teachers and apprentices, he grounded his schools in the Welsh language and geared them, in three-month bursts, precisely to the rhythms of living and working of hill communities of the poor. Backed by the money of Madame Bridget Bevan, wife of a Carmarthen MP, the schools were a brilliant success with adults no less than children. Starting in 1730, they were continued by Madame Bevan after Jones's death, until her death in 1779, when her will was challenged.

They even caught the attention of Catherine the Great of Russia. At the end over 250 schools were teaching 13,000 pupils annually. By 1761 the movement claimed to have taught 160,000 children and anything from 300,000 to 450,000 adults to read, out of a population which could not have exceeded 500,000. However inflated these claims, the movement clearly scored a success comparable to the more spectacular literacy drives of our own day.

A central fact of the eighteenth century is that by its final quarter, a majority of the adult population had probably become technically literate in Welsh. And the Welsh learned to read in an almost totally religious context. They learned to express themselves, indeed define themselves, in the language, imagery and concepts of the Bible and of Protestant sectarianism.

This was without doubt one source, though not the only or a major one, of the Calvinistic Methodist movement. Its origins in the 1730s, though located in the same stir of 'moral improvement', were independent of those in England. The instincts it shared with such movements everywhere and not least in the American colonies – where the revival led by Jonathan Edwards in 1739 occurred at much the same time and interpenetrated with it – were the more powerful in a Wales whose established Church seemed remote and cool and whose people were robustly indifferent or hostile. The movement began within the Anglican Church and for long remained within it, distancing itself from the older and somewhat disconcerted Dissent.

Young Anglicans, whether ordained or not, started to stand up in the open air and to bear witness, to ram home awareness of sin and, employing every device known to reach the senses as well as the intellect, to achieve that cataclysmic 'conversion' which had men and women 'born again'. Howell Harris, an outstanding preacher and organizer and a towering personality of somewhat psychopathic temper, started in Breconshire; Daniel Rowland, who could throw thousands into those public ecstasies which earned them the nickname of Holy Rollers, in Cardiganshire; William Williams, Pantycelyn, probably Wales's finest lyric poet, found his outlet in hymns which ultimately became irredeemably central to a 'Welsh way of life'.

They did not become that, however, for several generations. The movement's growth was slow and molecular, though highly organized from the start, through its local *seiat* (society) and its *sasiwn* (session), into a federal structure, a Church within a Church, firmly controlled from the centre. It was plagued by repeated heresy and secession. Howell Harris at one stage broke with the others and, playing the gentleman farmer, improver and militia captain, opened a religious community at Trefecca near his home. The Methodists remained resolutely within the Church of England, despite the hostility they encountered, especially in north and west, where the gentry organized mobs against them. One exhorter was thrown into the dog-kennels. Their Calvinism stemmed largely from Harris's service as a deputy to George Whitefield, during the latter's American missions. It hardened into a tribal identity, with orthodoxies, witch-hunts and sectarian fragmentation, directed in particular at Arminianism. Although John Wesley made repeated sorties into Wales, he and Harris in the end agreed to channel their energies separately. The final commitment of the Welsh to Whitefield led them to exclude the Wesleyans whenever they could.

As Methodism gradually accumulated a people devoted to 'vital religion', Dissent drifted in the opposite direction. As late as the 1800s a Baptist minister was hooted in the streets of Merthyr for trying to *introduce* hymns into chapel. Dissent's academies were open to the trade winds and the currents of Enlightenment, to Newtonian science and political economy. Their founding fathers had cut a king's head off, on principle; legally, they were second-class citizens. However respectable they became, their stance had necessarily to be somewhat political.

Furthermore, they had an important American dimension. Welshmen were everywhere in the New World, from the West Indies to furthest Canada. During the eighteenth century some made for Spanish North America. There were some Welsh merchants in New Orleans and a Rees family were prominent in New Madrid. The most striking of them made St Louis his base. This was Charles Morgan, a Welsh West Indian known as Jacques Clamorgan, who became the driving force behind Spain's last great enterprise in North America, the Missouri Company, searching up the unexplored Missouri to win control of the fur trade, break through to the Pacific and pre-empt the oncoming British and Americans.

Most Welsh people, however, had gone to America since the Restoration in organized denominational groups. John Miles had taken the Baptists to create Swanzey in New England and Welshmen were very prominent in Pennsylvania, even though Penn's promised Welsh Barony had never materialized. Thomas Lloyd of Montgomeryshire served as Penn's deputy and compatriots overflowed into the Welsh Tract in Delaware. There was a cluster of Welsh settlements served by Welsh churches in an arc from Meirion to Pencader. Arminian Baptists from mid-Wales moved to the colony alongside the Quakers and around 1700–1 were followed by an important group of Calvinist Baptists from Rhydwilym in the south-west who peopled the Welsh Tract. The Welsh grew in numbers and planted offshoots in the Carolinas, particularly on the Peedee river at Welsh Neck. Pennsylvania remained the Welsh heartland; a St David's Society was launched in Philadelphia as early as 1729 and Welsh books were published there, including the first biblical concordance.

Although migration faded in mid-century, the Welsh-American population became fairly substantial. American Baptists in particular were markedly Welsh in character. One of their oldest churches in Pennsylvania at Pennepek was served by a succession of Welshmen, having been founded by one, and Philadelphia First Baptist was opened as its daughter by another. Abel Morgan ran their well-known academy and from mid-century, the Baptists entered a cycle of growth. A prime mover was Morgan Edwards of Monmouthshire who rode hundreds of miles on circuit and wrote their history.

From 1762 Edwards was central to the creation of the Baptists' own college, Rhode Island College, later Brown University. One core of its library was bequeathed to it by William Richards of Lynn, a Baptist from south-west Wales who was an ardent supporter of the American revolution and published a defence of the atheism of the French. Edwards's colleague in the launching of the college was a remarkable Welsh-American, Dr Samuel Jones, a Glamorgan man in origin who served Pennepek from 1762 to 1814 and came to rank 'as a sort of bishop among the Baptists'. By 1786 Jones was claiming there were over 900 Baptist churches, many leading the advance into Kentucky.

Moreover, the Baptists remained in close contact with the homeland. Morgan Edwards returned to Britain to solicit funds for the college, and during the 1780s Dr Samuel Jones opened a correspondence with leading Baptists at home, which brings to light an intense transatlantic world. There was a two-way traffic in books, letters, information and ultimately people. This Baptist international had its own ships, four or five favoured vessels, notably the *Pigou* and the *Benjamin Franklin* of the Loxley family of Philadelphia who intermarried with Welsh and London-Welsh Baptists at home. Captain Benjamin Loxley had run the Continental Army's arms laboratory during the War of Independence and had been Benjamin Franklin's technician.

All the older denominations had these Atlantic links and close connections with the parent bodies in England. They were fully exposed to the tendencies which were working the old Dissent. The Carmarthen Academy of the Presbyterians succumbed early to heresies: to Arminianism with its relative autonomy for the human will, to Arianism, a partial denial of the divinity of Christ, and to Socinianism, its total denial, all of which affronted the

Calvinists. Its controllers moved the Academy around in a vain effort to stamp these out; in 1743 it split again and in 1755 the Congregational Board of London temporarily excommunicated it. It was in 1726 that Jenkin Jones from Carmarthen established a church in south Cardiganshire as an Arminian congregation and began a process that was to turn a district on the river Teifi into a persistent seedbed of rationalist heresy, a *Black Spot* to Calvinist demonology.

The schoolmaster–ministers of this persuasion, which tended to breed or to appeal to mathematicians and scientists, exercised a powerful influence. They carried the small Presbyterian denomination whose name came simply to signify liberalism in theology and politics. A particular conquest was of Independent communities in fairly affluent and literate Glamorgan and Gwent, with their comfortable Vale causes and their craggier hill chapels being taken over by workers in the new iron industry. Over a single generation, the Presbyterian families of the south-east, commercial and artisan in character, with a flow of recruits from the south-west, clustered around the new iron town of Merthyr Tydfil and made it the base for the launching of a new Unitarian denomination in 1802.

Most of the immigrants in Merthyr, however, came from the south-west and they came in hot for 'vital religion'. As Methodism grew, particularly in the last quarter of the eighteenth century, its modes and practices penetrated the Old Dissent and within that world a 'methodized' current ran stronger and harder than the 'unitarian' and in the opposite direction, away from rationalism and science and politics, towards passionate evangelism and systematically censorious personal re-formation. Blank if not hostile to politics, its leadership, particularly among Methodists themselves, could become intransigent Toryism. In the last quarter of the century the old sects went into crisis. The Baptists in particular, who in their upsurge rivalled Methodists as missionaries among the poor, entered a prolonged internal dispute from 1779 which twenty years later ended in schism.

The crisis was a crisis of growth. From the third quarter of the century the pace of growth within Methodism accelerates; from the 1780s Dissent follows. During the 1790s there were campaigns which resembled mass mission drives, and in the first years of the new century growth became torrential. When the Methodists finally withdrew from the Church under persecution in 1811, Nonconformists, old and new, by then accounted for some 15 to 20 per cent of the population. By the first religious census of 1851 they outnumbered Anglicans on average by five to one; in many places the ratio was seven and even ten to one. In the early nineteenth century the sects of Dissent threatened to become as much of a 'national Church' as Catholicism had become to the Irish. A people which around 1790 was still officially Tory and Anglican, over little more than a generation became a largely Nonconformist people of increasingly radical temper. It is one of the most remarkable cultural transformations in the history of any people.

A major irony is that, in the process, an old frontier reappears in Wales. For the victory of Nonconformity was the result of a crusade from south and east into the north and west. In the early eighteenth century, of some seventy Dissenting congregations on record, only ten were in the north, mostly in the north-east. The Methodist leader Thomas Charles who rooted his sect in north Wales and gave the Welsh Sunday schools their characteristic form (a species of directed democracy of exacting catechismic self-education) made Bala in Merioneth the centre of the creed, but he had come up from Carmarthenshire. At the great Baptist *gymanfa* or preaching festival in Nefyn in the northern Llŷn peninsula in 1792, a climax of the crusade, seven of the nine preachers were from the south. The greatest Baptist minister of his day, Christmas Evans, another southerner, made hitherto infidel Anglesey his fief. In the Dissenter breakthrough, it was the Methodists who made the running in the north and the west. The consequences were striking.

In 1823 Thomas Clarkson, the anti-slavery crusader, went on tour in Wales. As soon as he crosses from south-east Wales where normally radical Independents and Baptists and very radical Unitarians were legion, into Cardiganshire, the tone of his journals alters abruptly. Dissenters, now mostly Methodists, were much more under the shadow of an oppressive Establishment; the gentry would not sit with them on committees. In Caernarfonshire John Elias, a Methodist leader who towered over many Welsh minds like a pope with his bulls of Bala, dared not meet Clarkson at home; they had to meet in secret in Chester. Not until he reached north-east Wales could the circuit preacher relax. He immediately prepared special notes for his committee on this peculiar district. Eastern Wales, he claimed, was fifty years behind England in its politics, western Wales fifty years behind the east.

What does this mean, this re-emergence of an old frontier?

## Druids and Democrats

It means that Methodist advance, with Dissent following up, synchronizes with the advent of rapid economic change in general and of industrial capitalism in particular.

By 1796 the iron industry of Glamorgan and Gwent, with its mushrooming coal dependency, had outstripped Shropshire and Staffordshire, to produce 40 per cent of British pig-iron. Some of the largest and most advanced plants in the world ran in a clamorous belt along the northern rim of the south-east valleys. The 1790s saw a canal mania in both counties and ribbed them with tramways. Along one of the latter Trevithick's steam locomotive, the first in the world, made its run in 1804. Exemptions granted to the port of Newport created a sale-coal industry run on a shoestring by Welsh entrepreneurs. Entirely novel communities sprouted on the coalfield, drawing in population from the rest of Wales and starting the process which was to wrench its centre of gravity into the south-east. Monmouthshire's population increased at a rate faster than that of any other county in England and Wales; Glamorgan came third. Already the troubled south-west, with its riotous little capital of Carmarthen, was being transformed into the human matrix and service centre of a new industrial society in the south-east. At this stage the transformation of the north-eastern coalfield was scarcely less decisive, with Denbighshire and Flintshire moving rapidly into industrial capitalism.

The most unhingeing impact, however, was on rural west and north. The acceleration of industrial growth in England brought factors from Lancashire into the cloth country, to break the hold of the Shrewsbury Drapers. Petty local entrepreneurs appeared; there was a sharp pauperization during the French wars and a fairly rapid proletarianization. 'Machines are eating people,' shouted William Jones, Llangadfan; Voltaire's prophecy was coming true: soon there would be nothing but tyrants and slaves. The first cloth factories rose along the Severn, at Newtown, Llanidloes, Welshpool, even in Dolgellau. Rural centres of production like Llanbrynmair, a stronghold of Independency, went into prolonged crisis.

The crisis was intensified by the French war of 1793, with its press gangs and militia lists, taxes, levies, severe inflation and the closure of Barmouth. The new mode of production moved in massively even on this marginal agriculture. During the long wars, cultivation marched higher up the hillsides in Wales than it did during even Hitler's war. Modernization meant enclosures, the annual lease, rackrenting, the disrupting of traditional community. The 1790s were a decade of virtually continuous disturbance in the Wales which lay outside the coalfields, building up to peaks during the terrible years of famine prices in 1795–6 and 1799–1801. Waves of revolt broke across rural Wales to west and north in an arc of tension which follows the curve of the cloth country. Machynlleth, Denbigh, Llanbrynmair saw large-scale civil disobedience. Troops were repeatedly marching and countermarching through the little town of Bala, Mecca of Calvinist Methodism, and there were toasts to the French Revolution in its pubs.

The crisis in the south-west was more occult, a surface deference and quietism in matters political masking a society riddled with tension, secret societies and the growing alienation of an increasingly Nonconformist people from all establishments. Cardiganshire was hit harder by the population explosion than any other county in Wales. With its smallholders, hill farmers, squatters, lead miners and frustrated artisans encroaching without cease on the two-thirds of its stubborn soil owned by the Crown, it became a community of land-hunger and inching self-improvement, as were its sister societies in upland Carmarthenshire and north Pembrokeshire. In the post-war period, this was to be the most disturbed region in Wales.

Above all, it became a source of a distinctive migration movement which was one highly visible symptom of the crisis. From the sweep of semi-industrial rural Wales they went, along the curve of social tension from Cardigan and Carmarthenshire up through William Jones's country to Denbigh and the border. In the northern Llŷn peninsula, farmers and fishermen in revolt against enclosures decimated the population of their community in an independent movement into upstate New York, even as their compatriots made for new Welsh liberty settlements in Pennsylvania and Ohio. From 1793 there was a small-scale but steady flow, essentially of farmer–weavers and artisans, mostly Dissenter, swelling to major movements during the crises of 1795–6 and 1800–1. It was men of some small substance who went, while behind them thousands trapped in poverty clamoured to get away. The first native-born governor of the state of Ohio in the USA was the son of a man from the rebellious Independent weavers of Llanbrynmair.

This migration, millenarian in tone and strongly Dissenter in spirit, may have been one factor in the regional differentiation between the sects of Nonconformity which becomes a factor of major significance from this period. While the denominations were competitively present everywhere in Wales, it was the hinterland of Carmarthen, the textile districts around Llanidloes and, above all, the south-eastern coalfield, which emerged as centres of the more liberal, rationalist and radical doctrines: Unitarians, quasi-unitarian chapels among Independents, radical Baptists, Welsh revivalists and a fringe of Deists. In Merthyr Tydfil, in its Unitarian Association of 1802, its Cyfarthfa Philosophical Society of 1806 and its burgeoning world of *patriot* eisteddfods and chapel verse and musical festivals, such people were establishing some kind of institutional base.

To north and west, however, it was Methodism and its kin which won a local hegemony. This defined a distinct people no less, but in a kind of defensive withdrawal. It tended to lock its people away in a bunker. Not until it was forced to by the repression of 1811 did Methodism leave the Church; for long, it remained respectful.

One would hardly think so, however, from the correspondence of the gentry of north Wales during the 1790s. According to one distraught curate in Anglesey, whose report was passed to the king, 'hordes of Methodists' were 'overrunning north Wales' and 'descanting on the Rights of Man' (indeed some of them, in that place at that time, may well have been; the gentry of Glamorgan had reacted in a similar fashion a generation earlier). For what both Methodists and Dissenters offered, in the vacuum which had opened in Welsh life, was an alternative local leadership in a time of abrupt change widely experienced as human cataclysm.

What made this dislocation more serious was that this alternative society was being offered a new Welsh national ideology of radical temper and some new Welsh institutions to serve it.

This new Welsh nation was manufactured in London. The first *gorsedd* of Iolo Morganwg's directive elite of people's remembrancers was held on Primrose Hill; Jac Glan y Gors, Wales's Tom Paine, kept the King's Head in Ludgate. What the London-Welsh were offering their homeland was a radically new version of the old *brut*, transformed into a revolutionary doctrine of the democracy of the American and French revolutions.

The Abbé Pezron published his *L'Antiquité de la nation et la langue des Celtes* in 1703 and it gave a stimulus to antiquarian studies already under way on the manuscripts concentrated in the Clwyd Valley to the north-east. From this area came Edward Lhuyd, the earliest of the serious Celtic scholars and one of the best. The 'illegitimate' son of a squire in the Oswestry region, Lhuyd made his way to Oxford and became the second keeper of the Ashmolean Museum in 1690–1; careful observation, wide travel and a scientific approach made his *Archaeologica Britannica* of 1707 the foundation of all further study of the Celtic languages. He died before he could produce more, but Henry Rowland of Anglesey followed up with a highly influential study of the Druids in 1723.

An attempt to bring this work to a focus was made by the celebrated Morris brothers of Anglesey, particularly Lewis, who tried to re-establish a classic school of Welsh poetry by supporting the Augustan work of Goronwy Owen, a poet who characteristically made his way to America, and of Evan Evans (Ieuan Fardd), a poet who published some of the earlier texts. By mid-century, antiquarian studies were becoming something of a fashion under patrons like the Pennants. It was Welsh London which could power such interests with money and skills and Lewis Morris was to the fore in creating the London-Welsh society of the Cymmrodorion in 1751, to sponsor such work. Lewis Morris himself was a rather bilious sectarian and snob and the society in reality a bunch of successful philistines afflicted with the Welsh *pietas* of self-satisfied expatriates and adorned by a few aristocratic drones. During the 1770s and 1780s they yielded with some abruptness to the Gwyneddigion.

These were much more active and populist. They drew recruits in particular from Denbighshire, in the throes of its capitalist modernization. A crowd of bright young men came bustling through from Denbigh and elsewhere to people London's merchant houses, literary societies and intellectual taverns. A surprising number found a niche in the printing trade.

They reflect in a little Welsh mirror what was happening all over the Atlantic world, in the shift from academies to *sociétés de pensée* in France, the *amigos del país* of the Spanish world, the literary clubs and debating societies of the Anglo-American polity. Central was Owen Jones (Owain Myfyr) born in Denbighshire in 1741, who worked for years as a London currier and ended up the owner of a fur business and a wealthy man. He went up as a Welsh radical and stuck to his guns through William Pitt's repression and the witch-hunts of the war years, even as many of his erstwhile radical friends were running for cover like a different species of Welsh rabbit. He poured out his money in the service of Welsh history and literature, spending £180 on the society's edition of Dafydd ap Gwilym and over £1,000 on its mighty collection, named after him, *The Myvyrian Archaiology*. He helped send the brilliant Walter Davies (Gwallter Mechain) to Oxford and subsidized a host of others. The hardest worker was William Owen (who later, to secure an inheritance, added a Pughe to his name), Will Friendly (Gwilym Dawel), a Merioneth man educated in Manchester and something of a minor polymath in eighteenth-century style. An FSA, he edited the early poems *Llywarch Hen*, produced a Welsh dictionary between 1793 and 1803, published a *Cambrian Register* and a *Cambrian Biography*, translated *Paradise Lost* and was a pillar of the *Archaiology*.

Around them gathered a galaxy of stars: John Edwards (Sion Ceiriog), musician, astronomer, wit and professional gadfly; David Samwell (Dafydd Ddu Meddyg), surgeon to Captain Cook on the *Resolution* and the *Discovery*, accomplished botanist, amateur anthropologist and professional womanizer, who had made the first written record of the Maori language at Queen Charlotte Sound; John Jones (Jac Glan y Gors), who brought out pamphlets

in 1795 and 1797 which were Thomas Paine in Welsh and who coined the
expression 'Dic Sion Dafydd' to describe that familiar Welshman who,
on crossing Severn, becomes so English he makes the English feel foreign.

Meeting constantly in pubs, often riotous, sometimes raucous, generally
felicitous, their discourse at its best had something of the flavour of the
correspondence between John Adams and Thomas Jefferson. Appropriately so, because most of them were spiritual Americans, strong
supporters of 1776. When the fall of the Bastille in 1789 followed so hard
on the victory of Liberty in the new USA, most were swept into a millenarian
Jacobinism, as militant democracy was called. They revived the eisteddfod
and tried to make it a Welsh national affirmation. They had the engraver
to the new French National Assembly strike their competition medals and
tried to turn the festival into a radical academy. At a time among 'non-
historic' peoples when to publish a dictionary could be a revolutionary act,
they poured out dictionaries, registers, biographies, texts, translations and
established Welsh scholarship on a new, if distinctly shaky, basis. By modern
standards they were hopelessly romantic and unscientific (in which they
were typical of their times), but on their massive tomes, now safely
embalmed in the British Museum, a new Welsh nation was built. And it
was built on what they perceived as the principles which had liberated
America and were now liberating France. They formed a political club
in the euphoric early 1790s; Jac Glan y Gors wrote its song. It was a hymn
to the hero Madoc, who, having discovered America in 1170, took his people
out of an old brutal and corrupt world into a springtime of freedom in a
new one.

It was precisely here that their collaboration with Iolo Morganwg was
so crucial. 'Why take needless alarms?' Iolo once asked his long-suffering
wife Peggy, who used to comment on his vagaries in pungent verse. 'I do
not intend to publish my petition for the Abolition of Christianity until
long after I have finished with the work in hand...' Born in 1747 under
the name of Edward Williams, and a stonemason who went on incredible
tramping stints all over southern England (walking his horse from charity),
Iolo stands out now as one of Wales's most fecund, if maimed, geniuses.
His family would have interested the early D. H. Lawrence. His father,
intelligent and literate, was a working stonemason, his mother, aloof, frail
and a dreamer, a descendant of both a distinguished gentry family and
one of Glamorgan's dynasties of local poets. She never let Iolo forget his
twin cultural inheritance. Taught lexicographical and antiquarian skills
by local gentlemen, Iolo, from his base in the Vale of Glamorgan, raided
libraries and poets' houses wholesale, attached himself to Ieuan Fardd and

built himself, in the amateur fashion which was now inescapable for any Welsh scholar, into the most learned man of his day on the history and literature of the Welsh. He was much cherished by Southey and the English Romantics who saw in him an Original Bard out of their Celtic Twilight, an image he unscrupulously cultivated. His imagination was no less unscrupulous. A romantic and a forger in an age of romantic forgers in a good cause, the age of Ossian, the Noble Savage and the Druid, the age of Wordsworth and Blake, Iolo wove his own fabrications into his genuine discoveries to clinch his argument; he invented Welsh traditions the Welsh had never known. It has taken the heroic labours of a dedicated Welsh scholar of our day to cut Mad Ned free from his laudanum-laden fantasies.

In the process, however, Iolo is not seriously diminished. Some of the poems he fathered on Dafydd ap Gwilym, (to prove his affiliation to an ancient order of Druids in Glamorgan), are as good as anything the master himself wrote! His very forgeries convey a perception which no one else seems to have been capable of. He called for a Welsh national library, a national museum, a national eisteddfod; he was the first serious folklorist in Wales. He had an intuitive grasp of the historical function of Welsh traditions and of their functional utility to the half-starved and often self-despising Welsh of his own day. Welsh poets, he perceived, had not been 'poets' as the English used the word. They had been the rib-cage of the body politic, remembrancers, a collective memory honed for historic action. So he invented a *gorsedd*, a guild of those 'bards' who would be so much more than mere poets, antiquarians or historians, a directive and democratic elite of a new and democratic Welsh nation, conceived in liberty, deploying a usable past in order to build an attainable future (a kind of collective Owain Glyn Dŵr who'd served a proper apprenticeship, in short).

Many of the Londoners had the same instinct. The foremost Orientalist of the day was a Welshman, Sir William Jones; his researches seemed to suggest that the Celtic tongues were related to Sanskrit. Was Welsh the degenerate descendant of Earth's Mother Tongue? William Owen, who became a confidant of the millenarian Joanna Southcott, one of those prophetesses who people the times, joined with friends to invent a new orthography and purge Welsh of centuries of corruption and servility. In this he hardly differed from those typical new Americans, like Noah Webster who wanted to turn old Gothic English into the Esperanto of Liberty, and Benjamin Rush, landlord to the new Wales in the west, who wanted a New World medicine to be a new world medicine.

These obsessions ran into confluence with many of the fashionable interests of the time. The ghost of their distant compatriot, Dr John Dee, that Elizabethan protagonist of a British Israelism, returned to his homeland. His vast scheme for sixteenth-century regeneration had gone underground to live an increasingly bizarre life as Rosicrucianism (the Rose Cross, the Cross of the Tudor Rose). In the eighteenth century a highly scholarly but highly speculative and semi-scientific, semi-mystical version of it resurfaced on the fringe of the radical Enlightenment, to inform Freemasonry and those secret societies of Illuminati which the Counter-Revolution identified as the seedbed of the Revolution itself. The London Swedenborgians made contact with the quasi-religious house of the *Illuminés* of Avignon in the later 1780s, and these Welsh Londoners moved on the fringes of this circle of William Blake and the radical artisanry of the capital.

A whole new dimension was added to the misty perception of the past which Iolo and the Gwyneddigion were cultivating. Iolo came to see Druids as patriarchal figures of vast Celtic lands, charged with the Jewish Cabala, the language which God gave to Moses, antecedent to both Christianity and Judaism. Theirs was the original of Rousseau's Natural Religion, purged of superstition and priestcraft, unitarian in its belief in a single God, Masonic in its descent through secret societies of Enlightenment to the present. The medieval guild of Welsh poets thus became the last representatives in Europe of that libertarian Druidism. The Jacobin bards of the Welsh must resume the advance towards freedom and justice.

This millenarianism ran in harmony with the more measured, scholarly millenarianism which was coursing through orthodox religion, particularly Dissent, of which Dr Joseph Priestley, the chemist, philosopher and martyr to democracy, was such an exemplar. Morgan John Rhys, an active Baptist in Glamorgan and Gwent, was possessed by it. A committed American in spirit, he was militant in the campaign against the slave trade and for Welsh popular education. Like many others he saw the French coming hard on the heels of the American Revolution as a herald of the Last Days. He crossed to France to preach liberation theology. Driven home in 1792 by the outbreak of European war, he mobilized the Baptist Association of south-west Wales to translate into French an old and heterodox Puritan Bible and to print it *en masse*.

Inevitably the Gwyneddigion, who launched their freedom eisteddfods in the magic year of 1789 and held Iolo's first *gorsedd* in 1792, and who supported Morgan John Rhys's *Journal* which came out in 1793 even as Britain went to war with the Revolution, shuffled into loose alliance with men like Rhys, scattered across the brittle and increasingly bitter parishes of Wales. An unstructured but active collective intelligentsia began to form. The millenarianism of the Londoners could act as a unifying factor;

Unitarianism and Freemasonry run as underground currents throughout this first phase of a Welsh re-creation of themselves. It was a new and possessed *nation* which reached out to its half-aware adherents back home.

And a dusty time they had of it.

## Birth and Death of a Nation

Politics in Wales begin with the American Revolution. The first purely political publication in Welsh was a translation of a pamphlet on the dispute between Britain and the colonies. Even the John Bull balladmongers were disturbed by what they saw as a civil war. So visible were Welsh-American Dissenters in the struggle that the people back home thought that most of the signatures to the Declaration of Independence were Welsh! Five certainly were; David Jones, minister of Great Valley Baptist in Pennsylvania, had a price put on his head by the British, and John Rice Jones of Merioneth migrated to fight alongside the Americans in 1776 itself.

The war turned many Welsh Dissenters and a range of people who supported the liberties being fought for into spiritual Americans within British society. From this point, politics thrust its inquiring snout into the meagre book-production of the Welsh. In the 1760s there were some 230 books in Welsh; by the 1790s the total had climbed to nearly 500 and among them, the number of political texts multiplied sixfold. Over a hundred appeared, mostly in the 1790s, and their message echoed through the much larger numbers devoted to history, verse and, above all, to theology, sermons and hymns (600 and more out of a total of 1,300 printed between 1760 and 1799). David Williams, a celebrated Welsh Deist, dated the birth of Jacobinism in 1782 and located that birth not in France but in Britain.

It was out of this post-colonial crisis that the first serious democratic and popular movements grew. One strategic centre in Wales was Glamorgan, the wealthy county whose Vale nurtured not the usual scattered Welsh hamlets but nucleated villages which could cultivate urban graces. Bristol, an intellectually lively city, was the region's capital. Swansea was a cultivated little town. Cowbridge Book Society could disseminate important works and the new town of Merthyr, 8,000 strong and growing fast, could boast a bookseller taking weekly consignments from London. The Vale, anglicized in earlier days, was experiencing a Welsh-language revival. It was perhaps the interaction between Wales's two languages which made it so open and lively a place with a feel of Philadelphia about it.

The respectable opposition which emerged in Glamorgan from the 1760s yoked the old 'country' Toryism directed against the Court with the new

London radicalism, and the John Wilkes struggle gave it a focus. Sir John Aubrey was a member of the Hellfire Club and foremost in all radical campaigns; he was joined by Robert Morris and a cluster of Swansea industrialists and by Sir Watkin Lewes, a Pembrokeshire man with estates in Glamorgan, a member of the Ancient Britons and mayor of London in 1780. Lewes and Morris were raising petitions in support of Wilkes over 1769–71, and the Swansea people found allies among newer families coming to prominence in the Vale. Freemasonry gave them an organizational network. Throughout Wales the number of Freemasons' lodges increased sharply, from six in 1760 to sixteen in 1771. In Glamorgan they were built on the ruins of the old Jacobite society of the Sea Serjeants and allied Tory radicals with men from older Whig and deist circles like Thomas Matthews of Llandaff. No less prominent were Dissenters of the new, radical tendency. Dr Richard Price, son of an old Glamorgan family of Cromwellian Puritans, became Grand Master of the Bridgend Lodge in 1777. Dissenting ministers were reading Gerrard Winstanley the Digger, Vavasor Powell and Morgan Llwyd at this time, and Price moved rapidly towards unitarianism. Together with David Williams, a Caerphilly Dissenter who was to become a Deist, he had contacts with a propagandizing unitarian circle in Essex Street, London and with the Benjamin Franklin club there, and soon installed himself in the very radical group which focused on the Earl of Shelburne, whose Buckinghamshire estates Sir John Aubrey managed.

Also present in the Essex Street circle, however, were Iolo Morganwg and John Bradford, a deist dyer from Glamorgan. These men sprang from the creative bilingual artisanry and the aspiring lower middle class of the Vale, who developed at first in the shadow and shelter of the respectables. Both Iolo and Dr Richard Price were major publicists in a successful electoral campaign in 1789 which built on opposition to the American war and the new oligarchy in the county. Out of this world came men like Bradford, at ease in the literature of France and England and passionate in the cause of Welsh revival; William Edwards who built the single-span bridge at Pontypridd; Lewis Hopkin, a multi-purpose craftsman who trained a coterie of Welsh poets; Edward Ifan, a poet who became the first Unitarian minister in the hill country. This was the society which produced Jacobins in Iolo and Morgan John Rhys; and in Dr Richard Price and David Williams, two of the best-known transatlantic radicals of the age of Atlantic revolution. The former was perhaps the most celebrated political Dissenter, the alleged author of the Sinking Fund, a defender of the American and French Revolutions, whose sermons provoked Edmund Burke into writing his classic of conservatism, and a man formally invited over by the American

Congress to serve as financial adviser to the new republic; the latter was the author of a Deist religion which won praise from Voltaire, Rousseau and Frederick the Great, a friend of Condorcet and the Girondins in France, a man formally invited over to France to advise on its new constitution.

There were pockets elsewhere, in Denbighshire, for example, where Jac Glan y Gors was born. Jonathan Shipley, the absentee Bishop of St Asaph, was a friend of Benjamin Franklin and the father-in-law of the Orientalist Sir William Jones. The latter brought out a pamphlet against the American war in 1782 which was printed in Wrexham by his brother-in-law, the dean of St Asaph. A classic court case ensued in which the famous Erskine vindicated the rights of juries in libel cases. The region was drenched in democratic propaganda and the dean's acquittal was greeted by bonfires and popular rejoicing. A strong and often very radical popular movement developed around Wrexham and Denbigh. At the height of the troubles of 1795, as magistrates met at Denbigh to raise men for the militia and the navy, some 500 men in a military formation of fourteen squads marched in, took over the town, jailed the magistrates and forced them to renounce their project, before marching on circuit through the north-east to stop the export of grain. The leader was John Jones, a small farmer of Aerdden who made well-informed speeches in both languages, quoted Lord Camden in the Lords in 1776 and demanded a government responsible to the people. In the north-east there was a popular movement which was not only violent but highly ideological; they were making pikes there in 1800 and government feared insurrection.

There were others, grouped among the Independents of north Wales, the dissidents in Llanbrynmair, around contagious individuals like William Jones, Llangadfan. During the troubles of the 1790s people forced a magistrate in Bala to wear wooden clogs, a symbol of slavery borrowed from the French Revolution. Hundreds of people in Merioneth and Llanbrynmair met by night to demand a government of the poor, not the rich; papers went up on doors in Bangor calling for people to pray for a British defeat in the war against France.

Merthyr village in the south was said to be full of 'sturdy old Republicans'. Iolo Morganwg spent much of his time there; his son opened a school in the heart of its radical, Unitarian, Masonic, eisteddfod quarter (later its Chartist heartland). The devout in Merthyr had their boot-nails stamped in a TP so as to trample the infidel Paine underfoot. People like this could be found everywhere. A scattered minority at home, they were much more visible in the transatlantic perspective proper to British Jacobinism.

Their journey of hope was brief. Their democratic campaigns mounted to a climax in the celebration of the centenary of the Glorious Revolution of 1688 just at the point when George Washington took the presidency of the new American republic and the Bastille fell in France.

There was a brief but brilliant explosion of Welsh Jacobinism, in the liberty eisteddfods, the *gorsedd*, Morgan John Rhys's *Journal*, Jac Glan y Gors's pamphlets. Official Britain reacted strongly from as early as 1791. Its magistrates hounded Jacobins, its mobs wrecked their houses. In 1793 Britain went to war with France, in 1794 the leading English democrats were tried for treason, in 1795 traditional English liberties were suspended for the duration. These, too, were the years of the first implantation of modern industry in eastern Wales, north and south, the first cloth factories on the Severn, the closure of Barmouth, the social crisis running through north and west like rock fissures from an earthquake. They were years, no less, of a surging growth of Methodism which turned a face of brass to this new Welsh 'nation' to be copied by the more conservative or fearful leaders of Dissent. Morgan Rhys's journal was snuffed out after five issues and two attempts to restart it failed. The farcical French landing near Fishguard in 1797, when the Directory under the cover of its Irish campaign, dumped a gaggle of criminals led by a paranoid American, precipitated a run on the Bank of England already imminent, provoked a witch-hunt against local radicals, and strengthened the reactionary British patriotism. Jacobinism shrank from public view into private correspondence; William Jones's mail was opened by government agents. In this corner of a Britain disciplined by the suspensions of Habeas Corpus, patrolled by the Volunteers, deafened by 'God Save Great George Our King' sung five times over in the playhouses to drown 'God Save The Rights of Man', where could Welsh patriots turn but to that Land of Liberty where kindred spirits were waiting and where the Lost Brothers were even now ranging the Missouri?

These were the years of 'the rage to go to America', when the emigrants' handbooks came pouring from the presses. In Wales the migration already under way assumed utopian and dramatic form as Madoc suddenly returned to a people in travail. The old story of Madoc had been transformed into a myth of a tribe of Welsh Indians in the seventeenth century. In 1792 a French trader from Spanish St Louis came across a tribe on the Upper Missouri, the Mandans, and reported them to be 'white like Europeans'. The crisis at Nootka Sound in 1790, between Britain and Spain over rights to America, had already revived the old yarns, and a learned Welsh divine of Sydenham, Dr John Williams, published a sympathetic study of the legend in 1791. The report from the Missouri seemed a confirmation.

Jacques Clamorgan, Spain's Welsh West Indian in St Louis, immediately organized an imperial expedition into the west, while a minor outbreak of Madoc fever seized the USA. That passion hit Wales at a critical moment.

There was an outbreak of Madoc and America fever among its Dissenters and liberals. Christmas Evans raised his organ voice in protest against the Two Clever Talkers who were unhingeing the Godly in Wales, Mr Gwladaethwr and Mr Mynd-i-America (Mr Politician and Mr Go-to-America). Iolo Morganwg appointed himself missionary to the Welsh Indians, wrote their 'history' and presented a paper on them to the Royal Society. Young John Evans, a Methodist from Waunfawr near Caernarfon, threw up career and family, moved to a circle of Welsh Jacobins in London, crossed to America in the steerage along the Baptist network and entered the service of Spain and Jacques Clamorgan. He set off alone up an unknown Missouri with $1.75 in his pocket, was driven back, and enrolled as second-in-command to the Scottish explorer James McKay in the greatest expedition Spain ever sent up the river. Evans did indeed reach the Mandans; he lived through one of the worst winters on earth; he held those Mandans for Spain against the Canadians, helping indirectly to fix the future US–Canada frontier; he drew excellent maps which Lewis and Clark used on their major expedition only nine years later. He died of drink and disillusion in New Orleans at the age of twenty-nine.* Madoc and Jacobinism turned this young Welsh Methodist, who duly defected to the Baptists and the Freemasons, into a pioneer of American exploration and the last of the Spanish conquistadors in the New World.

After him two years later went Morgan John Rhys, giving up the unequal struggle at home. After a horseback tour of the entire American republic, he launched a Welsh freedom settlement at Beula, western Pennsylvania. And after both of them, with the Baptist network in the USA mobilizing to serve them, particularly during the desperate years 1795–6 and 1800–1, years of famine prices, mass riots, political witch-hunts and redcoats marching across north and west Wales, went Welsh families by the hundred, braving hideous sea-crossings with their 50 per cent casualties, Algerian corsairs and hostile British warships. They went, as many of them told the clerk in Philadelphia as they took out their American citizenship papers, to create *The Kingdom of Wales*.

Their frontier proved a frontier of illusion. After a heroic struggle, Beula was cracked by the simultaneous opening of the easier Ohio lands and the abrupt acceleration of emigration in 1801. The small town of Ebensburg

*There is a full treatment of the Madoc mythology in my *Madoc: the making of a myth* (Eyre Methuen, 1980).

171

(named after Ebenezer Chapel, Pontypool) was left as the people dispersed to found Welsh communities in Ohio at Paddy's Run and Welsh Hills and at Utica in New York state. But they shed their Cymric ambition. Back home the Jacobin nation was extinguished as the wars against the French Republic became the Napoleonic War. A new Wales being shaped by industry, Methodism and a measured Dissent had no place for such as Iolo and William Owen who were already beginning to look like creatures from another time. It was a hundred years before the new and reconstructed Welsh recovered their memory by an act of will.

And yet Jacobinism, however brief its moment of truth and fantasy, left a living and constantly renewed tradition which interacted with the new world of industry in increasing and intensifying power. The two strongholds of Jacobinism in the 1790s were Merioneth–Montgomeryshire and Merthyr–Monmouthshire; in the former it took wing towards the Ohio, in the latter it could find a home at home. It established a new political tradition around the textile towns and villages of mid-Wales, in the smouldering hinterland of Carmarthen and, above all, on the coalfield of the south-east.

In 1802 the Unitarians of south Wales organized themselves at Merthyr; in 1806 local democrats there, led by Unitarians, formed the Cyfarthfa Philosophical Society, Wales's version of the Lunar Society of Priestley in Birmingham. In 1810–11 the first trade unions appeared on the coalfield and the Methodists were driven by persecution at the height of the Luddite crisis to secede from the Church. In the 1820s the colliers of Monmouthshire organized their first unions and their Scotch Cattle resistance groups even as Dissenters started their first serious periodicals. In 1831 a working-class rebellion at Merthyr gave birth to the notion of 'a working class' and Unitarians were its political tutors. When the first working-class journal appeared in Merthyr in 1834, its editors were two Unitarians straight out of the Jacobin tradition, and Iolo Morganwg's son gave them one of his father's mottos which in time became the motto of the town itself; no strength but brotherhood.

Iolo Morganwg went back to his Vale to die in 1826, but he had spent his last years with his son in Merthyr. In the course of his lifetime he and the people he had tried to shape into a nation passed from one Wales to another, across the most dramatic dividing line in that people's history.

# 8 · THE CRUCIBLE

Look at this graph (p. 174), a simplified outline of Welsh population growth. Is there a peak more jagged in Snowdonia?

That right angle in the late eighteenth century is the population explosion. Together with the conquest of energy in steam ('Steam is an Englishman' they used to say in Europe) and the breakneck growth of industrial society, it created modern Britain, western Europe, the USA. Questions of cause are perhaps best left to diviners and necromancers or their academic equivalents, but in terms of the human race as a biological species occupying a particular stretch of territory in Europe and its offshore islands, that explosion turned everything that had gone before into a kind of prehistory. In Wales, it makes all those ages spaced out before the explosion look like Oxfam territory.

Consider some literally vital statistics. There were something over half a million people in Wales in the middle of the eighteenth century when, in every area, numbers started to multiply. From the 1780s, as iron strikes its roots into the east, the increase becomes cumulative. During the first half of the nineteenth century, it is breakneck. By 1921, when the world market which had spawned this society withdrew its favour and threatened to dismantle it, there were 2,600,000 people in Wales. Over little more than four generations, the population had nearly quintupled. And over little more than three generations, the human lifespan in those communities had virtually doubled. A people who, on average and at birth, could expect to die at thirty, could now expect to live to sixty. These changes seem to me to rank with the discovery of steam.

Already in the eighteenth century, Great Britain had made a marginal province into a sector of an imperial economy, in its copper, tinplate, plebeian cloth, the beginnings of iron, lead and slate. The 1790s saw the impact of the iron industry and an abrupt increase in numbers. The government started to count the people in 1801 and went on counting them every ten years. Until the census of 1841, every county in Wales registered a major population increase. Those to west and north, however, were already falling behind as they pumped people out into the north-east and, more particularly, the south-east. From 1841, those western counties recorded the first absolute losses and entered their long cycle of

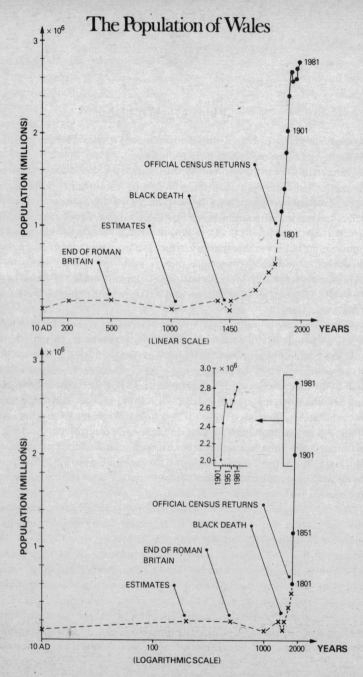

# The Population of Wales

Compiled by Dr. J. H. Williams. From 1801 totals are derived from
the official Census returns; earlier totals are estimates.

depopulation, to become 'rural'. Before 1841 Monmouthshire and Glamorgan were already running first and third in the growth race among the counties of England and Wales. From mid-century, the industrializing south-east sucked people in from the rest of Wales and from outside, until in the end nearly four-fifths of the people of Wales were lodged in that continuously renovating and increasingly English-speaking region. The centre of gravity of the Welsh population was wrenched bodily into the south-east. Gwynedd in the north-west became, with its slate quarries, another major export centre concentrating 90 per cent of British production, but the industrialization of the north-east ran into a ceiling. From the 1860s, the north-eastern coalfield started to lose people, while that of the south-east entered on a long phase of secular expansion which turned it into the maverick of British industrial society, moving competely out of step from every other region. The pacemakers were iron, coal and tinplate in the south; they were succeeded, in the high mid-century noon of the British imperial economy, by the significant world power of south Wales steel and rails. From about the 1880s, in a growth without parallel in Britain, everything that had gone before was eclipsed by the truly gigantic world empire of south Wales coal.

A modern scholar* has tried to capture the human reality of this in tables and graphs which make a picture. He has tried to relate variations in income in Wales to the process of industrialization by plotting variations in total livestock on the farms, and in the marriage rate in both Glamorgan, the heartland of coal, and Wales as a whole, against the selling price of coal, taken as the major determinant of the general level of prosperity. The image which results is striking. From the 1870s all the graphs move in harmony. In 1873 the coal-price graph abruptly shoots up into a Matterhorn figuration as prices reach their peak. The very next year, the marriage rate in Glamorgan reaches its maximum of 22.2 per 1,000 and the birth-rate 44.3 per 1,000. Not only in Glamorgan, but in Wales as a whole, the marriage rate starts to hug the price of coal. In 1874, the year following the price peak, the growth in livestock on Welsh farms reached its own peak, to climax again in 1891 when coal prices were at a new high. Between the 1870s and 1891 there was an increase of 25 per cent in the total of livestock on Welsh farms and of 33 per cent in acreage under permanent grass. And, mark this, this was during the terrible crises of rural Europe in the 1880s,

*Brinley Thomas, *Migration and Economic Growth* (Cambridge University Press, 1954 and subsequent revisions) and 'Wales and the Atlantic Economy' in the volume he edited, *The Welsh Economy: Studies in Expansion* (University of Wales Press, 1962).

precipitated by new American competition. In that decade rural Wales suffered its worst population losses by far; over 100,000 people quit the farms. Those who quit were, overwhelmingly, farm labourers. The number of farmers, generally small farmers, remained constant. In fact it was during this crisis decade, ravaged by severe political and ideological conflict in Wales, that the small farmers laid the foundation of that small-proprietor network which was to erode and by the 1920s supersede, the landlords. It was their labourers who took off, to industrial Wales during British export booms, to industrial England during booms in British home capital formation.

The conclusion seems inescapable. By the 1870s at the latest, Wales had become an industrial society in the sense that the terrible dominion of the harvest and seasonal cycle had been broken and it was the rhythms of industry which had become the ultimate determinants of social life. More significantly still, a critical feature of this whole process was the fact that Wales was completely out of step with every other region of Britain. What is distinctive about nineteenth-century Wales is the peculiarly *imperial* character of the formation of its industrial society and of the Welsh working class. The working population of Wales has been as much an offshore phenomenon as that financial capitalism of Britain to which it has been directly, if hardly intimately, related. The Welsh working class has been an offshore working class.

The key is the extension of a market towards a global compass and the dominant role of the new British capitalism within it. The near monopoly of British industry and commerce through much of the century and Britain's imposition of free trade on the Atlantic basin locked the British and US economies into an Atlantic economy which worked like a push–pull oscillator. Between 1846 and 1914 in that gigantic migration of the peoples which helped to build the USA into the greatest power on earth, over 43 million human beings emigrated from Europe to the Americas. Important in the absorptive capacity of the Americas, particularly the USA, was Britain; by 1913 nearly 70 per cent of the billions she had invested abroad was in the Americas. There were four major outflows of people from Europe to America; during 1849–53 and 1863–73, the great majority were Irish, Germans, Scandinavians and Italians driven to the new frontier of enterprise in America by the breakup of their own rural economies. The 1880s saw the great crisis of rural Europe. The Americans invented the harvester in 1872 and the binder in 1880; they completed their vital transport network, with substantial help from British money. While paying their labourers nearly six times the wages of labourers in the Rhineland, they could produce wheat in their north-west at forty cents a bushel and ship it to Germany where Rhineland wheat was costing eighty cents a bushel. During the 1880s, over 1¼ million people left rural Germany and over half a million quit Scandinavia; emigration became an Italian national habit and Denmark had to rebuild itself. The final peak came over 1903–13 when over 10 million Slavs, Jews and southern Europeans flooded across the Atlantic.

Central to this process was Britain. The outward pulses of British capital, of technological and human export, coincided almost exactly with the peaks of human migration from Europe. There was a close interaction between Britain, the major investing power, and the USA, the leading market for investment. During outward thrusts of capital from Britain and of people from Europe, the USA experienced a vigorous upswing in capital construction. At such moments the export sector of the British economy was at stretch, while in relative terms the home sector marked time. Conversely, in the downward swings in British lending and European migration, Britain experienced a boom in her own capital construction. This is what seems ultimately to have governed the flows of a rural population continuously displaced by the earthquake of industrial capitalism.

For the continental Europeans were joined by a quite massive outflow of human beings from the British Isles. To put it crudely, when the British export sector boomed, the displaced rural population of Britain, with others, tended to follow the thrust of enterprise to its new frontier abroad. Conversely, when the British home sector boomed, its export of human beings slowed; the displaced people of Britain could find a life at home. The peaks of these outward pulses of people from Britain were 1847–54, 1866–73, 1881–8 and 1903–13.

Every single people in the British Isles follows that pattern. With one outstanding exception. Every British people follows that pattern with the startling exception of the Welsh.

Ireland, of course, with its repeated demographic disasters, is unique in the intensity of its emigration, which could run to 200 per 10,000 of the population per decade, but it follows the rhythm, as does Scotland, often at 50 to 80 per 10,000. England has the lowest emigration rates (apart from Wales after the 1880s), reaching maxima in the low 20s per 10,000. Everywhere the crisis of the 1880s is very visible.

How does Wales fit? Briefly, it does not. Up to the 1860s, when it was losing people at a rate of 28–47 per 10,000 per decade, there was clearly a drain outwards, despite rapid industrialization, but from that moment,

Wales moves out of phase with England, Scotland and Ireland in a continuous expansion which reaches a climax in 1914. Where is the crisis of the 1880s in Wales? Rural Wales, shedding 100,000 people – nearly twice as many as in any other decade – certainly experienced a shake-out but while England's losses shot up to 23 and Scotland's to 58 per 10,000, the net rate of loss out of Wales *falls*, to a negligible dribble of 11 per 10,000. Moreover, it goes on falling, *irrespective* of any British or European rhythm, until, from the 1890s, Wales becomes a country of *net immigration*. In fact, during the remarkable decade just before the First World War, Wales becomes the only country to register a plus in the immigration tables outside the USA. In that tumultuous decade, when something like 130,000 people – and a mixed, polyglot, buoyant and innovatory people they were – flooded into the coal valleys of south Wales, Wales, with an immigration rate of 45 per 10,000, ranks second, by rate, only to the USA itself as a world centre of immigration.

The American statistics confirm the trend. Even more striking a picture emerges from the figures of internal migration within Britain. Taking England and Wales as a whole, the pattern is that suggested by the external flows. During the 1850s and 1860s some 1½ million people quit the rural areas. Expanding towns and colliery districts absorb a total equal to two-thirds of that; those leaving the country altogether equal a third. During the 1870s the British home sector is booming. There is a heavy outflow from the rural districts, but there is also a marked increase in the absorptive capacity of towns and coalfields. The emigration flow drops sharply. In the 1880s the rural crisis reaches its climax at a time of expansion in the export sector; the absorptive capacity of towns falls and there is a massive increase in emigration. The position is reversed during the 1890s, but in the astounding first decade of the twentieth century, as the rural exodus slackens, comes the climax for both British capital and European human export. Towns and coalfields (outside south Wales) themselves show a major fall and there is the most massive emigration yet.

Within Wales, on the other hand, the industrial sector (essentially the south Wales coalfield) expands most in those very decades when the industrial sector of Britain as a whole expands least. The population graphs of the colliery areas of England and south Wales are a veritable mirror image of each other; they run in opposite directions. Until the 1860s, Wales is losing substantial numbers of people. During that decade, the net outflow from Wales is actually greater than the outflow from the rural areas; this was the peak of Welsh emigration to the USA. From that decade the north-eastern coalfield around Wrexham starts to lose people; on the other hand, the holiday areas along the northern coasts start to expand. The outflow slackens during the 1870s but it is from the 1880s that the distinctiveness of Wales becomes overpowering. The rural crisis of the 1880s registers very sharply indeed, but there is an abrupt increase in the absorptive capacity of the south Wales coalfield. At this, a climax of British emigration as a whole, emigration out of Wales falls to a negligible level. In the following decade the absorptive capacity of the south Wales coalfield is a good deal less (this is a period of British home boom) but the scale of the rural exodus is much less and the holiday towns of north Wales, Llandudno, Rhyl and their kin are flourishing. The emigration rate out of Wales falls still further. And in the unhingeing 1900s, nearly 130,000 pour into south Wales and overall there is a net gain of 100,000 people.

As an export centre of the British economy, Wales, and especially south Wales, actually attracted people during those outward pulses which sent so many British people across the Atlantic; during British home booms, there was absorptive capacity within Britain itself. Naturally, it was not a one-to-one process. Though movement from north to south Wales was stronger and more frequent than has been assumed, the north Welsh would tend to drift into Liverpool and Merseyside or the Midlands. From south-west Wales, however, there was a permanent movement into the south-east and the evidence overwhelmingly suggests that, before the critical early years of the twentieth century, the working population of Wales was largely Welsh. The Irish tended to be segregated for religious and cultural reasons, but by 1900 assimilation was rapid. Large numbers of the English, and even the Spanish and Italians, who came in were absorbed so thoroughly that many learned the Welsh language – which partly explains the existence today of passionate Welsh-speaking nationalists who bear such ancient Welsh surnames as Millward, Reeve, Bianchi, Diez, not to mention Hennessy and Murphy.

This centrality to a British export economy made the Welsh the least emigration-prone of all the peoples of the British Isles. This fact jars against Welsh instincts and received wisdom. The *Cymry ar wasgar* (the 'exiles') are cherished in Welsh emotional life; they have their special day at the National Eisteddfod, a moment even more emotional than the Chairing of the Bard. There is reason for it. After the farmers and artisans of the 1790s went the tinplaters, ironworkers, colliers; Scranton, Pittsburgh, Youngstown, Edmonton, Calgary became household names in Wales. The US Immigration Service in 1875 was the first state institution in the modern world to recognize the Welsh as a distinct people. There is scarcely a family in Wales (including my own), certainly no extended family, which does not have its American and Canadian dimension. At one point, there were almost as many Welsh-language publications in the USA as in Wales itself. But this truth registers so powerfully on the Welsh imagination precisely because the Welsh, even the 2,600,000 Welsh of 1921, remained in objective terms a small people. It does not take many of them to create an American dimension. By any objective measurement, their emigrants were only a handful. In those years which sent so many across the Atlantic, for every 77 per 10,000 Irish who migrated annually, there were 20 Scots, 12 English and only 3 Welsh. In proportion to population, English emigrants to the USA were four times as numerous as the Welsh, Scots were seven times as numerous and the Irish twenty-six times. The Welsh did not need to emigrate.

If Wales had not been industrialized during the nineteenth century, its people would almost certainly have suffered the same fate as the southern Irish. Since the Welsh were so much fewer, any recognizable entity which could be called 'Wales' would have disappeared in the nineteenth century, its people blown away by the winds of the world. Instead, Wales retained a living people and sustained a massive increase in its numbers. The remarkable Welsh national revival of the nineteenth century would have been inconceivable without it. It is against this massive growth of an industrial Wales of British and imperial character that every other Welsh phenomenon must be set. What has come to be thought of as 'traditional', Nonconformist, radical Welsh-speaking Wales in particular, that Wales which created so many of the characteristic Welsh institutions, notably the educational, was in some basic senses a by-product of this industrialization, without which its success would have been impossible. On the other hand, that 'traditional' Wales was, in some other very real senses, a reaction against this new Wales. Its roots and its thinking and emotional life were in the other Wales which was being made marginal; its ideology grew from that marginal society – although most often through the agency of displaced and upwardly mobile middle classes who had climbed out of that populist tilth – the rural Wales which was in permanent crisis from 1841 onwards, which experienced an endless drain on its people and which lived, despite its subjective spirit, in objective dependency on industrial Wales.

Into that industrial Wales poured anything from two-thirds to three-quarters of the actually existing Welsh population. They shifted massively into the south-east. Once again it was in old Marcher Wales that innovation became the rule; once again the old frontier reappeared, this time sharply etched into the human landscape. These people were drawn into a society which was repeatedly modernizing and revolutionizing itself, planting

communities and uprooting them, building itself into an export metropolis
of a world economy and merging inexorably into the overarching culture
of the world language of English. This threatened to create two, and more,
'nations' out of a Welsh people.

The 'Wales' of what was at first a very real mind but which increasingly
became a 'Wales' of the imaginative will, was increasingly distanced from
the 'Wales' which actually existed on the ground. This process of
intensifying contradiction was infinitely worsened by the post-1920
depression which destroyed imperial Wales and, perhaps even more, by
the ensuing reconstruction of a survivor society. In our day, the
contradictions have become intolerable.

Beyond all this, the achievement of a new industrial society at such a
speed, in conflict and suffering, in liberation and an abrupt widening of
horizons, had effects on an old people which were as subtle as they were
profound. There are whole areas of human experience, among them the
most significant, which lie too deep for the historian's plumb line. The real
history of the modern Welsh has still to be written.

With one consequence, however, we in Wales cannot fail to be familiar.
This imperial Wales was the Wales of the grandparents of many of us. The
Wales we know and live in emerged from the wreck of that society after
the First World War and the painful attempt to rebuild which followed.
The results are imprinted on the psychology of many people in Wales. We
are living through the morning after a night before which lasted over four
generations.

# 9 · THE FRONTIER YEARS

Industrial capitalism,splintered Wales. Into a country which had long been dissociating into intensely localized cultures, came the intrusive and massively endowed entrepreneurs from England, Anthony Bacon, Crawshays, Guests, Homfrays, Wilkinsons, collaring a world market. Much of their capital came from the West India slave trade and the Indian empire. They exploited all the resources and all the people they could get hold of with a similarly irresponsible and single-minded fervour; their concentrations of people, their wage-lists, their housing schemes, their communication networks were all directed to the one end. North and south were directed towards the east and away from each other. It was easier for labourers to tramp from the south-west into the south-east than for their farmers to get their cattle there. Not until the south commandeered its own world market and developed its own ports and railway network was Bristol displaced. In the north that did not happen; its equivalent to Newport-Cardiff-Swansea was Liverpool.

Fragmented and divergent societies were propelled along different historic routes and into different historic time-scales. At any one point a man could be working, often as a skilled operative, in one of the most technically advanced industrial plants in the world and trying to live according to the rules of a modern society with a world language, while a brother or sister would be tramping after sheep in some barren and cloud-capped valley and trying to live according to the rules of a people's law, graced with the name of Hywel Dda, in a people's now essentially oral language. At a human level, these men and women who were being shovelled like small coal over the face of their country were united only by fragile and intangible threads; by the kinship and community patterns of that seasonal-becoming-permanent migration which had become a Welsh way of life, by a diffuse sense of identity, by a new identity born of conflict, by the strengthening networks of Dissent with its travelling preachers.

Ultimately these were to prove more powerful than steam-hammers. The Welsh created a new identity for themselves, yet again. This historically effective consensus emerged on a radically new foundation. Central to that re-formation was a specifically working-class consciousness which fought its way through rebellion to acquire a brief but potent maturity. After it had been neutralized and emasculated, the communal spirit it had engendered – suitably adjusted to a novel imperial context – could find a place alongside the appropriately reconstructed communities of its rural cousins, after their own rebellion had been contained, in a populist and radical Nonconformist People in whom its leaders saw the image of a new Welsh nation.

These creative responses, transcending the original challenge, were nevertheless *responses;* they followed the rhythms of the society which had provoked them. The focus of rebellion was the south which had been exposed to the full force of a frontier capitalism; as that capitalism settled into its comfortable imperial hegemony, the focus of realignment shifted towards the north and west.

## Sons of Vulcan and Daughters of Rebecca

Iron set the pace, running its furnaces along the heads of narrow trench valleys on the plateau in the armpit of the Brecknock Beacons and threading coal workings and other plants down those valleys. The ironworks, with the mushrooming settlements of their thousands of workers, ran in a clamorous arc from Aberdare and Hirwaun in the west, through the matrix of Merthyr, into Tredegar, Ebbw Vale, east to Brynmawr and down to Blaenavon, Pontypool, the beginnings of Pontypridd. Around the privileged port of Newport sprouted a sale-coal industry in the lower valleys of Gwent run by ambitious but marginal Welsh adventurers. Continuous technical development drove iron westwards into the already developed anthracite districts behind Neath and Swansea, themselves building on their world monopoly in copper, tinplate and its related industries. From the 1840s coal began to shift into the Aberdare and Rhondda valleys, carrying the customs of the colliers with it. A complex of small-scale subsidiaries and services sprang up around the rich and the blindly, wastefully exploited coal, ironstone and limestone; into them swarmed those half-forgotten people of Welsh history, the urban middle class and the Welsh plutocracy, into small plants and works, into coal, haulage, minor engineering, the professions, trade, commerce, the shopocracy, making fortunes in between strategic bankruptcies, looming over scurries of ambitious workers horning their way into a precarious, sometimes bandit, penny capitalism.

'Money was absolute trash,' said one contemporary as the whole region came alive with a buoyantly innovative technology and the radically new ways of life shaping themselves around it. Dowlais and Cyfarthfa were the biggest and most developed plants, a Mecca for migrant technicians and inventors. The highly skilled were at first imported and the practice persisted, but the region generated its own skills very quickly. Young mining apprentices were being taught Priestley's chemistry as early as the 1790s in the Unitarian chapels of Aberdare and Cefn near Merthyr; a master moulder at Cyfarthfa built his own planetarium as a change from his quadrant, thermometer and water gauge. Watkin George's great overshot water-wheel, 'the greatest wheel the world has seen', found its way into popular ballads, and it was Dowlais works which conferred on the human race the inestimable blessing of the steam-whistle. In 1804 Trevithick's steam locomotive made its run from Penydarren to Abercynon. They couldn't get it back up the slope and had to wait for Stephenson, but in most sectors these people were a vanguard. Their land was laced with canals, roads, tramways, many of them triumphs of engineering. There was a network of informal and formal training schools and circles knitted into a British pattern of recruitment and skill formation. By the 1830s south Wales was producing a small regiment of technicians, engineers, managers; it began to fertilize Pennsylvania in the USA and the Donetz basin in Russia. Its rails were to colonize the world, and after them went its capitalists, its merchants, its technicians; one of them, John Plumbe, was to give American railways their start.

The explosive emergence of an industrial civilization in the south-east transformed the south-west. Llanybydder, famous for its horse-fairs, started to specialize in pit ponies; the Teifi valley began to sprout woollen mills churning out flannel shirts for industrial workers; ripples of wage demands running outwards from the highly paid east sent circles of disturbance through parish after parish. People were moving out, at first in a seasonal rhythm, to colonize the east; Dowlais and tracts of Gwent were largely peopled by them. Even as its lead-mines declined, the little ports of the south-west were enlivened. The area remained politically quiet under its gentry, but its subterranean crisis got worse. The inflated agricultural prices of wartime had sent people swarming up the hillsides; population pressure building up in a region closing in on itself in the post-war depression kept them up there and stirred an underground struggle of farmers, squatters, displaced lead-miners, over cottages, pasture, right to common. There was an outbreak of sheep-rustling; farmers who bought additional farms found open coffins outside the door. A gnawing hunger for land possessed whole communities, brought them out against enclosures. The Dissent of the region, heavily penetrated by the newer Methodism, nevertheless began to move out of the defensive withdrawal of the west into militancy as its society slithered into an occult malaise and a growing disaffection from an Anglican magistracy.

It was this which tipped the already turbulent town of Carmarthen, with its printing press, its myriad small trades in novel capitalist crisis, its brisk Bristol Channel commerce responding to novel capitalist opportunity, its tribes of bloody-minded artisans simultaneously menaced and stimulated by the change, over the edge into a kind of secession from public order.* The endless faction feuds of the Blues and Reds, originally gentry-led mafias, took on a sharper tone as its hinterland was riven by the increasing tension between tenant farmer and landlord, Dissenter and Anglican. The crisis threw up one of the first recognizably Nonconformist radicals of Wales; the town was to produce Wales's first Working Men's Association dedicated to the People's Charter. A populist 'nation' was forming in miniature behind a language line and a religious line which was also a class line. Carmarthen became a transmission centre for dissidence radiating outwards to west and east.

When the labouring people of its hinterland moved east, they took their vivid popular culture with them. Not least they took their *ceffyl pren*, the wooden cock-horse on which they mounted offenders against community to parade them through village streets to the accompaniment of 'rough music'; they took their secret societies – not unlike the Terryalts of Ireland – which during the struggle against enclosures in the War of the Little Englishman of the 1820s in Cardiganshire could turn out 600 men dressed in women's clothes under Dai Smith the blacksmith to chase off an enclosing English gentleman, his soldiers and his hired goons. From this root sprang not only their own small farmers' guerrilla of the Rebecca Riots but the Scotch Cattle outlaw bands of Monmouthshire's ingenious colliers.

For the heartlands of this new civilization were the deeply scored valleys running down from high upland plateaux under the Beacons where God had clearly never intended human beings to live until the ironmasters corrected Him on the point. Those human beings struggled out of company towns in a mauled, moon-mountain landscape against all the odds to create some of the most remarkable working-class communities in Britain. Except in times of slump, they were always better off than their cousins in the west; wages, though they fluctuated wildly, were often six times those of farm workers, and the skilled men were among the worker aristocrats; most of

*On Carmarthen, D. J. V. Jones, *Before Rebecca: popular protest in Wales 1793–1835* (Allen Lane, 1973).

them lived better than small farmers. Their housing, too, while simple and sometimes crude, was markedly superior to that of the rural areas. But as the human inflow became almost unmanageable, throwing up communities everywhere, breeding semi-pirate and bohemian districts outside the law, a beady-eyed and enterprising middle class, speculators, jerry-builders, crooks, swarmed in. Alongside the reasonably adequate settlements provided by the masters for their skilled men, this cheapjack housing sprouted like killer weed in between pits and works, on tips, in every nook and cranny, in clumps, clusters, indescribable tangles. Sanitation and public services were non-existent, epidemics frequent. In the cholera of 1849, 1,400 people died in Merthyr alone. The infant death rate was murderous; three-quarters of those who died were children under five. The accident rate was high; work was hard and dangerous, life was dangerous. For a working-class child, life expectancy at birth was about twenty in the 1830s (though in places like Oldham it was seventeen). Shopkeepers, however, lived twice as long, and even in the working class, if you could get through your childhood, you could expect to outlive your country cousin. By the 1830s organized streets and squares were appearing, and if life could be short and often lived on a roller-coaster, it was also richer, fuller, more colourful, and above all more populous and alive, bubbling with novelty, than in the thin and often crabbed parishes of the west. Most of these people came and went on coming for what they called freedom.

They were ruthlessly exploited, by a system rather than by individual entrepreneurs, who were generally paternalist, providing houses, some schools, the odd church, sponsoring friendly societies; the exception was the small, murderously competitive Monmouthshire coal industry where master-man relations were usually poisonous. Popular protest was at first directed against the visible target of the shopocracy; not until the late 1820s did some sense of a structural predicament emerge. Most works were a mosaic of subcontractors, ranging from the master-craftsmen of tinplate through co-operative contracts with 'gentlemen puddlers' to the coal cutter and his team. The butty was a distinctive figure, a minor subcapitalist of working-class origin, and an ambiguous one, now a staunch defender of the rights of property, now a spokesmen for militant, if 'responsible' protest. There was a high proportion of skilled men, 15 per cent in copper, 25 per cent in tinplate, 20–25 per cent in coal and 30–40 per cent in iron. Many women and girls worked alongside the men, though among the skilled, women were already being shut off into the home in middle-class style, and girls by the thousand were still shuffled into domestic service.

The community was intensely Welsh and it was turning its incomers into that novel breed, the South Walian. The overlay of masters, an imported 'society', many shopkeepers, tended to be English. The Swansea *Cambrian* was launched as the first serious newspaper in 1804; the *Carmarthen Journal* followed in 1810; there was an efflorescence of newspapers during the Reform crisis after 1829 – the *Monmouthshire Merlin*, the *Merthyr Guardian, The Welshman* and others. Much official life was in English. At the eastern end of the coalfield in 1841 perhaps 40 per cent of the people may have been of English origin, but it dropped to 9 per cent in Merthyr and 3 per cent in Aberdare; the Severnside counties and Cornwall were already providing those who were to be such a formative force in south Wales society; there were Bristol shopkeepers, Jews, people from everywhere. The Irish were present from an early date and from the 1830s their influx grew strong, to become a flood after the Famine. But while the Irish remained to a degree shut into a ghetto by their poverty and their Catholicism, many of the others were absorbed into a vital society which acquired English as a necessary instrument. Lewsyn yr Heliwr (Lewis the Huntsman), charismatic hero of the Merthyr Rising of 1831, the haulier son of a butcher in a mountain parish, was fluent in English, though his oratory and common speech were Welsh; he taught his English fellow-prisoners to read and write their own language on the convict ship *John*. There was a wider command of literacy than might have been expected. Merthyr had been taking London newspapers from the eighteenth century, and from the 1830s there was a flood of them. Rebels holding people's courts during the Rising made out quasi-legal documents in English. But the language of the street, chapel, pub, whole areas of work, of cultural aspiration and political argument, was overwhelmingly Welsh; where the Welsh did not suffice, they invented a south Wales English.

The people's culture of morris dancing and maypole of the anglicized lowlands did not survive the transition to an upland quasi-urban life, but the old *ceffyl pren* of the west certainly did. So did the *cwrw bach* (little beer) festivals which acted as mutual loan rituals; the name attached itself to those myriad unlicensed beerhouses which were central to working people's life. These people had a passion for games, which ranged over the free, tawny moors; for ritual sexual relaxations, which did the same; for betting – they'd bet on anything, one man streaked naked through a wedding procession in Merthyr High Street for sixpence. Foot races, which seem to have been a tradition in the area, attracted huge crowds: one ran the length of the river Taff along a tramway. People would tramp twenty miles to watch one and bet on it, amid the boxing booths and the carnival accoutrements. Shoni Sguborfawr, a red-haired giant from Penderyn, claimed to be the fist champion of Wales. He had joined the army sent in after the Merthyr Rising and acted as a spy against the Scotch Cattle. He broke out and became a hero of 'China', the old heart of Merthyr village which had collapsed into a red-light district by the bridges, full of brothels, cheap lodging houses, drinking dens, dosshouses teeming with 'nymphs of the pave', tricksters, shysters, boys doing tricks for beer one jump ahead of the corrupt and blackmailing constables and such characters as the man selling aphrodisiacs who claimed to have been a (Welsh-speaking) Polish count born on a rock in Dublin harbour and who was to be transported to Australia under his baptismal name of John Jones. 'China' had an Emperor and an Empress to rule its 'celestial kingdom'; Shoni served as one briefly before lurching west from pub to pub to serve as a mercenary hero of Rebecca and her Children.

But 'China', cheerfully fleecing chapel deacons with the best, also teemed with ballad singers. The noble Lady Charlotte Guest herself, wife of an ironmaster, creator of schools and translator of the *Mabinogion*, was rumoured to smuggle herself in, heavily disguised, just to listen to them. Shoni's boon companion was Dai'r Cantwr, a hedge-poet. Ballad singers by the dozen flocked where the money was, which meant Merthyr, easily the largest town in Wales, and that whole sweep of Welsh people across the uplands of Gwent and Glamorgan. Some of them lived on the tips. The best was Dic Dywyll (Dick Dark), a blind singer from north Wales; selling his song-sheets on the streets on a Saturday, he could make more money in a week than a furnace manager. Dic even won an eisteddfod prize, though admittedly it was at one of the new eisteddfods of 1831 run by the Free Enquirers, a group which took its name from the Zetetics, subscribers to Richard Carlile's radical journal *The Republican*.

The eisteddfod had taken off from the 1820s. After 1819 Iolo's *gorsedd*, or a respectable form of it, had lodged in the ceremony itself. These official eisteddfods complete with the new singers of difficult *penillion*, paraded around Wales, to attract the favour of Anglican clergymen with antiquarian tastes and suppressed creative passion, Tory gentleman patrons and ironmasters trying to make themselves respectable. Lady Charlotte Guest sported her Welsh peasant dress and translated Welsh classics, Lady Llanover, wife to the ironmaster who gave his name to Big Ben, went further and invented a 'traditional' Welsh costume and a whole range of Welsh customs, as a kind of right-thinking aristocratic Iolo; many Welsh people, mostly those who would not have recognized a Welsh *cywydd* had they seen one, duly adopted the styles and dragooned or cajoled many of their social inferiors to do likewise, in the Welsh version of Scottish tartanry.

Meanwhile, Welsh people who dressed in a distressingly ordinary and undistinguished manner, including those who wore moleskin, staged their own eisteddfods around their multiple societies, which tended to coalesce into Cymreigyddion clubs; in Merthyr a half-dozen or so pubs held three eisteddfods each every year and published the winning verse and prose. The Cymreigyddion at Abergavenny turned the town into a potent and dread centre of this world (it seemed peopled with adjudicators). Upper-class patrons duly moved in, but not until the middle years of the century, with the victory of Temperance, good order, the new police and a Nonconformist Liberal consensus was the eisteddfod finally wrenched out of the pub and made respectable.

In the early days its great rival was the chapel, full of workers who formed friendly societies and clubbed together to build their own houses. By the 1830s the chapels totally overshadowed the Church in these areas: ninety-five chapels to twelve churches in the uplands. They were mostly Independents and Baptists, though Calvinistic Methodists were present in strength and Wesleyans penetrated along with immigrants from England. Before mid-century only the Calvinistic Methodists seem to have played the social control role unhesitatingly allotted to them by English historians. Even the distinction between 'pub people' and 'chapel people' which became common later was not firm; the early chapels first met in pubs. They were no doubt a minority, dedicated to the climb out of the 'roughs and rodneys' towards self-discipline, civilization and respectability. But they were also highly democratic in their inner life – they grew mainly through terrible doctrinal and semi-political splits – and they were strongly working-class from the start. They and their busy and popular Sunday schools offered more than a refuge. They were a training ground. Out of their verse and music festivals came the choirs and their intensely combative and competitive working-class conductors. Their composers achieved some fame, and the democratization of music (the 'movable doh' loomed over them like Pen-y-Fan in the Beacons) in Tonic Solfa (together with the piano, later the cultural hallmark of the self-improving and radical collier) gave them scope. Characteristically, one of them – and he one of the most famous choir-masters, a Dowlais collier from the age of eight – wrote one hymn to the tune of the English popular song 'Tom and Jerry' (women fled Zoar chapel as the devil entered); equally characteristically, the three acknowledged centres of this new type of popular excellence were Merthyr of the ironworkers and colliers, Llanidloes of the weavers and Bethesda of the quarrymen.

It was precisely through the popular culture, interpenetrating with the rival and yet kindred world of the chapel, that a political culture struck root, largely through the small but highly influential Unitarian causes which inherited the Jacobin tradition. Merthyr itself had three small but powerful ones, at Aberdare, Cefn and in the town itself. While Jones of Baptist Ebenezer was being hooted in the streets for trying to bring hymns into a respectable chapel, Cefn had its own string orchestra. They were central to the radical tradition as it developed; they took over local government in Merthyr at the height of the Reform crisis. They had their people and people like them in Gwent – Zephaniah Williams, mineral agent and pub-owner who hung a portrait of Jesus in his house with the enigmatic inscription 'This is the man who stole the ass...', who was a notorious Deist, who was involved with a Humanist Society (Dynolwyr) in Nantyglo which tried to extend the Welsh language to embrace modern industry and its world. Zephaniah Williams was to form political clubs, to serve as a leader in the Chartist rebellion of 1839, to be transported to Australia (where he made and lost a fortune). Dr William Price, the Druid of Pontypridd, who called his son Jesus Christ Price and burned his corpse on a pyre, to win legalization for cremation, was another Chartist, and a highly eccentric one. There were thousands less colourful or eccentric who were of the same mind. And it was out of this hybrid popular culture that many of them came. When Wales produced its first working-class newspaper in 1834, the bilingual *Y Gweithiwr/The Worker*, its editors were two Unitarians straight out of the Jacobin tradition and immersed in the new popular culture: John Thomas, Ieuan Ddu, an artist from Carmarthen who succeeded Iolo Morganwg's son as a schoolmaster in Merthyr, a sharp satirist of the eisteddfod and the chapel singing festivals, a collector and composer of folksongs and one of the finest music teachers of his day, who was said to have introduced Handel's *Messiah* to Welsh choirs and who was also one of the supporters of the Freethinker eisteddfods of 1831; and Morgan Williams, mathematician star of a family of harpists, a master weaver with a printing press, who was to become a leading Chartist. One of the journals the latter launched, *Udgorn Cymru* (Trumpet of Wales) of 1840, produced high-quality political argument in good-quality Welsh; it was run by a workers' collective, *Argraff-Wasg y Gweithiwr* (The Worker's Printing Press) and was successful enough to become a fully-fledged stamped newspaper before it was cut down in the general strike of 1842. Its English-language companion, *The Advocate*, was rather less successful.

Such people and such publications provided a frame of reference, encased popular action in political democracy. In themselves neither this nor a modernized Welsh culture nor the other world of chapel sermon and hymn could cope with the reality of boom and slump, episodic unemployment, constantly fluctuating wages, the long monthly pay which beggared budgets, the debt slavery of the truck shops. Industrial capitalism came hard and it was fought hard. People were trying to build community in the teeth of it. To those problems, no tradition offered any answer; they had to find their own. They had to walk naked.

Throughout the early nineteenth century a kind of radical triangle repeatedly reappears in Wales, linking the industrial valleys of the south-east, the south-west and the textile townships and factories of mid-Wales where differences were really only ones of scale. All of them were ultimately to be embraced in the Chartist movement.

The earliest rebellions belong visibly to the world of the 'moral economy' of the eighteenth-century crowd, a defence of the just price and the fair wage of the Freeborn Briton against the faceless pressures of the market. Such was the communal revolt over food prices in Merthyr in 1800–1, climax to a decade of such actions all over Wales; two miners were hanged and in the aftermath, an English leaflet found in the area links at least some militants with nationwide working-class insurrectionary movements which were exposed by the unmasking of the Despard conspiracy, which had planned to kill the king, seize the Tower and the Bank and precipitate national rebellion. During the Luddite crisis of 1811–12, the first trade unions appeared among the skilled men, the puddlers, even as a barracks was raised at Brecon to control them. The post-war depression, with its 40 per cent wage cuts, provoked in 1816–17 the most massive single action in the history of the nineteenth-century coalfield, with traditional forms of protest like the marching gang and demonstrations coexisting with embryonic unions, political actions and concerted movements sweeping to and fro across Monmouthshire and the Merthyr district. Once more, in the aftermath, there were revelations of connections with revolutionary movements elsewhere in Britain.

Throughout these years, through Unitarians, radical Dissenters and Deist heirs to the Jacobins, connections were forming around Llanidloes and Newtown, Carmarthen and the coalfield between working people and a radical lower middle class, but from the 1820s, 'the decade of the silent insurrection', it is the colliers of Monmouthshire who begin to take a proletarian lead. These lower valley communities were bleak and bare places, virtually single-class communities, locked in permanent conflict with sharp and shifty employers and trapped in quasi-permanent debt to the truck shops. Often people were distinguished from each other only by degrees of debt and the presence or absence of window-sashes in their houses.

But they were a vibrant and ingenious people, offering a home to popular poets in both English and Welsh, the barrack room lawyer and the physical force Chartist. Beginning to move into autonomous action during the ironworkers' strike of 1822, they began to make *control* their objective, over their work, their townships, their lives; they replaced consumer protest with producer awareness. By 1830 they were developing trade unionism and enforcing a sophisticated system of control over production and sales. They did not hesitate to use a friendly lawyer in their cause but they backed up their arguments with a terrorist organization, the Scotch Cattle.

The Cattle were an underground movement which worked in total Luddite secrecy; they clearly grew out of the *ceffyl pren* world. Offenders against community morality, blacklegs, overchargers, the over-ambitious (among them Thomas Rees, later a pillar of Nonconformist society) would be visited by a Herd (usually from another valley) under its horned Bull, the *Tarw Scotch;* the avengers wore animal hides, turned coats, women's dresses, and staged a ritual at a victim's door. There was a rhythmic drill of warning notes, trumpet calls from the hills, night assemblies, a destruction of dwellings or a symbolic breaking of an aspirant window-sash. Sometimes the victim would be beaten up. There was said to be a code of honour and the Bull could address proclamations to his '9,000 faithful children' (possibly organized in forty-five herds of a maximum 200 each, like the friendly societies). In court they supported each other in intransigence and secrecy, and court-rooms were frequently a theatre of mockery directed against all authority. This half-hidden movement with its black and puckish humour, which was highly effective and recurred over twenty years, was said to have been launched by a leader recruited by the Ned Ludd of the English and called Lolly – the Welsh Lol, Lord of Misrule, Charivari, Punch.

Between 1839 and 1843 his cousins suddenly appear in south-west Wales in the Children of Rebecca. The tensions of the district finally exploded in a rebellion of small farmers against middle-men and rack-renters, tithe-grubbing parsons and magistrates, which found its flash-point in the toll-gates erected to levy funds to support a new but inadequate system of Trust roads. They began as the Chartist movement was taking its rise in 1839, when a crowd dressed as women attacked a toll-gate north of Narberth in Pembrokeshire. Their leader Tom Rees, a fist-fighter known as Twm Carnabwth from his miserable little farm, could not find clothes to fit and borrowed some from a neighbour, Big Rebecca. But when the revolts broke out again over 1842–3 in the immediate aftermath of a Chartist general strike, they had found a more biblical warrant in Genesis . . . 'And they blessed Rebecca and said unto her, let thy seed possess the gates of them that hate thee . . .'

Within a few months south-west Wales had become ungovernable; there seemed to be no law west of Swansea. Bands of men dressed as women, frequently led by someone on a horse (often white), staged elaborate pantomimes before a gate and then destroyed it, returning again and again. Troops, police, spies, found her as hard to break as the Scotch Cattle. The scope of Rebecca, acting through her lieutenants – Charlotte, Miss Brown, Miss Cromwell – broadened; the hated workhouses of the new Poor Law were hit; fathers were compelled to take in 'illegitimate' children, youngsters to obey parents. Rebecca even forcibly reconciled estranged couples. In June 1843 Rebecca and her Children marched openly into the town of Carmarthen, led by Mike Bowen of Trelech, winking at his butties, brilliant in a white dress with locks of horsehair, and joined by the town's poor, attacked the Workhouse where a persecuted pauper girl danced a wild dance on a table and led them to their targets . . . 'The people, the masses to a man throughout the three counties of Carmarthen, Cardigan and Pembroke are with me . . .' ran Rebecca's proclamation to the *Welshman* newspaper in the September.

Oh yes, they are all my children. When I meet the lime-men on the road covered with sweat and dust, I know they are Rebecca-ites. When I see the coalmen coming to town clothed in rags, hard worked and hard fed, I know they are mine, these are Rebecca's children. When I see the farmer's wives carrying loaded baskets to market, bending under the weight I know well that these are my daughters. If I turn into a farmer's house and see them eating barley bread and drinking whey, surely, say I, these are members of my family, these are the oppressed sons and daughters of Rebecca . . .

At that moment Rebecca's people had begun to appear on the fringes of the industrial areas and it is almost certain that the author of the letter was Hugh Williams, who was a Chartist. Hugh Williams was a lawyer from mid-Wales who knew the textile districts. He was Richard Cobden's brother-in-law and a friend of the London-Welsh father of a free popular press, Henry Hetherington of the *Poor Man's Guardian*. He had set himself up near Carmarthen and his home was a storm centre of Rebecca. He had launched the first Working Men's Association in Wales at the town, wrote a book of Chartist verse, devised a Chartist tricolour and was the first representative to the Chartist Convention of the industrial valleys of the south-east. In his person, Hugh Williams linked Llanidloes, Carmarthen and the Valleys. The Chartist Orator of Freedom's Tricoloured Banner was also the grey eminence of Rebecca.

But there was no fusion; the secret meetings at the Three Horseshoes in Merthyr (duly shopped to the Home Office) failed to secure an alliance. The breaking point was precisely the class character of the movements. Rebecca essentially was a revolt of small farmers; they won the ear of Thomas Foster, correspondent of *The Times,* who gave them sympathetic coverage. The government commissions came down to remove some of their worst grievances, while the railways, the agricultural prosperity of mid-century and the funnelling off of their labourers brought more permanent relief. As soon as farm labourers showed signs of joining in, the local Rebeccas packed in the night rides, put on their Sunday best and went to mass meetings for the benefit of Mr Foster.

Chartists had little such support; there were plenty of middle-class people among them, but they had little purchase within the political nation and their whole ethos was working-class, with the Bastilles of the Poor Law a central enemy. The movement without doubt dates from the Reform crisis of 1829–34 when Britain came closest to civil conflict. The middle-class movement for parliamentary reform ran in rivalry with the new working-class movements of the National Union of the Working Classes and the trade union syndicate, the National Association for the Protection of Labour (NAPL). By 1830 the Scotch Cattle were already writing 'Reform' into their warning notes, but the real crucible was the ironworks settlements and their capital of Merthyr where society was more complex and where there was an established tradition of Jacobinism. The slump of 1829 plunged the working-class community of Merthyr into a debt crisis at the very moment when the tide of specifically working-class political propaganda came flooding into a town whose Unitarian radicals had taken local control in alliance with William Crawshay II, a radical ironmaster. The NAPL set up its first Welsh trade union at Newtown; a colliers' union affiliated to it moved into the north-eastern coalfield, to provoke riots. When its delegates moved on to Merthyr in the summer of 1831 they ran into mass political meetings organized by workmen who had been brought into action by Crawshay during the first general election forced by the struggle over the Reform Bill. There was an explosion.

Lewis the Huntsman led a classic natural justice rebellion under a red flag to restore goods confiscated from the poor by the debtors' court. When troops marched in from Brecon, the crowd, led by Lewis, attacked them head-on. They lost two dozen killed and over seventy wounded but they forced the military to abandon the town. There was a communal insurrection under arms. 'Remember Paris! Think of the Poles! . . . The thumb has stood over the fingers long enough, we will turn the hand upside down!' They spoke of rebellions in Lancashire, Yorkshire, London. They held the town for four days, defeated and disarmed the Swansea Yeomanry, beat back an ammunition train from Brecon. They were crushed after 450 soldiers, across levelled muskets, had faced down a crowd of 20,000 coming from Monmouthshire to join the revolt and after up to 1,000 troops had closed on the town. Lewis and several others were deported but only one man was hanged, Dic Penderyn, a young miner of twenty-three, for whom desperate pardon campaigns were fought and who after his hanging became and has remained the first Welsh working-class martyr. In the aftermath, the colliers' union of the NAPL swept the whole arc of the coalfield, to precipitate a bitter civil conflict which mobilized the entire working class and which was broken in the end by a merciless lockout and an unlawful denial of poor relief which starved them into submission.

From that point, for a decade or more, it was a militant working-class consciousness which governed popular life in south Wales and found an echo in the textile areas and the south-west. It billowed up repeatedly. It expressed itself in the Owenite Grand National Trade Union which again unified the coalfield in 1834 and produced Wales's first working-class paper, *Y Gweithiwr/The Worker*. It inspired the intervention of the voteless working-class to decide the contested Merthyr election of 1835 with their threat of a boycott against the Tory; it charged the resistance to the Poor Law. But as working people in the Merthyr complex enmeshed themselves with the emergent middle-class radicalism of the town and its *pas-de-deux* with the Liberal MP, the ironmaster Josiah John Guest of Dowlais who had taken the new seat given the area by the Reform Act; as Morgan Williams, spokesman for the popular movement, tried to launch newspapers in opposition to the resident Tory *Merthyr Guardian*, the colliers of Monmouthshire launched on their own independent action under the inspiration of the Chartist leader Henry Vincent.

Chartism entrenched itself in mid-Wales, around Carmarthen, in all the valleys, but it acquired a highly militant and conscious vanguard among the then well-paid workers of Gwent, who threw up their own leaders: William Jones of Pontypool, a former actor; John Frost, an ill-at-ease draper from Newport and a spokesman for an older, less proletarian radicalism; Zephaniah Williams of Nant-y-Glo; scores of less visible men like John Rees, a mason, Jack the Fifer who had fought as an American at San Antonio in Texas. When the Chartist Convention and the Petition failed during 1839, Llanidloes broke into riot but Gwent broke into insurrection.

Dragging John Frost with them, the colliers and ironmen launched a vastly ambitious plan for a 'Silurian Republic' which would take over the major towns, the ironworks and collieries, seize essential river crossings to block off the military and give the signal for a revolt throughout Britain. Division, bad planning, atrocious weather, a last-minute pull-out by Frost and some leaders in the North of England, and the great march was shot down and dispersed at Newport in November.

By this time, with military garrisons in five major south Wales towns, a middle class armed against them, at critical moments with cutlasses, with the press and the pulpits of all save some Independents, Baptists and Unitarians belabouring them, with their country the most heavily militarized zone in Britain, the Chartists were fighting against the odds. But by 1840 they had reformed within the National Charter Association, and launched the *Udgorn Cymru* and the *Advocate* at Merthyr; they battled on, to rise in strength again during the widespread strikes of 1842. Even when those broke, they remained a presence. And the struggle for the People's Charter and full political democracy burned itself into the memories of a whole generation, in its marching men in their blue waistcoats and marching women in their blue aprons, tramping provocatively into the churches, in their Chartist gun clubs and Chartist debating societies, their Chartist caves and their demonstrations, their young girls in white dresses and green flags. In the 1840s it was the moral force people who displaced the Gwent militants, and there were shifts in leadership and style after 1842. In the end, most of the best-known spokesmen began to drift into the new liberalism.

The Chartist effort of 1842–3 marked the end of an era. During 1840 the middle classes and the authorities in south Wales, not to mention the Cabinet, clamoured for the hanging of John Frost, William Jones and Zephaniah Williams; they were saved only by a liberal chief justice. The respectable press drenched working people in the spittle of a truly ferocious class hatred and contempt. But the storm of fear and hate passed. During the 1840s government sent in its commissions to report on this peculiar district, whose temper Chartism and Rebecca had exposed. In the late 1840s the first massive orders from abroad for rails coincided with the railway boom at home, to transform the economic climate. An abrupt change in atmosphere heralded a profound social change. That major realignment of society which characterized the pudding-time of Victorian and Imperial Britain began to register in Wales. The 'working class' of Chartism gave way to the 'working classes' of liberalism. Over the world of working people, hitherto something of a tumult, to quote a favourite

Welsh cemetery inscription, *fe ddaeth ddistawrwydd mawr,* there came a great silence.

There was no silence. In 1843, the year of Rebecca's march into Carmarthen on the heels of Chartism's general strike, the first radical newspapers appeared in rural west and north.

## *A Nation of Nonconformists*

In the August of that 1843 Hugh Owen, a young Methodist from Anglesey, a total abstainer and moral reformer, chief clerk at the Poor Law Commission in London and a leading luminary in a metropolitan circle of statisticians, actuaries and economists, published *A Letter to the Welsh,* which entered history. He called on them to organize primary schools and to apply for the Privy Council grants which had been created in 1839.

From that call grew a major and sustained campaign which was to enter Welsh historical mythology. Hugh Owen moved into nearly forty years of unremitting labour, to create primary schools, to establish training colleges to service them, to reorganize the Cymmrodorion society and the National Eisteddfod as efficient national institutions, to equip a Welsh middle class with grammar schools and a university. In fact he and the people who gathered around him set out virtually to create a middle class which was specifically Welsh and a Nonconformist clerisy which carried political clout; these were to move into the leadership of a 'nation' which was gradually accreting around a linguistic-religious demarcation line which was also a class definition. From this campaign there were to emerge some of the most representative institutions of the Welsh: Bangor Normal College, the University College of Wales at Aberystwyth, the first state secondary schools in Britain.

Like every other significant Welsh initiative before the 1880s, this Welsh nation took shape outside the political nation; it was an extramural nation. The Reform Act of 1832 gave Wales five additional parliamentary seats which accorded some recognition to the changing distribution of population: the counties of Glamorgan, Carmarthen and Denbigh got an extra member, the boroughs of Glamorgan were grouped around Cardiff and Swansea and the Whigs were forced to give a seat to Merthyr Tydfil. The industrialists, who had generally held themselves aloof from local politics, had nevertheless made an entry, and Josiah John Guest (iron) at Merthyr, Henry Vivian (copper) at Swansea, established a bourgeois presence, Canningite, Peelite and Liberal in tendency, which proved permanent. The wholly male electorate remained small, some 5.4 per cent of the population. Difficulties over registration procedures, which were strict, and social shifts, ensured that the electorate grew more and more unrepresentative. By 1852 the population had increased by 28 per cent, the electorate hardly at all; its proportion declined to 4.9 per cent. In the fifties and sixties the emergence of the middle classes, the labour aristocracy and the county-town shopocracy-artisanate pushed the electorate up by some 10 per cent, but the population had in the meantime increased by a further quarter. In 1867, in the 63,000-strong constituency of Merthyr, only one man in fifty-seven had the vote, and right across the heavily populated coalfields, working people were excluded from the political nation.

The borough franchise, the £10 householder, with the harsh registration clauses and the fading away of the old freeman vote, created a brutal class definition of citizenship, vested in the middle class with an increasing representation of the better-off and more organized workers, the indefinable 'labour aristocracy'. In the counties, the situation was more complex, but the net effect was to vest the vote essentially in the £50 tenant farmers, who were fairly substantial people, and leaseholders who, on the whole, were the professionals, the commercials and the craftsmen of the small towns – a vital factor in the politicization of non-industrial Wales. For in that Wales which had been made marginal by industrialization and which was steadily losing people, the power of the landlords was crushing. In Merioneth, twenty-one people owned half the land, and across west and north Wales generally, over half the territory was in the hands of 4 per cent of the population. The sheer weight and penetration of deference politics pinned the people to the ground; politicization itself demanded something in the nature of a mass rebellion, 'a peasants' revolt' as it was called (in totally misleading fashion), a political Rebecca. Dissent could provide the material for this, but it required something more; it was that 'something more' which opened the first breaches in Merioneth and registered what amounted to a major advance out of this trap into modern politics, by the quarrymen of north Wales.

In the urban constituencies the power of the industrialists was no less overpowering and omnipresent and it meshed into landownership as industrial magnates married into the quality; the Marquess of Bute in his Gothic revival of a castle at Cardiff was as big a 'capitalist' as any ironmaster and squatted on some of the richest real estate outside New York. But in fact, until the 1840s, the unenfranchised working class, organized by a militant middle class as well as its own leaders, had had major effect; John Guest's tenure of the Merthyr seat at first rested on a delicate triangular balance of forces; it was the rise of Chartism itself and its defeat which destroyed that balance; it was followed by the emergence of the white hope of liberalism, 'the respectable working man' which incorporated leading strata among working people in a general liberal consensus. From 1841 Guest looked as though he were holding Merthyr on a life-lease from the Almighty, and such shifts as there were, were within a broad-church liberalism. Only slowly did other industrial areas begin to approximate to this model, but society, particularly in the south, was complex and open; outsiders could horn in; the great seaports, as they mushroomed, could be maverick and mercenary, rather American in style. Cutting across the north-west – south-east shadow line was Dissent, around which it could, and did, prove possible to unite the local elites of working people and *gwerin* into what was potentially an historic force.

The British shift into an imperial hegemony, typified in the Great Exhibition of 1851, provided that force. Romantic Snowdonia in Gwynedd became one of the powerhouses of that imperial economy, no less than Gwent–Glamorgan. Caernarfonshire was the site of the most grotesque concentration of landlordism in Britain. Between them the Pennants of Penrhyn Castle and the Assheton-Smiths of Dinorwic owned a quarter of the county and strangled half the population in their leaseholds. They also controlled something like 90 per cent of Britain's slate. Anglesey had been a vanguard of industrialization. Thomas Williams, an Anglesey lawyer, building on the Swansea connection, had built the copper mines around Amlwch into giant enterprises with a world market; Williams himself was a ruthless muck-t'-brass capitalist straight out of the mythology; he ended up owning businesses in Cornwall, Flintshire, Swansea, Lancashire, Liverpool, the Thames valley and London; he became an MP for Great Marlow. The copper mines began to fade from mid-century, but by then, slate was taking off. The Pennants of slate were actually a bunch of Liverpool merchants who moved in on the older feudalism and modernized it. Penrhyn Castle, built on the backs of the blacks of the slave trade, soon towered over independent quarriers, and used its landlord power over tenants to create its working class. Slate in Caernarfon and Merioneth reproduced many of the features of coal and iron in the south. It was a major centre of British industry, far less 'remote' than many a south Wales valley. Railways had opened it up by 1848; steam ships were running from Liverpool, the region's capital, Telford's road and the Menai Bridge modernized the vital Irish route, and here was, for long, the strongest shipping fleet in Wales.

Its working class built villages, after often bitter resistance to enclosure, around chapels – Carmel, Cesarea, Bethesda itself. They held smallholdings but were no more 'farmers' than Montgomeryshire weavers had been. They dressed differently, talked, lived and thought differently. Their important towns, Bethesda and above all Blaenau Ffestiniog, were in fact virtually indistinguishable from the more Welsh and 'respectable' areas of the south. Dowlais, for example, or Heolgerrig, within the Merthyr complex, in their west Wales population and Welshness, their chapels and their measured but intransigent commitment to forms of liberalism, were very similar indeed to Blaenau Ffestiniog and Bethesda. Certainly, in the north-east, the relationship between Rhosllanerchrugog and its mother town of Wrexham was so reminiscent of that between Dowlais and Merthyr that it became (to anyone all-too-familiar with the ridiculous, customary and mutual north-south alienation) almost painfully comic. Similarly, the quarrymen of Gwynedd were as working-class as any tinplater or puddler. In the late nineteenth century they were to wage a class war whose sheer ferocity and tenacity were probably unique in Britain, certainly as harsh as the black year of 1926 in the south. The differences were ones of context and scale. Those in the north were totally immersed in the Welsh language and what had become its modern culture — 'Nid yw'r graig yn deall Saesneg,' they said, ('The rock doesn't understand English'). They were to be embraced in that middle-class revolt against an overpowering landlordism which took the form of a Welsh national revolt against alien magnates, an alien religion and an alien language, whose explosive force precipitated David Lloyd George into British politics and, ultimately, to Downing Street. The quarrymen formed their union in struggle in 1874 and were in the end to break into autonomy and a local power, but there simply were not enough of them to register fully within Wales as a whole; there were 16,000 quarrymen against 240,000 colliers.

Similar questions of scale imprisoned the other major centre of industry in the north-east. The coal, iron and chemicals of Wrexham, Ruabon, Holywell, Flint, Deeside generally, had taken off with the same force as the south-east; there was just as much turmoil there as in the south over 1830–1, in the battle of Chirk Bridge and other rebellions, as the NAPL colliers' union penetrated, before it moved south. Brymbo and Shotton were foremost in the shift to steel. But the coalfield was small and difficult; by 1850 even the trade with Ireland had declined and markets tended to be local and restricted. The industrial zone settled, but into a low-level stability rather marginal to north Wales life as a whole. People began to drift out in the 1860s and by 1913 there were only 15,000 colliers.

The region which played the role of the major cities of the south was Liverpool. Around an often near-monoglot Welsh core, an expatriate bourgeoisie and working population began to form in Liverpool which in effect took over regionally the old role of the London-Welsh. This English city (if 'English' is the correct word for Liverpool!) produced some of the most famous Welsh chapels, immensely popular poets and singers like Ceiriog, journals like *Y Brython*, Saunders Lewis, founding father of modern Welsh nationalism; David Lloyd George, a good Liberal, chose to be born in Manchester.

In the south, however, the rise of Swansea and the accelerating growth of Cardiff finally ended the hegemony of Bristol and established an autonomous polity. And it was a polity with world power. In 1837 the Waynes of Aberdare sank a shaft into the celebrated Four Foot Seam and Thomas Powell of Duffryn followed; John Nixon had noted that Thames steamers which ran on Welsh coal made no smoke; he moved in. From 1851 the Admiralty commandeered south Wales; in 1885 south Wales got its total monopoly there. South Wales coal kept the Royal Navy afloat. Aberdare and its valley rocketed into social and intellectual pre-eminence; from the fifties the Klondyke rush into the Rhonddas began. The railways, starting with Taff Vale in 1841, opened up the whole area – and its south-western companion zone – and the docks mushroomed along the coast.

The ironworks in the hills had been entering a difficult time when the rail boom hit them. Now, after a series of inventions – the Bessemer process, whose convertors multiplied in the northern works, and the Siemens process which required high-grade foreign ores and started to shift plants to the coast, the steel industry displaced iron, fusing with the tinplate works now clustering along the south-western edge of the coalfield. It was in these years that south Wales began to pull away into world power and to impose its economic dominion over the rest of the country. The valley entrances at Pontypridd and Pontypool grew into substantial towns. Dowlais and its related works opened subsidiaries in Bilbao in Spain and Hughesovka in Russia. Cardiff began to sprout its docks and to grow like an American boom town, breeding close rivals in Barry and outer suburbs in Penarth. Swansea rose on its hills out of a forest of ship-masts in its harbour and ringed itself with dependent settlements stretching from Port Talbot and Neath to Llanelli. By the 1870s the whole region was thickly colonized by people, skills, cities, institutions; Cardiff and Swansea came up fast to surpass Merthyr with its 60,000 inhabitants. The rhythms of industry finally displaced those of agriculture in the life of Wales as a whole; the country had become, alongside Lancashire, one of the first truly industrial societies in the world, and like Lancashire, it nested at the heart of an imperial economy.

This imperialism registered at all levels, some of them unexpected. As early as 1850 Wilkins, the 'workmen's bookseller' in Merthyr, was selling 189 copies of the *News of the World* to twelve of the Chartist *Northern Star*. The English Sunday newspaper was a direct outgrowth from the old chapbook world, with its sex and murder, its famous-last-words and crude woodcuts; it bubbled with the same brew — cheeky, populist, vaguely radical and full of that jolly British jingoism proper to an imperial working class, a music-hall in print. The English Sunday paper swept all competition from the field; it was the first mass medium and turned the inhabitants of Britain into the most newspaper-addicted people in the world. From the 1850s it started to establish that grip even on the Welsh Nonconformist mind, which it slowly extended and has never lost.

Some of the touring festivals of mid-century Wales, from showmen to the eisteddfod, rivet the eye. Mr Aldridge, 'the African Roscius', entertained the people of Neath with his rendering of 'Lubly Rosa' and 'Opossum up a gum tree', while Templeton's African Troupe of 'negro melodists' performed a farcical 'niggerized' version of Italian opera. Wombwell's Menagerie toured Wales with its far-famed collection of wild beasts, which included a few Zulus. While an eisteddfod at Tredegar offered a prize for an essay on 'The Consistency of the Volunteer Rifle movement with the principles of Christianity', Dr Thomas Nicholas, one of the heroes, addressed the National Eisteddfod on the need to establish public schools on the English model for the Welsh middle class. At the National Eisteddfod of 1865, as the Rector of Neath kicked off with the usual rhodomontade on the eisteddfod's ancient and magical presence among the Britons 'before foreign foe ever trod on Albion's soil', the 100-guinea prize was offered for an essay 'On the Origin of the English Nation', to illustrate its connections with the Ancient Britons. The adjudicator, who was Prince Lucien Bonaparte, found none worth a prize. (The new Welsh middle class were to prove themselves the greatest history-makers and myth-makers since Geoffrey of Monmouth, but even they had their limits!) A few years later the prize was offered for an essay on the efficacy of the eisteddfod as a means of disseminating the English language. Frederick Engels in Manchester was provoked into a direct comment: 'The English know how to reconcile people of the most diverse races with their rule; the Welsh, who fought tenaciously for their language and culture, have become entirely reconciled with the British Empire . . .' Engels understated it; they were not merely reconciled to Empire, they were enthusiastic junior partners in it. This was the Welsh atmosphere which drove Dr William Price finally into lunacy and the followers of Michael D. Jones into Patagonia, where in 1865, Welsh nationalists, despairing of their native country, set up in the Chubut valley what they intended to be a pure Homeland, a *gwladfa*, in a settlement which has retained something of its Welshness to this day.*

It was in this developing climate that Hugh Owen published his *Letter* in 1843. In the same year Samuel Roberts of Llanbrynmair, in north-central Wales, launched *Y Cronicl* (The Chronicle), while Gwilym Rees, (Gwilym Hiraethog) started *Yr Amserau* (The Times), twin voices of a rural Nonconformity moving towards self-assertion. Two years later Dr Lewis Edwards, principal of the Methodist college at Bala, whose library he built into a cultural institution of significance, published *Y Traethodydd* (The Essayist), a quarterly of genuine intellectual distinction. They had foundations to build on. The Welsh-language press of the Old Dissent had started with the Baptist *Seren Gomer* (Star of Gomer) of Swansea in the early years of the century, which was eclipsed by the powerful *Diwygiwr* (The Reformer) of David Rees of Llanelli from the 1830s, a middle-class Reform journal which offered Dissent's support to Chartism – Agitate! Agitate! Agitate! – and locked into a famous feud with the Anglican paper *Yr Haul* (The Sun) edited by a Nonconformist defector. Around them, a denominational press of some liberal temper began to circulate.

Characteristically, the break into print in north and west was once more a response. Central to the emergence of Welsh Dissent as a hegemonic force and to the celebrated 'radicalizing of the Methodists' was an abrupt renaissance of Anglicanism.

The crisis of 1832 had been peculiarly anti-clerical in temper and the first Reformed Parliament, with its clutch of radicals, had attacked the Church, particularly in Ireland. They were beaten back at the election of 1835 and the Church, in which a revolt against state control was stirring, moved to the counter-attack. This was particularly strong in Wales, which seemed to be slipping away altogether. The Church had already created the first Welsh institution of university standard in the 1820s, in St David's College, Lampeter, in the heart of Welsh Wales. It now launched a campaign to build churches, revive education and regain lost ground. The Pluralities Act of 1838 ended the curse of pluralism; tithes had already been commuted and had helped to provoke Rebecca; together with church rates and a host of petty restrictions, they continued to inflame Dissenters, but four reforming bishops of ability moved into the Welsh dioceses, headed by Connop Thirlwall at St David's from 1840; he stayed there for thirty years. Thirlwall, a towering intellect and the leading churchman of his time,

*People returning from Patagonia to the old country, speaking Spanish and Welsh, later found that they could not make themselves understood.

learned Welsh but scorned his inadequate clergy. Not until 1870 in St Asaph did Gladstone appoint the first Welsh-speaking bishop since Queen Anne. But powered in part by the high purpose, if rather low capacity, of the Oxford Movement which moved into west Wales (Keble gave a lectern to a church in Cardiganshire) and colonized Bangor diocese, Thirlwall and his kin revitalized the Church in Wales.

A striking and long-term consequence was that it was Anglicans above all who moved into the surging eisteddfod movement and the national revival, who proved to be the largest single group of subscribers to the new 'people's university' at Aberystwyth and who were some of the most committed to a Welsh nationality — a fact systematically eliminated from the overpowering *history* of modern Wales shortly to be composed by a triumphant Nonconformist populism. To them and to many steeped in their history, the Church of England in Wales was to be *yr hen fradwres* (the old traitress).

One feature of the Anglican drive, however, no Dissenter could ignore: it was capturing the minds of Dissent's children. Thomas Rees in his influential history of Dissent in 1861 warned that the Anglican schoolteacher was succeeding where the Anglican persecutor had failed. The Welsh Education Committee of the Church, headed by Sir Thomas Phillips, staunch coal-owner enemy of John Frost and mayor of Newport, but a passionate Welsh patriot (like many others, he loved Wales, it was half the Welsh he couldn't stand), raised £12,000 in three years and from 1837 the number of pupils in Church schools, static around the 25,000 mark, suddenly rose. Within a few years it doubled. By 1843, at a time when there were only two non-Anglican schools in the whole of north Wales, Church schools were servicing some 320,000 out of a total north Wales population of 396,000. The Anglican National Society, between 1846 and 1848, opened training colleges at Carmarthen and Caernarfon and won for the Church a decisive and persistent numerical and financial superiority.

It was this above all which stung Dissenters into action and moved Methodists, appalled at the 'Romanism' of the Tractarians, toward aggression. Government in 1833 offered small grants to the two educational societies, the National and the (in practice Dissenter) British Society. These, the Privy Council awards of 1839, Sir James Graham's contentious and apparently pro-Anglican scheme of 1843, the Teacher's Certificate of the Minutes of 1846,* generated intense sectarian conflict. Into this maelstrom

*On the immediate background to all the Welsh educational movements, see Brian Simon, *Studies in the History of Education 1780–1870* (Lawrence and Wishart, 1960), *Education and the Labour Movement 1870–1918* (Lawrence and Wishart, 1965), Asher Tropp, *The School Teachers* (Heinemann, 1957).

Hugh Owen hurled himself. He ran head-on into opposition from Independents and Baptists, deeply distrustful of all State action, among whom the new Anti-State Church society was capitalizing on the disillusionment with the Reformed Parliament. The Old Dissent embraced voluntarism, tried to build their own independent schools. They were strong in south and east and in those regions Methodists, too, were infected by voluntarism. After a conference in Llandovery in 1844, they funnelled money and energies into their campaign, backed up by the powerful Independents of Manchester and Birmingham and their press.

So the old frontier reappeared. It was the Dissent of the rural areas, suffocating in landlordism and draining its people away, and particularly the Methodists, who responded to Owen's repeated *Letters*. Within two years there were forty British schools in north and west Wales. Teacher supply proved a problem. Welsh students were directed to Borough Road in London, but the new teacher's certificate threatened to cut off its rapid output. The government sent an education commission into Wales which was to become notorious, and Dissenters, frightened at what might follow, created a Cambrian Education Committee and put through a hasty census to prove that in west and north Wales, at least, Nonconformists outnumbered Anglicans by seven to one.

The movement survived the explosion of Dissenter and nationalist anger which followed the education commission's report in 1847 and, in fact, the pressure relaxed. H.W. Lingen the bureaucrat succeeded Kay-Shuttleworth the social missionary at Education: English and Anglican schools were not to be thrust down Wales's dissenting gullet. By 1852 there were ninety British schools in north Wales and Borough Road was running courses in Welsh which carried a government bounty. From 1853 the voluntarist vision began to fade even in south Wales and the British movement struck roots there. In the 1860s training colleges were launched at Bangor and Swansea and by the time the board schools took over in 1870, there were over 300 British schools in Wales, handling 35,000 pupils. They were still heavily outnumbered by Church schools but they provided an institutionalized framework for the mobilization of a Nonconformist people, who were now moving rapidly towards hegemony over Welsh popular life.

They certainly rode a popular tide. The religious census of 1851 registered 1,180 places of Anglican worship in Wales as opposed to 2,769 chapels. Dissent, in all its manifestations, its large, effective Sunday schools, quite widely subject to democratic control, its broad belt of occasional or even regular 'hearers' as opposed to full members, in all probability accounted for some three-quarters of the population. From the middle of the century onwards, most Welsh people lived their lives within the orbit of, or in reaction to, the chapels. Their literacy, their world outlook, increasingly their politics, were deeply affected by the morality of the chapel, its often crabbed narrowness and its often sweeping spiritual vision, its populism, in both its warmth and its deacon-controlled and often mean-spirited tyranny, its social equality and its opening to talent, particularly in verse and music, its whole style and manner, fragmented by Dissent's sectarianism and made porous by multiple variants of or departures from Calvinism. A whole people did indeed form along this line; like the Czechs, they came to think of themselves as classless, a *gwerin*, to use the popular term. Everything outside them came to seem only half-Welsh, they were the *real* Welsh. As they became more radical in their politics, they came to feel that they, as a Nonconformist people, *were* the Welsh nation. Henry Richard, one of their leading spokesmen, put it in so many words, echoed by Gladstone himself, 'The Nonconformists of Wales are the people of Wales.'

It is necessary, however, to exercise extreme caution here. Nowhere is there such a perfect example of a 'superstructure' arising out of a 'base', in its turn to reshape that 'base'. It is in the very last years of the century, when the hegemony of Dissent seems at its most overpowering, that the most visible signs of decline register. Whole sectors of popular life remained outside the chapel, even for its members. A recent study of the incidence of civil marriage in Wales after 1837 brings to light a state of affairs which is inexplicable in terms of the received wisdom. Wales, like Cornwall and the North-East of England, emerges as one of three highly distinctive areas in Britain, with a strong tradition of informal marriage and an indifference to any sacramental connotation (itself a long tradition within the Baptists, for example, and oddly out of tune with efforts to oppose attempts to canalize all marriages through the Church). The incidence of civil marriage in Wales was extraordinarily patchy and bears no relation whatever to any pattern of commitment to the social styles of Dissent. As in Cornwall and the North-East, these differences disappear in the late nineteenth century, as all three areas correspond more closely to a British norm. These were precisely the years in which Nonconformity appears to blot out the horizon in Wales, and yet this incorporation in a British pattern takes the form of a shift towards ritual ceremony in marriage, focused on the Anglican Church, which is essentially a social rather than a religious ritual and which is, in itself, evidence of secularization. As its historian states, the evidence on civil registration calls seriously into question any Nonconformist hegemony over many aspects of social behaviour.*

Similar evidence can be gathered from many fields – sport, attitudes to law and order and sabbatarianism, education, personal interpretations of the Bible. This evidence is generally highly qualitative and of mixed origin. It lurks in the margins of one of Wales's few novelists, Daniel Owen, with the hints of the 'infidels' outside; it hovers ghost-like in that writing which grew into a specific genre in Welsh, the *cofiant* or minister's memoir: the lost father, the pious mother, the finding of salvation, the lapse back into satanism, the renewed struggle and the victory; all designed no doubt to strengthen and confirm the faithful but many, one senses, often directed to an invisible audience 'outside'. The point is, that audience *is* invisible. And such hints have to face an army of bare statistics and, of course, the overpowering material from the chapels and their ministers and spokespersons. That very monopoly is perhaps itself a warning. It was precisely the printed word which was most heavily colonized by Dissent. It is necessary to remember that on Census Sunday 1851, nearly a half of the Welsh adult population went to neither church nor chapel.

What is certainly true is that those absentees became historically invisible. Whatever culture they themselves generated (and it has still to be unearthed) it did not become an effective 'counter-culture'. Large numbers of them must have lived under the diffuse influence of the chapels they never went to. It is only in the 1890s that any serious 'counter-culture' becomes visible; then it is multiple in origin, though within popular Wales it started to take Socialist and more especially Labourist form, which in turn, of course, created its own historical unpersons.

Very striking is the regional differentiation within Dissent's hegemony. Wales as a whole was more massively provided with chapel accommodation than England; it has been estimated that the whole population could have been packed into pews without much discomfort. This overprovision in part reflects a dedicated sectarian fragmentation and, moreover, it was even more significant in the rural than in the urban areas. Here, the demographic history of Wales is central. That 'rural' population was in fact full of craftsmen, artisans, small professional people, shopkeepers, country solicitors, quarrymen as well as tenant farmers under the monolith of landlordism. Such people were to be central to a radicalization of

*Olive Anderson, 'The incidence of civil marriage in Victorian England and Wales', *Past and Present,* 69 (1975).

Nonconformity and its transformation into an instrument of struggle. But the population drain was constant and in the 1880s became very serious, with the labouring population the worst affected. There seems then to have been a measure of social simplification which turned whole tracts of popular Wales into a 'petty-bourgeois' sort of place. In these circumstances, Nonconformist penetration of and hegemony over the *gwerin* could become both real and overwhelming, even as that *gwerin* itself could come to serve as a mobilizing myth for a middle class which had climbed out of it and found its identity, in combat with landlordism, in that very fusion of Dissent and the popular. In the urban areas matters were more complicated, less subject to control. It was this, more than any doctrinal divergences between denominations (which became largely meaningless except in terms of an intricate and internal self-definition in social 'tribes' which people seem to have felt a need for), which largely accounts for the often significant deviations from a standard Nonconformist pattern. Before the 1890s, however, there is little doubt that the opinion-formers, in the middle class, the new working class, among the *gwerin*, were generated by the Nonconformist hegemony itself. It was in this manner that a Nonconformist people emerged as a Welsh 'nation'.

The nationalism itself was equally ambiguous. The Education Report of 1847, accurate enough in its exposure of the pitiful inadequacy of school provision, moved on to a partisan, often vicious and often lying attack on Welsh Nonconformity and on the Welsh language itself as a vehicle of immorality, backwardness and obscurantism. The London press, led by a racist *Morning Chronicle*, called for the extinction of Welsh. The venom injected into Anglo-Welsh relations then, by this ego-trip of three arrogant and ignorant barristers probably buttonholed by some militant clergymen, has never wholly ceased to operate, particularly since the propagandists of cultural genocide remain active. In Wales at the time, there was a massive explosion of anger and resentment, an endless parade of contradictory statistics. Dr Lewis Edwards, the popular preacher-journalist Ieuan Gwynedd, indeed the Anglican patriot Thomas Phillips, joined in. Scores of answers poured from the presses. The Saxon Night of the Long Knives was recalled as the Report was stigmatized as *brâd*, the Treason of the Blue Books. A form of Welsh nationalism, peculiarly Dissenter and Welsh-speaking, was stung into life.

That there was a surge of national feeling is undeniable. It is visible in all fields. The Cambrian Archaeological Association was established in 1846; the Baptists and the Independents were to form their autonomous Unions alongside the Methodists who had always been independent. The

Cymmrodorion Society and the National Eisteddfod were revivified. A popular song written by two Pontypridd weavers in 1856, 'Hen Wlad Fy Nhadau' ('Land of My Fathers'), was adopted as a Welsh national anthem – like its patron saint St David, never officially recognized by anybody else (particularly in Twickenham), but like him, irresistible.

Yet there was ambiguity embedded in it all; even the attitudes of the Blue Books find a suitably softened expression within the heart of the Welsh nation itself. The eisteddfod became increasingly popular from the 1820s, with a myriad local exemplars; after 1858 it was formally organized as a national festival; the railways gave it a great boost. It became not only an academy of poets and historians but a mass popular entertainment. The standards set by Goronwy Owen in the eighteenth century fixed the pattern of the central verse competition, popularized by the *Drych Barddonol* (Poets' Mirror) of 1839 by William Williams (Caledfryn). Poetry in the strict metres was to be impersonal, structurally formal, mainly descriptive. The results were remarkably, and occasionally tediously, uniform. But the pressures of its growing audience opened up the eisteddfod to all manner of influences; a middle-class group was trying to turn it into a social science association, and the dry formalism of its central competition became increasingly irksome. The influences of Kant and Hegel were registering in the *Traethodydd* and in 1855 there was an explosion of criticism by William Williams (Creuddynfab) in an influential book. There was a massive shift into a more free form, which allotted a transcendental role to the poet in his philosophical meditations; long, meditative poems became the norm. Sometimes these produced striking work as in the *Resurrection* of 1850 by Eben Fardd (Ebenezer Thomas) and, even more, in *The Storm* by Islwyn (William Thomas), but increasingly in the later years of the century, the genre was colonized by The New Poet, as he was called. He introduced a belated romanticism, which became steeped in religiosity and theology and tended ever more to reflect the rhetoric and the bombast of a Welsh Nonconformist triumphalism.

At the same time, the popular world was swept by a gale of folk and folk-ish music, artificial and real. The great choirs burst on the scene in full cry, a poet like Ceiriog transfers music from the harp to the piano and the concert stage becomes a central feature of life. Every other collier, quarryman and farmer seems to be a hymn- or song-writer. In this outpouring there was much of real quality and authenticity and much of it will live so long as a Welsh person lives; a lot of it was genuinely popular and pleased genuine people, but there was much that was drenched in gross sentimentality, superficial Welsh patriotism and a no less Welsh snobbery and British jingoism. Ceiriog, in particular, immensely popular, tuned his song precisely to the taste of a new middle class which could in fact carry a lot of people along with it.

What in truth happened was that the Welsh-language culture which was produced broke decisively with its own past; serious study of the Old Song of Taliesin and the prose works went into a decline. It was essentially an English and largely middle-class-cum-populist culture translated and transmuted. While it celebrated Welsh and increasingly complimented its own language for its exclusion of dangerous thoughts which English transmitted, while it sanctified the Welsh as a peculiarly religious and law-abiding people, built into it was a recognition of a peculiar and particular role for Welsh, as distinct from the English of business and success, which in practice confirmed the status of the language as subaltern and subject. It locked Welsh up in a particular world which was rapidly becoming marginal.

While many Welsh writers grumbled and growled at this self-mutilation, only one man really broke out of the circle. This was Emrys ap Iwan (Robert Ambrose Jones), a Methodist who was, I think significantly, of partly French descent. Very unusual among nineteenth-century Welsh people, he was fully European in his assimilation of literary culture. He coined the Welsh world for self-government, scorned both major political parties, dismissed Nonconformist ambitions and land reform as distractions and argued for national survival and renewal through self-government *(ymreolaeth)*. What he focused on were some truths which have been rediscovered only in our own day. Until quite late in the eighteenth century, while all Welsh writers wrote within the massive presence of Britain, many of their impulses and instincts were in fact *European* in their manner and often in their inspiration. It was as Britain pulled away from Europe into its unprecedented empire that Welsh was pulled with it. Emrys ap Iwan both sensed and reflected that pressure; in his own day he was an odd man out.

By this time a major literature in English was coming from Welsh pens; it was as weak in novelists as Welsh-language writing, and much of its creative work tended to figure as a regional variation on English literature. Some of the best writing was in fact in technical and engineering journals. A considerable contribution was made to history and criticism. The Merthyr literary circle produced a few gems. Thomas Stephens, a town chemist, wrote the first critical history of Welsh literature and the first serious analysis of the Madoc myth (which landed him in an eisteddfod scandal); Charles Wilkins wrote major histories of mixed quality. There were quite a few others rising out of an undergrowth of mythological and sometimes lunatic 'history', not all of which was as entertaining as Morien's Druidic history of Pontypridd: the eisteddfod itself was bilingual. There was little contact with working people. Report after report from the great *Morning Chronicle* surveys of 1850 onwards speak of a genuine hunger of Welsh people in the industrial areas, even more than in the rural, for a popular literature in Welsh which they could *read*. Very little appeared; popular Welsh stayed put in the spoken word and song and hymn. This was, in effect, the crisis of the sixteenth and seventeenth centuries all over again. By the late nineteenth century nearly a half of the population of Wales knew no Welsh. When they were fully admitted to the wealth of a world language like English, what role would the Welsh language play in their lives then? Here in the making was a cultural catastrophe for that language.

This was hardly the feeling at the time, any more than it was in the seventeenth century. On the contrary, the note was one of triumph against the odds. The blessed union with England was at last raising an old people up. But in the triumph there was frustration. This new nation was still struggling against the political odds of established society. It had to break in. The group of dedicated men who had formed around Hugh Owen during the schools campaign, backed up by people like David Davies, the mid-Wales entrepreneur, a great builder of railways and docks and national character, were confronted by the controversy over the Newcastle Education Commission of 1858 and the Revised Code of 1862. A massive clamour rose in England over the neglect of middle-class education; these were the years in which the public schools were reshaped. In 1848 Swansea tried to get a non-sectarian Queen's College, and as Anglican Lampeter was empowered to grant divinity degrees, the Welsh clergy of Yorkshire petitioned for a Welsh university. In 1854 Hugh Owen and his friends proposed a Queen's College for Wales conceived entirely in terms of a Welsh professional, technical and commercial middle class among whom the Anti-Corn Law League and other middle-class organizations had been working. The anglicized upper middle classes and gentry of Wales they had written off and out of the Welsh nation. Killed by the Crimean War, the scheme resurfaced in a plan for a teachers' training college. In 1858 this found a home in Bangor Normal. Arising directly out of the schools campaign, this located itself in the heart of that rural and Welsh-speaking Wales threatened with depopulation. The industrial south, becoming heavily enmeshed with English institutions, did not seem particularly to concern these people. Bangor had a struggle at first; one inspector said they had to hew the literate out of bare rock! The Welsh language disappeared from the curriculum within five years. But the establishment of the board elementary schools after 1870 transformed the College into a genuinely national college which could stand comparison with the best of the English. By 1900 it had become far more of an all-Wales college than its new neighbour the University College. Rugby football is one oblique indicator. Introduced by south Walians, it converted natives who came to mock and remained to play. In the classic Normal v. Varsity series which began in 1898, the latter never won a game before 1913; it was the Normal which was the national college.

Bangor Normal and its sister college for women at Swansea developed a quite extraordinary *esprit de corps* (like Aberystwyth after them). Its camaraderie even affected the staffing of some military formations during the First World War. It affected much more. By the 1880s Hugh Owen's middle class was appearing, though perhaps not wholly in a form he would have liked. In 1888 the teachers' organization decided to drop the word 'Elementary' from their title as 'humiliating'; they called themselves the National Union of English Teachers. So strong was the Welsh contingent already and so loud its outcry that the teachers decided to drop the offending 'E' altogether; so the NUT, in title at least, is a product of what was to become Wales's most characteristic profession.

On these men went, to transform the Cymmrodorion into a combination of Athenaeum, Rotary Club and statistical society, to try to turn the reorganized National Eisteddfod Association (which they grounded in permanent middle-class subscriptions to discipline the ebbs and flows of popular opinion) into a species of Royal Commission in permanent session (with a 'department of poetry and music' as an adjunct!) And, building on Thomas Nicholas's proposals, on they went, in 1867, to establish a University College of Wales in a disused railway hotel in Aberystwyth, one of the few genuinely popular universities in Europe. In response to a massive appeal, there was a rally all over Nonconformist and popular Wales; 100,000 subscriptions under half a crown, heroic gifts of hard-earned money from quarrymen and miners and commercial travellers, University Sundays in the chapels. The story of Aberystwyth became a national epic; in most Welsh minds it became the people's university of the Welsh. The reality behind the first drive was David Davies, hot for a no-nonsense 'mercantile college'; the largest single group of subscribers were Anglicans, with Methodists and commercial travellers on their heels. And this, paradoxically the most splendid voluntarist enterprise of them all, was soon in trouble. It was swiftly declining into a mid-Wales preparatory high school. It needed money and support like the British schools. That required the British state. Shortly after Aberystwyth opened its doors in 1872, the Tories came into power. But beyond this desert beckoned Gladstone, the High

Churchman who developed a remarkable sympathy for the Welsh and set himself to satisfy the Irish. The year Aberystwyth started, the Reform Act threw the franchise to large numbers of new men; the year its first students entered saw the Ballot Act. The political nation was opening up.

## A Political Kingdom

In 1859, there was a contested election in Merioneth; there had been only one other since 1794. This county, like Cardiganshire, was overpoweringly Nonconformist, its Methodism strong, yet it had become notorious for its reluctance to move against the no less overpowering presence of landlordism. Outside some small towns and a growing quarry district, the county's small tenants had been inured for generations to the subtle, all-engulfing squires' paternalism; it was presenting gifts to the Wynns after their mansion had burned down on the eve of the election. In Cardiganshire, society was more complex with some lively towns but there, too, a fine mesh of influence which had long since incorporated its old Unitarian nucleus, and the apoliticism of its Dissenters, coupled with a sense of isolation from British politics, turned the place into a desert for the new radical Nonconformists. Thomas Gee of Denbigh with its industrial core, a minister turned publisher, who merged his *Baner* and the *Amserau* into a powerful newspaper with a circulation of 50,000 and made it the classic voice of a radical Welsh Nonconformity, thundered rebuke, to no avail.

But in 1859, out of the blue, a lawyer, David Williams, was put up against W. E. E. Wynne, a celebrated antiquarian from the mighty Peniarth estate. Williams stood for Nonconformist relief and he got within thirty-eight votes of the Tory. This was unheard-of. Worse was to come. Landlords at Rhiwlas and other estates evicted a dozen or so tenants and raised the rents of others, because they had refused to vote as they were told. A few years later a wave of evictions hit Cardiganshire for the same reasons. The shock was indescribable. Never before had landlords felt the need to carry their 'screwing' that far. A mighty campaign blew up all over Wales; tenants who took the vacated farms were treated as blacklegs were in industry. The Merioneth evictions became one of the most potent images in a new national mythology of particularly Nonconformist character – and it coincided with Gladstone's great campaign of reforms for Ireland, where the parallels were obvious. For the first time, there was a major shift in Dissenting opinion towards the Irish struggle, and the landlords, for the first time, began to feel the ground shift under their feet.

The focus of what was at first a measured and cautious shift into a political disaffection, itself requiring a major psychological revolution, was Bala. Here was the celebrated Methodist college under Lewis Edwards, an Independent college under John Peter (Ioan Pedr), which taught French and German; nearby was an equally celebrated and strongly nationalist Independent, Michael D. Jones. Their students were swept into a religious revival which hit the county on the eve of the election – and brought some evangelical fervour into a community which 'liked their doctrines gloomy'. No wonder: under mountains which towered less high than their remorselessly paternalist landlords, the men lived a hard life and the women a harder, even in the relative prosperity which now embraced rural Wales but did not stop the outflow of its poor and fed-up. In a successful campaign to restore the town's incorporated borough status, which gave it a mayor, two Independents (a druggist and a grocer), mobilized many of the townspeople and, with the help of Lewis Edwards, moved into a careful reform campaign. It was the Romanism of the Tractarian Church and its candidate which moved them; how could such a man represent such a county? They made progress among the tenants, some of the lesser gentry, above all among the quarrymen to the north, most of whom, however, had no vote. The response from the landlords was crushing. Sheer terror drove many back into withdrawal and they got no further in the election of 1865. But then, on the wave of protest breaking over Wales, in came the Liberation Society, a national organization dedicated to the Disestablishment of the Church and an all-out attack on the grievances of Dissent. It frightened many with its radicalism but it had enrolled Henry Richard, a man from humble origin in Tregaron who was making himself into a spokesman for a 'Welsh people', and it worked with a hard-headed electoral realism. What that lot in rural Wales need, boomed Dr Thomas Price, a towering Baptist political operator in an Aberdare which boomed even more loudly, is a strong middle class. The Liberation Society, with its practised techniques, started to beef up whatever there was in Merioneth. More important still, the quarries caught the imperial tide. Blaenau Ffestiniog, a village built around an Independent chapel, became a town. And in 1867 came the Reform Act which tripled the electorate. Many quarrymen in particular got the vote. The central issue in the election of 1868 was the Disestablishment of the Irish Church, an issue of principle, voiced in the rhetoric of Gladstone and John Bright, whose echoes in Wales were loud and clear. With Bala and its radicalized shopocracy as the mobilizing force and Blaenau Ffestiniog as its heartland, the new radicalism forced the Tory to withdraw. The 'peasants' revolt' in Merioneth had been won by the quarrymen, marching appropriately behind that badge of the working class, their brass band. But there was a long way to go yet. More evictions followed all over rural Wales; the new Welsh MPs got a Ballot Act. A Gladstone government gave Bangor a university college, but it took another Reform Act, that of 1884 which turned Britain into a democracy, before, in 1886, Merioneth found its true man. Its voters elected Thomas Edward Ellis, the son of a tenant farmer near Bala, educated at Aberystwyth and Oxford and the shining hope of a new Welsh Liberalism. In him, Merioneth found a Hero and in Merioneth the new Welsh radicalism found a Hero County.

But it had been a long, hard business, a molecular growth, and it was even harder and slower in Cardiganshire. The new political consciousness broke in along the railways and through the press. The repeal of the Taxes on Knowledge in 1854 was followed by Gladstone's repeal of paper duties in 1861, and that remarkable phenomenon, the Welsh press, entered its golden age. There was an explosion into print. Its strongholds were on the borders of industrial and rural Wales – Llanidloes, Brecon, Trefecca, Abergavenny, Carmarthen, Llandysul, Caernarfon, Denbigh – supported by strong bases within the heartlands of commerce and their Welsh extensions into England and America – Merthyr, Aberdare even more, Swansea, Wrexham, Liverpool and, no less, London, Philadelphia and New York. Its 'overproduced' printers, like its 'overproduced' ministers, followed by its 'overproduced' teachers, straddled the shadow line and obliterated it. An ocean of pamphlet literature, newspapers – many of them to become celebrated – *Yr Herald (The Herald)*, *Y Gwron (The Champion*, literally *The Hero)*, *Tarian y Gweithiwr (The Worker's Shield)*, *Y Gwladgarwr (The Patriot)*, *Seren Cymru (Star of Wales);* magazines and critical quarterlies by no means always religious, flooded over Wales. Places like Merthyr, Swansea, Caernarfon, Denbigh at last became provincial capitals with influential papers. 'What we think today, Wales will think tomorrow,' they shouted from a bustling, militant and cultivated Aberdare and they were not joking. Because, with the press, came the Liberation Society, with its skilful management, and after it, the Reform League, striking once more for a vote for the workers. Chartists reappeared in Merthyr Tydfil and launched the *Merthyr Star*.

It was out of a reshaped industrial society that they came. Through the fifties and sixties, the new and respectable working classes emerged on the frontier of the franchise, in their co-operative societies, started in Aberdare in 1860, their serried ranks of friendly societies, their labour aristocracies. Beneath them the invisible made their way the best they could, into the army and navy or the boxing booths if there was no other way. The whole district was drawn deeper and deeper into a British manner of life. But it remained essentially Welsh, as the chapels expanded more and more deeply themselves into the working population, the new police finally brought places like 'China' under control, and the Temperance movement rallied both chapels and the eisteddfod to a Nonconformist populism. The historically visible working class embraced that fusion of Dissent and democracy which the redoubtable Baptist Thomas Price had already achieved in Aberdare, the model society for this configuration, finding a swiftly growing companion in the Rhonddas. They had to live under the control of such as H.A. Bruce (Gladstone's Home Secretary), a man of political presence, member of a legal dynasty enmeshed with the works masters who had towered politically for sixteen years over the valleys as any landlord in the west, but who had to walk a sight more carefully, indeed often had to tread as delicately as Agag.

It was this kind of society, finding its kindred across the shadow line in Dissent and its social ambitions, which was unleashed by the Reform Act of 1867. That Act brought household franchise into the boroughs and increased the county electorate by 50 per cent. In some areas the change was vital. In Denbigh, with its industrial base, the electorate tripled. In Merthyr the change was revolutionary. The electorate, in a constituency which covered much of the Aberdare Valley and 105,000 people and was given an additional member, rose from 1,387 to 14,577 to become the most democratic in Britain.

With the Irish Church and Nonconformist grievances central to the campaign of 1868, major change could be expected. The results were in fact sensational. In Denbigh the very radical barrister George Osborne Morgan, with Thomas Gee and his press behind him, won the second county seat to challenge Sir Watkin Williams Wynn, the King of North Wales. In Merthyr, H.A. Bruce was confronted with angry miners who had seen 300 of their people killed in pit disasters over the last fifteen years and had just heard of 168 men and boys blown to bits in Ferndale in the Rhondda. While the iron industry was hit by a depression, coal was booming and the colliers were inflamed by an attempt to introduce double-shift working. With the Chartists re-emerging and old Unitarians finding their voice again, working men began to form independent political organizations and to press their particular demands within a radicalism which added a secular dimension to a Nonconformist populism which was no less strong among them. Dr Thomas Price, who had been loud with accusations that industrialists no less than landowners, 'could screw three out of four of the electors from Cardiff to Holyhead', succumbed too readily to Liberationist pragmatism. He supported the Aberdare industrialist Fothergill, to some dismay, and seemed to be supporting double-shift. The normally united Liberal, Nonconformist and populist alliance was in disarray. In these circumstances, with working men discussing the writings of Ernest Jones, the Chartist friend of Marx and Engels, and suddenly become both angry and ambitious, the election committee in Merthyr, whose secretaries were three Unitarian and one Baptist minister and to which eighty-one Nonconformist congregations were affiliated, took the unheard-of step of inviting an outsider with no money and no local connections, a man already coming to be known as the Apostle of Peace, with great pull over Dissenters of radical temper but no parliamentary experience. The man who had to face Gladstone's Home Secretary and the Industrial Boss of the Aberdare Valley was Henry Richard of Tregaron, of the Peace and Liberation Societies. He moved in as 'a Welshman, an advanced Liberal and a Nonconformist'. More, he not only adopted all the most radical planks of the Dissenting platform, but came out openly for a completion of the Chartist programme and stood as the candidate of 'Wales and the Working Man', both good Dissenters of course. His campaign took off. Huge crowds spilled out from his meetings along the hillsides singing *Hen Wlad fy Nhadau*. Merthyr added to its list of heroes from its frontier prehistory, the first of its parliamentary heroes; Henry Richard swept to the head of the poll, pitching out Bruce to find consolation as the first Lord Aberdare and outrunning Fothergill, the middle classes' man, by 17 per cent.

And all over Wales, Blaenau Ffestiniog's brass band echoed; there was a critical shift in voting patterns, in Merioneth, Caernarfonshire, Denbighshire, Anglesey, Carmarthenshire. The Liberals won twenty-one seats to the Tories' twelve; Liberals had been winning overall majorities since 1857; the South, with some mavericks, had been a Liberal fief. But they had been Whiggish or industrialists. In 1868 a new kind of Liberal was moving in, with new forces behind him. It was the landlords who could now most clearly see the writing on the wall; it was the bishops who could see their notion of Wales getting out of control; Ireland was throwing a longer shadow. The election of 1868 was followed by a new wave of political evictions. A whole new roll-call of martyrs provoked a massive campaign which focused a Welsh hatred on the baron, the bishop and the brewer, the unholy trinity of Toryism. And it was increasingly a Welsh national hatred; these opponents were becoming enemies of a Welsh nation. That nation won the ballot in 1872.

The return of a Conservative government was simply another irritation. The Rhonddas now began to throw an even longer shadow than Ireland. As they boomed, so the pit disasters multiplied. The men marched into unionism and the Amalgamated Association of Miners (AAM), based in Lancashire, made headway in the early 1870s. The great coal combines were already beginning to form. From 1864, one bought out Powell's mines to create Powell Duffryn (nicknamed PD, Poverty and Death). Between 1872 and 1875, miners' wages were forced down by 25 per cent and the AAM went bankrupt. Out of its ruins emerged a patchwork of intensely localized unions under local satraps. As the pit and the chapel fused in Aberdare style, these threw up a remarkable leader, William Abraham, Mabon, a consummate operator, a thoroughly Welsh Welshman in the now approved style, Liberal, Nonconformist, an eisteddfod man. He was a charismatic figure; his face was ultimately to become an advertisers' image. Rowdy meetings he could quieten by breaking into a magnificent rendering of *Hen Wlad Fy Nhadau*. Significant in itself is the fact that this anthem could produce this effect at this time; even more striking is the fact that Mabon picked this trick up from 'old Mr Brown' of the AAM who was an Englishman!

Mabon, in tough negotiations with W. T. Lewis, head of the new coal owners' association, hammered out a seminal agreement in 1875 which set up a Sliding Scale to regulate wages according to the selling price of coal. This was the institutionalization of his Liberal concept of a unity of interests between masters and men. This, and the monthly holiday he won in 1888 for the men, Mabon's Day, were to be his memorials. They were to help make him the first Welsh working-class MP. And as working people carved out their place in this new Liberalism, Hugh Owen led the middle classes into action in one last battle. As soon as Gladstone got back, Hugh Owen in Lord Aberdare's study drafted a request for a public inquiry into Welsh higher education.

The Aberdare Committee, which included Henry Richard and Sir John Rhys, first Professor of Celtic at Oxford, met thirty-two times in fourteen towns, listened to 257 witnesses and published a volume of over a thousand pages with 20,000 questions and answers and twenty-five appendices. It was virtually a national petition. Owen himself put forward a distinctly French scheme for county secondary schools integrated into two university colleges at Swansea and Aberystwyth, presided over by a university of Wales and built on strictly middle-class and meritocratic principles. The Committee made a half-hearted attempt to focus a university on the already-existing Anglican St David's at Lampeter, but an aroused Nonconformity would not hear of it. The scheme which resulted was more messy and more British, but its consequences were epoch-making. Put through in the end in 1889 by the sympathetic Education Secretary of a Conservative

Government, it created the first secondary school system with state support in Britain. By the First World War, Wales had a network of 100 county schools, run on the rates and backed by the Board of Education, with a standard of teaching acknowledged to be superior to that in much of England. From the same Committee came two university colleges, at Cardiff and Bangor, both with state grants; they opened over 1883–4. The consequences were to be incalculable. A bubbling wealth of talent was set free – and in one direction, upwards.

And in 1881, under heavy pressure, the Commons passed the Welsh Sunday Closing Act which shut the pubs in Wales and later Monmouthshire on a Sunday. This was in fact the first British legislation since the Civil War to treat Wales as a separate nation. It speaks volumes, or perhaps liquid measures, in itself. The brewers got their come-uppance: so did many others, but they had their contrivances. It looked as though Henry Richard was right; that Welsh nation was the Nonconformist People.

Three years later came the Reform Act of 1884 and five years after that the Act creating elected county councils. In Wales this precipitated a legal revolution. The miner, the tinplater, the steel worker, the quarryman got the vote; there was a massive advance towards manhood suffrage. Seats were redistributed on a large scale. Glamorgan was turned from a two-member county with under 13,000 voters into five new divisions with 44,000; in Monmouthshire a two-member constituency with 7,600 voters became three constituencies with nearly 32,000. The Welsh county vote rose from 75,000 to over 200,000; the electoral landscape in places like Anglesey and Merioneth was transformed. Wales was overrepresented at Westminster and by a large preponderance of working-class single-member constituencies.

In a Britain which had become a democracy, this new Welsh nation crashed through the franchise barrier. The Welsh working man, in the person of Mabon, got to the Commons as the Liberal tide rolled irresistibly across Wales. George Osborne Morgan brought to an end 182 unbroken years of Wynn rule in Denbigh. Thomas Gee became chairman of Denbigh County Council. Throughout Wales the 300-year reign of the squires came to an abrupt end. The gentry went into a kind of internal exile as they were expelled no less forcibly from the history of their nation which the new men, in their new schools and colleges, set themselves to write. All over Wales, the bastilles went down before the ballot as the Nonconformist People entered its political kingdom.

# 10 · AN IMPERIAL DEMOCRACY

In December 1916 David Lloyd George became Prime Minister of Britain. The Welsh country solicitor, scourge of landlords and bishops and dukes, creator of a welfare system, familiar of press barons and the new rich of a novel society which thought in terms of masses, and a voice of the new populist and collectivist Liberalism of that society, was about to become the man who won the War and certainly the most remarkable, if not the greatest, statesman of the British Empire.

With him he brought a clutch of new men from Wales, to help staff his Whitehall executive and put through the shocking innovation of keeping the minutes of a war cabinet he had invented. Among them was Professor Thomas Jones (T.J.), the Methodist son of the company shop in Rhymney, south Wales, who had worked his way through the universities at Aberystwyth, Glasgow and Belfast, to make a distinguished academic career, had transferred to the great campaign against TB in Wales, had formed a Fabian and imperial intellectual circle in south Wales, and had launched its *Welsh Outlook* press, as he was later to invent other presses and cultural organizations, not least the Arts Council, in the service of his interpretation of social imperialism. Summoned to Downing Street in 1916 to serve as a deputy to Sir Maurice Hankey, he was to follow his Welsh master into that imperial transmutation during the twilight time of empire between the wars, in which he became a shadowy but very real grey eminence on the borders of the state and society, to write nearly all the speeches of Stanley Baldwin (except the bits about the pigs) one of which was hailed by the *Morning Post* as the very essence of true conservatism, to the huge and hidden glee of this Welsh Fabian; to work closely with the Astor family and become one of the celebrated Cliveden Set and to perform such manly late imperial services as trying to talk sense to Adolf Hitler and trying to install von Ribbentrop's son in Eton.

At much the same time, his control of patronage in his homeland was such that he was nicknamed the Minister for Wales; R.H. Tawney was warning rich men that a person carrying a red flag should herald the approach of this Robin Hood who was about to fleece them in the service of the Welsh; through him funds were funnelled into his shattered homeland

and into his favourite enterprise, the workers' adult college at Coleg Harlech in Merioneth. He regretted to his death his failure to become principal of his University College at Aberystwyth, when, in 1919, despite an application and a testimonial of unparalleled power, with the Prime Minister and General Smuts among his references, he met humiliation at the hands of Cardiganshire backwoodsmen who could not forgive him because he had stopped going to chapel. In the days when his native country came to the edge of despair, Tom Jones penned, anonymously, a satire in full Swiftian ferocity, outlining a Final Solution to the South Welsh Problem: the deportation of the population and the designation of the empty site as a Grand National Ruin.

The Wales he came from, and particularly its southern metropolis, was no less simultaneously Welsh-national and British-imperial. Ruin would have been in no one's mind in 1913, or even 1921. These men, with most, if not all their women trailing dutifully behind, strutted like fighting cocks through an economy which was perhaps the most buoyant and expansive in Britain. It found its most memorable human expression in what, after an initial struggle, had become its national game, rugby, the only field where it was possible to be simultaneously Welsh and a gentleman (normally a difficult undertaking), where doctor and lawyer could ruck happily shoulder-to-shoulder with miner and where Wales, safely lodged as a major directive element within imperial Britain, could hope to express its now self-confident identity in a continuous eisteddfod of Grand Slams and a continuous rugby-dinner chorus of God Bless the Prince of Wales (duly Invested at Caernarfon by a Lloyd George who was as inventive of Welsh traditions as any Lady Llanover or Iolo Morganwg). How much more Welsh was this than boxing, distressingly full of aliens and as brutal an escape route out of the poverty of south Wales as it was for blacks in the USA! How preferable to soccer, so irredeemably proletarian and English!

No less simultaneously Welsh, 'classless' and imperially British was the Magic Goat himself, leaping nimbly from the aggressive middle class of north Wales, now on the offensive against Anglican landlords and creating a Welsh nation in its own image, into the hymns around the piano in Downing Street and to the pinnacle of British imperialism at its moment of peril. They both rode the flood-tide of imperial and democratic Wales.

## Imperial Wales

In a south Wales which has lived for sixty years as a problem, it is difficult now to recall the atmosphere in which Professor Stanley Jevons of Cardiff,

Lloyd George's post-war City of Dreadful Knights, could see south Wales
in 1915 as an anticipation of California (and one worried statistician could
calculate that its capital's population might reach 20 million!). This
psychological blindness has in fact been a handicap to the creation of a
historiography and a cultivation of memory which have some contact with
reality. But around the turn of the twentieth century, south Wales was one
British region where growth was still breakneck and full of promise. It was
Old King Coal, of course, who was the kingpin; he had conquered the British
navy and his city had become the greatest coal port in the world. In 1921
he had at his command 270,000 miners, with their families, one Welsh
man in every four, four Welsh people in every ten.

But this was not simply a matter of coal export, huge though that was,
of John Cory's bunkers straddling the world and south Wales coal keeping
the greatest navy in the world afloat, staggering though these were. The
capital, the technology, the enterprise, the skill and the labour of south
Wales fertilized large and distant tracts of the world, from Montana and
Pennsylvania to Chile, Argentina and Russia. They helped to deflect the
economic development of Spain, wrenching the centre of its heavy industry
from its natural base in the Asturias to the region of Bilbao, where Dowlais
planted a subsidiary to snatch the high-grade ores and an even higher-grade
people, to scatter Spaniards around its own town and out to Abercrave.
South Wales firms bought up shipping companies and port capital in Rouen,
Le Havre, Brest, Hamburg, Marseille, Naples; for years Italy's economic
rhythms were those of its Welsh coal imports; the little town of Bardi near
Parma, with a few friends, specialized in colonizing Wales with their popular
restaurants, cafés and chip-shops, supplying some of Wales's most striking
dynasties and finding an immortality in Gwyn Thomas's novels. For years,
the real economic capital of Chile was Swansea, luxuriating in its nitrate
clippers and Cape Horners, though it was north Wales which rivalled the
Jacks to provide some of their most ruthless oligarchs to both Chile and
Colombia.

The entrepreneurial voice of south Wales, which, scorning its local
Liberal rival and a clutch of muscle-flexing challengers in north Wales,
Swansea, Newport and Liverpool, claimed to be the voice of Wales, was
the *Western Mail*. Its greatest editor was one of Cecil Rhodes's men, who
found Wales far more exciting and promising than Rhodesia, even though
he tended to confuse their respective natives. It was Cardiff which helped
finance and offered a base to Scott's mission to the Antarctic. The *Welsh
Outlook* could compare the Welsh to the Japanese as an old people finding
a new role and rejoice at their even more abrupt coming-of-age. After the

Klondyke climax of the First World War, a lurid and rollicking climax, all chicken and champagne bottles in the miners' tin baths, according to the *Mail*, lit by the roaring furnaces now sucked down to the populous coasts, the crash of the 1920s was all the more unhingeing in that it devastated a country on the crest of what had been a gigantic wave of ambition.

Presiding over this world in its imperial days, sucking it dry of talent and wealth, was the noble and squalid city of Cardiff, with Swansea and Newport at its heels. Cardiff, catching the town-planning fever and acquiring the huge Bute estate, cut a great green swathe through its heartland to raise the baroque palaces of its City Centre, alongside the prim but affluent and tall terraced houses of its bourgeoisie, to balance the merchant palazzi clustering around that huge and ponderous ideology in Bath stone, its Coal Exchange, with its vast chamber, its warren of offices, its slant-eyed dragons, right down in its docklands among the teeming and cosmopolitan peoples of Tiger Bay and Bute Street. This was the artery of empire and the jugular vein of capitalist Wales, within which every other Wales had to live. All along the coast the houses ran from Barry bunched around its great and rival docks, with its holiday strip of an Island, Penarth with its posh and prissy suburbia and its nascent Costa Geriatrica, past the developing beaches, through Port Talbot and its neighbours, all plants and works and people jammed into a huge sausage-dog of a long town somehow squeezing itself in between the mountains, into the sprawling, salty, hill and seaspray town of Welsh Swansea, with its great ships and old Cape Horn hands and its Dylan Thomas pubs, out on to the rim in rugby-mad Llanelli with its west Wales Welsh but no less imperial a sentiment. This was what Alfred Zimmern called 'American Wales' and what others called 'un-Welsh Wales', but what a good third of the Welsh people called home.

Up in what everyone except their inhabitants called *The Valleys* were the people who had raised these palaces. This was in no sense the dread and drear landscape of the 1930s that so many of us find hard to eradicate from our mind's eye. After the housing legislation of the 1870s, these communities, save the oldest right on the tops, took their familiar form, ribbon on ribbon stretching along the lower slopes above the railway, the road and the canal: houses tidy, uniform, often spacious, sometimes terraced on breathtaking sweeps of stone steps, tight, respectable, spotless and brightly painted. In and among them were the new symbols of affluence and self-assertion: the multiplying drapers and grocers, the Home and Colonials, the first chain stores, the vast, crowded and magic bazaars and emporia, the now massive and Gothic, Baroque, Rococo, Marzipan, you-name-it, chapels. There were public facilities, communal in scope, which neither working-class Cardiff nor anywhere on the coast could hope to match: huge, cavernous theatres and skating rinks – 'See you on the Ice!' and see everyone but everyone, from George Bernard Shaw, G.K. Chesterton and the Pankhursts to the Barry Dwarf, they did. Towering alongside the Temperance Halls were those buildings which were no less an ideology in stone, the Miners' Halls and Working Men's Institutes with their often massive libraries, focus of an intense social, intellectual, political and simply living, life.

These communities, intensely self-conscious no matter how imperceptibly the one ran into the other – 'Strangers they were, mun,' said a Tonypandy man, defensively recalling the Riots, 'They were strangers, mun, strangers from as far away as Gilfach . . .' – throbbed with Penny Readings, choirs, eisteddfods and *noson lawen* (ad hoc evening self-entertainment), debating societies, drama clubs, literary cliques. There was an extraordinarily rich, wide-open, very Welsh, very British, often travelled, if only in khaki, and increasingly American, popular culture which had invented its own language and which flourished no less in pub and boxing booth and pigeon meets and dog-race compounds, soccer and rugby fields (with baseball down in Cardiff), cricket matches, cat-and-dog in the streets, pitch-and-toss on the tips, railway trips, bikes, soon buses and charabancs to Barry Island and Porthcawl, Gilwern and Pontsarn, Llanwrtyd Wells (Llandrindod was a bit posh and English) and anywhere else the money would stretch, the road home marked by the hills and the pitwheels and some old Bessemers still roaring nearly 1,000 feet up.

This was the world of a majority of the Welsh people, a world carried, supported, fed, washed, coddled and clothed by its hard-working and resilient women, taken for granted as First Mate in the House by the Captain of the Ship at work. It was a people sustained by all the dense and interlocking networks of working-class life, with its bubbling world of imprisoned talent often marooned and mauled among the dark and bitter struggles, the harsh, hacking, unremitting labour, the disasters which could kill 300 men and boys at a time and blight whole communities. This was the distinctive, sardonic, complex, warm, picaresque, soft-hearted and malicious, hard-headed and cock-eyed, ambitious and heroic and daft world of the miners, whose disappearance has left south Wales a cubit shorter in spirit.

Across the shadow-line, now virtually obliterated by Dissent and Liberalism, rural Wales, settling after its huge blood-letting into a materially modest but psychologically ambitious pattern, rebuilt itself in much the same style. One can hardly see beyond the Victorian-Edwardian in its architecture to this day, except for those gentry houses stranded like obsolescent whales among a people which had swept past them. Scattered across an unyielding country, the houses, chapels, shops, small businesses, clustered in their tightly respectable knots, trim and brisk in the softer country, gaunt and limpet-like in those highlands from which human settlement was receding in a remorseless ebb-tide which left ruins and memories of a Welsh language that once was, as people were carried ceaselessly out. The small towns stirred with a new life, grouping their miniature garden and intellectual suburbs around Carmarthen, Bangor, Caernarfon, Aberystwyth. They blossomed more abundantly around Denbigh and its kin and looked slightly askance at Wrexham and Rhos, Ruabon and Deeside, with their dense settlements rehearsing the styles of the south-east in a different accent and sometimes a different language and living in the ever-extending shadow of Merseyside. Under that shadow rose the holiday towns along the coast, demotic Rhyl and aristocratic Llandudno and their exploited women. Breaking free of it were the fistfuls of quarrymen under Snowdonia, their towns built around chapels in the shadow of Penrhyn Castle, houses running in dungeon terraces under the mountains and the towering slate tips, typhus still ravaging them. From them and their women endlessly polishing brass and making tea and cramming the little rooms with pianos and dressers like their sisters in the south, the men walked to the canyons of the quarries wearing bowler hats and carrying umbrellas, to turn their lunchtime *caban*, a dark tunnel of spluttering candles and stewed tea, into an eisteddfod-cum-trade union of improvised verse, song, quizzes and debates. And along the sweep of the coast with its lively little towns and ships, with the hard upland life of small farmers and artisans behind, was the world of the seamen and the ministers, the Captains Cat and the Reverends Eli Jenkins, filling out into the richer south-west and shifting into different time-scales, different languages and different priorities in the open, busy and commercial Little-England-Beyond-Wales.

Out of this world, a new plutocracy had emerged: D.A. Thomas, to become Lord Rhondda the coal king, David Davies the top sawyer from the textile townships of mid-Wales and his no less committed kin in their Ocean Coal, the mandarins of Powell Duffryn, the new rich of the coastal towns in their Hanseatic palaces, Sir Alfred Mond of Monsanto crying 'Wales for the Welsh!'. Around, though some distance from them, were the other risen mandarins, more academic, but hardly less political – particularly the solicitors – of small-town, rural and aspirant working-class Wales. Beneath and sometimes alongside these were the new Welsh professional and middle classes, a pride of lawyers, the multiplying regiments of teachers, civil servants, drapers, a myriad salesmen and their colleagues, many seized with some sense of mission and self-fulfilment as they emerged from Board schools and county schools, universities and technical colleges to people half England, to reinvigorate their own Welsh-language press and to create a new English-language one, to plant their suburbs and imitation Hampsteads in Rhiwbina and Town Hill and Llanbadarn Road, while others moved resolutely into engineering, shipping, technological institutions. For the first time in generations, a new Welsh intelligentsia, from popular roots and strongly university-based, was creating a Welsh-language literature of high and original quality as their imperial and democratic kin of the world language of English invented a new genre.

This was a complex and basically contradictory people inhabiting a plurality of classes and social formations and languages who found an historically brief but potent moment of unity in the Liberal Wales of a Britain which had made itself a political democracy.

## A Nation and a People

Welsh political life in modern times, unlike English, has been characterized by relatively abrupt revolutions in personnel, ideology and style, which inaugurate long one-party eras, virtually *régimes* in the European sense. Only in the 1970s has that pattern been broken. The Tories ruled the roost until 1857; a Liberal majority succeeded, to become very powerful after 1868, and after 1884 to assume giant stature. In 1885 Liberals won thirty of the thirty-four seats and very rapidly became the 'Party of Wales'. There were minor setbacks in 1886, in the Liberal split over Irish Home Rule, and in 1895 after the humiliating collapse of the Liberal government, but the Liberals remained entrenched in twenty-five seats or so even then. In 1892 Welsh Liberals won thirty-one of the thirty-four seats, virtually to hold the balance in the Commons; they actually gained seats in the 'khaki' Boer War election of 1900 and in 1906 their triumph was total – not a single Tory MP was returned from Wales.

The 1880s brought in a new generation: Samuel Evans, a 'lawyer on the make' from mid-Glamorgan, an Independent rake who was a fierce spokesman for a politically rakish Nonconformity; Ellis Griffiths, an eloquent Anglesey barrister. There were three giants. Thomas Edward Ellis was for a while a national hero, a man of intellect and charm who died young in 1899 and became a figure of legend. The son of a tenant farmer of Bala, wreathed in the memory and mythology of the evictions, he had studied at Aberystwyth and Oxford, imbibing T.H. Green, Arnold Toynbee, Ruskin. He admired Cecil Rhodes and it was in Egypt that he was seized with a vision of 'the Wales that is to be' (Cymru Fydd). His was a highly unusual social imperialism which blended an empire in which Wales was to take its full place with a total immersion in what had become Welsh tradition, its poetry and its Methodism, in a strong populism which came to carry semi-socialist overtones. He was compared to Mazzini and Thomas Davis of Ireland and there are sometimes touches of a less bloodily sacrificial Patrick Pearse in him, despite his imperialism. He had an intensity and passion which echoed long after his death. He dominated Welsh politics to 1892; his service as a junior Liberal Whip from that year seemed an eclipse and to some a betrayal; and within seven years he was gone.

A Welshman of very different stripe was D. A. Thomas, later Lord Rhondda, member for Merthyr from 1892 to 1910, head of the Cambrian combine and Czar of the Coalfield. A formidable and intelligent spokesman for the industrialists and the Cardiff Chamber of Commerce, he was also a nationalist and a prime mover in launching the Cymru Fydd movement in 1892. He was a south Walian nationalist above all else and it was his resistance to north Walians and Lloyd George which broke it. He was a great antagonist of the miners in those battles which passed into popular mythology and his only unqualified success outside his business was his organization of local government and food supplies during the War.

Outshining all these was David Lloyd George, a solicitor who hurled himself and his incomparable oratory into the struggle against landlords and the church in the 1880s, became a 'boy alderman' and with his Labour and nationalist friend D. R. Daniel, the plague of the respectable. In 1890 he won Caernarfon Boroughs by the skin of his teeth at the age of twenty-seven and fought several knife-edge fights there before he turned it, most of Wales and half England with it, into his fief. Blazing, intransigent, a miracle worker, his was a genuine populist radicalism which was not tied to party. He had little sympathy with many of the issues stirring Welsh politics even though he had to pay lip-service; he was blank on Ireland, literature, education; hymns around the piano notwithstanding, he rebelled against the chapels of 'glorified grocers... and beatified drapers...' He was a freethinker, an unbridled opportunist, a committed social egalitarian and a magician who commanded passionate loyalties and provoked passionate hatred. Before he was transmogrified into the Imperial Wizard, he was, like Aneurin Bevan after him, a maverick and an utterly untypical figure in a Welsh theatre which could hardly hope to contain him.

This new breed of Welsh Liberals, organized in a Welsh Party in the Commons under the occasionally bewildered but always honourable Englishman Stuart Rendel, MP for Montgomeryshire, ran straight into the rural crisis of the 1880s. Those years which saw 100,000 people quit the farms and the fields, were years of hard battles, the Rebecca of north Wales. In a country hit by the great depression, which inflamed the grievances of tenant farmers, those battles were certainly real enough, but in economic terms they were shadow fights. There were tough times and the problems of security of tenure, rents and improvements were similar to those of Ireland, but matters were never so hard. Lloyd George and his friends invited Michael Davitt over, to leave his lasting impression; Thomas Gee could form a Land League and the burning Pan Jones even preach land nationalization. But in fact, underneath the great drop in plough acreage and the mass migration of labourers out, small farmers, heavily increasing their cattle stock and exploiting their new grass acreage as soon as the depression started to lift, were in these years laying the foundation of that society of small proprietors which was to be the ultimate inheritor. Ireland was employed as a metaphor. The real heart of the struggle became instantly clear from the start. As soon as crises hit, the first great revolt was directed at the tithes of the Church.

The Tithe War raged through the 1880s with a storm centre in the Vale of Clwyd, riots at Llangwm and Mochdre. Anti-tithe societies fought like guerillas, in riot, resistance, boycott. Soldiers had to escort English auctioneers of distrained property into Welsh villages. Out of the depression came an aggressive onslaught on a regime now alien to a new nation, mobilized by an impatient middle class and served by its new men in Parliament. Exploiting their strategic position in the Commons in 1891, the Welsh Liberals got a Tithe Act which unloaded the burden on to the landlords. Fight after fight was fought into the 1890s, against rackrenting, game laws, landlord oppression, above all against the insults which a State Church offered Dissent. Never before had Welsh issues been so forced on public notice, but the Wales that was thrust down English throats was the particular Wales of tenant and petty-bourgeois rural Dissent, mobilizing those of its people, its *gwerin*, who were not taking off in droves for the towns, behind its now permanently militant middle class. The labourers themselves found no spokespersons save for a few half-stifled words from an Anglesey journalist, J. O. Thomas; industrial Wales did not get a look in. It was as if the entire energy of political Wales was devoted to breaking the hold of 'alien' landlords and bishops over about a half of its land and a quarter of its population.

The battle produced the Land Commission of 1893 which sat for three years and whose Report, edited by the dedicated Daniel Lleufer Thomas, a scholar-publicist, was virtually a history of Wales and looms like Cader Idris over Welsh historians. The paltry legislation which resulted was a milk-and-water copy of Gladstone's Irish legislation but in reality the victories were political and ideological. It is doubtful whether there was an economic problem peculiar to rural Wales in those years. The frequent citing of Irish example was a political exercise in support of a movement which saw itself as a *gwerin* in national revolt. There certainly was a crisis for ordinary people in the countryside. They resolved it by moving out *en masse*. When the depression lifted, a slimmed down and reorganized society buttressed the growing strength of the small farmers. These were in no sense the struggles of a despairing peasantry. On the contrary, they were attack, aggression, advance by a rural people powered with the ideologies of a Welsh-speaking Nonconformity and its instrumental radicalism, marching against a squirearchy and an Anglicanism which this people's *own evolution* had made 'alien' in their own land.

The key position occupied by the Welsh MPs in the early 1890s thrust Welsh issues to the fore. They were all embraced under the Disestablishment of the Church in Wales. This had shifted from the general stance of people like Henry Richard and the Liberationists to presentation as a specifically Welsh national aspiration. In response, many Church leaders had to deny that Wales as a nation existed at all . . . it was just a 'geographical expression' according to one bishop, and Tory MPs started to wage a systematic campaign of denigration of everything Welsh. Not until John Owen, a Welsh-speaker from Llŷn, became Bishop of St David's did the argument of the Church switch to asserting, with reason, the very Welshness of the Church itself. From this point until 1914 Disestablishment and everything that went with it remained the core of official Welsh Liberalism, to dominate Welsh politics to the point of distraction.

Its companion creed, Home Rule, dissolved in the by now radically distinct social development of north and south. Tom Ellis had started to preach, together with two north Wales socialists, a new concept of nationhood, in which history, tradition, social culture, literature and political institutions would be yoked; he argued that the spirit of Wales in its local life was collectivist; he explained Robert Owen of Newtown in such terms; Wales was the land of '*cyfraith, cyfar, cyfnawdd, cymorthau, cymanfaoedd* . . .' ('custom, co-ploughing, co-protection, co-help, co-assembly . . .', to use some literal transcriptions), with the emphasis on the *cy-*, the *co-*. By 1888 the journal *Cymru Fydd* was preaching self-government. When its editorship passed to Owen M. Edwards the educator, in the following year, the emphasis shifted to culture rather than politics, but a novel note was injected by J. Arthur Price, an Anglo-Catholic who saw Disestablishment as a restoration of an organic community in Wales to overcome the divisive effects of puritanism and sectarianism – one brand of a novel nationalism which started to develop in High Anglican and even Catholic circles and which became a permanent though a minority theme, capable of either left- or right-wing development.

Though branches of a Cymru Fydd movement were launched, characteristically in London and Liverpool, it became serious only when it went political in the 1890s, which essentially was when Lloyd George got to Parliament. In the tense parliamentary situation, Lloyd George and D. A. Thomas at one time refused the Liberal whip because of the government's tardiness over Disestablishment, and both moved in on Cymru Fydd, whose membership mushroomed in centre and north and made its first lodgement in the industrial valleys. In 1894 a national league was formed and by 1895 the North Wales Liberal Federation had been taken over. The great stumbling block was the south, where the great bulk of the people and the wealth were. Characteristically, D. A. Thomas and Lloyd George, two larger-than-life figures in any case, quarrelled bitterly over the funds it was proposed to allot from Disestablishment. Thomas asserted that Glamorgan and Monmouth would be smothered by the Welsh-speaking west and north. Already the two societies seemed so far apart in social structure, modes of living and language that a massive reluctance to join in any 'Wales' which to them was alien became and has remained a dominant feeling in the south-east. This opened the door to an outright rejection of Welshness itself from the cities of the coast, notably Newport, Cardiff, Barry and even Swansea, which were both heavily English and heavily anglicized. Cymru Fydd found Swansea 'a howling wilderness', Barry 'intent on nothing but money-making', Cardiff 'lost'. This reflected not only the major divergence in hegemonic society but a growing radicalization of working people which was increasingly finding the politics of what was presented as Welshness irrelevant. The one area where Cymru Fydd made progress was in the industrial valleys, in the Rhonddas despite the uneasiness of Mabon, and in Merthyr, where the spokesman for the farm labourer was editing the *Merthyr Times*. Lloyd George worked the area with lectures on Llywelyn the Great, presented as an early apostle of Cymru Fydd!

The whole project crashed at a Newport meeting of the South Wales Liberal Federation, where a no doubt packed delegation howled down Lloyd

George and where the normally amiable Robert Bird of Cardiff, a Wesleyan businessman, asserted that the cosmopolitan south-east would never submit to 'the domination of Welsh ideas'. Packed or not, this meeting reflected a genuine and widespread feeling in the south which has become permanent. If a Wales as a political entity was to be created, it would have to be a different Wales from that envisaged by Cymru Fydd. By this time the Liberal government was collapsing and the party was to be out of office until 1905. All serious demand for Home Rule virtually vanished and Welsh Liberal politics came to focus on a single-minded but unifying project – an endless sectarian war over Disestablishment in which both sides seemed obsessed.

In 1906 it looked as though the Conservatives were going to follow the landlords and the Church clean out of the 'Wales' which Welsh Non-conformist Liberalism was establishing. Year after year Disestablishment was preached, got into Bills, floundered in parliamentary politics, to the final climactic campaign of 1912 – 14. All Wales was at one time apparently hypnotized by the great duel between Lloyd George and the Bishop of St Asaph: 'Last week, we had Mr Lloyd George here. We all know he's the biggest liar in Wales. But tonight, we have a match for him in the Bishop of St Asaph . . .' Many, one suspects, subjected to this deafening and often vicious clamour, might have felt disposed to echo Asquith: 'I would sooner go to Hell than to Wales . . .' But by September 1914 it was done and in fact the Welsh Church was revivified; the Bill passed. Hardly anyone noticed, a more catastrophic disestablishment had begun the month before.

In the course of this battle this new nation, frequently the butt of numerous English racists but often finding support from establishment figures who perceptively saw a cultivation of Welsh cultural nationalism as the best prop for a United Kingdom in its western fringe, had equipped itself with a whole range of institutions, primarily cultural and educational. A National Eisteddfod, organized on a regular annual basis from 1858, took familiar shape in 1880; the Cymmrodorion emerged as a national cultural society from 1872. From the 1880s the network of county schools thickened. University colleges at Cardiff and Bangor were opened in the early 1880s, while Aberystwyth survived to win its own grant, largely because of popular sympathy, particularly after a great fire, and because of the tireless efforts of strategically placed old boys working the system with a dedication to their old place which was to prove characteristic. In 1893, after a tough battle in the Lords over the sectarian exclusion of Lampeter, the three were united in a federal University of Wales, to be joined by the new foundation at Swansea in 1920. In 1896 a Central Welsh Board was created to manage Welsh secondary education and a separate department was carved out of the Board of Education under a typical, if remarkable, popular and academic hero, Owen M. Edwards, virtually the creator of the first modern, populist history of the Welsh. In that same year of 1907 Wales acquired a National Library and a National Museum.

The scope and the sweep of this movement, with its three great national institutions and its two generations of extraordinarily creative academics, generally coming out of the popular classes of Wales, are still breathtaking, even after a hundred years of indoctrination in their virtues. Behind the ritual chant of praise there is, in truth, a quite amazing reality. The serious study of Welsh life and letters was transformed as trained professionalism entered, to be serviced by people of creative ability: John Viriamu Jones, a brilliant English-speaking Welsh scholar from the Swansea area who served as head of the University College at Cardiff and of the new University of Wales; Sir John Lloyd of Bangor who wrote a classic history of medieval Wales; Owen M. Edwards, son of a Merioneth crofter who taught history at Oxford and poured out a flood of popular writings virtually to create one people's vision of Wales and its past. The list, particularly if extended into wider fields of intellectual activity, could be made to seem endless. While they often differed widely as individuals, however, the directive core of these people was locked into a particular view of Wales, its past, its present meaning and its future, which helped to shape the outlook of whole sectors of Welsh life, but made little or no contact with others even more central. What meaning would their work have had for what Lloyd George in a rage had called 'Newport Englishmen' and a south Wales sunk in 'morbid footballism'? A good deal more than might appear from such comments, in fact, but while the failure of communication was not that which such glib generalizations might suggest, the collapse of Cymru Fydd had in truth indicated that the triumph of this particular Wales rested on a major and intensifying contradiction. There was dislocation at its very heart.

During the early years of the twentieth century, when south Wales society was being turned upside down not only by mass immigration without precedent, which provoked some anti-Jewish, anti-Irish and anti-English riots in northern Gwent and Glamorgan, but by massive capitalist reorganization into combines and multinational corporations to be countered by a major upsurge of militant trade unionism, the central political issues of Liberal Wales appeared more and more irrelevant even in its moment of transcendental triumph in 1906. Even as a whole generation of young Welsh people in south and east moved powerfully out of both the Nonconformist tradition and the Welsh language, some of them into Marxism, it was often Anglicans and Catholics rather than Dissenters who elaborated on the one hand a much more organic and deep-sited, if disdainful and patrician, nationalism which looked with scorn on a 'nation of grocers' in its corrupt and hypocrite democracy and on the other, cultivated a slum-parson commitment to a Christian socialism.

In 1900 James Keir Hardie was returned from Merthyr as its second member to become the first Labour MP in Wales. By 1906 there was a handful of labourist Lib-Labs in the House and a slow but steady and molecular growth in local government. This hardly dented the Liberal buckler; most of them lived by Liberal tolerance and most of them were themselves broadly Liberal in outlook. The Liberal grip on Parliament was totally unshaken. Yet there is something increasingly unreal about it; it is as though Welsh Liberalism was becoming an inherited style much as Nonconformity had now become, despite its apparent 74 per cent predominance. The life was going out of it and routine was seeping in. Hansard and the press might be full of Disestablishment and other cherished policies, Welsh societies might still be stupefied by the after-dinner thunder of a glib and easy Welsh patriotism which was securely subaltern to its Britishness, but long before 1914, as records and reports from many sources make clear, such causes were coming to seem the obsessions of a minority. The responses among the majority were becoming glassy-eyed. That majority was still loyal to its party, passive or distracted, those who voiced impatience were a gaggle of marginal dissidents. But there was a massive divorce between ideology and reality, an ideology which seemed to thunder on in a life of its own and a reality of hard and often passionate concern among a Welsh people trying to fight their own way through to elbow room and dignity.

A hauliers' strike of 1893 heralded the emergence of a new and particular form of radicalism among working people. There were splits in the chapels and the Independent Labour Party moved in. There was a major growth of trade union formation in response to the combines and the amalgamations which, almost overnight in historical terms, turned what had been the least unionized district in Britain into the most. A strong, informed and ambitious militancy began to course through a minority in the colliery areas in particular. After the Tonypandy riots of 1910 a group of Welsh Marxists published a serious, well thought out and totally intransigent pamphlet, *The Miner's Next Step,* which was no less totally subversive of any capitalist order. This was light years away from a world outlook to which the Disestablishment of the Church was central. From the early years of the new century, at a time when coal-getting was harder and profits tighter, the coalfield lurched into a sequence of bitter conflicts which cut clean across the party lines set by Welsh Liberalism, even as the quarrymen of north Wales fought one of the longest lock-outs in history in a destructive civil war which took them, too, out of any Liberal consensus. Their shift was slow and painful, requiring a psychological revolution. The psychological revolution in the much more populous south affected only one part of its popular mind, but there, it was rapid and dramatic. Within less than twenty years sections of the leadership of the south Wales miners' union, itself becoming a formative power second to none within south Wales society, passed, in a series of abrupt lurches, from Liberalism to Communism.

What sort of a nation was it, then, that had triumphed by 1914?

## Gog and Magog Myths: gwerin and working class

Looked at in the long perspectives of a history which some of the Welsh fear may now be drawing to its close, the thrust of the late nineteenth and early twentieth centuries, comprehensive though some of its achievements were, and incalculable their consequences, takes on the character of an essentially middle-class drive to modernize Wales in its own image. To achieve this modernization, the new middle class, with its popular roots, had to present itself as and indeed believe itself to be, the hero-class of a nation, much as the French bourgeoisie thought of itself in 1789. The French of 1789 had their villain class in their 'aristocrats'; the Welsh middle class of the 1880s had its own villain class in the landlords and the Church.

They lived in Dissent, which had no inherently Welsh character, but which in nineteenth-century Wales could become the instrument and agency of mobilization and a specific social ideology. It was the integument which joined together a whole constellation of interests and passions in Wales which were potentially inimical to each other. It could serve as a non-class ideology which could create a national-popular will. The glittering climax of the imperial economy of Wales enabled the Welshness of Dissent to hold this congeries of societies and cultures together long enough to effect the major modernization. The very success of the economy subjected this synthesis to intolerable strain; by 1900 it was already beginning to come apart. The depression of the inter-war years destroyed the integument; it not only devastated an economy and dislocated a society, it killed the nation which Dissent had created.

From the beginning that nation had been badly skewed, largely as a result of its social and ideological origins. So overpowering has been the historiography which it created, so unquestioned did its assumptions become, that it is easy to overlook the extent to which all the hero enterprises of its textbooks, the educational drives above all, were originally rescue enterprises directed at a minority rural Wales in a permanent crisis of depopulation, a Wales which was becoming ever more visibly a minority among the Welsh.

One classic instance is the university movement of Hugh Owen which grew directly out of the British school campaign. Owen and his friends were obsessed with rural Wales and the middle class which had grown out of it. Other middle classes simply did not exist in their Wales. When they chose Bangor as the site of their Normal, the choice so offended many people in the south that numbers learned the Catechism and entered Anglican colleges. They chose Aberystwyth as the site for their people's university, said Owen, because, in his own words, it would be resorted to from all parts of north Wales. He then added, 'It was hoped, too, that the people of south Wales also would avail themselves of it . . .' Too . . . also . . . the very placing of prepositions resonates. The afterthought tone here stems from the central fact that Owen and his people thought, when they thought about it at all, firstly that the industrial areas were already fairly well catered for in an English context and secondly, that if they wished to follow suit, they would look after their own. In fact Owen assumed that, if a college were needed at all, it would be in Swansea. The fact that reality did not in the end conform to his expectations matters nothing; it is the expectations which open his mind. It is important to stress this point because a good deal of what has come to be considered an essentially Welsh historiography has made it invisible. The kind of modernization, *codi'r hen wlad* (raising up the old land) visible in rural, or perhaps more accurately non-industrial, Wales from mid-century on, the kind of populist epic which became part of the emotional make-up of many Welsh people – the image of the learned and cultivated ordinary person (usually a man, but not invariably), the stonebreaker who knows Vergil, the poor boy who gets to the university chair – had registered in the industrial areas at least a generation earlier and was to register again in a different form a generation later.

There is a classic and exemplary story about and by Sir Henry Jones, a celebrated hero who became a Professor of Moral Philosophy in Glasgow, where they are strong on such matters. As a boy, he once waited for hours at the roadside to see a *Bachelor of Arts* walk by, and was so overcome at the majesty of the spectacle that he could not speak. This nice tale is a commonplace in one Welsh folklore. What meaning would it have had a generation earlier in Dowlais, whose schools earned it the nickname of the Prussia of south Wales? What meaning in Swansea, in Wrexham, Cowbridge, Bangor, Ruthin? What meaning in 'frontier' Merthyr, where a Nonconformist middle class sent their sons, as a matter of course, to

Glasgow University after a stint in Unitarian schools near Bristol or the gentry school in Swansea?

The people of industrial Wales, however loosely defined, whether north or south, had largely been incorporated into whatever educational structure existed in Britain, prior to the Welsh university movement. The closest parallel to the Henry Jones trajectory in industrial Wales, of course, was the explosive entry of working-class talent into the educational systems in the early twentieth century. By that time a Welsh structure existed, but so did semi-alien but handy Cardiff, and the prestigious British system was more open than it had been.

What is striking about the whole educational campaign of 'Welsh' Wales is its strong list towards Methodism and more particularly towards west and north Wales. It never fully incorporated the complex reality of industrial Wales which came to embrace an overwhelming majority of the population. The universality of Welsh Dissent masked this predicament. The dissolution of this connection coupled with the increasing mutual alienation of Welsh-speaking and English-speaking Welsh, produced the most dismal results. A situation which Hugh Owen's and later generations accepted has come to be seen in an entirely negative and, in extreme cases, contemptible light. Large numbers of people, who in fact constituted a majority, were perceived as in some basic senses, un-Welsh, and the perception acquired retrospective force. The very name which contemporary and official Welshness bestows on the huge majority of the Welsh people is negative; they are *di-Gymraeg* (Welsh-less). The more arrogant, extreme or paranoid exponents of Welshness simply refuse to see any 'culture' at all in English-speaking Wales, or else they dismiss it as 'British' or even 'English'. The victims of this myopia cultivate an equally contemptuous and dismissive response. These attitudes operate within an overall context which is hostile and sometimes actively hostile to any Welshness at all. In this predicament, to the majority of the Welsh people, the history of Wales as presented by most of those most promptly recognized as Welsh, has been largely without meaning or relevance. They themselves have been slow to produce their own history, trapped in the Catch 22 situation generated by this kind of confrontation. Now that it is appearing, to the Welsh-Welsh it can seem either simply a branch of English History or an irrelevance to Wales. Both historiographies are in some senses parochial, even narcissistic; they hardly ever meet. This kind of schizophrenia threatens to extinguish not simply a Welsh nation but a Welsh people itself as an historic entity.

In practical terms, most of the institutions of Welsh education which are regarded as central to a Welsh identity have been situated within and in response to, regions and ideologies remote physically and ideally from the regions in which the majority of the Welsh lived and had their being. In this serious imbalance, a majority of the Welsh have never been possessed by, or entered into possession of, 'their own' national institutions. There was always a minority which did, across the shadow-line, but a minority it has been. From the moment of its triumph, a Welsh nation self-consciously institutionalized itself as a minority within the Welsh people. The structural contradiction proved increasingly intolerable to many of the Welsh people as they actually existed. In our own day it has become totally intolerable.

Public perception of a people in Wales for a century and a half has been expressed in two archetypal myths; both were powerful abstractions derived from reality and both became increasingly unreal: the *gwerin* and the *working class*. The idea of the *gwerin* passed into widespread and almost ritual usage at the moment when the notion of Wales it expressed was coming under severe pressure. The term is virtually untranslatable, as those who cherish it stress, although many languages have its equivalent, all equally untranslatable. Perhaps the Spanish *pueblo* approaches it, particularly since the latter can be used to describe both a place and the people who live in it, a practice common in Welsh and Welsh English.

The *gwerin* in the form it assumed from the late nineteenth century was not and is not a class, certainly not a proletariat, to which it is often opposed (in such contexts of course the use of words bears little relationship to their actual meaning). The *gwerin* was a cultivated, educated, often self-educated, responsible, self-disciplined, respectable but on the whole genially poor or perhaps small-propertied people, straddling groups perceived as classes in other, less fortunate societies. Welsh-speaking, Nonconformist, imbued with the more social virtues of Dissent, bred on the Bible and good practice, it was open to the more spiritual forms of a wider culture and was dedicated to spiritual self-improvement. It cherished many of the 'traditional' habits of Welsh culture, derived ultimately from the poets' guild, nurtured country poets, skilled in verse and wordplay; it was learned in a somewhat antiquarian manner, interested in letters, and cultivated a deep pacifist patriotism, controlled by religion. The *gwerin* deeply respected learning and rejoiced in the local boy who got to Oxford, provided he did not forget himself. Sir Henry Jones was once directly challenged by his chapel in a congregational letter sent to Glasgow. Had he been so misguided as to preach the non-divinity of Christ? 'Certainly not,' said Sir Henry, 'I would deny divinity to no man.' This *gwerin* was the heart and soul of the Welsh nation who cultivated a respectable and genial commonalty, free from the 'side' and the 'snobbishness' so characteristic of the English. It was a warm, mutually supportive, often cosy and rather amateur sort of fellowship within a hard, pushy, beady-eyed general society dominated by the English and their language, philistine and commercial. The original and demotic word for business in Welsh, as in many other European languages said to be 'peasant' in spirit, is an insult.

That this image departed rather dramatically from the reality, even of rural Wales, hardly needs saying. Even within village life, it made invisible those familiar characteristics savagely satirized by Caradoc Evans's *My People* of 1915 with its 'mean vignettes of a sly, crabbed peasantry' to whom hypocrisy was a way of life. Nevertheless, it was not as remote from reality as it may seem; it would hardly have been so effective if it had been. In many parts of Wales, thanks in no small measure to the very depopulation, a Nonconformist totality could embrace a community as comprehensively as conformity a small American town. Nor was it by any means confined to rural areas. Many communities in industrial Wales, particularly those of the colliers, were similar. The removal of landlords, squires, parsons and a thin upper class from the kind of nation the *gwerin* represented, as would a similar operation in some small Spanish *pueblo,* would leave that nation a non-class, or rather one-class, human community – much as the Czechs, for similar reasons, perceived themselves to be. Its new middle classes would be essentially a service bourgeoisie of academics, ministers, professional men. ('The services, teacher, doctor, preacher, apart from working with your hands, the only honest jobs,' as I was once told by an old lady on a Dowlais bus.) Growing out of and still emotionally immersed in the world represented by the chapel, its wider culture, chapel-derived intellectual journals, they would be sufficiently close to their roots to enable this one-class spirit to persist, despite the obvious and glaring contradictions of outside reality. Not only in village and small-town Wales, but in whole areas of industrial society, the concept of the *gwerin* seemed capable of infinite extension and indeed institutionalization. The *gwerin* was the natural form for a Welsh polity. Originally, the Welsh had only one word for both democracy and republic – *gwerin-iaeth,* the rule of the *gwerin.* They had to invent *democrat-iaeth* for constitutional monarchy's sake.

The styles of this *gwerin* have in fact become, or at least were until very recently, Welsh national styles. The apocryphal Welsh brain surgeon and Welsh bricklayer meeting in London, to this day, immediately constitute a small conspiracy, demotic in manner; a populist discourse is *de rigueur.* The style infuses much Welsh humour; it tends to flood the television screen when the more effective representatives of Welsh politics appear on it. A great deal of its style was simply taken over, lock, stock and barrel, by that other archetype which succeeded it, the *Welsh working class,* normally English-speaking and normally referring only to south Wales (and to a 'south Wales' which has become an ideological rather than a strictly geographical definition – 'Go back to south Wales!' they once shouted at marching demonstrators in the town of Haverfordwest, further south than which it is difficult to get in Wales). However remote this *working class* was and is from the *gwerin,* however indifferent or hostile it may be to the Welsh language, it has shared many of its populist attributes. A *working-class* community could nurture a similar sort of internal commonalty, could critically assimilate an Aneurin Bevan precisely as its predecessor did a great preacher. To the charismatic hero, of course, feet of clay are essential; the sceptical eye of the listener remains sceptical through the tears which flow from it. It could find it as hard to forgive Roy Jenkins his manner of speaking (every healthy Welshman keeps his vowels open) as the *gwerin* could any other Dic Sion Dafydd. It has shared that sly, mild, levelling malice which is so characteristic a feature of our gallant little nation.

Nor has this *working class* failed to follow the trajectory of the *gwerin* from reality into power and on into a limbo of unreality. The reality behind the abstraction was the identity of workplace, trade union and community, so strong a feature of mining communities, and on a smaller scale, of the quarrymen, particularly during the years of disaster. It acquired real power and was buttressed by an Alp of Marxist and Marxisant theoretical analysis denied the *gwerin.* Over the last twenty years it, too, has moved into a rhetoric which seeks to deny reality. This *working class* is still thought of in terms of a male who works his forty hours at least and outside the workplace is serviced by women, a totally unreal and irrelevant perception in a working population 45 per cent of whose workers are women. In the General Election of 1983 over half the working population voted against the Labour Party. The phenomenon was widely described in the sentence 'The working class is in retreat'! The resemblance to the years immediately before the First World War is uncanny. The term *working class* is used by spokespersons in the last days of Welsh Labour precisely as the term *gwerin* was used in the last days of Welsh Liberalism.

It was in the last decade before the War, when anything resembling a *gwerin* was fast disappearing from Welsh earth, that the *gwerin's* self-appointed voices filled the Welsh air. This was precisely the point at which a *working class* started to break in, because, however styles might resemble each other, realities were totally different – different in context, in manner of thinking and speaking and organizing, different in language and culture. In content the worlds of the *gwerin* and the *working class* were as remote as was the Aberystwyth Restaurant in Tonypandy where they drafted the *Miner's Next Step* from the town which gave it its name. In order to assert its own Welshness, the *working class* had to break the hegemony of the *gwerin* and prise loose its mental grip. The Rhondda valleys scarcely existed as a full human community in the 1860s. They became a stronghold of Welsh and Dissenter populism, Mabon's land, a *gwerin*. By the 1890s Nonconformity was already in decline. How many years make a tradition? How many traditions make a nation?

Some historians see a watershed moment in the last great popular religious revival, that of Evan Roberts. Welsh Dissent had been singularly free of breakaway movements like the Primitive Methodists. Perhaps the closest parallel had been the Mormons who scored major successes in industrial Wales in mid-century and led a remarkable migration across the Atlantic. The Revival of Evan Roberts, starting from Loughor on the Glamorgan–Carmarthenshire border in November 1904, swept over Wales for eighteen months and particularly affected south Wales. While it sent people packing into the chapels and had spontaneous Bible readings and prayer meetings breaking out everywhere, many ministers were soon alarmed by the anarchic passion of its evangelism which swept away denominations and asserted a popular identity which made the strange, mystical figure of Evan Roberts briefly a power in the land. 'Maybe it was the last attempt by ordinary Welshmen', says one historian, 'to make of religion what it had once been – popular, non-clerical, unlearned, unsophisticated, enthusiastic, organic in the community and Welsh in language.' Maybe, says another, it was a point of transition from 'Welsh peasants' into a 'British working class'. *

Certainly many miners were seized by the Revival's vision of social apocalypse. Arthur J. Cook, who was to become the miners' leader during the General Strike, was possessed by it. Arthur Horner, Wales's most distinguished Communist, was to begin as a boy preacher. It was followed by the crushing electoral victory of Liberalism and the first major advance of Labour. If I may be permitted a personal note, two collier uncles of mine who had been rather routine members of an Independent chapel and Liberal voters, were swept up in it. Their passion did not last, but they remained total abstainers from alcohol for the rest of their lives – and they moved straight from the Revival into the Independent Labour Party.

'Keir Hardie had a meeting on the Dowlais Tips last night,' ran one

---

*Ieuan Gwynedd Jones, *Explorations and Explanations: essays in the social history of Victorian Wales* (Gomer Press, 1981) and David Smith, *A People and a Proletariat: essays in the history of Wales 1780-1980* (Pluto Press, 1980).

ILP report. 'After prayers and hymns, he preached the sermon.' 'Lluoedd Duw a Satan sydd yn cwrdda nawr', they roared at those meetings. 'Mae gan Blant eu cyfran yn y Rhyfel Mawr' ('The Hosts of God and Satan go into battle now. The Children have their place in this Great War.')

## An Alternative People

In the folklore of Labour which ultimately displaced Liberalism, to become in its turn the political expression of a people who were the real Welsh 'nation', there are stations of the cross parallel to Dissent's roll-call of victims and victories: 1893, the hauliers' strike and the coming of the ILP; 1898, a six-months' stoppage and the formation of the South Wales Miners' Federation, affiliated to the Miners' Federation of Great Britain; 1900, Keir Hardie takes the second Merthyr seat and John Hodge nearly captures the intensely Welsh constituency of Gower; 1905, Enoch Morell becomes the Labour mayor of Merthyr; 1906, six Labour MPs of differing kinds win seats in Wales; 1909, the South Wales Miners' Federation (the Fed) affiliates to Labour – and on through the War until Labour moves swiftly to parliamentary control in south Wales and holds twenty seats there even in the catastrophe of 1931. By 1966 there were only four seats in Wales which were not Labour; its hegemony was virtually as total as that of the Liberals in 1906.

Reality was not so simple. In the areas of experience where the ballot box channelled action, the Liberal presence was ubiquitous and overpowering. Labour men made their way within it; even Keir Hardie operated under the tactically benevolent shadow of D.A. Thomas. The advance of Labour was slow and painful, the product of many local struggles and local deals in which a local power and prestige were at stake. In a myriad elections at all levels, Boards of Guardians, local councils, Parliament, Liberal organizations, strongly entrenched and often exclusive, had often to be chivvied and cajoled by national Liberal powers into admitting working men's representatives to a necessary junior partnership. It was a gradual process and the kind of Labour leadership which emerged, despite its irresistible thrust for independence, was in personal style, morality, general approach, virtually indistinguishable from that of the more populist leaders among the Liberals. The new Labour people were still children, even if bastard children, of imperial Wales.

In industry, however, intolerable pressures forced conflicts which became more and more fierce and which turned the years immediately before the War into years of pitched battles of an unprecedented intensity.

Consequently the south Wales coalfield, in particular, in the slow tenacity of its traditional politics and the extraordinarily combative practice of its industrial struggles, came to resemble contemporary and equally contradictory Catalonia in Spain. As the combines mushroomed, so did trade unions. Lewis Afan had started a tinplaters' union which, through repeated success and collapse, built up strength, while Charles Perry of Pontypool and Henry Parfitt of Neath were foremost in establishing the Amalgamated Society of Locomotive Engineers and Firemen (ASLEF), three of whose original six branches were in Pontypool, Tondu and Neath; it was the Swansea branch which proposed the creation of a political fund. The Amalgamated Society of Railway Servants (ASRS), ancestor of the National Union of Railwaymen (NUR), recruited heavily; Richard Bell of Merthyr became its general secretary and it was on the Taff Vale Railway that the legal counter-offensive against the unions precipitated the crisis which led to the formation of the Labour Party. General unions swept into south Wales and there was a rapid growth of trades councils. As early as 1891, 5 ½ per cent of the Welsh were members of trade unions, as opposed to fewer than 4 per cent in England and fewer than 3 per cent in Scotland.

The new intransigence registered first in an unexpected quarter. The resolutely respectable quarrymen of the north had a desperate struggle to get their union recognized at all by the politically neanderthal Baron Penrhyn and had to fight their way forward against ice-age opposition from a colonial mind. Conflicts over unskilled labour, the import of blacklegs, sub-contracting, spilled over into a demand for a minimum wage which was flatly rejected and forced a lockout in 1896 which lasted over a year, drove the men back to work on the old terms, but created a crisis atmosphere. About the same time, the huge workforce in coal erupted. Rising to the climax of its expansion, south Wales coal was a high-cost and labour-intensive industry. Its wasteful pits thrust deeper and deeper and ran into frightful geological problems; pressures mounted on profits as the endless waves of immigrants came pouring in. The work got more dangerous. There had been eight major disasters, each killing over 100 men, between 1856 and 1900; in 1894, 250 men were killed in the Albion Colliery, Cilfynydd; in the dreadful Senghenydd disaster of 1913, 439 died. After virulent conflict between a fairly paternalistic D. A. Thomas and a coal-owners' association headed by Sir William T. Lewis which was almost as chisel-faced as Baron Penrhyn, the coal companies lurched into cut-throat competition and the miners were subjected to speed-ups and endless detailed erosion of wages in continuous haggling over work in difficult places. None of the miners' leaders was in any way radical. The major protagonists, Mabon and

242

William Brace of Monmouthshire, were both Lib-Labs but they clashed over forms of industrial action. There were eight small unions, only three of which had wholly independent funds; Mabon held to the Sliding Scale and local independence and was heavily enmeshed with the employers, while Brace pressed for harder collective bargaining and links to the miners' federation in Britain. In 1897 the tension exploded, the union denounced the Sliding Scale and there was a harsh six-month lock-out. This set a pattern which was to become familiar: poverty, soup kitchens, national appeals, bleak intransigence, a bubbling of political groups and a permanent struggle for power within the miners' union. The men were beaten, Mabon's Day was lost. Within a month of this defeat, they formed the South Wales Miners' Federation with over 100,000 members and affiliated to the Miners' Federation of Great Britain (MFGB); the Fed was to govern the lives and loyalties of the miners up until the Second World War.

The struggle of 1898 was a solvent of tradition. At every level in south Wales, the lodge, the chapel, the family, the club, the native and the immigrant, there was conflict and a massive breakout from the old order. It heralded twenty-eight years of virtually continuous struggle, in which among the miners, leadership after leadership was repeatedly displaced by new men and new ideas in escalating conflict – 'Move on or move out.' The Fed and the ILP carried the struggle into the north around Wrexham and Rhos and within a year the quarries of north Wales crashed into what was virtually a communal conflict and a civil war.

'You can't face your creditors? Then walk backward,' said an English under-manager to a Penrhyn quarryman in distress. It was essentially against this kind of colonial control, against Steward Big-Mouth, Ceg-Mawr, against the denial of any rights to their union, that the quarrymen rebelled. Penrhyn's refusal to permit union dues to be collected at his quarries precipitated suspensions, riots, a calling in of the militia and a lock-out which started in November 1900 and was to last for all of three years in a bitter intransigence which has few equals in history. Every elected authority in Gwynedd rallied to the quarrymen and there was a national campaign of support. Elected police committees could not control their own police. Tory and Anglican magistrates defied the democracy of Welsh Nonconformists. They sent dragoons, infantrymen and Merseyside police against Bethesda and its villages. They persecuted and blacklisted. They sent in free labour. Up went the union cards in the windows: *nid oes bradwr yn y tŷ hwn* (no traitor in this house). *Cynffonwyr* they called the blacklegs, flatterers–stool-pigeons–men with tails. They were driven out of chapel into church, out to the villages of Sling and Tregarth, out of community

— 'Let not one of them or one of their sons marry a Welsh woman!' they shouted about people who were Welsh themselves – a shout which was to echo over south Wales for a generation. The Reverend Morgan of St Ann's, Bethesda compared it to the horrors inflicted on loyalists in Ireland. In the end they broke in total defeat and their industry broke with them. 'For half a century, the workers of Wales have been used to push up the middle class,' said one of their leaders and a big chapel man, William Arafon Williams, W.H. — 'Let the worker take care of his own welfare first and be in a knot one with the other . . . The workers of England have shaken off the middle class and have taken the workers of Wales into that knot with them.'

If the resolutely Liberal quarrymen could start talking like this, what of the colliers in the south, already in turmoil? Ironically, the Fed, with the winning of a conciliation board, achieved some respectability in 1903. But with the threat of blacklegs even more potent, this union had to organize a huge working population in intensely selfconscious villages and valleys. It tried to go on operating in terms of consensus and a social darwinism, but real power lay with the twenty autonomous Districts which were compelled to try to make themselves organizers of whole communities. Local leaders became satraps; men like the able and powerful Vernon Hartshorn in Maesteg, or the meteoric C. B. Stanton of Aberdare, a literally pistol-packing syndicalist who in 1914 suffered an instant conversion to jingoism and broke Keir Hardie (it is difficult not to think of Mussolini).

From 1908 this leadership ran into the first of successive waves of revolt as demands for a minimum wage, an eight-hour day, state control, workers' control, nationalization bubbled up and militants could ride repeated rank and file rebellions. In 1908 the miners supported the strike at Ruskin College in Oxford which threw up the Plebs League and the Central Labour College and launched the first serious movement of workers' self-education. The syllabus was demanding, rigorous with Marx and Marxist classics, Joseph Dietzgen, science, biology and Marxist history. Nowhere did their movement win such support as in south Wales, with its passionate and dedicated local classes. Two generations of men passed through it, among them names which were to loom large: Aneurin Bevan, Jim Griffiths, Morgan Phillips, Ness Edwards. Most were to end in the Labour Party but a good third of the graduates ultimately became Communists. Reinforced by the Marxist literature coming in, often from Scotland through the Socialist Labour Party, often directly from America with its celebrated publishing house of Kerr in Chicago, this tide rose dramatically, especially in the Rhonddas, east Glamorgan and Monmouthshire and was to achieve

European significance in its classic *Miner's Next Step* of 1912; it produced the first Marxist history of south Wales in the 1920s. European in intellectual content and semi-syndicalist in inspiration, American in its sources and supplementary reading, this new creed was also an alternative culture. It had no contact whatever with the chapel or the Welsh language. A new world was being transmitted entirely in English.

At the time of the first language census of 1891, little over half of the population knew Welsh. By 1911 the proportion had fallen to 40 per cent. This held at around 36 per cent to 1931 but after the worst trough of the inter-war depression and the Second World War, there was a sharp fall to 28 per cent in 1951. Another steep fall in the 1960s brought it to the crisis level of 20 per cent. At this level, in 1981, it roughly stabilized and showed some signs of growth in particular areas among the young.

There had been considerable English-speaking strength in Wales from early days, outside south Pembrokeshire, clustering along the borders and lowlands with pockets around commercial centres in the heart of Welsh Wales, and later in the holiday zones along the north coast. A capacity to read English was widespread, but English as a mortal threat to popular Welsh was geographically restricted.

There was clearly an erosion of Welsh through the nineteenth century. A good deal of industrial Wales was operatively bilingual by mid-century. Industrialization and people were, of course, focused on the south-east, where anything from two-thirds to three-quarters of the people were concentrated at different times. This unbalance could produce paradoxical results. As late as 1951, 54 per cent of the Welsh speakers (715,000) were actually in the south-east; until very recent times, the heartland of Welsh speech in terms of number has ironically been in the most English-speaking areas. But while Welsh speakers were a mere 20 per cent of Glamorgan's population in 1951, they were 75 per cent of Merioneth's. The old frontier here assumed its most bleak and enervating form.

The two major collapses of the Welsh language have some clear explanations. In the late nineteenth and early twentieth centuries, the sheer mass of the immigration could no longer be assimilated; a high proportion came from western England, Scotland and Ireland; there were Spaniards, Italians and other Europeans, some West Indian, African and Asian groups. In 1909 at a meeting of the Rhondda district of the Fed, the chairman asked, 'Is there anyone here who wants the resolution in Welsh?' The reply – 'Everyone here understands English.' The Rhondda retained a strong Welsh-speaking population, but the trend in the District minutes is clear. In 1901 it printed its rules in English and Welsh; between 1901 and 1907 summarized every report in Welsh; from 1908–11 they simply gave a synopsis of the minutes in Welsh. In October 1928, a time of great distress, the resolution was put 'That the Welsh translation of agenda be deleted for the present . . .' This process is most visible in the eastern half of the coalfield; the anthracite remained resolutely Welsh-speaking, though the coastal towns had been English for a long time. Similarly the decline in the 1930s was the product of the hideous drain of people out of Wales. More generally, of course, a Welsh language had to try to live with a world language of probably unparalleled richness.

There were negative factors. Many of the school-teachers in the new schools practised cultural genocide; the *Welsh Not* slung around a child's neck to accompany his or her punishment for speaking his or her own language has become notorious. It was not very effective but it enormously reinforced the image of Welsh as an inferior and gutter tongue. More generally, the language suffered from its lack of social prestige; a 'kitchen language', many of its practices merely oral at the popular level, it was treated with scorn and, with the advance of English education, with vilification. Certainly a significant number of Welsh school-teachers, presumably suffering from a tribal self-contempt and a species of shame, saw it their duty not simply to introduce their students to the world of the English language, but to eradicate every trace of Welshness they could get their self-justifying hands on. This was by no means restricted to the Welsh language; there was a sustained attempt to induce self-contempt into a population of English-speaking Welsh largely outside what their mentors considered orthodoxy and an all-too-successful effort to blot out the history of the Welsh as something primitive and contemptible and best forgotten; a process which without doubt helped to make the Welsh a people without historical memory and one which continues. This constitutes a *trahison des clercs,* a treason of the intellectuals, whose parallel can be found only among such peculiar breeds as the anti-Semitic Jews.

These processes operated amid the widespread assumption that English was essential to success and achievement and Welsh useless in this respect. Few of the heroes of the nineteenth century actually taught their sons Welsh (Hugh Owen did not). Many of the new secondary schools quite consciously set out to incorporate their students wholly into the world of the English language, an admirable ambition in itself, but one which seems often to have been interpreted in a manner which required the elimination of Welshness. During the Depression, as family after family, aided by sympathetic Labour local authorities, tried to get their children out of the pits via the examination obstacle race, and Wales became notorious for its over-production of school-teachers, these trends became both serious and self-contradictory.

These negative processes, however, have been exaggerated. From the 1880s government policy shifted into a fairly sympathetic attitude towards the Welsh language, there was quite heavy pressure from education authorities, and within both primary and secondary schools there were many teachers, increasing in number, who did not succumb to the fashionable lunacy; several schools were major influences in Welsh studies. The roots of the change-over lay deeper in the structure of social living itself.

No one can miss the sense of liberation which swept over many young people at this time on being admitted to a world language of infinite scope, the language of Chaucer, Shakespeare, Shelley and Dickens. English poets start to figure as Welsh Christian names, with Byron rivalling even Handel. More immediately the admittance was to the language of Jack London, Melville, Upton Sinclair, Sinclair Lewis and a host of American writers. The American thrust of 'anglicization' in south Wales, at the popular level, is quite striking; this, after all, was a democratic English. The abrupt widening of popular horizons from the Edwardian period onwards, particularly in popular entertainment, was no less American. Popular song and, of course, the cinema, were to be more potent still. In many ways the 'anglicization' of popular Wales (even in its Marxism) was a function of the Americanization of popular England. Outside the educated middle classes, and even frequently within them, large numbers of new English speakers did not acclimatize themselves to what was considered mainstream English culture; many still do not. This was as much a structural as an ideological influence. The predicament of working people in Wales over the previous generations had resembled that of working people in industrializing America as much as anything else. Zimmern's tag of 'American Wales' points to a truth. And increasingly, American was to be the language of urban people.

Beyond all this, there is that intangible factor which every person in Wales is familiar with. Wales is a small country where everyone seems to know everyone else and interests are often parochial, hermetic and suffocating. There is frequently a yearning for occasional and sometimes permanent escape, a feeling that could lead one college principal to say that coming home to Wales was like going back into jail, and Dylan Thomas to tell his Fathers what they could do with their Land.

What could Welsh offer in this situation? The very mental processes of 'anglicization', the excessive commitment to those values considered English or British which were most broadening and also most instrumental and self-serving, had already been entrenched within the Welsh language itself. More concretely, that language was very much the language of the chapel, of political interests which seemed irrelevant, of a rather meagre recent literature which did not connect. Ironically, it was at this very time that Welsh-language culture was entering its twentieth-century renaissance, in the new dramatic, forceful, high-quality writing of such as T. Gwynn Jones, W. J. Gruffydd, Silyn Roberts; it was too early for Gwenallt, whose work was supremely relevant to industrial south Wales. But such people were by then remote. Most of the Welsh-language literary culture of the time *was* irrelevant to a majority of the Welsh people, as irrelevant to living concerns as a folk museum to Mardy Lodge.

Perhaps most central of all is an issue which seems to have been underplayed. The people who poured into the Plebs League classes and swotted up their Dietzgen and their Engels's *Anti-Duhring* were rejecting *all* orthodox education as bourgeois, whether it were offered in Welsh, English or South Walian. They were a minority, often a small one, but always a minority of contagious individuals and they generated an attitude of mind. On a much wider scale, the language question was hopelessly enmeshed with the social conflict. It was precisely against the world which the Welsh language had come to enshrine, at least in its official aspect, that these people were rebelling. In many places at different times in the coalfield, the Welsh language was that of conservatism and accommodation. Again, matters should not be exaggerated; there was never any bloc transfer. Many areas of rooted militancy remained thoroughly Welsh-speaking. The outstanding example was the anthracite coalfield, but there were plenty of enclaves within the most English-speaking districts. What is striking here is that their kind of Welsh, the Welsh of populist and socialist radicalism and an unconscious, undisciplined and easy commonalty, found less and less purchase *within* the official Welsh-language world itself. It lived long, however, like the Law of Hywel, because it was a genuine people's language, and remained so even when those people went Communist.

Moral and intellectual hegemony, itself denying a demotic Welsh of this brand the possibility of development, passed to an English which was invariably, for thousands of people, the language of militancy, self-assertion and a rejection of servility. The brilliant and effective Plebs League tutors like the mercurial, foul-mouthed and hypnotic Nun Nicholas, that Mark Starr who could have been a historian of quality, the great Noah Ablett, south Wales's leader lost to drink, found and preached liberation in and through the English language.

The molecular growth of Labour at a local political level and the repeated quasi-insurrectionary explosions within the coal industry also, then, represented the break-in of a new culture. From 1910 the confrontation became a drama. The struggle between the Cambrian Combine of D. A. Thomas and the colliers, the irreconcilable class conflict over 'abnormal places' in which the most basic interests were at stake, precipitated the Tonypandy Riots of 1910, large-scale battles with the police, a selective sacking of the town, face-to-face confrontation with the military, all rapidly celebrated in song and ballad, and a bitter struggle, out of which came the *Miner's Next Step* calling for a complete break with customary practice, the end of private ownership, the end of 'leadership' itself (in a kind of socialism which was to go into eclipse after the 1920s) and the centralization of the union under continuous rank-and-file control. The world of the ballot box remained relatively undisturbed and within the Fed this kind of militancy was contained, but it ran strongly right into the War years and in 1915 powered a strike in the teeth of jingoist patriotism which forced Lloyd George to a surrender and imposed a measure of state control over the coal industry which hiked the Fed to a position of unparalleled power and influence.

The War, of course, was an unhingeing shock of the first order, above all to the pacifist and small-nation pieties of Welsh Liberalism. A whole sector of Liberal opinion, dismayed by Lloyd George's performance, transferred to Labour and took its Liberalism with it. The Labour movement was split. The great majority rallied to the War; there was much jingoism to enliven the patriotism, some chauvinist riots, and mass recruitment. But there was resistance, both from Christian pacifism and from revolutionary socialism and Marxism which at times fused. Several Nonconformist districts in north Wales yielded to the recruitment drive only after a tour by Lloyd George, while a minister in the mining community of Cwmgiedd near Swansea stopped all recruiting with a single sermon. There was quite significant repression. More generally, in those intangible ways which cannot be analysed, the War at every one of its levels of disruption and disorientation unhinged a whole generation from its certainties. It was the War which killed Liberalism just as it dismissed the all-seeing eye of the Freemasons' God from trade union banners.

In the last grim months which debouched in hideous anti-black pogroms in Cardiff, there was an equally grim rally to the British nation, but also a tendency for the labour movement to reunite. People who, in truth, inhabited a different mental universe altogether, strengthened a revolutionary and totally dissident militancy. Arthur Horner, exemplar of a disaffected generation, crossed to Ireland to fight for the Citizen Army of James Connolly. Imprisoned on his return, he was promptly elected checkweigher by Mardy Lodge in the Rhondda. An emergency conference in 1917 actually wrote the abolition of capitalism into the rule-book of the South Wales Miners' Federation and, on a brief surge of working-class sympathy, it momentarily adhered to the Red International of Comintern. This was a spasmodic and minority trend, but at moments of high temper it could carry a majority. More permanently significant was the political advance of Labour which, while it shared some general emotions and commitments with the revolutionary socialists and rode on the tide of post-war ambition, retained its essential heritage of the morality and style of the Liberal dominance it was displacing.

Its advance was temporarily checked by the post-war prestige of Lloyd George. The Welsh Liberal Party, committed to him, won twenty-one out of thirty-six seats in Wales, though there were nasty civil wars, especially in Cardiganshire, and much of the coalfield was now lost. But in an electorate which had been considerably extended and opened up and within which women were now advancing, the collapse of the Coalition brought disaster for the Liberals. They lost another eight seats to Labour and shrank to a handful of family constituencies in rural Wales. The Conservatives inched back into Wales, particularly on the coasts and the borders, and the Labour Party advanced methodically to supremacy in south Wales. It was very much a regional party at this time. By 1923 Labour was polling over 50 per cent of the votes in Monmouth, Glamorgan and Carmarthen, while in the other ten counties the Liberals polled 56 per cent, a higher share than they had won in 1906. But after a check in 1924, the advance of Labour seemed remorseless. In 1929 only one Conservative was elected in Wales; the Liberals took ten seats and Labour towered over the country from its bases on the coalfields in north and south with twenty-five MPs.

As a socialist won the University of Wales seat, it was in a world transformed that the Disestablishment of the Welsh Church went into effect, to liberate and energize that Church, but to register as a total anti-climax. All the old struggles seemed to be coming to an end. Under the hammer-blows of taxation, war finance, the inflation and the artificial boom of the immediate post-war years, the great landlords finally gave up. In the Welsh sector of Europe's 'green revolution' they sold out and the era of the great estates came to an end. The magnates followed the Church and the Tories out of 'Wales' and the Welsh smallholder finally came into his own. The Labour political hegemony over the industrial south was quickly becoming a regime as all-embracing as the Liberal had been. A small Communist Party began to make headway among the unions and a socialist ILP bubbled in a frustrated evangelism. Riding an even more powerful tide was the miners' Federation. By 1921 it had organized 200,000 men out of a labour force now numbering no fewer than 270,000. Strong in its wage policy, its membership, its commitment to the labour movement, it awaited with confidence the implementation of the Sankey Commission's Report which would liberate the miners as the farmers had been freed. Yet another Welsh people, with the Labour movement inheriting the role of Liberalism, moved in turn into its kingdom.

They marched instead into a blizzard which killed their Wales stone dead.

# 11 · THE DISMANTLING OF WALES

> I stood in the ruins of Dowlais,
> And sighed for the lovers destroyed
> And the landscape of Gwalia stained for all time
> By the bloody hands of progress.
> I saw the ghosts of the slaves of The Successful Century
> Marching on the ridges of the sunset
> And wandering among desolate furnaces,
> And they had not forgotten their humiliation,
> For their mouths were full of curses.
> And I cried aloud, O what shall I do for my fathers
> And the land of my fathers?
> But they cursed and cursed and would not answer
> For they could not forget their humiliation.

So Idris Davies, the boy miner from Rhymney who, like so many, became a teacher in London and, with T. S. Eliot's commendation, published *Gwalia Deserta* in 1938. In the following year, unemployment in what had been the steel town of Dowlais stood at 73.4 per cent and commissioners reported that half the adult male population was surplus to the needs of existing industries and services. In its mother town of Merthyr unemployment stood at 69.1 per cent and the planning organization Political and Economic Planning (PEP) proposed that the whole population be shipped out to the river Usk. It suggested that the same solution would have to be applied to Ebbw Vale, Abertillery, Blaenavon, Bargoed, Mountain Ash and a score of other places, where something like 40 per cent of the Welsh had until recently lived. The central core of the population of Wales had become redundant.

So, apparently, had much of the rest of the country, outside the north-eastern coalfield, Swansea and tinplate and some sections of the anthracite coalfield, some firms and offices in Cardiff. Most of the small farmers had become pensioners of the Milk Marketing Board and the banks and there was a general *sauve-qui-peut* into teaching, any nice, clean jobs that were going and into the shadow-world of the No-Good Boyos. Women were streaming out to the servants' quarters of the English south-east in a 'maiden tribute' and men, women, whole families, were decamping to Dagenham,

Slough, Canada, anywhere where there was work and some dignity, leaving their valley townships to break down under the strain – 'Up here the rates are so high, they make everyone look short', said Gwyn Thomas – and thousands of people to scrub along under the fish-eyed scrutiny of under-managers, Means Test Men, public assistance boards, in a purgatory of sustained and inquisitory humiliation which burned itself into the memory even of their grandchildren. Leaving them, too, to fight and fight and fight again, to shape a movement whose power and colour transformed south Wales into some mythic heartland of a *Working Class*, to leave a memory which governed Welsh political life until the 1960s.

Officially 430,000 people left, in reality about half a million; overwhelmingly, they came from devastated south Wales and what had been the centre of imperial Wales. Nearly a quarter of a million came in, overwhelmingly non-Welsh, largely elderly, often retired, *rentiers,* an overspill from an affluent elsewhere, making for the holiday coasts and the little, emptied villages, where property was almost as cheap as people. A population of some 2½ million lost a fifth of its natives and saw one economy and society destroyed; it gained a tenth from new people and saw another economy and society transformed. And over the whole, even the tinplate on the coast, even Swansea with its poets and musicians, even the north-east now disappearing into Merseyside, fell a pall of neglect and depression, a collapse of social capital and a dismal legacy in bad housing, ill-health, poor environment. Whole areas of Wales became and have remained problem areas.

It was the central role of Britain in a world market which had created modern Wales with its offshore working class. That class was left stranded by the eclipse of British coal, the switch to oil, the contractions of British steel. What Wales experienced between the two Wars was a major reconstruction of that British and world economy, which left it a battered, sub-standard and lopsided region under a peculiarly rigid economic regime. Government action finally began to make a little progress towards reconstructing Wales itself in the late 1930s, though the unemployment level did not fall very much from the shattering 32 per cent of the worst moments after the 1929 Depression until that saving power, the War. Wales went into the Second World War with an officially insured working population of just under 600,000. The bulk of it was still concentrated in the south-east. Most of it, some 144,000, a quarter of its workers, was still in coal. Sixty-six thousand were in metals. The old basic industries still accounted for not far short of 40 per cent of the working people, overwhelmingly male. More general engineering and manufacture had inched up from their low proportion of a fifth. Shops, stores, offices and that range of services called distributive accounted for around 15 per cent.

During the War there was another major adjustment as industries were dispersed. By the end of it there was a huge amount of factory floor space available in Wales; its women, who had played a major role in the mass movements of popular resistance and had been driven to become wage-earners of the last resort during the depression, poured into the factories and the pubs to form an unprecedented 40 per cent of the working population. With the peace they moved or were moved out, though thousands now shifted into those jobs like teaching and nursing which they had already started to colonize. In 1946 coal had slithered to 116,000 and some 18 per cent of the workers and for the first time had been surpassed by general manufactures which accounted for nearly a fifth; metals had also slipped back, but government service now accounted for one worker in ten.

It was in the brief period from 1945 to 1948 that the Labour government seriously applied the idea of social planning and social engineering in the interests of Wales considered as a community, that short interval when the overpowering dominance of America governed the processes of recovery throughout Europe and which lurched into serious trouble, resolved only by the Marshall Plan and the Cold War and the wave of devaluations over 1947–8. From that point on, there were only two moments when social planning in the full sense was seriously considered; in a period of tension in the late 1950s and over 1964–6, in the first years of a Wilson government committed to modernization, when it foundered in conflict between a new Welsh Office backed by the Treasury and planning authorities which were intended to be the voice of community. Otherwise state planning, with an eye to regional rescue, served the industry which carried it. Wales, of course, shared fully in the massive spiritual transformation effected by the coming of the Welfare State, the National Health Service, the restoration of dignity and honour to a degraded people. It shared in the growing, apparently endless prosperity of the long capitalist boom of the 1950s and 1960s, when people seem to have entered a new era, though there were repeated hiccoughs. That boom was plagued in Britain by the structural and persistent weaknesses of its old economy, and by the recovery and rise of Germany and Japan.

From the late 1960s, the overdeveloped ten nations of the world ran into more and more severe crises through the oil and energy dislocations, the mushroom growth of new industrial peoples, the growing divergence between a global north and south, the currency lunacies precipitated by heavy Third World and Soviet bloc indebtedness. New technologies and new techniques stimulated a major relocation of industries with branch plants scattered out among hitherto untapped reserves of unorganized working people. The processes of production were dispersed around these plants, with control concentrated at the centre, normally located within existing complexes of political and financial power: a practice which rapidly became international. The shift out from the cities, the rise of multibranch and multinational firms, the growing integration of a still stumbling Britain into Europe, all tended from the late 1960s onwards to reshape Britain around its highly developed core running from Bristol in a great arc through the 'sun-belt' past London and out to Cambridge. The rest had to adjust to this heartland. All was immeasurably intensified by the adoption of policies of monetary rigour and capitalist discipline by the Labour government under International Monetary Fund (IMF) pressure after 1976 and made into a kind of crusade by the Conservative government which came in on a wave of popular support in 1979 and won a crushing electoral majority in 1983.

The consequences in Wales have been revolutionary. While the unbalanced concentration of people in the south-east persists and turns the area into a sub-standard and atomized dormitory, the interplay of these drives in industry with government action directed at easing them and where possible producing employment, with popular and increasingly localized responses, and with cultural complexities arising from language conflict, is shaping new regions in Wales. Cardiff and its region have grown into a subordinate metropolis, almost totally deindustrialized, with waves of public services succeeded by waves of private services. The only region in Wales where men's non-manual earnings are higher than the British average, it is increasingly a branch extension and dependency of the London–Bristol axis. The central and eastern valleys of south Wales saw a growth of branch-plant manufacture in the 1960s and into the 1970s. Foreign multinational corporations in particular have nested here and throughout the south. By 1974 they were employing anything from a quarter of Welsh workers in coal and petroleum products, mechanical engineering and vehicles, to a third in chemicals and electrical engineering; they were mainly American, with Europeans coming up behind. Since then the Japanese have entered in force; of thirty Japanese firms which opened branches in Britain between 1967 and 1981, seven chose south Wales. In the 1970s, however, the growth of manufacture in eastern south Wales was checked and public services have developed.

Western south Wales, focused on Swansea, saw its steel and heavy industry hammered, with a powerful concentration of services in the city itself. Central Wales running along the eastern border has nearly a half of its working people in services, but employment in small-scale but often technical manufacture has mushroomed, as the region has become a state-managed outpost of the English Midlands. The older north-eastern core of industry was slow to change until disaster overtook its steel and related industries and the area slid into the dismal flux of proud Merseyside. Along the north Wales coast, unique in Wales, there was a major growth of both industry and services but the great industry is tourism which employs many low-paid women. North-west Wales, the old slate area, followed the fluctuating pattern of the south-eastern coal relic at first; manufacturing, usually by British branch-plant firms, penetrated and there has been a growth in services, but it is tourism and the transformation of the district into a leisure reserve which catch the eye. So they do in the south-west, where self-employment is even more marked than in the west as a whole and where services have made great strides. Throughout the west and much of rural Wales, a farming population seems to have derived benefit from the European Common Market.

In consequence, the working population of Wales has been turned upside down, in so rapid and drastic a manner that the change has not yet fully registered on the consciousness and the discourse of Welsh politics.

By 1961, when the population of Wales had finally been prised painfully back to the level it had reached in 1921, the largest single group of workers in Wales was in the distributive trades; they just pipped the number of colliers, each about 11 per cent of the working population. Next came professional and scientific services, which in Wales means education and medicine, with 10 per cent, followed by metals with 9. Electrical and other engineering was substantial with 5 per cent, and over the rest, older trades and services still predominated over the new. The working people were still largely male. From the middle of the nineteenth century, women who had been so central to working people in the eighteenth century had been eased out of the ranks of wage-earners. Their place was within the home, where they exercised real but subordinate power. Throughout the late nineteenth century, the proportion of women of working age who actually went out to work as wage-earners fluctuated between 26 and 29 per cent. Mostly they went into domestic service or dressmaking, though nurses and teachers began to appear at the turn of the century, overproduced in Welsh custom, as the general proportion declined to 22 per cent. Their centrality between the 1920s and the 1940s did not last. By 1961 it was still only 28 per cent of Welsh women over fifteen who were officially recorded as being in work or actively seeking it.

From that point, their rate of entry into the working population has exceeded that of any other group in Britain and it is forecast to go on exceeding it into the 1990s. For it was from the 1960s that the working population of Wales was transformed and, in the depression which followed 1979, severely cut down. The transformation is best caught in some simplified tables of the distribution of working people between the extractive industries (mining, quarrying, agriculture), manufacturing, and the whole range of service industries, public and private. Official figures over 1968 to 1983 project an immediate image (see Table 1).

Most visible is the total collapse of the old basic industries. In 1982 miners were only 23,000, a little over 2 per cent of workers; steel accounted for some 38,000, a bare 4 per cent. Between them, the old standards now account for little more than one in twenty Welsh working people.

Table 1: The Welsh Working Population 1968 – 1982

| Date June | Total | Sectors of Employment (in thousands) | | |
|---|---|---|---|---|
| | | I | II | III |
| 1968 | 992 | 102 (10.3%) | 409 (41.2%) | 481 (48.5%) |
| 1969 | 974 | 94 | 409 | 471 |
| 1970 | 968 | 87 | 416 | 465 |
| 1971 | 962 | 78 | 413 | 471 |
| 1972 | 973 | 75 | 412 | 486 |
| 1973 | 1000 | 73 | 421 | 506 |
| 1974 | 993 | 70 | 422 | 501 |
| 1975 | 997 | 68 | 403 | 526 |
| 1976 | 996 | 67 | 391 | 538 |
| 1977 | 997 | 65 | 393 | 539 |
| 1978 | 1015 | 64 | 395 | 556 |
| 1979 | 1022 | 60 | 399 | 563 |
| 1980 | 987 | 60 | 373 | 554 |
| 1981 | 914 | 59 | 319 | 536 |
| 1982 | 900 | 58 | 295 | 546 |
| December | | | | |
| 1982 | 884 | 59 (6.7%) | 286 (32.4%) | 538 (60.8%) |

I = Extractive, i.e. agriculture + mining and quarrying.

II = Manufacturing, i.e. food, drink, tobacco; coal, petroleum and chemicals; metals; engineering and allied; textiles, leather and clothing; other; + construction and gas-electricity-water.

III = Services, i.e. transport and communication; distributive; financial, professional and miscellaneous (entertainment and personal); public administration.

Manufacturing has fallen to 286,000, fewer than a third. Towering overall are the service industries, with nearly 61 per cent of the working population. The largest single group are those in educational and medical services and of those no fewer than 71 per cent are women. In 1921 the largest single group of Welsh workers were 270,000 colliers; in the late 1970s, they were 118,000 women: teachers, nurses, cleaners, ancillary workers. In the Tonypandy of the *Miner's Next Step,* 49 per cent of the registered workers were women; in Treorchy of the Male Voice Choir, 57 per cent. The Rhondda militants of today are women protestors at Greenham Common missile base.

The rise of women workers by number has been as remorseless as a slow rock-slip in a crumbling pit (see Table 2). In December 1982 there were some 884,000 people officially at work in Wales, the lowest total for decades; a whole young generation is moving as relentlessly into a life without work as we have known it as any of the Hywels and Blodwens of Idris Davies in the 1930s. In manufacturing industry 286,000 people work, often at low production and part-time, and the number shrinks. Nearly 540,000 people are in services: local and national government, shops, stores, offices, private firms, hotels, pubs, clubs, entertainments. Of the core working population, 45 per cent are women. Of these some 42 per cent are part-time, moving in and out of work according to the rhythms of child-birth and rearing. The pressure on them mounts. Women go on working beyond retirement age in larger numbers than men. In 1981 3,000 women over seventy were officially reported at work in Wales. In the shadow land of the informal economy and with the multitudinous return of the No-Good Boyos, no one knows exactly what is happening.

What is clear, however, is that seeping through the fragmentation into new regions in which everyone fights for themselves, there is a remorseless drain of people and activity to the coasts, which are now coasts of Europe, a drain which sucks the life out of Wales's hollow heart to the point of vacuum. In the future looms a reconstruction of the public sector in a country which lives by it, virtually the whole of whose middle class is embedded in a British state and its local agencies, which subsidize the cultural Welsh nationalism of important groups within it. Beyond that looms the new technology, the coming of robot labour and perhaps the end of work as we have known it.

This restructuring has seen an overpowering Labour hegemony take shape and start to collapse, a myth of a *Working Class* by which a majority of the Welsh have lived take off into a limbo of meaninglessness, the rise of a passionate Welsh-language nationalist movement which has scored major successes and turned Wales into an officially bilingual country, only to provoke an angry and fearful backlash from hundreds of thousands of Welsh people who use English, in which confrontation the very idea of *Wales* itself goes out of the window. In a triple sequence of elections in 1979, the Welsh electorate not only rejected any notion of Welsh self-government by 47 per cent to 12 per cent and turned its back on a concept of Europe, it swung harder to the Conservatives than any region in Britain outside London. In 1979 the Welsh electorate halted and reversed what had been the dominant political trend in Wales for 150 years. In the General Election of 1983 they drove harder still against Labour. By 1983 every political tradition to which the modern Welsh people in their majority had committed themselves was bankrupt. Wales itself seemed once more to be dissolving into a congeries of disparate societies in these two western

Table 2: *Women in the Welsh Working Population 1968 – 1982*

| Date June | Total ('000s) number of people in work | Women %age Total | II and III Total | II and III Women ('000s) | Women %age II + III |
|---|---|---|---|---|---|
| 1968 | 992 | 32.8 | 890 | 315 | 35.4 |
| 1969 | 974 | 33.4 | 880 | 315 | 35.8 |
| 1970 | 968 | 34.3 | 881 | 322 | 36.6 |
| 1971 | 962 | 34.6 | 884 | 324 | 36.7 |
| 1972 | 973 | 35.1 | 898 | 334 | 37.2 |
| 1973 | 1000 | 36.4 | 927 | 355 | 38.3 |
| 1974 | 993 | 37.4 | 923 | 363 | 39.2 |
| 1975 | 997 | 38.1 | 929 | 373 | 40.0 |
| 1976 | 996 | 38.4 | 929 | 375 | 40.4 |
| 1977 | 997 | 39.0 | 933 | 383 | 41.1 |
| 1978 | 1015 | 39.5 | 951 | 395 | 41.5 |
| 1979 | 1022 | 40.0 | 962 | 403 | 41.9 |
| 1980 | 987 | 40.1 | 926 | 390 | 42.1 |
| 1981 | 914 | 42.5 | 855 | 383 | 44.7 |
| 1982 | 900 | 42.0 | 841 | 373 | 44.4 |
| December 1982 | 884 | 42.7 | 824 | 371 | 45.0 |

*Sources:* Tables 1 and 2 are derived from official figures in *The Digest of Welsh Statistics 1980 and 1981* (Welsh Office, 1981–2); *Regional Trends 1982* (Central Statistical Office, 1982); *Census 1981: County Reports* (Office of Population Censuses and Surveys, 1982); *Employment Gazette 1982–4* (Department of Employment).

peninsulas, whose future, whose very existence as coherent and tolerable human societies was beginning to seem problematical. We have run off our maps.

This has happened within the space of a single lifetime. I was born in 1925. My parents, like many others, were school-teachers from working-class families. Brothers, cousins, friends were colliers often on the dole. The talk at the supper table of my childhood in Dowlais was of Labour and the ILP, what to do about the Communists, of my uncle's latest Welsh-language play on the Welsh radio, our local fascist Arthur Eyles and his rather more menacing colleagues abroad – and, we were convinced, bunching around Neville Chamberlain and 'his' police officers at home – of the ethics of canvassing for headships among an overpowering Labour council noted for both heroic service and unheroic nepotism and petty corruption, of TB (*y dicai*) and diphtheria (the Dip), which took away one of the children and nearly took both, of the *noson lawen* (folk-nights) at the chapel and the scholarship to Aberystwyth, of the fights with the fascists on the Bont and how difficult it was to discuss the performance of the Spitfire in Welsh. When my mother descended on Cardiff and its posh shops, she took care to employ, loudly, what she fondly imagined to be an Oxford accent, to show we were as good as any of *that lot* down there. At the end of her life, in those shops, my mother would, equally loudly, use her excellent Welsh, to watch the assistants apologize and know we were better than *that lot*. But she found the Wales she was in strange beyond belief and I think she was glad to get out of it.

By the 1980s the Wales which The Successful Century had invented was being dismantled by the force which through that black fuse drove the power, and no one, in his or her heart, no matter what clichés old and new they might parrot in diminishing conviction, knew what was going to happen to us, we who had lived in these two peninsulas, as a people, somehow or other, for a millennium and a half.

# 12 · CATACLYSM AND COMMUNITY

On Sunday, 3 February 1935, the valleys of what was still called industrial south Wales started to come alive with movement. Knots of people gathered around banners: local committees of action, churches, chapels, co-operatives, women's groups, the Salvation Army and the British Legion, Sunday schools, shopkeepers, teachers, printers, ministers, shop-assistants, the miners, the unemployed. In and about them moved their organizers, Labour and Communist and ILP, the National Unemployed Workers' Movement, (NUWM), women in groups and as individuals. Bands formed up. Lewis Jones, the Communist spokesman for the NUWM, a man of spirit, once the only comrade present at a Moscow meeting who did not stand up when Stalin came into the room, captured the moment in his novel *We Live,* based on his 'Cwmardy' which is the Rhondda.

At the bottom of the hill, before turning into the square which led to the rubbish dump, where the other pit contingents of the Combine were waiting, Len looked back. His eyes glowed with what he saw. The street behind him looked like a flowing river of human beings on which floated innumerable scarlet banners and flags . . . Although directly in front of the band, he heard running beneath its thrumming wails the deep monotone of countless boots tramping rhythmically on the hard road . . . When the front of the demonstration was two miles advanced and on the summit of the hill to the east of Cwmardy, people were still pouring into the assembling field. Len lifted his head sharply into the air when he fancied he heard the distant strains of music in the direction left of the demonstration. He turned to Mary and the workman next to her. 'Can you hear anything?' he asked. They both looked simultaneously past Len and he, seeing their amazement, turned his head to look in the same direction. He drew his breath sharply and his perspiring face went a shade whiter. The mountain which separated Cwmardy from the other valleys looked like a gigantic ant-hill covered with a mass of black, waving bodies. 'Good God,' the man next to Mary whispered, 'the whole world is on the move . . .'

On that Sunday, the population of south Wales seems to have turned out on to the streets. There were 60,000 to 70,000 in the Rhondda marching to Tonypandy; Aneurin Bevan spoke to thousands at Blackwood; Pontypool saw the biggest meeting it had ever had, 20,000 listening to Ernest Bevin. There were marches and meetings in Neath, Briton Ferry, Merthyr, even

in Barry. Down the Aberdare Valley, 50,000 people marched to Mountain
Ash in a procession two and a half miles long through wind and rain . . .
the local reporter, one of the very few even to report this colossal
demonstration, was thunderstruck – men and women wore their Sunday
best, young unemployed were in shiny shoes and even yellow gloves, young
women wore their hats, high heels . . . it was like a Gymanfa Ganu or a
Sunday School rally, 'a cry from humanity for humanity. The Government
cannot refuse to listen to the cry of the people . . .'

'The world's brow was hot,' wrote Gwyn Thomas the novelist, who was
in the march, 'and we were out to fan it with banners. We suggested a
possible definition of Wales as a non-stop protest with mutating consonants.
Navels distended by resting banner-poles became one of the region's major
stigmata.'

Something of the order of 300,000 people marched that day. One person
out of seven of the entire population of Wales was out in those valleys. It
was the greatest demonstration Wales has ever known. There had been
nothing like it in the history of the Welsh and there has been nothing like
it since. A whole community stood up and said No.

They were saying No to the Unemployment Assistance Board Act of
1934–5. They had had enough of unemployment and emigration, of Public
Assistance Committees haggling over threepence for children's milk, of
young girls going off to London and young men putting their heads on
the railway line, enough of Means Test Men and National Government
10 per cent cuts in benefit. Now they were confronted by a government
bent on restoring expenditure within strict limits, on curbing the autonomy
of local officials and on ramming through draconian measures, directed
in particular at sons or daughters who might pick up a few shillings from
petty profiteers swarming in like rats around a grounded ship. Their
regulations would drive children of earning age out of the house in sheer
self-defence. The legislation was a direct threat not only to what self-
government they had left but to the family most of them lived by. They
took to the streets against the Slave Act as others of their kin were doing
all over Britain, though none to quite this communal extent.

It was the women who carried this broken society on their backs and
on the next day, the women around Merthyr organized another march
behind Ceridwen Brown of Aberdare and her friends. Griff Jones, a
Communist who was to fight alongside Ceridwen's son in Spain, saw thirty
with banners in the little village of Pengarnddu alone. By the time they
reached the bottom of Dowlais, there were hundreds of women, some
carrying babies, with men running to support. The demonstration massed

before the Unemployment Assistance Board (UAB) offices. Clerks in the windows pulled faces and the women went in. They wrecked the offices and burned the papers, ripping phones off the walls. A well-respected Quaker, John Dennithorne, tried to quieten them but they shouted, 'Come down, Old Bug Whiskers!' A Party man, a Cardiff Greek, tried to speak; they wouldn't hear him. They would listen only to Ceridwen Brown from Aberdare and a local hero everyone knew as Jack-Williams-the-Communist from Dowlais. They smashed the UAB offices, to horrify even the Labour MP, the fiery radical S. O. Davies himself, whose opinions were such that no Welsh nationalist or communist party stood much chance in Merthyr while he was around. He denounced them as a rabble – and was promptly shouted down by ILP-ers and Communists.

Over in Blaina, the demonstrations also blew up. The children of Nant-y-Glo refused to go to school and the shopkeepers shut up shop. 'Take all necessary measures,' their Labour MP George Dagger told them. In the valley of the Ebbw Fach, there were seventy in the Communist Social Club and fifty in the Communist Women's Club; the valley had Communist district and county councillors. People unleashed a guerilla war against a tough police led by Superintendent Baker. They marched on Abertillery singing 'We'll make Queen Mary do the washing for the boys' and 'Who's afraid of the Big Bad Wolf?' at the Superintendent. Twelve of them were acquitted after they claimed that anti-royalist songs were unlikely to disturb the peace of Abertillery. The big demonstration was planned for the offices at Blaina after authority had refused to listen to the Communist councillor Phil Abrahams. The Brynmawr and Nant-y-Glo contingents were already there, when the Blaina and Abertillery squads came up past the Blaina Inn. Out of it came the police flailing batons; there were guerilla battles all over the valley heads; Clarence Lloyd and his brother went into hiding on a farm near Abergavenny. At the trial, three American Rhodes Scholars supported them and D. N. Pritt defended them. Six got four to six months, three Communists of the NUWM got nine and Phil Abrahams was stripped of his civic rights for ten years.

On a smaller scale, this was happening in many places. And on the day after the women's rebellion in Merthyr, Oliver Stanley announced in the Commons a stand-still order on the new regulations. They did not come into effect for eighteen months, and then in modified form. This is the only known occasion in the thirties when popular protest, aligned with parliamentary opposition, led most memorably by Aneurin Bevan, actually stopped a government such as that one in its tracks. South Wales had been in the forefront. And from that moment, despite the continuing horrors, there is no mistaking the sudden lift in morale in south Wales. It can be sensed everywhere and carried these people into their liberating World War on a surge of socialist and Labour hope. What God himself seemed to have abandoned, these ordinary men and women defended, and they saved the sum of a human society in the valleys of south Wales for a bob on the benefit.

## Resistance

For fifteen years, south Wales was an arena of conflict. That arena was, in objective terms, strictly limited geographically and socially. Swansea, with its anthracite, steel and oil, was quite flourishing, with a lively press, a circle of writers and artists and musicians around Dylan Thomas, Daniel Jones, Vernon Watkins, Fred Janes, Mervyn Levy; there were new housing estates and a Guildhall. There were jobs and life all along the coast, though opportunities were narrow. The north-east got a boost from Courtaulds rayon and an extension of steel-smelting, and the north coast resorts were expanding. Much of rural Wales moved at a slow pace, its politics locked into the family wars of the Lloyd George clan who dominated the ten or so Liberal seats outside the coalfields.

Throughout the period and through all areas, the long-term and molecular processes were under way, in particular the rise of new middle classes, notably professional in character, through the heroically defended and developed schools, the university, the law, the new radio broadcasting; others on the fringe of law and morality in a dissolving society had their ways and means. The middling sort, so newly emerged from a populist tilth, could have their golf and tennis clubs even in stricken Merthyr, hold bridge parties and go on holidays to the English south or Welsh cruises to the Celtic lands. There was a breathtaking efflorescence of adult education classes, some of them terrifying in their appetite, local drama groups, eisteddfods. Sir Malcolm Sargent would conduct the Three Choirs Festival at Mountain Ash. These were the years of Ivor Novello from Cardiff. The Sunday School outing became a national institution; spectator sport flourished, notably soccer and rugby, and Glamorgan got itself a county cricket club. Tommy Farr's battle for the World Heavyweight title with Joe Louis was a national epic, characteristically of frustration. We was robbed.

Robbed we had been and no one could avoid the fact. Thomas Jones and his friends launched the adult education college at Harlech, there were repeated campaigns against TB and other diseases, major efforts by the

Quakers and other charities. The stream of reports and analyses seemed endless. This was a highly complex and contradictory society in which a new social formation was taking shape. But the pain and misery and the anger at its heart could not be dodged for a minute, not when the medical officer of Pengam reported that children were contracting rickets in their mother's womb, not when the suicide rate shot up so abruptly, not when what had been the heartland of the Welsh population was torn out. When Treforest and the new industrial and housing estates at last began to rise in the late thirties, they rose in a south Wales which had almost totally committed itself to Labour and a determination so to remake British society that nothing like this could ever happen again. It was, moreover, a Labour hegemony of a highly distinctive kind, wreathed in passionate left-wing talk, shot through with Marxism and great blood-red dreams of brotherhood, with at its side a small but highly influential Communist Party and all around it a tradition of pro-Soviet feeling and bitter class battles. The *Working Class* seemed to have become an organizing principle for a Welsh people.

Before the War, the ILP around Keir Hardie, with its aggressive paper *Llais Llafur* (Voice of Labour) in Ystalyfera and the *Merthyr Pioneer* under its radical and Welsh-speaking Independent minister T. E. Nicholas (Niclas Glais), and its scattering of dedicated candidates, had preached a socialism parliamentary in character but revolutionary in intention and radical in practice. Out of the early battles in the coalfield had come a clutch of revolutionary socialists, semi-syndicalist in style. All had passed through the crucible of the War, when many had been persecuted. Many like the South Wales Socialist Society passed straight into the new Communist Party, which was small but full of activists, including Niclas Glais, particularly among the miners. It moved forward through its International's fluctuations around the theme of the united-front-from-below, in its Minority Movement among the unions, its NCLC training schools and classes, in sharp, sometimes allied, often tense relationship with the Labour Party. Within the Gothic structure of that Party, the ILP went into its dervish dance of continuously frustrated principle. The Labour Party itself represented a total transformation of the south Wales society it was conquering – 'Mae Leysh wedi mynd Bolsh' ('Leyshon's gone Bolshevik') meant joining the Labour Party after 1918. In 1922 it contested twenty-eight of the thirty-six Welsh seats and got nearly 41 per cent of the vote; by 1929 it was getting 44 per cent and in the disastrous year of 1931 actually inched up to 45 per cent, riveting itself on the coalfield and supplying sixteen of the Labour Party's forty-six MPs. It was overpoweringly a trade union party; of its sixteen MPs in 1924 thirteen were trade union officials, twelve of those miners. Mostly they were an undistinguished but hard-working oxgang of labourers, like their councillors back home who, in multiple battles, were emerging as defenders of their communities in disaster. The Labour Party, hit as hard by the depression as anyone else, grew as a kind of tribal defence mechanism against ruin, its professed socialism taking on a Utopian and moralistic distance. New men entered in 1929, W. G. Cove of Aberavon, an aggressive school teacher, and Aneurin Bevan of Ebbw Vale on his quest for power, whose voice was to echo over Wales and Britain and half the world before he was done. In 1934–6 in came two very Welsh MPs, James Griffiths of Llanelli from the anthracite, President of the Miners' Federation, a gentle giant and, unlike Aneurin Bevan, committed to a more traditional and populist Wales; and S. O. Davies of Merthyr, a meteor who had been in the Minority Movement and could embrace a species of Welsh nationalism and a species of communism in a Welsh socialism which had him repeatedly excluded from the parliamentary party. During the thirties the Labour Party not only grew more strongly socialist in tone and rhetoric and style, it seemed to present a quasi-revolutionary left-wing, often pro-Soviet face which belied the inner reality of its rank-and-file middle-of-the-road trade union loyalists. This was the product of that particular constellation of forces which found a focus in 1935.

Working people came out of the War full of the ambitious, quasi-revolutionary temper which was sweeping Western Europe. The Communist Party, the Minority Movement in the unions, the NCLC classes focused a Marxist temper. They ran straight into the direct offensive of the coal-owners to cut wages and control labour which threw whole communities into conflict. In 1921 the South Wales Miners' Federation (SWMF) urged the Miners' Federation of Great Britain to affiliate to the Red International of Trade Unions. S. O. Davies of the Dowlais district and the leader A. J. Cook worked to organize it; Borodin himself, fresh from Comintern in Moscow, is said to have consulted the Ynyshir Unofficial Reform Committee which controlled the Rhondda district of the Fed. The initiative failed, but it launched the radical wing of the miners into that 'proletarian internationalism' which was to be their hallmark for the next two generations.

And after the shattering let-down of the sabotage of the Sankey Commission and Black Friday, two new Combines in the anthracite region launched an attack on established working practices.* This intensely Welsh district exploded, with the Spaniards at Abercrave giving a lead in militancy.

There was an overturn of society, splits in the chapels, mass riots around Ammanford against blackleg labour; the mobilization of whole communities, wholesale victimization; over 200 miners were tried, nearly sixty jailed. The owners dismantled one pit rather than compromise, but the men held like grim death to the 'seniority rule' (first in, last out) which was the essential shield against victimization and the manipulation of the unemployed and gave workers a measure of control. The radicalization of the anthracite region, indeed its social and political transformation, given its less severe slump, was to prove significant; it was to be the base for a counter-offensive into the more devastated areas and for an intelligent and highly influential Communist leadership.

All local conflicts were swept up into the trauma of the attack on living standards, the General Strike and the long, harsh seven-month lock-out which followed. To the TUC, south Wales was a Class One region; to Wil Paynter, a passionate young Communist, 1926 was Year One. The spectacle of the Fed lodges, with the co-ops and the women's groups, mobilizing whole communities to run south Wales themselves was for many a deathless vision of a workers' power which could be attained.

Do you remember 1926? That summer of speeches,
The sunlight on the idle wheels and the deserted crossings,
And the laughter and the cursing in the moonlit streets?
Do you remember 1926? The slogans and the penny concerts,
The jazzbands and the moorland picnics,
And the slanderous tongues of famous cities?
Do you remember 1926? The great dream and the swift disaster . . . **

The dream of workers' power and the jazz bands and football matches with the police soon dissolved into the long agony of the seven hard months. The communal kitchens and the controlled working of outcrops by the Glynneath Soviet Level began to crumble as thousands of half-starved families were driven to turn the outcrops into small businesses with outlets in Cardiff, as more and more were forced back to work, to face councils of war, hundreds of angry women throwing stones, muffling them in white shirts and frogmarching them out. Captain Lionel Lindsay of the Glamorgan police resumed his long war with the miners. There were

*Government response to the Sankey Commission ruled out nationalization of the coal industry and virtually abandoned it to a socially irresponsible entrepreneurial rationalization, while the 'Black Friday' of trade union tradition refers to the breakdown of the alliance of the miners and the transport unions under government pressure in 1921. The miners were to be even more isolated in 1926.
**From Idris Davies's *Gwalia Deserta* (Dent, 1938).

eighteen major battles and innumerable skirmishes. Everywhere women were to the fore with their whiteshirting and their whitewash; an extraordinarily ingenious and bitter struggle raged for weeks on end, with 'ghost trains' of blacklegs being ambushed and decoyed, serried ranks of police charging crowds. At Glyncorrwg and Cymmer in the Upper Afan valley, where over 140 children had to go to school barefoot, there was a kind of civil war. Hundreds of men and women filed into the police courts, hundreds of supporters followed them; they were drilled in their evidence, the women told just how to lay down their gloves before they answered questions. Scores of them filed into the jails, to be greeted as heroes and heroines when they came out. It was a community action. But it was a community divided against itself, for who were these 'blacklegs' but their former butties?

South Wales now entered that travail which Bethesda and the quarries had known for three years; the miners lived with it for ten. The Fed went into the General Strike an army and came out of it a rabble. Over 70,000 deserted. The Combines moved in, practised wholesale and sustained discrimination, ruthlessly exploited the unemployed, set community against community. A South Wales Miners Industrial Union was created under their auspices, William Gregory at its head, specifically directed against the 'political' SWMF; it made gains in western Monmouthshire and eastern Glamorgan. By the end of the 1920s the Fed was fighting for its life.

> 'Ay, ay, we remember 1926,' said Dai and Shinkin,
> As they stood on the kerb in Charing Cross Road,
> 'And we shall remember 1926 until our blood is dry.'

The fight back was hard and bitter. Arthur Horner in the Rhondda started his long struggle for one big union. It was his base at Mardy in the Rhondda which created the best known of the Little Moscows. Not very different in truth from most other coalfield villages, including those in its own valley, it was always equipped with its Conservative Club, Boy Scouts and Carolina Coons. The intransigence it shared with other villages was deliberately canalized by the militants of the Fed and the NUWM, by people like Dai Lloyd Davies and Horner, into the creation of a counter-community. Derived from the past, this community was translated into a Welsh sector of a proletarian international with its Young Pioneers, its secular funerals (red ribbons and hammer-and-sickle wreaths) comrades Bessie Baker and Wharton reporting back to the Lodge on their visit to Workers' Russia in the firm tones of thirteen-year-old proletarians. Mardy, rooted as it had to be in the Union Lodge, became a myth because it lasted longer. But its styles were present wherever there were Communists and there were some everywhere. In the face-to-face conflict with Labour enjoined by Comintern's Class against Class policy between 1929 and 1934, Rhondda CP took over the Labour Party locally, was confronted with another, stood Horner as parliamentary candidate against Labour and in one very fierce conflict against Will Mainwaring, one of the authors of the *Miner's Next Step,* in 1933 got within 3,000 votes of victory. By that time, Horner had seen the Mardy lodge virtually expelled from the Federation, and the Communist Party reduced to impotence by Comintern's policy. He shuffled almost inevitably into the heresy of 'Hornerism', renewed that working within the major organizations which finally came to fruition in the Popular Front which had become a reality in south Wales before it was officially adopted by the International. There were many short-lived Little Moscows, wherever the demands of struggle became so intense that a counter-community became necessary. At the height of the battle against non-unionism, Bedlinog, one of those mining villages where you need magnets in your boots to stand upright, at one time elected a Communist Chamber of Commerce, a rather striking anticipation of Eurocommunism.

That was at the peak of the struggle over Taff Merthyr. The names of those years now read like battle honours on the banners of the NUM: Taff Merthyr, Nine-Mile Point, Bedwas. It was a desperate, hard fight to unhinge the 'non-political' union, regain members, establish credibility among the unemployed in an industry being driven by utterly intransigent coal-owners. It is a story of infinite patience, persistence, care, resolution and where necessary ruthlessness in what had the makings of a civil war. It is a story of remarkable leadership: James Griffiths who became president of the Fed in 1934 and directed it; S. O. Davies, the fervent Labour agent; unemployed leaders of outstanding mettle like Wil Paynter and very noticeably a whole generation of Communist militants like Paynter, Dai Dan Evans of the anthracite, a model for many more, with the genius of Horner in the van. The ritual was endlessly repeated, the strikes and arguments, the brass bands, marching crowds, women in the lead everywhere, the police charges, the court cases, the pilgrimage of political prisoners, the banners like the one at Treharris which at one time became a permanent theatre for these battles – 'You have suffered for a principle. We are proud of you.' The process climaxed in those dramatic stay-downs which caught the imagination of a generation, the long, wretched hours underground, the drama at the pit-head, the upcoming to a triumph. From 1934 onwards the Fed was reorganized with a rank and file executive, unemployed lodges and a more effective structure. It successfully harnessed community to its purpose and, in its shrunken industry, it won. This was one essential core around which the popular mobilization of 1935 formed.

But that mobilization also demonstrated the limits of the Communist initiative. On the crest of that wave the CP, with its new *Daily Worker* offering powerful support and its *de facto* Popular Front approved, with its membership nearing 3,000, moved forward, with its intelligent, learned, hardened, crusading yet earthily practical men and women, with all its dependent organizations, to run into a blank wall of Labour hostility. A violent reaction from the TUC and the British Labour Party broke the shift towards a popular front in Wales. There was a major rally of the faithful around the social democratic flag. Chapel ministers rose up against the threat of Communism in the valleys; one resorted to the ultimate terror weapon and warned that the Communists would abolish Sunday School trips to Barry Island. Throughout 1935 there was a marked hardening of the Labour position in south Wales. At the disappointing General Election in the October, the Communist candidate in the Rhondda slipped well back.

Aneurin Bevan got into trouble. After Hitler's coming to power and the new police measures adopted by the government, there was a widespread fear of fascism. The local variant struck roots in south Wales. There was a scattering of them along the coasts and pockets inland. An eccentric Communist in Merthyr, who had a strong following among the most isolated and depressed communities and remained a hero to them, Arthur Eyles, became a convert and there were regular battles around the town. Over 1933–4 Bevan proposed the formation of worker defence militias against these and the police and there was some drilling around Tredegar; the Communists were organizing their own, and held aloof, but all such initiatives were promptly smothered by the Labour Party which was to go on to expel Bevan and his colleagues in the Socialist League.

The Communists, however, continued to ride the swelling international tide. The greatest moment of glory was the Spanish Civil War. In a country which had plenty of working-class Spaniards and established links with Bilbao, the Civil War struck an even deeper chord than it did elsewhere. In all, 174 volunteers from Wales fought with the International Brigade; thirty-three of them died. The majority were south Wales miners, 122 of them, with thirty-four more from the coal ports. Nearly all of them were Communists or communisant. To serve in Spain became as much a mark of honour as to have gone to jail for the cause. Lodges raised money; a poverty-stricken people gave milk, money and goods to the Spanish Republic and took children from the Basque Republic into sanctuary even as Cardiff ship captains tried to run the Franco blockade. Lewis Jones the writer spent his energies on the cause; he dropped dead from exhaustion after addressing over thirty street meetings on Spain, in the week Barcelona fell. His novel *We Live* reaches its climax with the departure of his hero (Communist, of course) for Spain. He had intended to complete the trilogy with the returned volunteers leading a revolution. Characteristic in its irony: the movement of which he was a leader had already reached its real peak. Its membership was to soar during the World War and the epic of Soviet resistance, but its power and its limits had already been defined in the years of the Popular Front. Its great base was the Miners' Federation, which by 1939 represented some 135,000 miners, sponsored thirteen MPs and was present in most local authorities. Its executive council was more powerful than the local Labour Party. Communists were entrenched within it; Arthur Horner had become its president in 1936 and proved a highly effective one. Communists had their own miners' journal and in a wider field, through their classes, their subordinate organizations, their active role, formed a real presence. It was their actions more than anybody's which had charged the Labour movement in south Wales with its peculiar temper and its internationalism. But within their own society they had become a distinctive subculture, hated by many, admired by many, tolerated as a dynamic force by most. The great majority in south Wales remained encased within their Labour loyalties, though the gloss they put on them was often communisant in tone. In the great surge of pro-Soviet feeling during the War, the Nazi-Soviet Pact and the isolation of Communists during 1939–41 were temporarily overlain; it nearly carried Harry Pollitt to parliamentary victory in the Rhondda in 1945. But with the onset of the Cold War, and the ambiguous examples of Czechoslovakia and Yugoslavia during 1948, the Communist Party dwindled quite rapidly and its own divisions over the Parliament for Wales campaign confirmed its isolation. It remained entrenched within the new NUM fashioned broadly after Horner's image, and continued to develop its distinctive sub-culture within it, to flower even into a bilingual Miners' Eisteddfod under Dai Francis. But politically, as the Cold War began to lift somewhat and as its new programme came out in 1951 as the first of the Eurocommunist manifestos, the Party tended in practice to operate as a pressure group on the edge of Labour, with its newspaper virtually indistinguishable from a left-wing Labour paper except for an apparently unaccountable fondness for Bulgarian ballet dancers. Its residual prestige, however, was such that, pariahs elsewhere except in Scotland, Communists in south Wales found themselves in the disconcerting predicament of having become almost as respectable as an eisteddfod.

## Commonwealth

It was Labour which moved forward to embrace most of the popular loyalties, first of the south Wales coalfield, later of Wales as a whole. It had trouble with the ILP. The divisions over the catastrophe of 1931, the secession of the ILP, its flirtations with the Communist International, brought some very bitter conflict within the ranks of Labour. The ILP produced militants as active as the Communist Party during the Hunger Marches which left Wales from 1932 to 1936; it sent its men to Spain, characteristically to lean to the POUM (the independent Marxist party in Catalonia which George Orwell supported) rather than the Communist-run International Brigade's choices. These people, socialists and often revolutionary socialists by instinct, found themselves trapped between historic millstones they could not resist. The ILP remained a power and a dissident power for some time, to plague both Labour and the Communists and to challenge parliamentary candidates with the cry of treason. They could not hold the running. By 1932, just as Jennie Lee surrendered to the argument over virgin impotence put by Aneurin Bevan, even Dick Wallhead, its former chairman and MP for Merthyr, rejoined the Labour Party. The ILP, however, continued to run as a kind of underground memory within the Labour movement, to resurface in a very striking manner in the late 1960s.

The Labour hegemony was rooted in the endless work of its devoted servants in the constituencies. In the campaign against TB, working with central funds and charities, the local Labour councillors proved infinitely more energetic than their nondescript rural counterparts whose problem was even worse. They put colossal effort into education, even though their funds were stretched to the limit. Merthyr contrived to make 90 per cent of its secondary school places free, and it was imitated; Newport and Swansea fought stern battles against Board of Education means tests. The remarkable success of Labour local authorities in this one field alone would have earned them the loyalty of a generation. In every crisis they did their best to defend their people against impossible odds; Bedwellty Board of Guardians was suspended for its humanity. The Labour people had no ideological inhibition about working within every institution and with every charity going. They won an entrenched place in them all, the developing commitment of a middle class newly emerged from working-class origins, and parliamentary votes which in the valleys towered like pyramids over the landscape. The experience of the Second World War enormously strengthened this hold, as Welsh people dispersed through England to serve as red tracer in the bloodstream, to appear for the first time as something other than comic in the realist films of those years: in the Welsh characters who appear in such as *Millions Like Us,* in the sentimental but in some respects powerful *Proud Valley* graced by Paul Robeson, in the film reconstruction of the Lidice massacre in Czechoslovakia set in a Welsh mining village and peopled by genuine miners (Communists to the van). Labour emerged into the triumph of 1945 with its Welsh members central to it, in James Griffiths, Aneurin Bevan, Morgan Phillips, the ranks of Welsh MPs from Wales and many other constituencies. It could rally something approaching a national mobilization in Wales in the building of its Health Service and Welfare State which transformed the lives of millions; Aneurin Bevan, author of the Health Service, could canalize the fiercer passions of a committed minority in his losing struggles for socialism in 1951 and during the long conflict within the party. By this time, as Labour reached its British national peak in 1951, within Wales it rolled relentlessly on to establish itself as the nearest thing to a 'party of Wales' since the Liberals in the 1890s.

Through years loud with promotion schemes for industry and new towns, Labour continued to advance. By the 1920s it had already established itself among the quarrymen in the north-west, where in Caernarfon, their leader R. T. Jones ran the Liberals a close second; there was heavy Labour voting in Merioneth and Anglesey. From its industrial bases, Labour could take Wrexham and from time to time snatch Carmarthen. It emerged in 1945 with twenty-five seats and was poised to make inroads into the Liberal west as Lloyd George's party crumbled (Megan, most radical of his children, went over in Carmarthen) and the Conservatives edged back in along the southern coasts and in anglicized areas. In 1945 Caernarfon finally fell, to Goronwy Roberts; in 1951 Merioneth and Anglesey followed. With the two coalfields secure and, in the south, held by crushing majorities, something of a north-west/south-east axis developed, yoking the two most non-Conservative areas of Wales; Labour's advance was remorseless no matter what its internal turmoil. The climax came in the dazzling Wilson victory of 1966. In that election, only four seats in Wales were not Labour and one of those was Liberal. It looked like 1906 all over again.

Labour, however, could not hope and did not intend to re-create that kind of Welsh-national formation. Its thrust was resolutely British and centralist. It proved highly reluctant to sanction any distinct Welsh organization. A south Wales regional council was formed in 1937, but mainly to combat Communist influence. Not until 1947 was there a Council of Labour for Wales. At the first rather ridiculous 'Welsh Day' in the Commons in 1944 Aneurin Bevan mocked any thought of Welsh separatism and he echoed the overriding sentiment of Welsh Labour thinking. The Home Rule commitments of Keir Hardie and the early ILP and Clause IX of the Labour Party constitution were abandoned; there was a deep and principled hostility to any kind of nationalism, after the Nazi experience, a total commitment to a centralized British social democracy in which the Welsh would find their place.

The one shift in this direction on the Left came from the Communist Party and a handful of Labour dissidents. The Communist Party had been blank on any national issue, largely because its membership had little concern with it, partly because such nationalist movements as existed were overpoweringly linguistic and narrow or were developing a right-wing analysis akin to that later enshrined in Vichy France. There was a major change after the Seventh Congress of the International which formally initiated the Popular Front in 1935. Idris Cox, a strong, well-read even by Communist standards, and effective man who edited the *Daily Worker* between 1935 and 1937, was also a man of strongly Welsh temper; after serving as an organizer at various times from 1927 he returned in 1937 and wrote *The People Can Save South Wales,* a popular front pamphlet which sold 20,000 copies; in the same year a small north Wales district was established which grouped some of the most dedicated and some of the least widely known activists in the country. Niclas Glais brought out a shortlived *Llais y Werin* (People's Voice). In 1938 the Central Committee of the Communist Party recognized that it had mistakenly analysed Welsh nationalism, and the Districts combined to produce a bilingual pamphlet for the Cardiff Eisteddfod calling for a united front to embrace nationalists. The next year the CP took on board the right to self-determination of Welsh and Scots and the party committed itself to support of the Welsh language and a whole series of devolutionary measures. Over the next ten years its press produced at least twenty different pamphlets on such themes and at the first all-Wales congress at the end of the War, where 44 per cent of the delegates were Welsh-speaking, the Communist Party came out with a strongly devolutionist statement.

This ran into very heavy weather. Arthur Horner, committed to his NUM concept and adopting a similar position in all fields, strongly opposed any Welsh-national diversion and was supported by Harry Pollitt, though not by R. Palme Dutt, the grey eminence. Matters came to a head with the Parliament for Wales campaign, launched by the Welsh language pressure group Undeb Cymru Fydd in 1950, which secured the support of five Welsh Labour MPs, got some response in the valleys but very little generally and produced a bill proposed by S. O. Davies, who was saved from yet another expulsion by Aneurin Bevan. In the CP, W. J. Rees wrote a pioneering paper outlining the first serious attempt at a Marxist history of Wales and Welsh nationality and arguing the case for a federal structure in Britain with the Lords replaced by a House to represent nationalities and regions. The paper was shelved and after Idris Cox, on the instructions of the Welsh Congress, had joined the Parliament for Wales Committee, he was displaced from his office, appointed to the International Department and sent to Iraq. The Communist Party fell in line with Labour.

Here, both parties were reflecting and reinforcing a grinding dissociation in Welsh society. What to the capitalist economy of Britain was a difficult but necessary adjustment was thrusting the communities of Wales under a steam-hammer and, in the process, what had been considered the central components of its identity were being shovelled off into redundancy. Welsh Nonconformity came sick out of the War; it entered a steep decline which has proved irreversible. There were still some 400,000 in the chapels in the 1920s and the old religion held on hardest where the Welsh language persisted, notably to west and north, but the decline, breeding impoverishment, was cumulative and robbed Dissent of influence. The pathology of decay began to register; there was a crisis in Methodism over the expulsion of a heterodox but powerful preacher, Tom Nefyn; Sunday golfers at Aberdyfi were physically attacked in 1927. Most efforts to tune Nonconformity to an increasingly appalling modernity failed and it tended ever more to shrink dourly back into a defensive tribal mentality, obsessed with symbols like the 'Welsh Sunday'.

For the Welsh language was shrinking with it. By the census of 1921, the proportion of Welsh speakers had fallen below 40 per cent; ten years later it was down to 36 per cent. It was less the speed of the immediate decline than the multiplying symptoms of an acceleration which drove many desperate. The many Welsh speakers in the industrial areas were rapidly becoming an ethnic minority as the huge displacements of population worsened all prospects, and the desperate struggle in the south locked a whole people into a totally British commitment, almost into a nationality, a radically non-traditional identity of its own. The language was receding into a western and northern rural margin. This truth was partly masked by the still living reality of a popular oral Welsh which united many, but this was visibly giving way among young people as, in a flood of English and American books, magazines and films, native publishing was

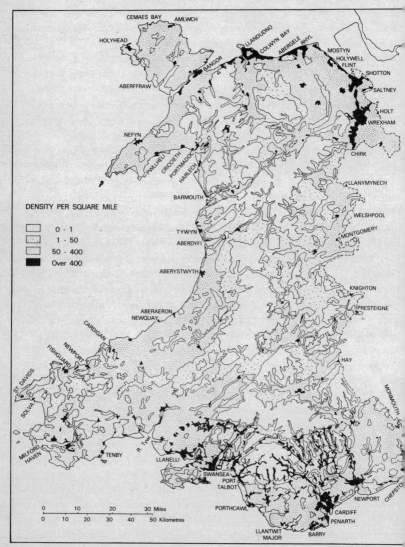

DENSITY PER SQUARE MILE

| | |
|---|---|
| | 0 - 1 |
| | 1 - 50 |
| | 50 - 400 |
| | Over 400 |

CEMAES BAY  AMLWCH
HOLYHEAD
LLANDUDNO
COLWYN BAY  ABERGELE  RHYL
MOSTYN
HOLYWELL
FLINT
SHOTTON
BANGOR
SALTNEY
ABERFFRAW
HOLT
WREXHAM
NEFYN
CHIRK
PWLLHELI
CRICCIETH
PORTMADOC
HARLECH
LLANYMYNECH
BARMOUTH
WELSHPOOL
TYWYN
MONTGOMERY
ABERDYFI
ABERYSTWYTH
KNIGHTON
PRESTEIGNE
ABERAERON
NEWQUAY
CARDIGAN
HAY
NEWPORT
FISHGUARD
ST DAVIDS
MONMOUTH
SOLVA
MILFORD
HAVEN
TENBY
R. Tywi
LLANELLI
SWANSEA
PORT
TALBOT
NEWPORT  CHEPSTO
PORTHCAWL
CARDIFF
PENARTH
LLANTWIT
MAJOR  BARRY

0    10    20    30 Miles
0  10  20  30  40    50 Kilometres

6.   DISTRIBUTION OF POPULATION, 1951
(after Margaret Davies, *Wales in Maps*, University of Wales Press, 1958).

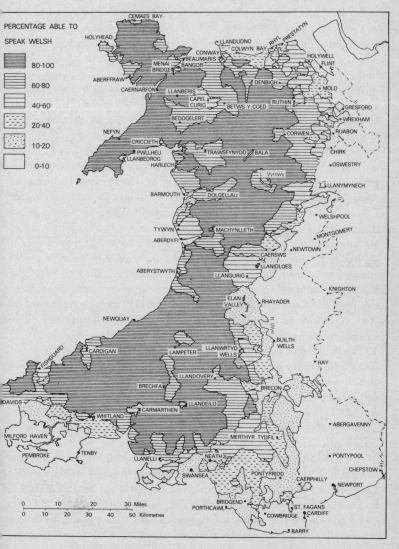

PERCENTAGE ABLE TO
SPEAK WELSH

80-100
60-80
40-60
20-40
10-20
0-10

7.   DISTRIBUTION OF WELSH SPEAKERS, 1951
(after Margaret Davies, *Wales in Maps,* University of Wales Press, 1958).

struggling. A note of desperation, and among some, of fierce commitment, entered nationally minded politics.

In what has proven to be the most persistent and painful irony of twentieth-century Wales, this shrinking in the popular base of Welsh coincided with a brilliant resurgence in the quality of its literature. As the older generation gave way, men like T. Gwynn Jones and W. J. Gruffydd, both installed in academic chairs, were creatively active. There were formidable younger poets like D. Gwenallt Jones, moving from a left-wing socialism that had landed him in a pacifist's prison cell during the War towards a sympathy for the Catholic ideals of the organic community. A channel for much of this energy proved to be the journal *Llenor* (Letters), edited with combative zest by a critical W. J. Gruffydd, which was particularly scathing about the eisteddfod, dismissed as a peasant festival riddled with addled Methodists. A galaxy of writers circled around the *Llenor,* the poets Williams Parry and Parry-Willams, the critics Saunders Lewis, Griffith J. Williams and Ambrose Bebb. The novel at last found a home in Wales in the profound and often disturbing work of Kate Roberts with its tense and dark explorations of northern life, in the lighter vein of T. Rowland Hughes, a man who like the hero of one of his more genial stories moved from north to south (and characteristically into the BBC) but rooted himself in the experiences of the quarrymen. They were supported by whole new schools of academic work, strongly buttressed by the press and the Board of Celtic Studies of the University. The incomparable essayist R. T. Jenkins, meticulous scholars like Griffith J. Williams and Ifor Williams, with a small army behind them, revivified that Welsh history which fewer and fewer of the Welsh people read or were permitted to read. Many writers found a lodgement in the new radio services for which the redoubtable Rhys Hopkin Morris won a degree of autonomy from 1937. While the programmes were at first overloaded with religion and eisteddfodic folklore, a whole new school of writers, in both languages, playwrights and entertainers, successors to the old story-tellers, emerged. Welsh radio (to be followed by television) grew into a real power, a major force in Welsh life and a vital institutional focus of patronage and enterprise. During and immediately after the Second World War it established itself as a central institution among the Welsh.

What became the morally dynamic and dominant power in Welsh writing, however, was work by a handful of authors who came to exercise an influence out of all proportion to their numbers. Even their opponents often found themselves compelled to argue in terms of a discourse which these people enforced. Writing in Welsh was suddenly invaded by Europe and by a particular, right-wing, traditionalist and often Catholic Europe in which the work of such as Maurice Barrès, Charles Maurras and Action Française loomed large. The list of translations into Welsh during these years (and later) makes quite extraordinary reading, when set against the human realities of Wales at the time and the nature of the traditions it had come to consider national. What makes this even more remarkable was that, at much the same time, a wholly different Europe was invading Welsh minds which thought in English.

While most secondary schools taught a mainstream French culture and while there were plenty of Liberal and socialist Francophiles among writers in Welsh, such as R. T. Jenkins and W. J. Gruffydd, a whole world of reading and writing in English formed around the European Left. The Left Book Club, the Popular Front, the Communist Party, many public libraries open to popular pressure, generated a whole culture, politically based but embracing a very wide field in literature, art, popular philosophy and science which tended in practice to focus around debates on Marxism, anti-fascism, a broad International, with a powerful assertion of contemporary European history. The quite massive inflow of American creative and often radical writing, while distinct in origin, reinforced the effect. This Popular Front culture, quite strongly represented among the 750,000 books held by 109 workers' institutes, was widely diffused and, to a considerable extent, determined the terms of discourse among most English-speakers. Often rich, exacting and imaginatively stimulating, it was nonetheless (at least from the perspective of the present) highly sectarian.

Most striking is the degree to which the rival European sectarianism commandeered the world of Welsh-language writing. Without doubt, the sheer power of Saunders Lewis was the root cause. His simultaneous commitment to an utterly intransigent nationalism and to a radical reappraisal of Welsh tradition through its literature was grounded in a firm and focused ideology which saw Wales as a nation of Europe, and of a Europe defined in terms of Latin Christendom and the lost values of the Middle Ages. This gave his criticism a power and an apparent coherence which blasted through the received styles of Welsh writing. Moreover, he was himself a major artist, particularly in that genre rare in Wales, the theatre, and verse drama in particular. In a long sequence of critical essays, often brilliant, cogent prose work and plays, generally through his own creative work rather than in any sustained theoretical exposition, he recast the whole shape of Welsh history in Idealist terms around a concept of Christendom, Latin culture, an aristocratic tradition and an organic community. He became a Catholic convert in 1932 and dominated a tiny Nationalist Party. Allied to him were men like Ambrose Bebb, French in formation with close connections in Brittany who thought in similar terms and was deeply influenced by Charles Maurras, and J. E. Daniel, whose voice was harsher than Lewis's. So remote had Welsh-language writing become from Europe that analyses of this kind were a shock and seemed to elevate discussion of Welsh nationality to an altogether higher plane. This and his own ability in the end gave Saunders Lewis an influence over Welsh writing reminiscent of that established by Benedetto Croce over Italian. But this was a Croce who savagely divided his own people.

Lewis and Bebb entered politics as two young academics. Bebb, the son of a prosperous Cardiganshire farmer, was trained at Aberystwyth, Rennes and the Sorbonne and burst on the scene in the early 1920s virtually as a Welsh spokesman for Action Française with a Breton accent. 'Aim accurately; strike clearly. Above all, be strong, be powerful. The age of Lenin! The age of Mussolini! Indeed, it is a Mussolini that Wales needs . . . And coming he is . . .' Lewis shared the impatience with 'Welsh chatterboxes'; in a startling speech in 1923, he called for military discipline, a training camp, five years of drill and prison martyrs. It was in an atmosphere dominated by echoes of the Bolshevik revolution, Fascism and Sinn Fein that Lewis, Bebb, G. J. Williams and Elisabeth Williams at Penarth formed a secret society, Mudiad Cymreig (Welsh Movement) in 1924, to join with a Home Rule Army created in north Wales, to form a Plaid Genedlaethol Cymru (Welsh Nationalist Party) at the Pwllheli Eisteddfod in 1925 and to attempt to impose the ideology of their Mudiad on the party.

The new party, getting off the ground at a summer school the following year, followed the Mudiad in committing itself to a total rejection of all British parties and of Westminster, to work within Welsh local authorities only and to a campaign to enforce Welsh as Wales's only language. For five years the Party would not use English; some of its powerful writing, by Bebb, appeared in a Breton magazine. A poor showing at an election fought in Sinn Fein style forced a reappraisal from 1930. The Party launched an English language journal, adopted Dominion status as an objective and accepted linguistic equality if only as a transitional programme. A visit to the stricken Rhondda, 'the worst hell in Europe', the year he became a Catholic, deeply affected Saunders Lewis. He launched Thursday Dinner Clubs, to give the unemployed at least one good meal a week and called on party members to give up one of their weekly meals and contribute a regular sixpence. He himself gave a tenth of his income to the fund which launched four centres, starting at Dowlais in 1936. The Ten Points which Lewis got the party to adopt as its social policy in 1934 reflected Catholic thinking and anticipated the practices of European Christian Democracy.

While the Mudiad faded, its people remained at the centre. Saunders Lewis, born in Wallasey in Merseyside, the son of a Methodist minister, and wounded during the War as an officer in the South Wales Borderers, was a shy, aloof man, who distrusted leadership though he was driven by strong elitist instincts. He tried nine times, in vain, to resign from the headship of the party. Political leadership was thrust upon a man who was essentially a creative writer, critic and moralist. By now a towering figure in Welsh writing, he served as president of the party for thirteen years and was identified with it in the public eye.

A more subtle man than Bebb, he disliked the notion of 'independence', and favoured a medieval concept of limited sovereignty in 'freedom'. Although he identified Action Française as the nationalist party of France and some of the vocabulary of Maurras entered the discourse of nationalist leaders, Lewis denied any affiliation. It was Maurice Barrès he cited; Barrès's *Le Culte du Moi* had inspired him in 1916 and Lewis's first play echoed Barrès's novel *Colette Baudoche*. Emrys ap Iwan and the Irish Renaissance were more immediate exemplars. Lewis was deeply conservative, a monarchist, a believer in leadership by a responsible elite; his philosophy was rooted in his idea of Christianity and Tradition with an idealized Welsh fourteenth century of cultured gentry at its heart. Under him, the party called for a nation of 'small capitalists', co-operation, the deindustrialization of south Wales and the restoration of agriculture as the basic industry of Wales. The Welsh language remained central. Despite the party's official position on bilingualism, Lewis's own position and that of the people around him was clear. 'We cannot therefore aim at anything less than to annihilate English in Wales . . . It must be deleted from the land called Wales: *delenda est Carthago.* '

These were unusual people to find at the head of a party full of former Liberals and Labour people and stiff with pacifists and Nonconformist ministers. Drs D. J. and Noëlle Davies, dedicated workers of socialist temper, who looked to Denmark and Scandinavia and elaborated a complex and researched programme of co-operative economics for Wales, argued repeatedly for a more fraternal approach to the English-speaking Welsh, often called 'English' in this party, and for a transfer of its base into the industrial south-east. Men from very different traditions like Iorwerth Peate, embodiment of Llanbrynmair Independency, a student of folk culture who would ultimately give an international journal the Welsh title

*Gwerin,* or A. O. H. Jarman, an Arthurian scholar who was to suffer for his pacifism during the Second World War, were often at odds with the leadership; Peate in fact resigned, as did others. A *Mudiad Gwerin* at Bangor struggled to assert a socialist perspective, as did others. But in fact, during the thirties, the right-wing tonality of the party strengthened, as did the Catholic presence around its journal *Y Ddraig Goch* (The Red Dragon). It was commitment to the Welsh language and to Wales and admiration for the intellectual stature and moral integrity of Saunders Lewis which attracted so many writers and kept this in reality, incoherent movement going to the War.

During the thirties the party became even more of a right-wing force. Its journal, rejecting any and every English political position, refused to resist Hitler and Mussolini, ignored or tolerated anti-semitism and, in effect, came out in support of Franco and Salazar, despite agonizings from its left wing, despite the fate of Basques and Catalans, despite the deaths of Welsh men in arms for the Spanish Republic. Saunders Lewis rejected both capitalism and fascism, but reserved his scorn and often biting polemic for Liberals, Labourites and Socialists. He claimed to respect Communists as the only worthy opponents, and it was Marxism which remained the living enemy. J. E. Daniel, who was peculiarly tortuous in his comments on the international scene, made no bones about it: 'Whatever is the enmity between Fascism and Democracy, it becomes friendship in the face of the great enemy Communism. That is the lesson Hitler is trying to teach Europe . . .' For him, as for Lewis, the struggle was between Communism and what they called European Tradition, an idea made explicit in Lewis's later play *Brâd* (Treason), on the July Plot against Hitler.

This introduced a sharp division into the world of Welsh-language writers whose work was itself considered, in traditional style, central to political life. This was as nothing, however, compared to the abyss opened up between Welsh nationalism and the outlook of the Popular Front Wales of the European Left, sometimes dismissed as Maurras's *métèques,* metics, half-members of the community. In one desperate poem of 1939, *Y Dilyw (The Deluge),* which was centred on Merthyr and Dowlais, Saunders Lewis conjured a frightful nightmare of a people who had forsaken the old world and had gone whoring after the false religions of commerce and its usurers, only to slither into a morass of despair, as apocalypse loomed in Europe. The verse crawled with lurid and offensive images and put self-lacerating words in the mouths of servile men, dismissed as a gutless crew who were no longer Welsh.

This was the voice of Calvo Sotelo in the Spain of 1936, informing most of his people that they were unfit to enter the castle of the Spanish spirit he and his friends were erecting. In the European civil war which burned from Austria through Spain to engulf the Continent between 1934 and 1944, the only communication which proved possible between cultures as opposed as these was that which exists between a bullet and the brain it lodges in.

In the crucial and murderous year of 1941 Saunders Lewis published *Byd a Betws* (The World and the Church) which rejected the war against Nazi Germany in terms of the Welsh nation and in terms which would have made it acceptable in the collaborationist Paris of Otto Abetz. The European civil war ran right through the heart of literate Wales. Ambrose Bebb, French in his *alter ego,* totally opposed to Nazism and appalled at the pro-Hitler attitude of Breton nationalists in 1939, found it running through his own spirit; he withdrew from the party of which he had been a founder. In view of what happened in Europe at the time, not least in Brittany, to its Nationalists, its Communists and to plenty of its people who were neither, it is as well for Wales that there was an English Channel in 1940.*

There was only one moment at which this party and its leader struck the resonant frequency of the Welsh. It was a moment of martyrdom. The RAF established a bombing school at Pen-y-Berth in the Llŷn peninsula. In response to protests in England at its original site, they had moved it to Llŷn over equally cogent protests from Wales, a recurrent English habit over the next forty years. In 1936 Saunders Lewis, the Reverend Lewis Valentine and D. J. Williams, a Fishguard school-teacher, all members of the Nationalist Party, set fire to the airfield buildings and gave themselves up to the police, as a national and pacifist gesture. After the jury had failed to reach a verdict in Caernarfon Assizes, the government transferred the trial to the Old Bailey, where the prisoners refused to give evidence in English. They were sentenced to nine months' imprisonment.

Their action won them immense popularity; there was a national outcry. Lloyd George himself, normally a hammer of nationalists, joined in. They passed into Welsh-language discourse as 'Y Tri Llanc' (the Three in the Fiery Furnace; coinage of the phrase was claimed by a popular Welsh-

*Readers can find the full text of *Y Dilyw,* in English translation by Professor Gwyn Thomas, in Gwyn Jones (ed.), *Oxford Book of Welsh Verse in English* (Oxford, 1977); there is copious quotation from Saunders Lewis, Ambrose Bebb, J. E. Daniel and many other nationalists in a scholarly and balanced book, D. Hywel Davies, *The Welsh Nationalist Party 1925–45* (University of Wales, 1983), and the movement is set in wider context in K. O. Morgan, *Rebirth of a Nation: Wales 1880–1980* (Clarendon and University of Wales, 1981). There is a sympathetic treatment of Saunders Lewis's work in Alun Jones and Gwyn Thomas (eds.), *Presenting Saunders Lewis* (University of Wales, 1973) and an interesting short essay in Chapter 27 of Emyr Humphreys, *The Taliesin Tradition* (Black Raven Press, 1983).

language playwright from Dowlais on its slime of snail, who was a left-wing socialist). On his release, Saunders Lewis was vindictively hounded. A play of his, *Buchedd Garmon* (The Heritage of St Germanus), had been broadcast on St David's Day so that he could hear it in Wormwood Scrubs, but he was now persecuted; he was sacked from his university lectureship at Swansea. In 1939, after repeated attacks on him as a Catholic, and confronted by a party which was coming apart at the onset of war, Lewis retired from the leadership and withdrew from public life into private study and teaching. J. E. Daniel took over, but it was clear from the middle of the war that leadership would pass to Gwynfor Evans, a pacifist and Nonconformist of stature, and that the party would emerge a very different organization.

In his later work, as with so many other embattled writers on all sides from the thirties, there is a post-facto recognition in Saunders Lewis of absent sensibilities, notably in a play *Esther* about the extermination of the Jewish people in Europe. His analysis of Welsh literature and the elaboration of his particular historical perspective on Wales strengthened. He grew into something of a national saint and guru and was to make a decisive intervention in Welsh life in the sixties. He was finally appointed to a teaching post at the University College of Cardiff and recently, with some quiet but significant ceremonial, he was offered and accepted a Doctorate of the University of Wales.

In terms of Wales and what were considered its traditions, nothing in Saunders Lewis changed except the modes of action he recommended. The major effect of his writing was to establish a particular view of the history of the Welsh, as refracted through their literature, as an extra-mural but often overpowering orthodoxy, and to rivet a particular notion of *tradition* on the minds of Welsh writers. Since this was also the high-tide of the F. R. Leavis controversy in England and the pre-eminence of T. S. Eliot, the effects were long-lasting.

In particular they poisoned relations between younger writers in Welsh and an extraordinary profusion of Welsh writers in English in these years, which the Welsh Academy recently characterized as a First Flowering. In many ways the initiator, in 1915, was Caradoc Evans, who had an almost Joycean way with language and who in his *My People, Capel Sion* and the rest pilloried rural and small-town and Nonconformist Wales in so merciless a manner as to repel the bulk of his compatriots, but with a power which commanded a hypnotized attention. By the time he had finished with them there was not much left of the *gwerin* or any of its traditions. 'Like a bad smell coming in through the window,' said Gwyn Jones, but 'the war horn was blown, the gauntlet thrown down, the gates of the temple were shattered . . .'

But whereas all the writers in English who burst on the scene in these years were in revolt, sometimes angry and disgusted revolt against some aspect or other of what had come to be considered Welshness, and some of them experienced the familiar difficulty of English-speakers in Wales in placing themselves at all (several of them could write effectively only when they were out of 'the jail'), the work which emerged most directly from Welsh working people in those years was, if anything, work to celebrate unjustly scorned and invisible Welsh men and women. This was as true of the torrential, almost uncontrollable Jack Jones, whose rolling, rollicking, Dickensian books reflect a personal life hardly less so, as of Lewis Jones, with the Nant-y-Moel teacher Mavis Llywelyn at his side, who produced some of the most wrought and effective of the genuinely working-class novels, and of Bert Coombes, the Wolverhampton man who worked for forty years in the pits of south Wales and who in *These Poor Hands,* which sold 60,000 copies through the Left Book Club in 1939, and its successors, wrote out of work experience with a classical directness and power.

The people who have registered are that cluster of poets who have been saddled with the title Anglo-Welsh – Vernon Watkins of Swansea, Glyn Jones of Merthyr, Idris Davies of Rhymney, Alun Lewis of Aberdare and a small army of others, doubling as essayists and critics like Gwyn Jones, son of a Blackwood miner who became an Icelandic scholar, a short-story writer of genius, a trenchant critic and a professor of English. His journal the *Welsh Review* set a high and rigorous standard to stiffen the ebullience of Keidrych Rhys's *Wales* and the catholicity of *Dock Leaves* edited from 1949 by Raymond Garlick and continued as the *Anglo-Welsh Review* under Roland Mathias. There were the prose writers like Geraint Goodwin of Newtown who explored a little-discussed region, Glyn Jones, the black and bubble-brilliant Gwyn Thomas and the enigmatically powerful Rhys Davies from Clydach. There were in truth a myriad of them, from whom the world figure of Dylan Thomas took off into a stratosphere. There was much to-ing and fro-ing about 'traditions' (a disease it seems to have been impossible to escape in these years) and their exact location in this or that, which at this distance seems a waste of good writing time. They certainly formed an intense little world, circulating around the BBC in London and Wales, Griff's Bookshop, an informal athenaeum off the Charing Cross Road in London, and on the frontiers of the academy and bohemia. While its borders were blurred, these people represented the explosive emergence of a multi-faceted Welshness which expressed itself through an English language often handled with superb mastery and which was unlike not only writing in Welsh but anything else Welsh people had hitherto written in English. Glyn Jones, almost alone, tried to see Wales whole in both its languages; most writers in Welsh, and most in English, tended to drift apart, many of them into mutual incomprehension and hostility.

During this critical time, therefore, the major creative writers in Wales were hopelessly dispersed and divided. The Urdd Gobaith Cymru, a Welsh youth movement launched in 1922 by Ifan ab Owen Edwards, son of the educator, was an effort in one sense to straddle the divide by enrolling young Welsh people in the service of the Welsh language, Christian morality and what were considered to be Greek ideals. Of all the Welsh language movements, this was the most successful. It ran classes, eisteddfods, summer camps and cruises, encouraged the publication of books in Welsh and circulated its own journal. By 1934 it had 50,000 members. It launched the first Welsh-language school in Aberystwyth under Norah Isaac in 1939. It certainly established its presence throughout Wales. By the 1960s it had been drawn into a passionate Welsh-language campaign which may have shifted its impact.

For it was in the next generation, after a major shift in language distribution and social perceptions, that a wholly novel set of attitudes developed quite rapidly out of this intensifying dichotomy to provoke both dramatic development and violent controversy. Late in the thirties a long campaign to turn the National Eisteddfod into a monoglot Welsh festival won acceptance for the principle. The rule started to go into effect from 1951. At the time, it was felt to be part of a general revolt by Welsh people to reassert themselves and their identity and, while there was widespread apathy among people long removed from that kind of world, there was no opposition. By the 1970s the anomaly which closed the national festival of the Welsh to four-fifths of the inhabitants of Wales had become a painful issue over which tempers were lost. That cruel chronology repeated itself everywhere.

For after the Second World War, a whole generation of the Welsh moved into a quite novel prosperity and an unprecedented integration into British society. The decline in both Nonconformity and the Welsh language accelerated. People were living in a cultural climate which was expanding, international, well-nigh universal and strongly American. They appeared to be moving swiftly out of most attitudes hitherto considered specifically Welsh.

All the greater the surprise when, in July 1966, a mere three months after Labour's greatest electoral triumph in Wales, Gwynfor Evans, leader of what was, in effect, a new Plaid Cymru (Party of Wales) won the Carmarthen seat by a small but decisive majority over a Labour candidate who was himself of strongly national temper and had been, in his youth, a leader of a short-lived Welsh Republican Movement.

## *Identity*

The victory of Gwynfor Evans in Carmarthen in July 1966 opened a decade of political instability. The giant Labour majorities in the valleys of south Wales started crashing. In March 1967, in Rhondda West where the Labour majority was normally of the order of 80 per cent and everyone else ritually lost deposits, Plaid Cymru secured a swing of 30 per cent and cut the majority to just over 2,000; in Caerphilly the following year, the Plaid scored a swing of 40 per cent and reduced the Labour majority from 21,000 to under 2,000. In 1969 elaborate ceremonies greeted the formal Investiture of Prince Charles as Prince of Wales, to a tumult of public acclaim and a tumult (largely in Welsh) of public mockery; at the same time, confronted with a much more menacing rise of Scottish Nationalism, the Labour government appointed a Royal Commission on the Constitution. At the General Election of 1970 the nationalist tide seemed to be halted. Plaid Cymru lost Carmarthen and its usual string of twenty-five deposits. But its vote topped 75,000 and 11 per cent and it registered unexpected strength in some of the valleys. The most startling result in Wales, however, was in Merthyr Tydfil, where the veteran S. O. Davies refused to retire and stood against the official Labour candidate, an engineering trade union officer. S. O.'s people formed an Independent Labour Party and amid considerable turmoil the Merthyr electorate returned him with a 7,000 majority. Furthermore, after S.O.'s death, at a by-election in 1972, Emrys Roberts the Plaid candidate won nearly 12,000 votes, scored a 37 per cent swing and cut the normally huge Labour majority to 4,000. In January 1973, after years of struggle led primarily by left-wing and Welsh spokesmen in north and south, including Dai Francis the Communist secretary of the south Wales area of the NUM, a Wales TUC was established, with limited autonomy. In the 1974 General Election the Labour Party for the first time in decades fell below 50 per cent in its vote. The Conservatives rose to an eight-seat representation. Plaid Cymru, though it seems to have lost ground in the southern valleys, only just failed to recapture Carmarthen, while in north Wales its candidates scored striking successes. Dafydd Wigley, an able and radical cost-accountant, took Caernarfon, and Dafydd Elis Thomas, a college lecturer and the most radical socialist in the Welsh political scene, captured Merioneth. As the new system of county, district and community councils ground cumbersomely into operation in 1974, over loud yelps of pain, to make Wales one of the most heavily governed and least self-governing regions of Britain, Plaid Cymru in 1976 swept the board on Merthyr council, in a body of thirty-three, reducing the Labour representation from twenty-five to eight; in nearby Rhymney it took control of the district council. In the meantime, in 1972 and 1974, the miners in their first national strike in a generation had fought their dramatic battle, putting the country on a three-day week and unhingeing the Heath government. 'This time we'll win,' they had said in 1972. No one in Wales needed to be told what last time they meant. A new spirit came into Wales with the miners' strike. An even newer one had entered earlier, after the formation in 1962 of Cymdeithas yr Iaith Gymraeg, the Welsh Language Society, whose young people stormed all over Wales, staging sit-ins, wrecking TV masts, generally making life hell for any kind of official, the most visible Welsh and visibly Welsh signal of the onset of the great wave of revolt in the late sixties. It felt as if an ice-field were breaking up.

The major factor, without doubt, was disillusionment with the Labour Party and increasing disaffection from the Labour movement. The abrupt reversal of Labour government policy in 1966, after the high hopes of 1964, seemed a culminating disappointment after long years of diminishing relevance and diminishing socialism in the Party's policies, internal debate and inner life. The Labour hegemony in Wales had hardened into oligarchy. Social democracy had become a recognized career structure in the life-cycle of able and ambitious Welsh people. It provided a framework for social life. It was present in people's lives in a manner reminiscent of the southern states of the USA. It had certainly been characterized by a more humanitarian, civilized and educated society, by a genuine concern and an effective welfare state, by a genial and easy populism in style. It was also characterized by accommodation snug within the system, with its political mechanisms becoming an arena for rivalry and agreement between pressure groups, its parliamentary representatives becoming more and more middle-class and professional and dependent on the support and manipulation of powerful trade union and locality controllers. The system seemed to be closing up; in some places, where a real local party organization existed at all, it was often difficult to join; the party was degenerating into a vote-winning machine which came to political life only during elections; in between times, it appeared to many to be simply a caucus of power-brokers. It was also characterized by the customary Welsh blend of high thoughts and low thinking, by widespread petty corruption and nepotism which during the corrupt property boom of the 1960s threw up some spectacular scandals. A radical investigative journal, *Rebecca,* could live, and register an increasing if irregular circulation, solely on leaks and exposures from this world. Labour in Wales continued to produce or sustain striking and impressive political leaders, from James Griffiths and Cledwyn Hughes to Leo Abse, from James Callaghan to Neil Kinnock; it was massively represented at the centre. In Michael Foot as Aneurin Bevan's apostolic successor at Ebbw Vale after 1960, it nurtured a much loved and honoured socialist. But within Wales, all life seemed to be draining out of it. Coveys of socialists and radicals bubbled at the edges, the Communists laboured at the union militants, but it is characteristic that the party and its trade union organization in Wales moved massively into the right-wing and conservative sector of the movement. During the passionate inner struggles of the 1980s Wales was a country whose Labour constituency parties chose Denis Healey in preference to Tony Benn.

In this, at least, they adequately reflected the country their party still overwhelmingly represented. It is clear now that over the past dozen years and more, Wales has become a right-wing country which is moving relentlessly to the right in its politics. No doubt the roots lie in the profound and swift social changes which have accompanied the major adjustments of an increasingly multinational capitalist economy in its British theatre. These began to operate in the mid-sixties but did not fully register in public awareness until the late seventies. The old basic industries have virtually collapsed, miners and steelworkers between them are now hardly 6 per cent of the working population. Pit closures on the grand scale without doubt powered much of the late sixties rebellion. The intense class and community consciousness of the former mining valleys can resurface in a striking manner during crises which evoke memories, but by and large has dissolved. Women have entered the working population *en masse* and now constitute 45 per cent of it; most of them are employed as an under-class of low-paid, under-organized labour subject to a gender discrimination rooted not least in the very cultural formation of the historic Welsh working class itself. Families and regions struggle to maintain their hold on the prosperity of the last two decades which, in spite of mounting unemployment and mounting pressure on the poor, persists among those with jobs. The massive extension of consumer capitalism, its imagery and its values, its sweeping advances in technology, the explosion in information industries and the intensifying privatization of existence around the television screen and the computer have generated attitudes and values remote from any of the recent traditions of Wales. There are whole new ranges of professional and technical people for whom some far horizons widen even as human society within Wales itself loses coherence. The radical changes in the family, the growth and subsequent dislocation of a specific youth culture, the rise of feminism, have broken many patterns. Overall, there was increasing frustration and humiliation at apparently inescapable economic failure and national inadequacy which made a mockery of all social projects and bred a yearning for a decisive change of direction. A society which in Wales had been cast in a distinctive and peculiar mould was dissolving into something new.

What is striking is that, in the valley heartlands of Labour, this initial breakaway should at first take the form of a rally to Plaid Cymru. Throughout the late sixties in the valleys the ghost of the old ILP walked abroad. Older people in particular harked back endlessly to earlier days and resurrected the memory of ILP stalwarts as shining models of socialist virtue, precisely to contrast them with a grisly present. 'Dick Wallhead was the best MP Merthyr ever had . . .' (a major injustice to S. O. Davies). It was an Independent Labour Party which defeated the official candidate in Merthyr in 1970. It was Arthur confronting Iddawg the Embroiler of Britain and his 'little fellows' again . . . 'Lord,' said Iddawg, 'at what art thou laughing?' 'Iddawg,' said Arthur, 'I am not laughing; but rather how sad I feel that men as mean as these keep this Island, after men as fine as those that kept it of yore . . .'

Plaid Cymru started its transformation into a social democratic party with the withdrawal of Saunders Lewis into a rather embittered isolation and the election of Gwynfor Evans as president in 1945. A graduate of Oxford and Aberystwyth and an Independent, Gwynfor Evans was a pacifist of charismatic quality who could strike many chords in Wales. A younger and forceful generation entered with the switch to social democracy in the 1950s. But whereas the Party built up some strength in the Welsh-speaking areas and registered a presence in some of the south Wales valleys, its parliamentary record was one of marginality and lost deposits. It was in its abrupt breakthrough over the late sixties and early seventies that it equally abruptly became a distinctly modern and radical movement, less concerned with language and cultural issues, moving rapidly into a European Left and provoking crises within its own ranks in the process. It did not maintain its parliamentary advance; it slipped back to somewhere below 10 per cent of the parliamentary vote in the seventies but began to establish itself in local government, to develop systematic theory and to create cadres of largely young activists who appeared to be much more lively than those of other parties.

The new Plaid, however, ran head-on into a bewildering and often bizarre maze of contradictions generated by the growing crisis over the languages of Wales. A grinding sense of neglect and under-representation had been growing for years, as both the Labour Party and the Conservatives had consistently refused Wales any measure of self-government. Both parties had fobbed off a ridiculous sequence of nominated and futile consultative bodies on an increasingly frustrated country. The Conservatives had compounded the offence by creating a phoney Minister of Welsh Affairs in fulfilment of a vote-catching promise in the 1950s; the first incumbent of this largely ornamental office was Sir David Maxwell Hamilton-Fyfe, promptly christened Dai Bananas, and he had been succeeded by such implausible Welsh luminaries as Sir Henry Brooke and Sir Keith Joseph. While James Griffiths, supported by Cledwyn Hughes and like-minded people within the Labour Party, had pressed for further measures of self-government, they had run into intransigent resistance from most south Wales Labour MPs committed to the centralist drive of traditional Labourism and accurately reflecting a profound sense of alienation from what had become official Welshness, centred on the language, among their constituents. The long and dismal history of indifference and contempt towards English-speaking Welsh people which had been a disturbing feature of Welsh nationalism and much language-focused Welsh national feeling since the days of Saunders Lewis's early polemic, was duly reaping its dragon's teeth of a harvest.

The scandal of Tryweryn in the fifties and sixties sharpened the tension. It was the powerlessness of Wales which was exposed here. Liverpool corporation decided to build a reservoir at Tryweryn in northern Merioneth and to drown a Welsh-speaking community of peculiar cultural significance to Welsh speakers in the process. There was no authority anywhere in Wales which could challenge the decision and Liverpool were free to do what they liked with the water, resell it if they wished. A campaign of protest and opposition built up; every Welsh Labour MP in the Commons, including those most hostile to nationalism, voted against the scheme. To no avail. It was at this point that violence entered Welsh nationalist politics. Passive demonstrations having failed, some people resorted to sabotage when a successor dam went up at Clywedog for Birmingham. Control over its own water became and has remained an inflammatory issue in Wales.

Far more serious, however, was the decline in the Welsh language and the apparently swift elimination of a Welsh identity. The opening of cinemas and public houses in Wales on a Sunday, while passionately fought in a hypocrisy almost comic on both sides and resisted by Nonconformist sects now in headlong retreat, hardly stirred the blood or brain, but the hammer blows of repeated census returns certainly did. By 1961 Welsh speakers were down to 25 per cent of the population, by 1971 to a bare 20 per cent. The crisis appeared terminal. It was at this point that Saunders Lewis returned to public affairs; in the BBC Wales Annual Radio Lecture in 1962, 'Tynged yr Iaith (The Fate of the Language), he called upon Welsh people to make the salvation of the language their central, indeed only, priority and to be prepared to use revolutionary means to achieve it. The response has been remarkable. The Welsh Language Society moved into action as soon as it was formed, to open twenty years of non-violent direct action against offices, roadsigns, TV masts, with sit-ins and an infinite variety of demonstrations. Like predecessors in the thirties they filed in their turn through the law courts into the prisons. While Plaid Cymru and other nationalist organizations held aloof, there was much human overlap, and the heavy colonization of Welsh institutions, particularly in the media, by Welsh-speaking professional people ('sons of the ministers') proved of powerful occult assistance, not least on the judicial bench. Around this campaign, which assumed the character of a crusade, developed all sorts of movements: a major drive to create Welsh-language primary and secondary schools, Welsh-speaking college hostels, special posts for the teaching of Welsh, demands for an all-Welsh college, and for positive discrimination in favour of Welsh. There was a crash programme of modernization for the language, the invention of a Cymraeg Byw (Living Welsh) to assist learners, the grouping of Dysgwyr (Learners) into an organization, a widespread copying of the dramatic techniques employed by the Israelis to make Hebrew a living as well as an official language which achieved considerable success. The new Welsh Arts Council directed subsidies towards an ailing Welsh publishing world. Step by step a Labour government, followed by a Conservative, was forced to yield; a Secretary of State for Wales in 1964, a major Language Act in 1967, a whole series of autonomy measures and finally, after a strong and sometimes violent campaign, climaxed by a threat by Gwynfor Evans to fast unto death over a broken Conservative pledge, the very recent creation of Sianel 4 Cymru, the Welsh 4th TV channel, in fact a bilingual channel taking Channel 4 programmes but one which broadcasts a major Welsh output at peak viewing times and clears the Welsh language off all other channels. Within, around and distinct from this drive a whole world of Welsh language publishing, film production and infinite varieties of pop, rock, youth and urban music mushroomed.

The consequences have been extraordinary. In response to a militant campaign whose hunger is by definition insatiable, the British state, ruling a largely indifferent or hostile Welsh population, has in a manner which has few parallels outside the Soviet Union, countenanced and indeed subsidized cultural Welsh nationalism. Wales is now officially, visibly and audibly a bilingual country. The equal official status of Welsh is nearing achievement. Whole Welsh-language structures, serviced by an effective training and supply apparatus, exist in education, administrative life and the media. The issue of the Welsh language, in many fields of Welsh action, blots out all other political considerations.

The consequences have been contradictory. There has been a wave of support for the enterprise from English-speakers, the heaviest demand for Welsh schools has come from English-speaking Glamorgan, the language courses are full. On the other hand there has been a growing resentment, impatience and anger which has taken the form of an increasing dislike of the Welsh language itself which at times and in places has become a kind of hatred. An English-speaking working class, neglected and treated with shoddiness, its necessities, not only social but cultural, scorned, not least by some leaders of the Welsh language movement, sees a British state subsidizing the Welsh language production of what is to them a middle-class minority. They see bilingual language qualification shutting off areas of employment for their children. They perceive Welsh-language schools as nurseries of a new order of privileged beings who employ Welsh and particularly the new language of Cymraeg Byw much as the Irish middle class has used official Gaelic and the medieval clergy used Latin, to manufacture a new oligarchy. They see subsidies going everywhere except to their culture.

In this litany of complaint there is much mythology which spokespersons for the Welsh language movement can rebut with statistics. It is, however, evidence of a much deeper malaise which is much more ominous: the denial of Welshness to the English-speaking Welsh, an exclusion which is becoming rapidly and increasingly, and inevitably a bitter *self-exclusion* of the English-speaking Welsh from the Welsh people and nation. The adjective 'Welsh' is increasingly applied, outside and inside Wales, only to the Welsh-speaking component of the people, which is one-fifth of the actual number. A new shadow-line runs across the face of Wales.

Some of the contradictions which have resulted are grotesque. Welsh historians turn away from a project to reissue an invaluable series of broadcasts because the BBC will not and says it cannot publish in both English and Welsh; in the cause of the Welsh nation, four-fifths of the Welsh people are denied effective access to their own history. In a country many of whose school-teachers still apparently consider the history of the Welsh unworthy of attention, this seems a kind of treason. Over the line, militants of the south Wales miners, union of the late Dai Francis who was a Bard of the Order of the Gorsedd at the National Eisteddfod, refuse to attend a CND rally because they hear the dread sound of Welsh. To escape that sound, thousands and thousands of TV aerials train on Somerset and Merseyside. Welsh now having been removed from the major popular channels, little or nothing about Wales in English replaces it, while the creation of Sianel 4 brings bitter complaints from people in the English-speaking valleys half-deprived of Channel 4. The list could be extended indefinitely into the limbo in which most of the Welsh are being corralled. Essentially, English-speaking Welsh people are increasingly being denied membership of Wales. Such people constitute four-fifths of the Welsh population and over two-thirds of those who could be considered biologically Welsh. What sort of Welsh nation or even Welsh people is going to survive this?

Whom the Gods wish to destroy they first afflict with a language problem. Or to quote Thomas Paine on Edmund Burke, theorist of the organic community, 'He pities the plumage and forgets the dying bird.'

These half-hidden resentments against a vaguely liberal consensus which it had been impolite to break, found a sudden release, in a manner reminiscent of London dockers' response to Enoch Powell's first speech on black immigrants, in the black farce of Devolution. A cogent and effective proposal for an elected Welsh assembly to arise out of the reorganization of the counties, had been formulated and presented by Cledwyn Hughes back in the sixties; it got nowhere. The proposal which emerged in the 1970s was an afterthought to the response of Labour to the challenge from Scotland. It was an ineffective compromise which won no enthusiasm. After endless parliamentary agonies, it was submitted to a referendum on St David's Day, 1979. It was resisted by a huge bloc of opinion, ranging from the representatives of that capitalist enterprise which had long since abdicated any regional role and surrendered to the multinational and multibranch corporations, to the populist and anti-intellectual press. It was fiercely opposed by a bloc of south Wales Labour MPs led by Neil Kinnock and Leo Abse, who played largely on fears of the Welsh language and (rather oddly) of corruption, fears of being taken over by north Walian Welsh speakers with double-barrelled names, fears of losing hold on Britain. The campaign in support lacked conviction; Plaid Cymru itself was caught in a cleft stick. There was a multiplicity of motives: Caernarfon almost certainly did not relish rule by a Cardiff it quaintly described as socialist;

Merthyr Tydfil would have cherished such a prospect as little. The Westminster Parliament seemed the only forum within which these fragmented peoples could co-exist. The illusory quality of many of the arguments was remarkable even for Wales; it was an unreal war over an unreal proposal. One major reality, however, was a wholesale popular revolt against the kind of Wales being presented and created through the medium of the Welsh language campaigns. It was a revulsion entirely negative in content and style.

Far more than a Welsh-language Wales was being rejected in 1979. Opinion polls alongside the Referendum showed the Conservatives running at a level unprecedented for a century. In 1976 came the economic crisis and yet another crashing surrender of the Labour government to the British financial establishment and to the International Monetary Fund – yet another reversal of direction. In a half-willed, half-hidden manner, the Labour government adopted those policies which the Conservatives under their radical new leadership were enthusiastically embracing as a way of life. Not since the 1940s could the Labour Party seriously have been considered a socialist party. In the 1970s it ceased to be a social democratic party. It was not clear just what it was. It was no longer clear what a Labour Party was for. In a Wales plagued by economic difficulties, whose working population had been transformed at a speed too swift for its traditional institutions to handle, whose public life seemed to be dominated by arguments over languages which the majority found irrelevant or offensive, there appears to have occurred that phenomenon much cherished by Marxists, an historically effective mutation of consciousness.

It registered brutally and abruptly. In a triple series of votes, the Welsh electorate in 1979 wrote *finis* to nearly two hundred years of Welsh history. They rejected the political traditions to which the modern Welsh had committed themselves. They declared bankrupt the political creeds which the modern Welsh had embraced. They may in the process have warranted the death of Wales itself.

# 13 · TRAVAIL'S ACRE

In the Devolution Referendum on St David's Day 1979, Wales voted by 956,000 to 243,000 against an elected Welsh assembly. The supporters were strongest in the north-west, at 22 per cent, and weakest in Glamorgan –Gwent at 8 and 7 per cent, but everywhere there was a crushing rejection; only some 12 per cent voted in favour. In June, in the heartland of institutionalized Labourism, there was a heavy vote against the European Common Market. In the General Election of May, Wales located itself firmly within *The South* of Britain. At a time of heavy swings to the Conservatives everywhere, the heaviest swing of all, outside London, was in Wales. The Tory tide swept irresistibly through rural west Wales in particular. It was the real force which unseated Gwynfor Evans in Carmarthen to Labour's benefit. It lapped around the heels of the solitary remaining Liberal in Cardiganshire and rose to menace Dafydd Elis Thomas of Plaid Cymru in Merioneth. It achieved an expected win in Brecon but scored two unexpected triumphs, ending generations of Liberal predominance in Montgomeryshire with a highly implausible candidate and parachuting a Sussex solicitor into Anglesey, Mother of Wales, to snatch the seat with a swing of no less than 12 per cent. In the industrial heartlands of Labour, the swing to the Conservatives was the second strongest in Britain. Majorities were too massive for seats to be lost but the Tory tide rose menacingly. For the first time in two generations it became possible to envisage standard British two-party contests in some of those fiefs. The only strong counter-tendency was in Caernarfon, where Dafydd Wigley of Plaid Cymru massively strengthened his majority. Labour was driven back into the coalfields; now only marginal Carmarthen lay outside.

It would take time for a breakaway such as this to translate itself into losses of seats; Labour remained, with twenty-one seats out of thirty-six, 768,000 votes and 47 per cent of the electorate, a massive presence, but the Conservatives, with eleven seats, 526,000 votes and 32 per cent, had reached a position they had last technically occupied fifty years earlier and in reality had last enjoyed only in the 1870s. They swept with such force through non-industrial Wales in particular, that they obliterated landmarks which had been familiar for generations. For Labour, confronted with an oncoming English normality in its strongholds, there was a whiff of 1931 in the air. Moreover, the elimination of Welsh peculiarities and a powerful simplification strongly suggested an integration into Britain more total than anything yet experienced. One Welsh TV political correspondent wondered aloud whether he ought to resign. Welsh politics had ceased to exist. Wales had finally disappeared into Britain.

One effect of this abrupt reversal of two hundred years of history was equally abruptly to cut off an intelligentsia from its people. In this generation, in sharp contrast to the last, creative writers in Welsh and in English had started to draw together. Curiously, as younger Welsh writers began to move out of the kind of universe which the work of the Saunders Lewis school had created, younger writers in English ('sons of the miners') started to move into it and to adopt a firmly nationalist position. While Welsh speakers, assisted by subsidy, lent committed support to a struggling but very active publishing community, the English speakers had to dog-paddle vigorously in an eddy of the great world ocean of the English language. Major efforts went into drama and a whole range of arts; twin academies and a writers' association came into existence, the Welsh Arts Council was furiously active; but two attempts at new political-literary journals in English failed and the crisis of representation, everywhere acute in the paralysis of parliamentary democracy, remained painfully serious for the English-speaking Welsh.

Moreover, while there had always been exceptions and in recent times, numerous ones, most Welsh intellectuals since the eighteenth century had served as organic intellectuals, in some senses as the articulators of the consciousness of social groups and classes whose dimensions were national. The votes of 1979 dramatically registered the end of that epoch. While the ideologies of technical, managerial and administrative groups remained opaque but clearly without any Welsh specificity, the most visible and creative formers of educated opinion among the Welsh were rejected by their people, tossed into a ditch of irrelevance.

Almost immediately Wales was fully exposed to the Conservative crusade and the radical restructuring of an increasingly multinational capitalism in Britain. The Welsh working population reached a peak in 1979, when 1,022,000 people were at work, 55 per cent of them in the service sector and 42 per cent of them women in the core industries. The run-down of the coal industry continued and was followed by a sharp reduction in steel. Between June 1980 and June 1982, the official working population fell by no fewer than 106,000. The most catastrophic losses were in steel which lost half its workers and plummeted to 38,000. There were heavy losses of about a quarter in chemicals and textiles; engineering threw out 16,000 workers, construction over 11,000 and general manufacturing over 9,000. The distributive trades shed about 3,000 people and transport and communications over 5,000. Public administration, however, lost fewer, around 3,000, while a whole range of services in insurance, banking, entertainment, leisure trades and educational and medical services actually gained over 4,000 workers.

In consequence more men than women lost jobs at first, particularly over 1980–1, though much women's work was part-time. During 1982 unemployment was heavier among women, but the overall result, in terms of number, was by June 1983 to increase the proportion of women at work within the central areas of the economy to 45 per cent. By June 1983 the official working population of Wales, at 882,000, was at perhaps its lowest level in modern times. There was a high level of unemployment and particularly serious was the wasting of a whole generation of young people. Some 279,000 people were in manufacturing, numbers of them on short-time, and nearly 550,000 in services. Getting on for a half of the working population were women and of those, over 42 per cent were part-time. There had been a substantial growth in the informal and extra-legal economy and in the numbers of women over retirement age who were at work. The entire Welsh working population was beginning to take on the character of 'women's work' and of an informal, partly casual, unstructured labour force, perhaps an intimation of what was going to become a general experience in an age of robot production.

The Wales TUC, weakened and losing both numbers and funds, seemed incapable of adequate adjustment and response. Its autonomy is strictly limited. Of an income of £33,000 in 1980, nearly £20,000 was a grant from the British TUC. In that year, its nominally affiliated membership totalled over 580,000, nearly 60 per cent of the official working population. Three-quarters of its membership came from eight trade unions. Totally dominant was the Transport and General Workers Union with 118,000 registered membership, followed by the engineers with 78,000. These two unions accounted for a third of the Wales TUC and were closely followed by the general and municipal workers, the local government officers and the public employees, with the shop-assistants and miners bringing up the rear. Their response to the transformation of the working population varied, with the National Union of Public Employees (NUPE) perhaps being the most prompt. Overall, the organized workers' movement seemed encased in a perception of a 'working class' which had become a myth. Certainly, what was striking, to anyone reared in the traditions of the *Welsh Working Class*, was the puny response from Wales to the repeated calls for protest and action from British trade union and Labour organizations. The People's Marches for Jobs and other demonstrations were in Wales pale wraiths in contrast to those in England. The exceptions, as usual, were the south Wales miners, who by 1984 were, with growing public support, fighting a struggle as hard and as dedicated as any in their history.

And as the Labour Party plunged into its internal crises, Plaid Cymru and the Communist Party, in a manner which had become traditional, followed it. The rise of the Left within the Labour Party was matched by a leftward shift in Plaid Cymru which wrote a socialist state into its programme for Wales and, within the Communist Party, by a remarkable opening up of its journals to wide-ranging debates. The recovery of the centre-right within the Labour Party after the secession of the Social Democrats was paralleled by the formation of the Hydro Group to wrest control away from the socialists in Plaid Cymru and by a fairly abrupt tightening of Communist Party ranks around its Labour-centred orthodoxy.

There seemed to be little response from a population readily accepting the values and arguments of the new dispensation. All human life in radical political action went into the multiplying women's groups, ecology-directed movements, above all CND which acquired much more weight and spirit in the valleys and elsewhere than any merely political body. Here again the role of women was striking, particularly among Women for Life on Earth. The protest camp at Greenham Common missile base was started by a march of women from Cardiff.

Around the language issue the clamour and the turmoil continued. The Census of 1981 revealed that the proportion of Welsh-speakers had slipped back to 18.9 per cent, but that the decline in the Welsh language had dramatically slowed and was probably coming to a halt. There were marginal increases in the number of Welsh speakers in the most English-speaking areas such as Gwent and Glamorgan, though this probably reflected a divisive social differentiation. Most serious was the continued decline in the heartlands of the language, notably in the south-west, where the fall was 6 per cent. There had been a hardening, however, visible in Ceredigion (Cardigan) and parts of Gwynedd and there were the first unmistakable signs that the crusade was beginning to take effect among young people. Overall, out of a population of some 2,790,000, around 550,000 were Welsh speakers. There was intricate regional diversity. In parts of Wales, notably the west and the north-west, particular districts, individual villages, individual streets, in the last resort, even individual pubs, have virtually seceded from British community, to create a tribal map as complicated and, in extreme cases, almost as necessary to physical safety, as a Belfast city guide.

The continuing threat to the *bro* or Welsh heartland has precipitated the creation of a new organization, Adfer (Reconstruct), with a swathe of intellectual supporters, dedicated to the building of a monoglot Welsh *gaeltacht* in a western *bro* and to the construction of a shrunken but ethnically pure economy and society on the basis of a Welsh self-sufficiency. This movement tends to see only the Welsh-speaking *Cymry* as truly Welsh; the remainder, unfortunately the vast majority, are described by Offa's English term: *Welsh,* an unhingeing if elegantly symmetrical other face of the coin to the anti-Welsh British chauvinism which is present in some Labour areas, not least on the Left.

In these circumstances, a people which had been deprived of its historical memory and whose children are still widely denied effective access to it in their schools, seems to have been seized by a hunger for its past. Local and amateur historical societies have proliferated while the academic study of Welsh history has become a major intellectual force. Alongside the *Welsh History Review* has appeared the journal *Llafur* (Labour), organ of a Welsh Labour History Society which successfully marries academics and workers, traditional and novel styles, and scored a major success when, with help from the Social Science Research Council and the south Wales area of the National Union of Mineworkers, it rescued what was left of the magnificent miners' institute libraries, which were being sold off without compunction to hungry hucksters (who also gobbled up a celebrated library at Bala-Bangor Theological College) and set up a well-equipped and efficient South Wales Miners' Library at the University College of Swansea as a centre for adult education, active research and also as a kind of shrine, complete with a memorial to the fallen of the Spanish Civil War. Parallel to this movement, in a way, there is Cofiwn (Remember!) a strongly nationalist group dedicated to remembering everything which, and anyone who, could help the Welsh build themselves into a nation. While heartening, all this is also disturbing; one wonders whether it is some kind of symptom. We are living through a somewhat desperate hunt after our own past, a time of old militants religiously recorded on tape, of quarries and pits turned into tourist museums. This recovered tradition is increasingly operating in terms of a Celebration of a Heroic Past which seems rarely to be brought to bear on vulgarly contemporary problems except in terms of a merely rhetorical style which absolves its fortunate possessors from the necessity of thought. This is not to encapsulate a past, it is to sterilize it. It is not to cultivate an historical consciousness; it is to eliminate it.

Even more disturbing, however, has been the response of an establishment in crisis. The University College of Swansea, forced into financial cuts, promptly proposed to lop off the South Wales Miners' Library. In the effort to save it, the miners themselves are the major protagonists. Cofiwn has itself become historical evidence; it is subjected to police surveillance and harassment. All those accoutrements of creeping tyranny, the remorseless erosion of the rights of the jury, the emasculation of that Freeborn Englishman who was promoted into a Freeborn Briton, which have long disfigured the landscape of the English inner cities, have now appeared in Wales.

They have done so in response to an undercurrent of violence which has been getting stronger. The sabotage of reservoirs yielded to a bombing campaign during the Investiture of the Prince of Wales, in which two bombers blew themselves up and a little child was mutilated in an accident (Cofiwn remembers the first but not the second). A Mudiad Amddiffyn Cymru (Welsh Defence Movement) which was behind it, with a Free Wales Army as public theatre, has been succeeded by other shadowy organizations, little groups with big names, Meibion Glyn Dŵr (Sons of Glyn Dŵr), Guardians of Wales, The Workers' Army of the Welsh Republic (whose initials in Welsh spell Dawn). Weapons were acquired from the former Official IRA. There has been a major campaign of arson, which continues, against second and holiday homes in western Wales which are themselves a grinding grievance among a hard-hit people, who lend passive support and whose humour tends to run to jokes about England's Glory matches and the title of an old and once popular school textbook, *Flame-Bearers of Welsh History*.

A major police action against the arson campaign, Operation Tân (Fire) produced a chorus of complaint over violations of civil rights, telephone-tapping, the use of provocateurs and other familiar charges. Recently there has been an even more serious attack on elementary liberties in police action directed against a small Welsh Socialist Republican Movement. Members of this movement, whose stalwarts ranged from serious Marxist analysts of Welsh society to practitioners of a street theatre of flag-burning and Provisional Sinn Fein styles, were accused of involvement in a bombing campaign against army, government and Conservative party offices. In the course of the action, which provoked strong complaint from the moderate *Western Mail*, several of the accused were held for up to sixteen months without bail, and after a trial in which the credibility of the police was the major issue, most of the defendants were acquitted. Several police officers were accused of fabricating evidence and confessions and of trying falsely to implicate the Merioneth MP Dafydd Elis Thomas in the bombing. Enquiries have been instituted, but protest from the generality has been muted and if the object was to break up the Welsh Republicans, it appears to have succeeded. In the media and in government projects for the unemployed such as those financed by the Manpower Services Commission, there is evidence of the beginning of a witch-hunt, directed in particular against nuclear disarmers and feminist militants (who are characteristically often identical).

Across a Wales whose public atmosphere was thus becoming unpleasant in many respects, broke the trauma of the Falklands War. The impact on Wales was direct, in the disaster to the Welsh Guards at Bluff Cove and in anxieties over the Welsh communities in Patagonia in the Argentine. Plaid Cymru was the only political party apart from the Communists totally to oppose the war from the beginning and it evoked some response. On the other hand, there is little doubt that the War gave the same impetus to British patriotism, nationalism, even chauvinism, and to the Conservative party, as it did elsewhere.

As a general election loomed, with Labour in visible disarray, and with the appreciably calamitous effect of the new policies on the Welsh economy, together with the possible fortunes of the new Liberal–Social Democratic Alliance, the only matters of speculation, it was on the left wing of the national movement that awareness of the bankruptcy of traditional attitudes seems to have registered. Cymdeithas yr Iaith Gymraeg, the Welsh Language Society, adopted a strongly libertarian-Marxist statement of aims and moved into more social action; a National Left within Plaid Cymru also assumed a libertarian-Marxist style and tried to establish contact with ecological, peace and women's groups, while within the latter a strong and independent, radically novel, often intransigent and sometimes disconcerting (to males) political style emerged.

In the Wales of 1983, these could be but marginal movements. The great majority remained locked within what was now essentially a trinity of parties. The General Election of June 1983 exposed the myth that Wales, or to be precise south Wales, was still some kind of 'heartland of Labour'; it registered even more visibly Wales's presence with *The South* of the British geography of politics. In Wales, the Labour vote fell by 9.8 per cent, a fall exceeded only in East Anglia and the South-East; it ran level with London again. The Conservative vote fell by only 1.7 per cent; there were lesser falls only in East Anglia, the South and Yorkshire. The Labour vote in Wales fell by over 178,000, the Tories' by 24,000; the great victors were the Alliance whose vote rocketed by over 200,000.

The Conservatives, with a candidate of Ukrainian descent and strong right-wing views, took the Cardiff West seat of George Thomas, the former Speaker, and the marginal seat of Bridgend, swept most of Cardiff and again pressed very hard throughout the rural west, to end up with thirteen seats out of thirty-eight. Plaid Cymru, while disappointed in the valleys, broadly held its marginal line, establishing itself firmly in the north-west, holding Caernarfon and Merioneth and moving into second place in Anglesey; it registered potentially significant votes in Carmarthen,

Caerphilly, Ceredigion, Llanelli and the Rhondda. The success of the Alliance was spectacular. It more than doubled the former Liberal poll, reached 23 per cent of the electorate, won two seats and came second in nineteen out of the thirty-eight. Labour's defeat seemed to be slithering into rout even though it retained a score of seats. It dropped nearly 10 per cent of the poll and is now markedly a minority party overall, at its lowest level since 1918. It held on by the skin of its teeth not only to Carmarthen but to Wrexham, a former stronghold. In the fourteen seats which now cover its traditional base in the south, one fell to the Conservatives, six registered anti-Labour pluralities and became three-party marginals. The Alliance came second in ten and, in the Rhondda, won 8,000 votes without even campaigning. Seven remain which give Labour over 50 per cent of their votes. Of the old 20,000-majority familiars, only a traditional three remain: Rhondda, Merthyr Tydfil and what used to be Ebbw Vale (Blaenau Gwent). They stand like Aneurin Bevan's memorial stones on the Pound above Tredegar and they are beginning to look like the Stonehenge of Welsh politics.

Ahead, a country which largely lives by the British state, whose input into it is 10 per cent of its gross product, faces a major reconstruction of the public sector; a country whose industries remorselessly disperse and make casual and feminize their working force faces the prospect of a renewed depression or a recovery, either of which will intensify the process; a country whose young people are being dumped like rubbish in town and country faces the prospect of a large and growing population which will be considered redundant in a state which is already considering a major reduction in the financial burden of welfare.

Small wonder that some, looking ahead, see nothing but a nightmare vision of a depersonalized Wales which has shrivelled up into a Costa Bureaucratica in the south and a Costa Geriatrica in the north; in between, sheep, holiday homes burning merrily away and fifty folk museums where there used to be communities.

This is without doubt a nightmare. Some human society will obviously survive, though what kind it will be, no one can tell. What seems to be clear is that a majority of the inhabitants of Wales are choosing a British identity which seems to require the elimination of a Welsh one. There is irony here since the reconstruction of the British economy and society is no less clearly getting rid of Britain as we have known it. Britain as we have known it appears to have started its own long march out of history. This history of the Welsh may close then with the intriguing thought that the Welsh, First of the British, look like being the Last.

## *Walking Naked*

The Welsh have danced among these giant cogwheels before. Wales has always been now. The Welsh as a people have lived by making and remaking themselves in generation after generation, usually against the odds, usually within a British context. Wales is an artefact which the Welsh produce. If they want to. It requires an act of choice. Today, it looks as though that choice will be more difficult than ever before. There are roads out towards survival as a people, but they are long and hard and demand sacrifice and are at present unthinkable to most of the Welsh.

In that Welsh making and remaking of themselves, a sense of history has been central. The Welsh or their effective movers and shapers have repeatedly employed history to make a usable past, to turn a past into an instrument with which a present can build a future. It was once done in terms of myth, it has been recently and can be again done in terms of history. I am a Welsh man (even Adfer, I believe, would grant that) and I have tried for thirty years to be an historian. I am by instinct, training and commitment turned to such work. But in these days without precedent and without promise, I must confess that I often succumb to what Aneurin Bevan once called, in capital letters, The Invasion of Doubt.

I write these words in a blistering summer in one urban corner, congenially cosmopolitan, ringed appropriately by a hospital under threat, a Conservative Club and a funeral parlour. When I walk to the river, which is my river, here a canal running under the giant Le Corbusier stands of what used to be called Cardiff Arms Park before inflation set in, in this city which I am assured, all appearances to the contrary notwithstanding, is the capital city of my country, I cannot shut out a voice many of us have heard before, from that country which, among the contumacious crew of little Celtic peoples, has often played the role which France has played among the Latins.

William Butler Yeats immersed himself in the history and the mythology of the people to whom he belonged and whom he wished to serve by remaking them, an enterprise which carried him into some disconcerting company. At length, having, as he put it, 'swayed my leaves and flowers in the sun . . . through all the lying days of my youth', he 'withered into the truth' and in 1914 he published some poems under the chilling title of *Responsibilities*. One of them, these days, I find I cannot put from my mind.

> I made my song a coat
> Covered with embroideries
> Out of old mythologies
> From heel to throat;
> But the fools caught it,
> Wore it in the world's eyes

As though they'd wrought it.
Song, let them take it,
For there's more enterprise
In walking naked.

One thing I am sure of. Some kind of human society, though God knows what kind, will no doubt go on occupying these two western peninsulas of Britain, but that people, who are my people and no mean people, who have for a millennium and a half lived in them as a Welsh people, are now nothing but a naked people under an acid rain.

# EPILOGUE:

*The Welsh Hill Country*

Too far for you to see
The fluke and the foot-rot and the fat maggot
Gnawing the skin from the small bones,
The sheep are grazing at Bwlch-y-Fedwen,
Arranged romantically in the usual manner
On a bleak background of bald stone.

Too far for you to see
The moss and the mould on the cold chimneys,
The nettles growing through the cracked doors,
The houses stand empty at Nant-yr-Eira,
There are holes in the roofs that are thatched with
    sunlight,
And the fields are reverting to the bare moor.

Too far, too far to see
The set of his eyes and the slow phthisis
Wasting his frame under the ripped coat,
There's a man still farming at Ty'n-y-Fawnog,
Contributing grimly to the accepted pattern,
The embryo music dead in his throat.

R. S. Thomas, *An Acre of Land,* 1952.

This fine poem was originally directed at a particular group of people
in a particular corner of Wales. Read as metaphor, it now seems to me
to have wider significance.

# FURTHER READING

A proper bibliography would require an additional volume. After some agonizing, I have decided to restrict this list to works in English, basic texts, some general essays and the more accessible of my colleagues' studies (and, I fear, my own) which seem to me essential. Many carry their own booklists in Welsh, English and other languages.

*Reference*

There is a *Bibliography of the History of Wales* (University of Wales Press, 1962) with supplements in the *Bulletin of the Board of Celtic Studies, Welsh History Review* and occasionally in *Llafur,* journal of the Welsh Labour History Society. *The Dictionary of Welsh Biography* (Oxford University Press, 1959) may be supplemented by Joyce M. Bellamy and John Saville (eds.) *The Dictionary of Labour Biography, vols. I-VI* (Macmillan 1972–82). Alun Morgan has produced a useful *The South Wales Valleys: a guide to literature* (Tŷ Toronto, 1974). E. G. Bowen, *Wales: a Physical, Historical and Regional Geography* (University of Wales Press, 2nd edn, 1967) and D. Thomas (ed.), *Wales: a New Study* (David and Charles, 1977) are very helpful. On writing in Welsh, there are annual reports in *Studia Celtica* (and a major survey in Welsh, Thomas Parry and Merfyn Morgan (eds.), *Llyfryddiaeth Llenyddiaeth Gymraeg* (University of Wales Press, 1976)). Brynmor Jones has produced a *Bibliography of Anglo-Welsh Literature 1900–1965* (University of Wales Press, 1970). W. T. R. Pryce gives a bibliographical guide to the Welsh language in the *Bulletin of the Board of Celtic Studies* for November 1978 and there are helpful annual reports from the National Library and National Museum of Wales.

*Basic Texts*

Probably the best way into the history of Wales for a newcomer is still a collection of broadcast talks, A. J. Roderick (ed.), *Wales through The Ages,* 2 vols. (Christopher Davies, 1960, several impressions in paperback since). A. H. Dodd, *A Short History of Wales* (1977) was a Batsford book. There are two works widely acknowledged as standard: J. E. Lloyd, *A History of Wales from the Earliest Times to the Edwardian Conquest,* 2 vols. (Longman Green, 1911 and later editions) – he also wrote an important book *Owen Glendower* (Clarendon Press, 1931) – and David Williams, *A History of Modern Wales* (John Murray, 1950, revised by Ieuan Gwynedd Jones, 1977). Kenneth O. Morgan, *Rebirth of a Nation: Wales 1880–1980* (Clarendon Press and University of Wales Press, 1981) is the first volume of a series to be published jointly by the universities of Oxford and Wales.

*General*

There are a number of general studies, collections of essays, etc. which should prove stimulating. These include Prys Morgan, *Background to Wales* (Christopher Davies, 1968), Brinley Jones (ed.), *Anatomy of Wales* (Gwerin Publications, 1972), Glanmor Williams, *Religion, Language and Nationality in Wales* (University of Wales Press, 1979), Emyr Humphreys, *The Taliesin Tradition* (Black Raven Press, 1983), Gwyn A. Williams, *Madoc: the making of a myth* (Eyre Methuen, 1980) and *The Welsh in Their History* (Croom Helm, 1982), and, most recently, Dai Smith, *Wales! Wales?* (Allen and Unwin, 1984).

It would be a good idea to move straight into *The Mabinogion,* trans. Gwyn Jones and Thomas Jones (Everyman, 1948, paperback 1972), Gwyn Jones (ed.), *The Oxford Book of Welsh Verse in English,* (Oxford University Press, 1977), Anthony Conran and J. E. Caerwyn Williams (trans. and ed.), *The Penguin Book of Welsh Verse* (Penguin, 1967), locating yourself in Gwyn Williams, *An Introduction to Welsh Literature* (University of Wales Press, 1978) and Thomas Parry, *A History of Welsh Literature,* trans. Idris Bell (Clarendon Press, 1955). Many worlds are opened up by Glyn Jones, *The Dragon has Two Tongues* (Dent, 1968), Gwyn Jones, *The First Forty Years* (University of Wales Press, 1957), Gwyn Jones and Islwyn Ffowc Elis (eds.), *Twenty-five Welsh Short Stories* (Oxford University Press, 1971), Alun Richards (ed.), *Penguin Book of Welsh Short Stories* (Penguin, 1966) and the trilogy of novels by Raymond Williams, *Border Country* (Chatto and Windus, 1960), *Second Generation* (Chatto and Windus, 1964), *The Fight for Manod* (Chatto and Windus, 1979), his political thriller *The Volunteers* (Eyre Methuen, 1978) and his testimony in *Politics and Letters* (New Left Books, 1979).

Very useful short texts and studies of writers are published by the University of Wales Press in its bilingual St David's Day series and in the Writers of Wales series brought out by the University in conjunction with the Welsh Arts Council, which together with the Welsh Academy, is preparing a major Companion to Welsh writing and sponsoring many studies of Welsh arts and music.

*Texts*

From a very large number of books and articles, I single out the following which seem to me essential, indeed in some cases, epoch – making, roughly in chronological order.

Peter Salway, *Roman Britain* (Oxford History of England *(sic!),* 1981)
Wendy Davies, *Wales in the Early Middle Ages* (Leicester University Press, 1982) and her article 'Land and power in early medieval Wales', *Past and Present,* 81 (1978)
David Dumville, 'Sub-Roman Britain: history and legend', *History,* 72 (1977)
G. R. Jones, 'The Tribal System in Wales: a Re-assessment', *Welsh History Review,* 1 (1960–2)
  'Post-Roman Wales', in H. P. R. Finberg (ed.), *The Agrarian History of England and Wales* vol. 1, part 2 (Cambridge University Press, 1972)

Leslie Alcock, *Arthur's Britain* (Allen Lane, 1971)

E. G. Bowen, *Saints, Seaways and Settlements* (University of Wales Press, 1977)

Thomas Jones Pierce, *Medieval Welsh Society,* ed. J. Beverly Smith (University of Wales Press, 1973)

R. R. Davies, *Lordship and Society in the March of Wales 1282–1400* (Oxford University Press, 1978) and his articles 'Colonial Wales', *Past and Present,* 65 (1974) and 'The Twilight of Welsh Law', *History,* 51 (1966)

Ralph Griffiths, *The Principality of Wales in the Later Middle Ages:* vol. 1: *South Wales, 1277–1536* (University of Wales Press, 1972)

Glanmor Williams, *The Welsh Church from Conquest to Reformation* (University of Wales Press, 1976)

*Owen Glendower* (Oxford University Press, 1966)

*Welsh Reformation Essays* (University of Wales Press, 1967)

Frances Yates, *The Occult Philosophy in the Elizabethan Age* (Routledge & Kegan Paul, 1979)

P. J. French, *John Dee, the World of an Elizabethan Magus* (Routledge & Kegan Paul, 1972)

A. H. Dodd, *Studies in Stuart Wales* (University of Wales Press, 2nd edn, 1971)

Geraint H. Jenkins, *Literature, Religion and Society in Wales 1660–1730* (University of Wales Press, 1978)

Philip Jenkins, *The Making of a Ruling Class: the Glamorgan gentry 1640–1790* (Cambridge University Press, 1983)

Brinley Thomas, *Migration and Economic Growth* (Cambridge University Press, 1954 and subsequent edns) and 'Wales and the Atlantic Economy' in the volume he edited, *The Welsh Economy* (University of Wales Press, 1962)

David Smith (ed.), *A People and a Proletariat: Wales 1780–1980* (Pluto Press, 1980)

David J. V. Jones, *Before Rebecca: popular protest in Wales 1793–1835* (Allen Lane, 1973)

Gwyn A. Williams, *The Search for Beulah Land: the Welsh and the Atlantic Revolution* (Croom Helm, 1980)

*The Merthyr Rising* (Croom Helm, 1978)

David Williams, *The Rebecca Riots* (University of Wales Press, 1955)

David Howell, *Land and People in Nineteenth Century Wales* (Routledge & Kegan Paul, 1977)

Ieuan Gwynedd Jones, *Explorations and Explanations: essays in the social history of Victorian Wales* (Gomer Press, 1981)

Kenneth O. Morgan, *Wales in British Politics 1868–1922* (University of Wales Press, 3rd edn, 1980)

Merfyn Jones, *The North Wales Quarrymen 1874–1922* (University of Wales Press, 1981)

Hywel Francis and David Smith, *The Fed: a History of the South Wales Miners in the Twentieth Century* (Lawrence and Wishart, 1980)

David Smith and Gareth Williams, *Fields of Praise: the official history of the Welsh Rugby Union* (University of Wales Press, 1981)

Peter Stead, 'Working-class leadership in South Wales 1900–1920', *Welsh History Review,* 6 (1973)

John Davies, 'The End of the Great Estates and the Rise of Freehold Farming in Wales', *Welsh History Review,* 7 (1974)

D. Hywel Davies, *The Welsh Nationalist Party 1925–1945: a call to nationhood* (University of Wales Press, 1983)

Robert Griffiths, *S. O. Davies: A Socialist Faith* (Gomer Press, 1983)

Dot Jones and L. J. Williams, 'Women at Work in the Nineteenth Century: parallels and differences', *Llafur,* 3 (1982)

Gwyn A. Williams, 'Women Workers in Contemporary Wales 1968–82', *Welsh History Review,* vol 11. no. 4 (1984)

# Index

Aberafan, 90

Abercrave, 222, 266

Aberdare, 183, 184, 187, 190, 201, 215, 216; valley, 183, 201, 216, 262

Aberdare, 1st Lord, 216, 217; *and see* Bruce, H. A.

Aberdare Committee, 218

Aberffraw, 18, 67, 79, 85

Abergavenny, 93, 100, 189, 215

Abertillery, 252, 263

Aberystwyth, 98, 110, 112, 225, 286; University College, 197, 204, 212–13, 218, 221, 231, 235

Abraham, William, *see* Mabon

Abse, Leo, 289, 294

Act for the Better Propagation of the Gospel in Wales, 134–5

Act of Supremacy, 118

Act of Union, 119–21

Action Française, 279, 280, 281

Adam of St Asaph, 69

Adam of Usk, 107, 109

Adam of Wales, 69

Adfer, 299–300

*Advocate, The,* 190, 196

Aetius, 23, 24

agriculture/farming: early, 2, 6, 8, 18, 48; medieval, 62, 64, 66, 73–4, 89, 99; modernized, 63, 139, 141, 144–5, 151, 160–1; 19th century, 175–7, 184, 194, 201; 20th century, 252, 256, 281

Albion, 1, 123

Alfred, king, 58

Amalgamated Association of Miners (AAM), 218

Amalgamated Society of Locomotive Engineers and Firemen (ASLEF), 242

Amalgamated Society of Railway Servants (ASRS), 242

Ambrosius, 24, 25, 26, 39, 45, 56

Ambrosius Aurelianus, 25, 45

America: discovery and colonization of, 57, 123, 124–5, 127, 136, 137, 145, 155; emigration to, 138, 140, 141, 156–7, 161, 170–2, 174, 176–7, 178, 179–80, 240; name, 115

American influence: cultural, 223, 224, 247, 275, 279, 286; economic, 254, 255

American Revolution, 142, 145–6, 149, 151, 162, 164, 166, 167, 168–9, 170

*amobr,* 52, 91, 92

*Amserau, Yr,* 203, 213

Aneirin, 37

Anglesey, 3; early history, 2, 7, 13, 14, 17, 35, 36, 38; Northmen, 56, 57; medieval, 67, 84, 93, 105, 107, 112; Dissent, 137, 159; industry, 143, 149, 199; politics, 217, 219, 273, 296, 302

Anglicanism, *see* Church of England

anglicization, 130, 230, 247–8

Anglo-Saxons, 26–7, 38

Anglo-Welsh poets, 285

*Anglo-Welsh Review,* 285

Anian, Bishop, 77

anthracite coalfield, 183, 246, 248, 252, 264, 267

Anti-Corn Law League, 211

antiquarian studies, 123, 126, 129–30, 153, 162–3

Archenfield, *see* Ergyng

Arianism, 136, 157–8

aristocracy: early, 15, 22, 30, 43, 49, 53, 54; medieval, 80, 82, 85, 93, 100; 17th and 18th centuries, 142, 146, 149

*Armes Prydein,* 56–7, 58

Arminianism, 136, 156, 157–8

Armorica, 22, 25

Arthur, Arthurian tradition, 13, 25–6, 28, 31, 36, 37, 40, 45, 54, 70, 71–2, 123–5, 290; Return of Arthur, 56, 103–4, 115, 117, 121, 125, 131

Arthur, prince, 113, 117

Arts Council, 220; Welsh, 292, 297

Asquith, 231

Asser, 43, 58

Assheton-Smiths, 199

Athelstan, 57, 58

313

General and Municipal Workers' Union, 298

General Strike, 267–8

gentry, squirearchy, 88, 90, 92, 95, 98, 99–100, 104, 105, 108, 109, 115; 16th century, 118, 119, 121, 122–3, 125, 126, 127–31, 132; 17th century, 133, 134, 136, 137, 138, 139; 18th century, 141, 146–50, 162; 19th century, 159, 184, 211, 213, 219, 229

Geoffrey of Monmouth: *History of the Kings of Britain,* 71–2, 104, 123, 129, 131, 153

Gerald the Welshman, 38, 43, 53, 63, 68, 69, 70–1, 77

Germans, 15, 19, 21, 24

Germanus of Auxerre, St, 22, 23, 24, 25, 29, 39, 41, 45, 56

Germany, 176–7, 254, 282

Gildas, 20, 22, 23, 25, 26, 27, 33, 34, 37, 53

Gladstone, W. E., 204, 206, 212–13, 214, 215, 216, 218, 229

Glamorgan, 3, 5; early history, 7, 31, 32, 42; medieval, 66–7, 71, 78, 83, 92–3, 97, 105, 109, 115; 16th century, 122, 127, 128, 130; 17th century, 132, 133, 136–7, 138; 18th century, 143, 144, 146, 147–9, 158, 160; 19th century, 175, 188, 197, 219, 230; 20th century, 232, 244, 245, 250, 293, 296, 299

Glorious Revolution, 136, 139, 169–70

Glynneath Soviet Level, 267

Glyncorrwg, 268

Glywysing, 31, 32, 40, 43, 55; *and see* Morgannwg

*gorsedd,* 140, 162, 165, 166, 170, 188

Gouge, Thomas, 154

Gower, 30, 112, 135, 241

grammar schools, 129, 197

Great Britain, 127, 139, 141–3, 151, 173

Great Sessions, 119–21, 122–3, 150

Greenham Common, 258, 299

Greys, 90, 93

Grey, Reginald, lord of Ruthin, 105, 106, 109

Griffith ap Nicolas, 116

Griffiths, James, 244, 266, 269, 273, 289, 291

Gruffydd, W. J., 248, 278, 279

Gruffydd ap Cynan, 57, 65, 69

Gruffydd ap Llywelyn, 59–60

Gruffydd Llwyd, 104

Gruffydd Llwyd, Sir, 96, 97

Guest, Lady Charlotte, 188

Guest, Josiah John, 195, 197, 198–9

Guto'r Glyn, 115, 129

*Gweithiwr, Y,* 190, 195

Gwenallt, 248, 275

Gwent (kingdom), 10, 16, 29, 30–1, 32

Gwent (region), *see* Monmouthshire

*gwerin,* 152, 199, 206, 208, 228–9, 237–40, 284–5

*Gwerin,* 282

Gwilym ap Gruffydd, 116

Gwriad, 55

Gwydion the Magician, 6

Gwynedd, 2; kingdom, 18, 20, 28, 33, 34–8, 47, 55; 59; feudal state, 62, 66, 67, 73–86; region and county, 88–9, 104, 115, 175, 200, 243, 299

Gwyneddigion, 163–7

Gwynn Jones, T., 248, 278

*Gysegrlan Fuchedd, Y,* 94

Hakluyt, Richard, 125

Hanmer family, 90, 106, 107

Hanoverians, 139, 148

Harlech, 93, 110, 112, 115, 132; college, 221, 264

Harold, king, 59, 60

Harris, Howell, 155–6

Harrison, Colonel Thomas, 134–5

*Haul, Yr.,* 203

Haverfordwest, 119, 145, 239

Healey, Denis, 289

Heledd, princess of Powys, 38, 40

Helen Luyddog, 14, 20, 61, 125

'Hen Wlad Fy Nhadau', 209, 217, 218

Henry I, 65–6

Henry II, 63, 66

Henry III, 82–3

Henry IV, 105–12 *passim*

Henry V, 88, 110, 112, 114, 116

Henry VI, 116

Henry VII, 103, 116, 117, 118, 123, 124

Henry VIII, 117, 119

Henry Hotspur, 107, 110

Herbert, family, 115, 117, 126, 128

Herbert, William, Earl of Pembroke, 115, 116

Herefordshire, Welsh, 132; *see also* Ergyng

Heroic Age culture, 9–10, 18, 31, 37, 54, 70

High Kings of all Wales, 47, 55–8, 59–60

60, 62, 63, 125, 131; 19th century, 179, 180–1, 182–3, 214; 20th century, 236, 303–5
*Welsh Review*, 285
Welsh Socialist Republican Movement, 301
Welsh Sunday, *see* Sunday closing
Welsh Tract, 156
Welsh Trust, 138, 154
Welsh Wales (Pura Wallia), 64, 72, 73–9, 80, 92, 93, 236–7
*Welshman, The,* 187, 193
Welshness, 230, 236–7, 240, 285, 286–7, 291, 293
Welshpool, 107, 160
Welshries, 72, 80
Wesley, Wesleyans, 156, 189
Wessex, 5, 7, 27, 32, 55, 57, 58
*Western Mail, The,* 222, 223, 301
Westminster, 67, 76, 129
Whigs, 138, 139, 142, 148, 150, 151–2, 168, 197, 217
*White Book of Rhydderch,* 94
Whitefield, George, 156
Whitland, 78, 107
Wigley, Dafydd, 287, 296
Wilkes, John, 149, 168
Willem of Ghent, 71
William I, 60–1, 65
William III, 139
Williams, D. J., 283
Williams, David, *Deist,* 168–9
Williams, Elisabeth, 280
Williams, Griffith J., 278, 280
Williams, Hugh, *Chartist,* 193–4
Williams, Ifor, 278
Williams, John, Archbishop, 128, 132
Williams, Morgan, 190, 195
Williams, Thomas, of Anglesey, 143, 199
Williams, William (Caledfryn), 209

Williams, William (Pantycelyn), 155
Williams, Zephaniah, 190, 195, 196
Wilson, Harold, 254, 273
women: status of, 9, 42, 50, 51–2, 75, 91, 224, 225, 250; employment of, 144, 186, 239, 252, 254, 256, 258, 289, 297, 298; protest by, 258, 262–3, 267, 268, 269, 299
women's groups, 267, 299, 302
Worcester, Marquises of, 127, 132, 137
workers' institutes, 279
working class, 172, 176, 183, 185–96 *passim,* 198–200, 208, 215–16, 219, 223–4, 253, 289, 293; archetypal myth, 237, 238–41, 253, 258, 265, 298
Working Men's Associations, 185, 193
working populations, 176, 179, 252–8, 297–8, 303
World War I, 181, 220, 223, 249–50, 265
World War II, 160, 253, 264, 271, 273, 278, 283
Wrexham, 131, 137, 144, 169, 200, 215, 225, 243; elections, 273, 303
Wroth, William, 133
Wroxeter, 14, 17
Wynns, 122, 149, 150, 213, 219
Wynne, Ellis, 153

Yeats, William Butler, 304–5
Yeomanry, 99, 100, 147
Ynyr Fychan, 96
Young, Dr Gruffudd, 87, 110, 111, 112
Ystrad, 89
Ystrad Tywi, 34, 66

Zimmern, Alfred, 223, 247
Zosimus, 22

# MORE ABOUT PENGUINS, PELICANS
# AND PUFFINS

For further information about books available from Penguins please write to Dept EP, Penguin Books Ltd, Harmondsworth, Middlesex UB7 0DA.

*In the U.S.A.*: For a complete list of books available from Penguins in the United States write to Dept DG, Penguin Books, 299 Murray Hill Parkway, East Rutherford, New Jersey 07073.

*In Canada*: For a complete list of books available from Penguins in Canada write to Penguin Books Canada Ltd, 2801 John Street, Markham, Ontario L3R 1B4.

*In Australia*: For a complete list of books available from Penguins in Australia write to the Marketing Department, Penguin Books Australia Ltd, P.O. Box 257, Ringwood, Victoria 3134.

*In New Zealand*: For a complete list of books available from Penguins in New Zealand write to the Marketing Department, Penguin Books (N.Z.) Ltd, Private Bag, Takapuna, Auckland 9.

*In India*: For a complete list of books available from Penguins in India write to Penguin Overseas Ltd, 706 Eros Apartments, 56 Nehru Place, New Delhi 110019.

*A Choice of Penguins*

## THE AMATEUR NATURALIST
### *Gerald Durrell with Lee Durrell*

Meadows and hedgerows, shrublands, deciduous woodlands, marshlands, rocky shores . . . These are just some of the habitats which world-famous naturalist Gerald Durrell and his wife Lee open up for the aspiring naturalist.

For each environment they provide a delightful and detailed guide to what to look for, where to look for it, how to interpret what you see, and what to take home for further study.

Each chapter has a unique colour photo of one day's findings in the chosen habitat, and instructions on how to preserve, propagate, dissect and display these objects, as well as useful information, among other things, on how to take a lichen scraping and care for a wounded bird.

'One of those rare books that fires and inspires' – Susan Hill in the *Daily Telegraph*

## 'MISS READ'S' COUNTRY COOKING

Apple Amber, Summer Chicken with Peas, Ginger Pudding, Potted Port, Zabaglione . . . Simple or sophisticated, traditional or new, 'Miss Read' has culled her recipes from a wide range of sources.

Grouped into spring, summer, autumn and winter, she has put together a seasonal feast – although she has not neglected the modern conveniences of frozen or tinned food – which will delight and satisfy the most exacting cook.

# THE KINGDOM BY THE SEA
## A Journey Round the Coast of Great Britain
### *Paul Theroux*

Paul Theroux's round-Britain travelogue is funny, perceptive and, said the *Sunday Times,* 'best avoided by patriots with high blood pressure . . .'

After eleven years' living as an American in London, Theroux set out to travel clockwise round the coast and find out what Britain and the British are really like. It was 1982, the summer of the Falklands War and the Royal Baby, and the ideal time, he found, to surprise the British into talking about themselves. The result is vivid, opinionated and – as you'd expect from the author of *The Great Railway Bazaar* – absolutely compulsive reading.

'He describes it all brilliantly and honestly' – Anthony Burgess in the *Observer*

# THE PURPLE DECADES
### *Tom Wolfe*

'Tom Wolfe is quite easily the most entertaining and interesting commentator on the American scene' – Auberon Waugh in the *Daily Mail*

'Tom Wolfe . . . the dude in the white suit, the man who rapped us with "Radical chic" and the "Me-decade", the man who reached Parts of the Typewriter that other Reporters never rumbled . . . Here, anyhow is a retrospective collection of his work, 21 essays and extracts, from 1964 to 1981, running through the whole mad circus of his American sub-cultures – from Surfers, Acid Freaks, West Side Divorcees, and Soho Bohos, to Astronauts, Moonies, Manhattan Socialites, Mid-Atlantic Men, Pop Painters and Down-Filled People . . . immensely exhilarating to read' – Richard Holmes in *The Times*

'He is basically a comic writer . . . he comes close to that other great hick, F. Scott Fitzgerald' – Stanley Reynolds in *Punch*

'He irritates all the right people . . . And as for weathering, they've *improved*, these famous pieces' – Peter York in *New Society*

## POLITICAL TRIALS IN BRITAIN
### *Peter Hain*

Is law enforcement founded on political decisions?

Peter Hain examines this crucial issue, analysing overtly political cases involving official secrecy, conspiracy, public order, trade unions, Northern Ireland and race relations, and challenging the whole notion of the law as an impartial and technical instrument.

'A well-documented argument that discretionary power is exercised by the police, prosecuting authorities, magistrates and judges as a weapon to intimidate, discredit and exhaust those who "threaten the social and political status quo" ' – *The Times Literary Supplement*

'A valuable hunting ground for those who want to attack the alleged impartiality of the arms of the state' – *Tribune*

## MORE ROUGH JUSTICE
### *Peter Hill and Martin Young with Tom Sargant*

Breaking all audience viewing records for television current affairs documentaries, *Rough Justice* has provoked a storm of public interest and outrage. Following the first series, four men convicted of murder were released from prison. In *More Rough Justice,* (based on a further television series) the authors have reopened three further cases:

* A teenage boy is found dead with stab wounds; after hours of police questioning, his mother confesses to the murder
* A girl's body is found hidden in an oil tank; a worker at the plant who admitted that he knew her is convicted of murder
* A young woman is murdered *en route* to a railway station; even her family believe that the local train-spotter, now ten years into a life-sentence, is innocent

With the help of lawyers and forensic experts, Martin Young and Peter Hill set out to discover what really happened. Their findings – in an outstanding piece of investigative journalism and detective work – provide detailed and disturbing evidence to suggest that in all three cases there has been a serious miscarriage of justice.

# LABELS
## *Evelyn Waugh*

Evelyn Waugh chose the name *Labels* for his first travel book because, he said, the places he visited were already 'fully labelled' in people's minds.

But even the most seasoned traveller could not fail to be inspired by Waugh's quintessentially English attitude and by his eloquent and frequently outrageous wit. From Europe to the Middle East to North Africa, from Egyptian porters and Italian priests to Maltese sailors and Moroccan merchants – as he cruises around the Mediterranean his pen cuts through the local colour to give a highly entertaining portrait of the English abroad.

Written in 1929, *Labels* is a splendid example of the genius that was to make its author the greatest writer of his generation.

'He will be admired as long as there are people who can read'
– *Daily Telegraph*

# THEY WENT TO PORTUGAL
## *Rose Macaulay*

Henry Fielding sailed there with his household – at an all-in cost of £30 – in search of a cure for dropsy, jaundice and asthma. Later on, William Beckford anticipated orange-scented, wine-soaked afternoons and a fanfare from Lisbon society, while the Portuguese sent Byron into one of his inexplicable black rages, and Palgrave and Tennyson, both thickly bearded, found the climate rather too hot . . .

Rose Macaulay's wonderful book rambles down the centuries like a kind of Cook's Tour, from the pirate-crusaders, through sailors, poets, aesthetes and ambassadors, to Anglican, Roman and non-conformist clergymen, the port wine trading pioneers and the new wave of romantic travellers. The result is one of the most fascinating and unusual travel books ever compiled – a wonderful mixture of literature, history and adventure, by one of our most stylish and seductive writers.

# THE PELICAN SOCIAL HISTORY
# OF BRITAIN

*General Editor: J. H. Plumb*

This highly acclaimed new series is a fresh and comprehensive survey of British society since the Middle Ages that takes full advantage of the enormous increase over recent decades in our knowledge of almost every aspect of social history.

*Already published:*

# ENGLISH SOCIETY
# IN THE EIGHTEENTH CENTURY

*Roy Porter*

'Hugely enjoyable to read ... his writing glows even when dealing with statistics, and positively crackles when expressing the vigour and zest of what has rightly been called the age of exuberance' – W. A. Speck in the *Observer*

'A brilliant work of synthesis' – John Brewer in the *London Review of Books*

# BRITISH SOCIETY SINCE 1945

*Arthur Marwick*

'Packed with useful information ... an enjoyable, readable, usable achievement which leads the field' – John Vincent in the *Sunday Times*

'A highly stimulating and compelling book which can be read with considerable enjoyment' – *Yorkshire Post*

*and*

British Society 1914–45
*John Stevenson*

Sixteenth Century England
*Joyce Youings*

# A CHOICE OF PENGUINS

☐ **The English House Through Seven Centuries**
**Olive Cook** £9.95

From Norman defensiveness and Tudor flourish to Georgian elegance and Victorian grandeur, this beautiful book records and describes the wealth of domestic architecture in Britain. With photographs by Edwin Smith.

☐ **The Daughters of Karl Marx** £4.95

The letters of Jenny, Laura and Eleanor Marx: 'An enlightening introduction to the preoccupations, political and personal, of the Marx family' – Lionel Kochan. 'The tale they tell is riveting' – *Standard*

☐ **The First Day on the Somme**
**Martin Middlebrook** £3.95

1 July 1916 was the blackest day of slaughter in the history of the British Army. 'The soldiers receive the best service a historian can provide: their story told in their own words' – *Guardian*

☐ **Lord Hervey's Memoirs** £4.95

As an intimate of the Royal Court – and as a particularly witty and malicious raconteur – Lord Hervey was ideally equipped to write this sparkling account of royal personalities, politics and intrigues, 1727–37.

☐ **Some Lovely Islands  Leslie Thomas** £5.95

The islands off the coast of Britain, and their islanders, are celebrated in this delightful book by well-known novelist Leslie Thomas. With photographs by Peter Chèze-Brown.

☐ **Harold Nicolson: Diaries and Letters 1930–64** £4.95

A selection of Nicolson's famous diaries and letters. 'A brilliant portrait of English society ... a touching self-portrait of a highly intelligent and civilized man' – Kenneth Clark

# A CHOICE OF PENGUINS

☐ *A Colder Eye* **Hugh Kenner** £4.95

A study of the modern Irish writers. 'Anyone interested in language, in theatre history, in, indeed, the great comic literature of Joyce, Beckett and O'Brien will find this a highly enjoyable read' – *Punch*

☐ *The Europeans* **Luigi Barzini** £2.95

Witty, stylish and provocative, this is a veteran journalist's-eye view of the past and present character of the British, French, Germans, Italians and Dutch. 'Fascinating . . . read it immediately' – *The New York Times*

☐ *In Search of Ancient Astronomies* **Ed. E. C. Krupp** £4.95

Forming an introduction to archaeo-astronomy, a series of new essays on the world's most spectacular ancient monuments, from Stonehenge to the pyramids. 'Outstanding . . . accessible even to the beginner' – Patrick Moore

☐ *Clinging to the Wreckage* **John Mortimer** £2.25

The bestselling autobiography by the creator of Rumpole and the playwright author of *A Voyage Round My Father*. 'Enchantingly witty . . . England would be a poor place without Mr Mortimer' – Auberon Waugh

☐ *Chips: The Diaries of Sir Henry Channon* £4.95

'Chips' Channon, M.P., knew everybody that was anybody. Here, from the abdication of Edward VIII to the coronation of Elizabeth II, he serves up history with an irresistible 'H.P.' sauce of gossip and glamour.

☐ *The Miracle of Dunkirk* **Walter Lord** £2.95

'This is contemporary history at its most readable' – *The New York Times*. 'It gives an effective new polish to the golden legend' – *The Times*

# A CHOICE OF PENGUINS